Horror and the Horror Film

New Perspectives on World Cinema

The **New Perspectives on World Cinema** series publishes engagingly written, highly accessible, and extremely useful books for the educated reader and the student as well as the scholar. Volumes in this series will fall under one of the following categories: monographs on neglected films and filmmakers; classic as well as contemporary film scripts; collections of the best previously published criticism (including substantial reviews and interviews) on single films or filmmakers; translations into English of the best classic and contemporary film theory; reference works on relatively neglected areas in film studies, such as production design (including sets, costumes, and make-up), music, editing, and cinematography; and reference works on the relationship between film and the other performing arts (including theater, dance, opera, etc.). Many of our titles will be suitable for use as primary or supplementary course texts at undergraduate and graduate levels. The goal of the series is thus not only to address subject areas in which adequate classroom texts are lacking, but also to open up additional avenues for film research, theoretical speculation, and practical criticism.

Horror and the Horror Film

BRUCE F. KAWIN

ANTHEM PRESS
LONDON · NEW YORK · DELHI

Anthem Press
An imprint of Wimbledon Publishing Company
www.anthempress.com

This edition first published in UK and USA 2012
by ANTHEM PRESS
75-76 Blackfriars Road, London SE1 8HA, UK
or PO Box 9779, London SW19 7ZG, UK
and
244 Madison Ave. #116, New York, NY 10016, USA

British Library Cataloguing-in-Publication Data
A catalogue record for this book is available from the British Library.

Library of Congress Cataloging-in-Publication Data
Kawin, Bruce F., 1945-
Horror and the horror film / Bruce F. Kawin.
p. cm. – (New perspectives on world cinema)
Includes bibliographical references and index.
ISBN 978-0-85728-450-1 (pbk. : alk. paper) – ISBN 978-0-85728-449-5 (hardback : alk. paper)
1. Horror films–History and criticism. I. Title.
PN1995.9.H6K39 2012
791.43'6164–dc23
2012016159

ISBN-13: 978 0 85728 449 5 (Hbk)
ISBN-10: 0 85728 449 5 (Hbk)

ISBN-13: 978 0 85728 450 1 (Pbk)
ISBN-10: 0 85728 450 9 (Pbk)

This title is also available as an eBook.

In memory of Frank McConnell and Stan Brakhage

The night can sweat with terror as before
We pieced our thoughts into philosophy

—W. B. Yeats, "Nineteen Hundred and Nineteen"

CONTENTS

PREFACE

I have a blood disorder similar to hemophilia, and my father was a hunchback. I came to the horror film naturally. I thought it addressed the terms of my real world as well as my imagination. It seemed to me that in a horror film anything could happen, anything could be dreamt of and shown, while all the other movies were stuck in the known world.

I was scared of a lot of things, and a horror film calmed me. I'm still afraid of excessive bleeding and I remember—or more exactly, can't forget—vomiting spaghetti-like balls of clots after my tonsils were removed, and a doctor using big forceps to snip off the scabs that were closing my throat as the thick blood built up beneath them. As hands or matched parts fit together, the horror film met my fears with its world full of fear. It offered an alternative and a complement to anxiety with its made-up anxiety. It lived up to the energy inside me. Sometimes it scared me—the first mummy film I saw, *Pharaoh's Curse*, gave me bad nightmares at 11, but I still enjoyed it. The thrills and visions, especially the look of a new monster, compensated for the risk of nightmares. They were by far my favorite movies, and this book attempts to convey a mature appreciation for them along with a comprehensive view of their values, their narrative strategies, their artistic achievements, their relations to reality and fantasy and their claims to profundity and cinematic power.

The horror film is a construct of fear and revulsion, and this vivid, sometimes gruesome book examines the frightful and disgusting in the clearest possible terms. These observations are based on close viewings of the films, and not on what has been written about them. The films are the key data here; this is not a survey of horror criticism and theory, although relevant earlier work is of course acknowledged. Instead it is a fresh, comprehensive look at how the horror film frightens, disturbs, shocks and revolts the viewer, the effect and the art of it and some of the good that comes from it.

The book begins with an overall look at the genre, an introduction to the horror experience and some recurring ways it has been structured in cinema. The book then examines the subgenres of the horror film, each one organized by the brand of horror central to it, which is most often embodied in a monster: hence the sub-subgenre of the vampire movie within the subgenre of the supernatural monster movie. This taxonomy proves to be a clear and simple way to organize the whole genre, and to cover many key films across its history, all the way from *A Terrible Night* (1896) to *Scream 4* (2011). At the end, there is an added discussion of two closely related genres that have the ability to integrate horror into their worldviews—that is, the comedy and the documentary. I have designed this to be a complete description of the horror film, although there will always be new monsters and threats. This book is addressed to horror enthusiasts, to film scholars and to general readers who have yet to be convinced of the importance of the genre.

I am very grateful to those who read earlier drafts of my book: Rick Balkin, Ann R. Cacoullos, Christina Dokou, Katherine Eggert, David Glimp, Lori Janssen, Stephen Graham Jones, Lise Menn, Wayne Phillips, Cathy Preston, Michael Preston and Harold Schechter.

Boulder, Colorado
December 2011

LIST OF FIGURES

Part I

APPROACHING THE GENRE

1

HORROR

The horror in a horror film is as essential as the West in a Western or the humor in a comedy. This book concentrates relentlessly on the nature and expression of horror, both in reality and in the cinema.

Overview

Horror films can be profound fables of human nature and important works of art, yet many people dismiss them out of hand, are too disgusted or frightened to watch them, or are simply reluctant to discuss them.[1] One reason is that horror itself resists formulation and can be difficult and unpleasant to contemplate. The material is awful, a nightmare no one wants to come true. Horror can be filled with violence, cruelty and gore. It can scare us badly. It can be inexpressible, nameless. It can make us want to vomit. And it can be disturbing. The horror film can bring uncomfortably close the worst that could ever happen—to a character or to ourselves. It can explore forbidden aspects of human psychology. It can present dark beauty or sick fantasy. It can be sexist. It can be stupid. It can be badly produced. Arousing both terror and repugnance at once, it can be revolting in its moments of greatest power, when it shows us what we do and do not want to see. It can make us unable to express what we have seen. It can transgress and transcend limits. It can make the repellent, the terrifying and the creepy compelling. It can have the raw theatricality of a freak show. It can make a composition out of violence, blood and shadow, and can charge an image or a moment with the suspense and power of the unseen—with fear or awareness. It can offer a place for the fantastic and the uncanny[2] to play, a place for monsters, lost places, things that cannot be, things from here and not from here. It can go to the limits of violent, insane human behavior, or it can open a way for the supernatural to intrude. It can put us in touch with old emotions and reactions: fight or flight, fear of the dark, the need for community.

It can give pleasure to feel how frightening and repulsive a scene is, how extreme, how expressive, and it can satisfy the critic and the fan in the viewer to appreciate how well it lives up to the potential of the genre. We want the film to shake us up, to thrill us, to show us wonders, to frighten us, to make us wince, to give us chills, to build tension in us and release it, to give us characters in terrible situations, to observe the imperatives of the genre (of which the most important is to be frightening) without being excessively formulaic, and to be unsettlingly familiar as well as original. For all the genre's use of formula and the repetition of figures and images that establish its traditions, the horror film has a license to be profoundly inventive and original. We are engaged with the genre for the blood and shock, the adrenaline and relief, the fantasies and creative leaps and more, but also for the powerful images and scenes that can arise in a world where nothing is impossible and horror must find visual expression. The range of the creative horror image is potentially endless. We may even need it and be drawn to it. The circle of civilization surrounds the fire where stories are told, with the dark at its back—even if the fire has become a screen.

Origins

The nightmare, playing out our deepest fears while we sleep, is a universal human experience. Horror films, which often include nightmares, are the nightmares of the cinema, but horror has been an important genre for millennia, in literature, folklore, and high and popular culture.[3] Among the oldest written stories is the attempt to come to terms with death in the Babylonian *Epic of Gilgamesh*; the *Odyssey* is full of monsters such as the giant, man-eating Cyclops; English literature finds its first monsters in *Beowulf* and includes the horrific blinding scene ("Out, vile jelly") in *King Lear*; children have long been told fantastic tales of wonder, danger and evil; sheets passed out at public executions went over the crimes in graphic detail; folk songs and ballads often made murder vivid and death an expressive state. Horror is old, an old concern and an old source for tales. It is far older than the Gothic novel, let alone science fiction (even though many literary critics and historians correctly observe that the codified genre of horror was a late arrival); it may even be said to have been part of the narrative arts before horror was given a name. How could it not be significant? Horror is part of our response to the world. It runs through and determines many of our oldest tales as well as our movies. Suspicions about the supernatural are as old as religion if not older, and the horror story may have begun there—or in some tale of an animal attack. The Devil is a creature of the imagination, but before him came—and he may be said to have been created to organize—a host of unknown things in the night as well as in nightmares.

Defining Horror

Horror is a compound of terror and revulsion.[4] Imagined horror provides entry to a made-up world—one that could be richly, fantastically imagined or dead-on realistic— where fears are heightened but can be mastered. In doing so, it accesses a core of fears we may share as humans, such as the fear of being attacked in the dark, as well as some fears that are specific to culture, such as the fear of water associated with the power of ghosts in many Japanese horror movies.[5] It also calls on a vast range of the revolting, from guts to vermin, and much of the art has depended on making an image, a monster or an event both scary and repulsive. Above all, the horror film provides a way to conceptualize, give a shape to and deal with the evil and frightening. Some fears may be potential, lying dormant until a horror film arouses them; some may be created entirely by the movie, just as showers became frightening to many after *Psycho* (Alfred Hitchcock, 1960, US) and some may be part of our daily, conscious experience. Evil, too, may be encountered in ordinary life or engendered in fiction, though in the movies it is often presented as a supernatural force or embodied in a supernatural being. It is also embodied, of course, in human characters who are fundamentally malicious, regardless of their sanity. Akin to the disgusting spectacle that may be hard to watch and that may frighten us as much as the idea, fact or face of evil, fear contributes to the art, look, coherence, intensity, range and overall project of the genre.

As a genre, the horror film is defined by its recurring elements (such as undeath, witches, or gross, bloody violence), by its attitudes toward those elements (such as that transgressing limits is dangerous) and by its goal: to frighten and revolt the audience. Analogously, one could say that the Western is defined by such recurring elements as gunfights, horses and the Western landscape, and an attitude that there is a proper time for violence, and the basic goal of dramatizing the conflicts of frontier life.

The major subgenres—films about monsters, supernatural monsters and humans—are based, as we shall see in Part II, on the nature of the threat, and so are the sub-subgenres. (The genre is, of course, the horror film.) Within the subgenre of the supernatural monster movie are the sub-subgenres of the ghost film, the zombie film and so on.

The determining effect of genre on versatile material is significant. For example, imagine a scene in which two young lovers decide to go swimming in a remote lake. They don't see anyone around, and they feel safe. But this is not a horror movie, so they *are* safe.

To define the core of the genre, it is important to take a look at the word and its history. "Horror," according to the *Oxford English Dictionary*, begins its career in English as a roughness or ruggedness; there is something uneven about it. It also means "a roughness or nauseousness of taste, such as to cause a shudder or thrill." Nausea remains part of the horror response, part of the definition—and so do the shudder and the thrill. Roughness and nausea are linked to disgust and revulsion, for horror often provokes a gut reaction as the belly tightens up in shock or turns over to vomit. In *The Texas Chain Saw Massacre* (Tobe Hooper, 1974, US), when Pam sees the horrific artwork made of bones and feathers, she vomits. "A horror" also means a shuddering or shivering, especially "as a symptom of disease," but in Latin the verb *horrēre*—the source of "horror"—means to tremble, shiver, shake or shudder, not necessarily because of disease, but in some cases because of fear; it also means to loathe and to dread as well as to bristle, to stand on end as hair does, and to be rough. The hair-raising shudder is part of the term. The fullest and most lasting sense of the word is in place by the late fourteenth century: "a painful emotion compounded of loathing and fear; a shuddering with terror and repugnance; strong aversion mingled with dread; the feeling excited by something shocking or frightful."[6] Beginning in the late fifteenth century it is also used to signify "a feeling of awe or reverent fear (without any suggestion of repugnance); a thrill of awe, or of imaginative fear,"[7] a usage that touches on the heights to which fear can lead the imagination, an important aesthetic consideration, which also provides a link with our sometimes ineffable response to the sublime.[8] There it is: rough, nauseating, dreadful, frightening, hair-raising, repulsive, unspeakable, nameless, loathsome—an odd foundation on which to build an art.

Yet it is an art, one that depends on the successful evocation and manipulation of fascination, revulsion and fear, and that may present to us scenes and realms of fantastic, dangerous, uncanny beauty. A film with a particular monster or threat usually is built around a particular fear or set of fears,[9] including the outright fear of the monster and what it can do, as well as of what it represents, evokes, symbolizes or implies. The vampire picture is built around the vampire, and the vampire comprises all the fears and horrors for which it provides a form, an embodiment: the horror of drinking blood, the fear of losing blood, the fear of contamination or infection, the fear of being bitten, the horror of wanting to drink blood, the fear of death and the horror of undeath. Or the fear might be in response to endangering some less tangible aspect of being or behavior that we value, such as our free will. Or it might be a response to something new that the film has shown or implied or triggered—a guide that leads us into the world of horror, as if into the dark. Fears can be grouped according to their objects: fear of the unknown (which includes death and the dark), fear of the self (one might turn into Mr Hyde) and the largest category, fear of others, which can range from the fear of a real snake—the sight or sound of which instantly activates the brain's amygdala, where feelings of anxiety appear, according to current research, to be stored[10]—to the fear of an unreal vampire.

Taking It All In

Our eyes widen at the image of horror, taking it in, feeling awe at the awful. Those moments—when we must look at what we dread to imagine or think we cannot bear to see—are the pulse of the genre, moments of revelation and clarity. We are faced with the monster at the height of its power, the terrible event, the truth of the situation, the realized intuition, the threat that hid in the dark. In *The Texas Chain Saw Massacre*, a film rich in fundamental examples, such a horror moment comes when Leatherface (Gunnar Hansen) hangs Pam (Teri McMinn) on a hook and then starts to saw up an earlier victim. Another comes when we see Sally's (Marilyn Burns) unbelieving look of shock, fear and revulsion when Grandpa (John Dugan) sucks her bleeding finger as if he were a baby, a scene perverse in its confusion of milk and blood. Her eyes wide but tightly focused on her finger in the old man's mouth, she offers one example of the look at horror (Figure 1). When watching this scene, it is almost impossible not to try and pull one's hand away. A more understated example of horror at its peak and the consciousness of it (in this case an aroused moral consciousness) comes in *Salò or The 120 Days of Sodom* (Pier Paolo Pasolini, 1975, Italy/France) when the pianist sees the final torturous killings and silently jumps out of a window to her death.

There is an unforgettable horror moment in *Black Sun 731* (T. F. Mou, 1987, China), better known as *Men Behind the Sun*, a PRC[11] film, about the atrocities performed on Chinese prisoners during the Second World War by Japanese doctors in the Manchurian medical research facility, Unit 731. A woman has her hands and arms thawed in warm water after they have been frozen solid in a frostbite experiment. To demonstrate the destruction of tissue, a doctor suddenly strips the flesh off the woman's arms and hands down to the bone. The woman holds her skeletal arms in front of her and screams, her eyes wide open and staring at the bones and at the bag of flesh that hangs from one of her hands (Figure 2). We see the evidence and imagine the depths of the subjective horror she feels, but we also see her and her arms together as an objective horror, and

Figure 1. *The Texas Chain Saw Massacre*: Looking at horror.

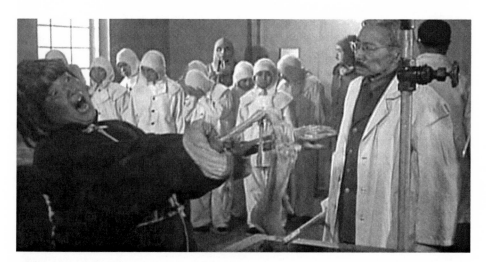

Figure 2. *Black Sun 731*: The spectacle and the look.

thus we look at the spectacle two ways: with our own vision and with a vision mediated through the character who sees and reacts to it. This reacting figure recurs throughout the genre. In a horror scene, someone is usually looking at or screaming at or hiding from or intuiting the horror, giving the audience a character through whom to experience the fear, a way in.

Spectacle and Suggestion

Not every resonant horror moment has to be shocking. Many of the best scenes, and many considered the more artful, are subtle. It is not necessary to display the horrific event, or the monster or the violence on the screen, even though one of the advantages of the horror film in comparison to horror tales and literature is that it can *show* the monster, or whatever parts of the story can be rendered as images (although horror literature may have the advantage in imaginative or abstract power, like evoking disembodied fear). But what is shown to the audience may be not a gorging zombie but a creepy night wind in the trees, an image that has, in many stories and movies, been used to imply impending danger or a supernatural presence. The art of such a shot is not one of spectacle but one of suggestion.

Film can draw on either or both ways of conveying horror. For example, there are two sequential killing scenes in *The Descent: Part 2* (Jon Harris, 2009, UK). In both cases a human is attacked by a monster in a cave. In the first scene, we see the spectacle of the monstrous humanoid taking a bite out of a man's neck, blood spurts and all. In the next scene, where a woman is apparently slashed to pieces, the monster is shown as a shadow on the cave wall, and the victim and her wounds are implied or evoked when blood splashes onto a flashlight. The sounds of both scenes are violent and keep the monsters and victims vividly present, but these sounds can still be divided according to their purpose in each scene: to make the shown wound more realistic or to evoke the unseen.

One of the first things to examine critically about a horror film is whether it depends more successfully on spectacle or on suggestion. Certainly there has been a tendency throughout the history of the horror film to increase the degree of spectacle and to make those visions of horror increasingly realistic, subject to the censorship and other expectations of the time. What cannot be shown must be implied, and much of the art of the horror film has developed as a means of suggesting—in shadows, for instance—what might be hidden in shadows.

It has long been recognized that the films Val Lewton produced at RKO offer superior examples of suggesting horror rather than directly, overtly presenting it. In *Cat People* (Jacques Tourneur, 1942, US), for example, he avoided the onscreen transformations seen in the previous year's *The Wolf Man* (George Waggner, 1941, US), and in *Cat People*'s pool scene it is clear that the cat-woman shredded the swimmer's robe in the offscreen locker room, but not whether she was a cat when she did it—an example of how suggestion can embrace ambiguity. A more run-of-the-mill but still effective use of suggestion can be found in *Village of the Damned* (Wolf Rilla, 1960, UK), when a military official looks at the offscreen face of a man who has been burned. We can see from his reaction how bad the burns must be, but we do not see the burned face for ourselves. While the increasingly graphic sex and violence that began in the 1960s have led to a less restrained use of spectacle in the horror film, suggestion has continued to play a key role. In *The Uninvited* (Lewis Allen, 1944, US), suggestion builds until the ghost is completely revealed and spectacle becomes more dominant, and much the same happens with the monster in the far later *Super 8* (J.J. Abrams, 2011, US).

Lewton's *The Body Snatcher* (Robert Wise, 1945, US) offers a great moment of suggested horror when a grave-robber (Boris Karloff) kills a blind street singer (Donna Lee) after she walks into complete shadow. All we see is the night street and the shadow, and all we hear is her singing suddenly cut off as the killer stops his coach and silently chokes her. The abrupt end of her song, conveying her murder, is violent in its implications but not its presentation. Upsetting and cruel, the scene also presents a rich moment of horror beauty and a memorable use of the fear of the dark.

What we see is rendered problematic in the horror film, for we may or may not enjoy what we see or being put in the position to see it. People do not cover their eyes when reading a horror story, but many do when watching a graphic or frightening horror movie, afraid or unwilling to see the image before them. Like the problem of unwelcome or resisted vision, the problems and solutions the genre has raised for itself are acutely cinematic: to work intensely with our fear of the dark, for example, or to charge space with a sense of the uncanny or troubling (as Carl Dreyer said, a room changes when we know there is a corpse behind the door[12]). Horror is among the most cinematic of film genres, a playground for showing and hiding. Movie images are projected shadows, present and not present, an ideal medium for making us see the fantastic and the impossible or a record of the real. The horror film can give form to a threatened or threatening space, provoke terror or apprehension with a sound, set and manipulate a frightening or eerie mood and show a monster or a gross event in all its immediacy. It can summarize, realize and deliver a disgusting and repellent horror, as does the sound made by the woman in *Dumplings* (Fruit Chan's contribution to *Three…Extremes* [Fruit Chan, Takashi Miike and Park Chan Wook, 2004, Hong Kong/Japan/South Korea])—as she chews the barely formed bones of finely chopped fetuses stuffed in dumplings so that she can look younger. *Black Sun 731* shocks us with spectacle, and *Ringu* (Hideo Nakata, 1998, Japan), also known as *Ring*, shows us the ghost, while *The Body Snatcher* hides a murder in a field of black. Image and sound can charge the darkness that hides a horror object with the fear of the unknown or the dreaded, and both the atmosphere and the threat— which both are crucial—lend themselves to being shown in whatever light is available or hidden in the visually tangible darkness.

A spectacle can horrify, but so can an idea, an atmosphere or an implication. The horror film often constructs a conceptual framework that provokes a shudder as it falls into place, exemplified at the end of *Rosemary's Baby* (Roman Polanski, 1968, US), based on the novel by Ira Levin, or *Dead of Night* (Alberto Cavalcanti, Charles Crichton, Robert Hamer, and particularly Basil Dearden,[13] 1945, UK), or in the chilling moment when the viewer of *Peeping Tom* (Michael Powell, 1960, UK) finally understands how the victims are killed and the rationale behind it. The genre depends as much on the unshown as it does on the shown. Thus, one of the best things about *The Haunting* (Robert Wise, 1963, US), adapted from Shirley Jackson's much more frightening *The Haunting of Hill House*, is that the film never lets us see the ghost. Likewise, much of the art in the opening of Lewton's *The Leopard Man* (Jacques Tourneur, 1943, US) is devoted to frightening us with darkness and sudden sounds before it unleashes a violence that is shown only indirectly: instead of seeing the killing, we see the victim's blood running under a door, and as the blood follows the gaps between the floorboards, it starts to form a cross.

Nightmares and Forbidden Texts

Nightmares can be dangerous, opening the dreamer to a world of horror, and they and their visions can be of an unknown that, as it gradually becomes defined, brings or predicts destruction. A recurring dream turns into a trap for the dreamer in *Dead of Night*. John Baxter (Donald Sutherland), in *Don't Look Now* (Nicolas Roeg, 1973, UK/Italy), has psychic powers he does not recognize, misunderstands a vision of his own funeral and fails to pay attention to a ghostly visitor, which contributes to the death of the hero. *Don't Look Now* is an excellent example, down to its title, of how the horror film problematizes vision. Another film in the same vein, *The Last Wave* (Peter Weir, 1977, Australia) is about a lawyer, David Burton (Richard Chamberlain), beset by prophetic and visionary dreams as well as waking visions. He confronts the reality of the supernatural and his own role as a doomed prophet, then faces or has a vision of the great wave that will destroy him and his world and— if one takes the cosmic view of catastrophe—provoke a fresh start.

A character can even die in a dream. At the end of *The Ugly* (Scott Reynolds, 1997, New Zealand) a therapist, Karen (Rebecca Hobbs), is at home in bed when she sees her patient, Simon (Paolo Rotondo), standing before her. Simon is, as we will see in the next chapter, the monster in her bedroom, and through the window she can see other figures from Simon's dream world. He then slits her throat. She wakes up, and then realizes it was a dream. She goes back to sleep, and the wound opens in her neck. As she bleeds to death, unconscious, we see Simon leave her bedside. The quietly opening wound makes clear the power of dreams to extend into the horror film's reality, without offering any explanation of how the dreaded and perhaps impossible events are happening— a narrative decision that can be crucial to a dreamlike horror's effectiveness and that maintains the integrity of the unknown.

Some nightmares can be compared to forbidden texts, for they show what should not be seen. A forbidden text is one we are not meant to open, and we may feel drawn to or repelled by it. Such a text can be a book, like the *Necronomicon* in Lovecraft's fiction, or a document like the Scroll of Thoth in *The Mummy* (Karl Freund, 1932, US), that carries information meant never to be read or known. The person who reads it and perhaps acts on it is usually destroyed. There may be a curse on anyone who opens it, as there is on the case containing the Scroll of Thoth, and its words, read aloud, may invoke or bring to life the horror it concerns, as do the words on the tape in *The Evil Dead* (Sam Raimi, 1983, US) or the spell to revive the dead in *The Mummy*. The document may also merely be difficult to find and dangerous to act on, like Frankenstein's notebook in many of the Universal sequels to *Frankenstein*, a notebook whose information helps bring the Monster back to a powerful state, and that usually proves destructive to the doctor by providing the means to attain forbidden knowledge. A forbidden text makes its horror happen. The tape in *The Evil Dead*, which is a forbidden text as well as a manual like the *Book of the Vampire*, both activates the monsters and tells one how to deal with them; it is found in a cellar that can be chained shut.

Some horror films reflexively present it as dangerous to attend a horror film—the forbidden text as an audiovisual structure—where something like the events in the movie might happen to members of the audience, as in *He Knows You're Alone* (Armand

Mastroianni, 1980, US), where a woman is knifed through the back of her seat while the horror climaxes onscreen, and *Demons* (Lamberto Bava, 1985, Italy), where a barbed mask wounds and infects its victims in the same way on the screen and in the auditorium where the movie is being screened. Some horror films present forbidden visions as limited narrative structures that one would be better off not to consult yet cannot avoid, and some of these visions are dreams that may foretell or constitute horrors.

Completely different from the forbidden text are the accessible sacred text, with its correct words and effective ritual formulas (which is how it's presented in most films) and the scientific text (which could be a lecture or a body of notes) that dispels mystery and advances knowledge with experiments and interpreted facts. The nearest the forbidden and scientific texts approach each other is in Frankenstein's notebook, for the purely scientific text does not generate horror (at least not without some prodding) though it is often used to explain a horror. As opposed to science fiction, the horror genre is full of things people are not meant to know, though many characters pursue that knowledge anyway. In a horror film, a forbidden text will always be opened.

Real and Imagined Horror

Both real experience and art can have aspects that are frightening and repulsive. Horror is not confined to the fictitious. To be horrified is a real if not common experience if one lives in a peaceful time and place. When we are absorbed in a horror film, we respond to the things in it we know are impossible and also to the correspondences between the horrors intrinsic to the film and those of the real world. Noël Carroll has found it necessary to distinguish "art-horror," where the horror object is imaginary, from "natural" or real-world horror, where what provokes fear and disgust is something real and where aesthetic enjoyment is, he feels, ruled out.[14] But actual horror can be a component of fictional horror by reference or implication (or by inclusion, as in the Italian cannibal movies), and this is a concept horror often evokes; we may relate what we see on the screen to what we know of real horror, and start running through our fears of the real world even while we are immersed in the monstrous and the impossible. There are no 40-foot spiders, but there *are* spiders, and the gigantic one in *Tarantula* (Jack Arnold, 1955, US) is more frightening than most of the big bugs in movies because real tarantulas were used when shooting the optical effects, with slowed-down but authentic movements that anyone with a fear of spiders could recognize. We may think of the lethal sharpness of our own kitchen knives when we watch a slasher use one, or consider the pain and abjection inherent in real torture when watching the victims being tortured in *Salò* or *Hostel* (Eli Roth, 2005, released 2006, US).

Part of what a violent image signifies, then, is the concept of real violence. But in a commercial narrative film it also signifies unreality, that none of this is happening, that the creative and destructive imagination is in charge, that this is only an illusion in a movie produced according to professional standards. Some critics and theorists, Carroll among them, have preferred to limit the genre to the monstrous and the imaginary, so that horror films would be obligated to feature unnatural or fantastic monsters (which would leave *The Texas Chain Saw Massacre* and *Psycho* not as horror films) rather than unsupernatural humans, who may be consigned to thrillers.[15] While I agree with Carroll that a horror film needs a monster or a figure that focuses and embodies the horror—or even a disembodied and undefined force, as in *The Exterminating Angel* (Luis Buñuel, 1962, Mexico)—I believe that there are more kinds of monsters in the genre than he allows. I propose that the scope and subjects of the genre depend on how one defines the films' central threats, their horror figures or monsters. For instance, Leatherface is a human horror figure (in other words, *Texas Chain Saw* certainly is a horror film, and the "monsters" in it are human ones) and, as said before, there are three major subgenres within the horror film, depending on the kind of threat: monsters without supernatural characteristics (Godzilla), supernatural monsters or forces (Kharis) and monstrous humans (Leatherface).[16] I also propose that the genre can draw on real as well as imagined horror, much as *Black Sun 731* draws on the reality of Unit 731[17] or *The Body Snatcher* draws on the history of grave-robbing. *Night and Fog* (Alain Resnais, 1955, France), a documentary that contains authentic footage of atrocities, shares many aspects with the horror film and could be called a horror documentary. *Night and Fog* is about the knowledge of horror and what can be learned from it, an attempt (in the shot that tilts slowly up the immense pile of female victims' hair, for instance) to find a way to acknowledge and conceptualize horror, to comprehend it, to contain it in a shot, though this may prove impossible. It does not set out to horrify us in the fictive manner of what Carroll would call an "art-horror" film, but it remains a film that inspires horror. And so, what it reveals about horror, and the problems of thinking about it and adequately showing it, is also valid for the dramatic film. The narrative film *Cannibal Holocaust* (Ruggero Deodato, 1980, Italy) is an extreme example of realism that does not come from the documentary, but includes real horror in order to make the rest of the film appear more authentic—as in several scenes in which animals are killed on camera. In addition, to shift from the atrocious to the great, it is crucial to its effect and meaning that *Freaks* (Tod Browning, 1932, US) has a cast of real freaks.

Endings

Before going on to examine systematically the ways horror has been realized in all its narrative modes and categories, we need to take a further introductory look at the horror film's changing concept of the normal and how it may be threatened—and at its closed and open endings, some of its formulas and recurring elements, its beauty, its reflexivity, its appeal and the ways it takes advantage of being denigrated and ignored, as well as some particularly resonant recurring images, structures and strategies.

Both the movies that work more with the unshown or suggested and those that work more with the shown project a world whose status quo is threatened by an incarnation of danger, a shape taken by a fear. The status quo can be the safe, familiar lives of the characters and their (usually stable) sociopolitical world, or it can be a nice day with no unusual problems or any state of order and calm (or disorder and discomfort, but not because of the monster) that the movie may finally reestablish. It can also be the universe as we know it. Robin Wood has called this threatened state (which, he has argued, may depend on psychological repression and on oppressive sexual politics) the "normality" that is threatened by the monster.[18] Of course, constructs of normality date films as readily as new cars; any vision of the norm is something that changes with time, varies with culture and in practice is rarely as monolithic as it sounds. In ancient horror tales like *Beowulf*, the hall where Beowulf and the others celebrate their deeds and lie down to rest is part of the established way of things. Grendel, the monster from the outside, breaks into the hall, tearing the warriors to pieces. With the eventual killing of Grendel and his mother, the human norm is restored.

But for Beowulf there will be one more monster, a dragon. At the end of the poem the hero will die, and an age with him; by the end of a horror movie, the normal world may or may not have been restored, and the monster may or may not have been destroyed. Even after death, the monster's having existed may lead to further consequences—not just in a sequel, but in the last minutes of the original picture. The resolution that followed the climax may be undone in the final shots. The unsettling of things may have become permanent. The conventional ending, the closing of the wounds opened by the presence and actions of the monster, is reassuring. It becomes a ritual with ritual power, as it declares the world once again a safe place for humanity to flourish. In particular the core of the norm, reproductive sexuality, may flourish (the reason so many horror movies end with a view of a potentially fertile couple and also the reason so many sexy couples are threatened), and so may the underlying, civilizing order. Even if the world as the characters know it has been destroyed, the hero and heroine can embrace, a sign of fertility and continuity but also a minor comic ending, for as Lord Byron observed in *Don Juan*, a tragedy ends with a death, but a comedy ends with a marriage.[19] The world may also be made safe through the destruction of the monster not in a comedic ending but in a tragic one, as in *Nosferatu: A Symphony of Horror* (F. W. Murnau, 1922, Germany) or *Gojira* (Ishiro Honda, 1954, Japan, also known as *Godzilla*; US version, *Godzilla King of the Monsters!*, 1956). The conventional ending offers a return to a state of rest and stability— even if it is full of rubble and death—after the intrusion and destruction of the threat.

At the conclusion of *Frankenstein* (James Whale, 1931, US), for example, Henry Frankenstein (Colin Clive) is recovering from his injuries, and the wedding is being planned again or at least is expected by the baron, who makes the closing toast, hoping for a grandson. This insures romantic continuity and the survival of the species, that is, our species, as the Frankensteins will presumably give birth to normal children. With the Monster (Boris Karloff) destroyed and with Henry in no mood for further experiments, the norm has been restored. There will be no more constructed monsters, as babies will be made in the usual way, nor will there be any more disturbing of the dead, as the natural processes of death and decay will be left to continue. Death is back in its place, in charge of its domain. Nature will follow its course, an interplay of birth and death. The whole movie has led us to come to terms with this, with the normal world of natural reproduction and natural death, rather than to indulge our desire to change the rules.

However, after the success of the shock endings of *Carrie* (Brian De Palma, 1976, US), *Halloween* (John Carpenter, 1978, US), and *Friday the 13th* (Sean S. Cunningham, 1980, US), it became commonplace to have the threat be vanquished in a climax but then to follow that with an ending that undermined the sense of resolution, much as had the unexpected ending in *Night of the Living Dead* (George A. Romero, 1968, US)[20] or the open ending of *The Birds* (Alfred Hitchcock, 1963, US). Like Carrie's hand, the horror would jump back into view and become present again. The ending of the original *The Hills Have Eyes* (Wes Craven, 1977, US) makes it clear that the last villain has been killed; yet the last shot of the remake (Alexandre Aja, 2006, US) makes it clear that there is at least one surviving deranged outsider watching the closing scene. Such open endings have become expected, mitigating their impact, but most of them still aim to send the audience out with a shock of unresolved fear, to carry the chill outside. Compared with the conventional ending, the post-*Halloween* ending shows the horror as completely accomplished rather than defeated, and it implies that safety and the norm cannot be restored, at least not for these characters. This is how *Cloverfield* (Matt Reeves, 2008, US), the remake of *Friday the 13th* (Marcus Nispel, 2009, US) and many others end. The real surprise now is when films like *Hostel Part II* (Eli Roth, 2007, US) and the remake of *The Last House on the Left* (Dennis Iliadis, 2009, US) have closed, happy endings. Perhaps, as the world becomes more unsettled, we are starting to feel the need for more resolution in our horror endings.

Recurring Elements

Genres include recurring elements, figures and situations, and their repetition from one film to another is part of the pleasure. An original approach to the ghost story still has a ghost in it, and that ghost brings along with it ghosts from earlier works, with new opportunities to work with or against genre formulas. The same opportunities arise in recurring situations, such as being surprised by a killer, threatened by a mad scientist or chased by a monster, which need to avoid clichés to be effective.

A recurring figure in many horror films is a person who knows the secrets and the terms of what is going on: the gypsy Maleva (Maria Ouspenskaya) in *The Wolf Man* or Dr Van Helsing (Edward Van Sloan) in *Dracula* (Tod Browning, 1931, US). This figure is usually older than the other characters and sees things that more conventional people would deny, like the old drunk in the graveyard near the beginning of *Texas Chain Saw*, who says that he's seen things around there nobody talks about and that some people would be well advised to listen to him. An equivalent of this well-informed figure is the *Book of the Vampire*, a text that under this title or a similar one makes its first film appearance in 1922 in *Nosferatu*[21] and plays an important role in *Vampyr* (Carl Dreyer, 1932, Germany/France). At first, it is a book or document that explains what a vampire is and contains instructions for destroying one. In later films it need not be a book, or about vampires; in *The Evil Dead* it takes the form of a tape recording about demons.[22] The important thing is that it's an authoritative, supernatural instruction manual, laying out the nature of the monster with which the characters are confronted. The older, wiser or more insightful One Who Knows what is going on, the Maleva or Van Helsing who may have special access to magic, science and ritual, is a type. The old drunk in *Texas Chain Saw* functions as the One Who Knows, but in contrast to that type, he is incompetent because he is a drunk, and no one thinks to ask him what happened in the graveyard or what else he might be talking about. He is a formulaic figure played against formula. We need the background of other films to recognize him, and we are stimulated, even glad, when our conventional expectations of him are frustrated. Such figures—conceived against type or reinforcing formulas, though some manage to do both—appear throughout the genre.

Beauty

Horror can lay claim to beauty. Writers from Edgar Allan Poe to H. P. Lovecraft have argued that the most important element of a horror story is atmosphere. A setting and tone may be unsettling and still be masterfully rendered; they may also demand to be called beautiful in their own terms—the terms of horror. There is a haunted pool in *Beowulf*:

> 'Tis an eerie spot! Its tossing spray
> Mounts dark to heaven when high winds stir
> The driving storm, and the sky is murky,
> And with foul weather the heavens weep.[23]

This eerie image, constructed out of unpleasant elements, sets the tone and lays out the terms for a place where dark things happen. One can also take from *Beowulf* a powerful image composed of violent material:

> There Grendel suffered a grievous hurt,
> A wound in the shoulder, gaping and wide;
> Sinews snapped and bone-joints broke,
> And Beowulf gained the glory of battle.[24]

This is a spectacle of gore, a celebration of tearing body parts. It contributes to the theme of heroic violence, and its beauty can be found in its immersion in the extreme. Both kinds of image—the eerie setting and the grisly spectacle—abound in the horror film, though the former is usually the one called atmospheric. It is also worth noting this vivid evocation of fear in Coleridge's "The Rime of the Ancient Mariner":

> Like one, that on a lonely road
>   Doth walk in fear and dread,
> And having once turn'd round walks on,
>   And turns no more his head:
> Because he knows, a frightful fiend
>   Doth close behind him tread.[25]

And from the same poem there is a memorably unpleasant image:

> The very deeps did rot: O Christ!
>   That ever this should be!
> Yea, slimy things did crawl with legs
>   Upon the slimy sea.[26]

Effective atmosphere conveys a conviction about the world in which the film takes place: that we are confronted with a frightful sphere that has its own rules, such as that people can turn into wolves under the spell of the full moon or that death can fail.[27] Part of the atmosphere associated with the werewolf can be found in that moon, that sign of night, in the disturbing nature of its spell and in the notion that it could cast a spell at all. It sets the tone. Less subtly, relentlessly, the tone is set in *Texas Chain Saw* by the monumental sculpture made out of corpses by the hitchhiker (Edwin Neal)—an example within the film of horror art—and soon the atmosphere is enriched by a soundtrack of running engines, squawking chickens and screaming people. The scene in which the doctor (Jan Hieronimko) is smothered to death in flour is a beautiful moment in *Vampyr*, a triumph of white, and there is beauty in the terrifying, arresting, perfectly realized shots in which the vampire's victim, Léone (Sybille Schmitz), turns her head to follow her sister, Gisèle (Rena Mandel), her eyes gone evil. The image feels evil.

Reflexivity

Horror can be full of things we never want to see done or to feel, yet there we are, watching. Reflexivity—a reference to the horror film from within a horror film, or more universally, the conveyed impression that a work of art is aware of itself as a work of art, either as part of a tradition or as a self-directing structure—has many uses in the horror film, and one of them is to make us conscious of our potentially voyeuristic, sadistic or masochistic position—to call attention to the moral, aesthetic and psychological aspects of filming and watching horror, of putting the frightening in a narrative frame and a visual one, of looking. Another use of reflexivity is to put the horror in a frame or on an inner screen where it can be homaged or analyzed, considered as an illusion, compared with a nightmare—another limited narrative field that contains a horror—and related to its previous appearances on film. Many horror movies ask us to consider why we have decided to attend this spectacle of the frightful, the gruesome, the violent, the disturbed—why we have chosen to have a nightmare, to share the experience of a madman or his victim, and so on. *Mad Love* (Karl Freund, 1935, US) opens with such a question, when a woman angrily asks her date why he has taken her to a horror show. Midway through the much later *Funny Games* (Michael Haneke, 1997, Austria), one of the killers asks the audience a similar question about what we want from the film, a film that actually interrogates the desire for violence.

Appeal

There are many reasons people like horror films. They may take us back to a campfire or a comic book, to an early experience of the power of narration, to what "a good story" meant to us. They may take us back to early experiences at the movies, where the unfamiliar, challenging, mysterious and awe-inspiring images of horror and fantasy films may have helped to define our impressions of the fabulous. Their images may have been among the first resonant images we were aware of receiving from the movies. To revisit them or to see new horror films may be to renew those thrills with a sense of having come home, of returning to a founding and forbidden text—forbidden in the sense that it offers secret knowledge, to be used only within the ritual of the genre, but also in that it reflects what is widely considered inferior taste, giving us the pleasure of seeing and enjoying something we should not. More simply, they may have contained the first film images that frightened us and therefore stuck with us, or such images may have been parts of films in other genres, like *The Wizard of Oz* (Victor Fleming, 1939, US). They may take us back to the defining moments of Western culture, when pity and terror were the crucial and cathartic responses to tragedy. In the East, they may take us back to the defining separation and interpenetration of worlds, like those of the mortal and the ghost. They may help us to relive, in a controlled context, the trauma of puberty (the subject of many horror films, not just those about werewolves[28]) or to experience the fear of death when there is no danger of the movie's events' killing us. To use an overfamiliar but apt image, they may offer the roller-coaster experience of generated and controlled fear. It can be a pleasure to endure a controlled danger in the theatre as much as in the amusement park.

The defense of horror films most often offered by filmmakers is that they allow us to work out our fears and stresses through identification and catharsis, that they offer a purge for aggression and anxiety, that we can use them to blow off steam. Some critics say this cathartic process helps us fit into our prescribed social roles, to become calm when we had been in a heightened state and to see that the status quo has survived the eruption of the horror object, the apparently unkillable, undispellable threat, as a regime may survive a revolution. We may want this sociopolitical reassurance—or we may, on the contrary, enjoy the film as a revolutionary site, a narrative field in which politics and the status quo may be called into question. The horror film can take extreme chances because, as John Carpenter once observed,[29] nobody is paying attention to it. The horror film's generally low budget and reputation keep it below the radar, both of producers and of many reviewers. Anything can happen, and any position can be taken. Some people like horror films, then, because they may be politically radical, psychologically revelatory or poetically interesting. They have a history and an iconography that are fascinating to follow. They make art out of horrific material, and they assault the body in particular because it is a powerful site of identity as well as of eroticism and pain. Horrific cinematic uses of the body can be as subtle as Pam's naked back in the early parts of *Texas Chain Saw*—foreshadowing the scene in which a meat hook is sunk into her unprotected back—or as blatant as the gore in *Blood Feast* (Herschell Gordon Lewis, 1963, US).

Horror films also resonate, politically and personally, with what we know of some extremes of human behavior, and in this they are relevant to an understanding of the world. They grapple with the important mysteries of sex and death and they may even give us a feeling of temporary power over death. They may express a nostalgia for contact with the spirit world and can give us a chance to visit the Land of the Dead, like the hero of an epic. They develop the imagery of horror to a high degree of complexity, subtlety and mutual reference, revealing the labyrinth of the art, an art that depends on fear and the inevitability of dealing with fear. In *War and Peace* Tolstoy wrote of the line between opposing armies:

"One step beyond that line, reminiscent of the line separating the living from the dead, and it's the unknown, suffering, and death. And what is there? who is there? there, beyond this field, and the tree, and the roof lit by the sun? No one knows, and you would like to know; and you're afraid to cross that line, and would like to cross it; and you know that sooner or later you will have to cross it and find out what is there on the other side of the line, as you will inevitably find out what is there on the other side of death. And you're strong, healthy, cheerful, and excited, and surrounded by people just as strong and excitedly animated." So, if he does not think it, every man feels who finds himself within sight of an enemy, and this feeling gives a particular brilliance and joyful sharpness of impression to everything that happens in those moments.[30]

The horror film allows us figuratively to cross Tolstoy's line between life and death—and to engage what frightens us with our perceptions keen. Fear is part of the energy with which we cross the military line or its equivalent, and being afraid is one of the reasons we have to cross it. Advancing on the unknown is an essential part of life, though it risks death. For only the living can risk death—and they may enjoy constructing a story or a movie about how they made fear their companion, how they lived with it and let it decide, for a while, the terms of their existence.

Frames and Windows

This book will go on to investigate many things: the fears the horror film stirs up and the art of frightening people; the horror film's range and its often serious themes and concerns; some of its recurring or related figures, icons and devices; its use of point of view and reflexivity; its occasional overlap with such genres as science fiction and comedy; its use of dreams and rituals; how it is filled with references to its own intrusion into our consciousness; how monsters, events, situations and settings evoke and become symbols for what we fear or are made to fear; how the genre may take human nature for its topic and concern; the ways film techniques can create horror and stimulate fear; certain plot devices, such as the interrupted honeymoon, and the reasons for them; the most important kinds of monsters and what we fear and find emphasized in them; and the reasons it may be valuable and rewarding to be horrified. It will deal with these matters by looking at a number of the most significant horror films in terms of the fears they evoke and the horrors they reveal, many of which are founded in particular monsters, for no matter how the movies diverge, fear and monstrosity are at their core. The films that are discussed have been selected because of their excellence and historic importance, or simply because of the resonant threats and images they contain. Brief plot summaries are used as tools of analysis and to orient the reader who hasn't seen the films.

The rest of this introductory section concentrates primarily on narrative frames, such as the uses of inner storytelling devices and of reflexive structures, because they open so many important aspects of the horror film in general, and because they form a link with horror literature that reveals some of the genre's key ongoing narrative strategies and techniques. The narrative within a narrative has been used to enhance horror since Henry James's "The Turn of the Screw" and Mary Shelley's *Frankenstein*. So has the narrator who is mentally disturbed or whose perspective has been disoriented by a horrific experience, as in Sadegh Hedayat's *The Blind Owl*. And so have windows, dreams and other inner framing devices that may, by setting part of the story within limits, render its reality ambiguous and its unrealities more effective. The horror film has played with reflexivity and inner framing from *King Kong* (Merian C. Cooper and Ernest B. Schoedsack, 1933, US) to the *Scream* series (Wes Craven, 1996–2011, US). The influential *[REC]* (Jaume Balagueró and Paco Plaza, 2007, Spain), itself influenced by *The Blair Witch Project* (Daniel Myrick and Eduardo Sánchez, 1999), foregrounds the use of a video camera and thereby intensifies the claustrophobic nature of the events, and heightens the sense that what one doesn't see outside the limits of the viewfinder may be fatal. There is also the general sense that we put horror in a frame in order to distance and protect ourselves from it, and that defense operates in the cinema as well as in literature and in reactions to real trauma—although there are movies like *Salò* in which a distancing device (in that film, the reversed binoculars) brings the horror closer and makes it more intense. To look at a frame is also to look through it, to examine the genre's vision of itself and the nature of the threat it reveals to the viewer.

As a more visual means of introducing the horror genre and the rich intricacy of its uses of tradition, suggestion and repetition, one recurring image calls out to be examined in detail: that of the monster at the bedroom window, a model of the intrusion of horror into our consciousness as we watch a horror movie. Both the everyday world—the

Figure 3. *Bride of Frankenstein*: The Monster at the window.

established one of the fiction—and the world open to dreams are touched by the arrival of horror. As we shall see in the next chapter, the window frame may contain a monster's image as if it were being dreamt of or as if the monster were being seen directly, or the frame may turn reflexive and contain the monster as in a tale or a work of art. In both cases, and as a literal window, it provides access and an interface—even when the window is not in a bedroom (Figure 3), as in this frame from *Bride of Frankenstein* (James Whale, 1935, US). The bed, when it is present, signifies the potential for sexual activity and for dreaming. The window puts fear in a frame, whether it is a narrated frame like a nightmare or a visible rectangle that separates and brings together the known world of the bedroom and the unknown world of the monster.

2

THE MONSTER
AT THE BEDROOM WINDOW

Tarantula

Tarantula concerns the experiments of Professor Gerald Deemer (Leo G. Carroll), who with his late assistants has been developing a radioactive nutrient that has led to rapid development and abnormal growth in animal test subjects, notably a gigantic tarantula that escapes during a fire in the lab in Deemer's house in the desert. The isotope they added to their nutrient, Deemer says late in the film, "triggered" the nutrient into "a nightmare." There are indeed many scenes in *Tarantula* that can remind one of nightmares, such as when two men are running from the spider at night and can't get away, but one implication of Deemer's line is that the whole experience is comparable to a nightmare: that *Tarantula*'s events are as frightening as those in a nightmare and could happen only in one (which lets the viewer compare the horror film to a nightmare) and that they have been overtaken by the equivalent of a frightening dream turned real, a horror that has erupted into the waking world with a monster that is, like the Monster in *Bride of Frankenstein*, "a nightmare in the daylight." The use of the word "triggered" links the science fiction premise of the film to the 1950s' fear of uncontrolled atomic technology. This monster movie has aspects of both science fiction and horror, but horror predominates.

Stephanie "Steve" Clayton (Mara Corday), a graduate student, becomes Deemer's new assistant. One night she is studying in her second-story bedroom, wearing a robe. The tarantula approaches the house—perhaps, like the Frankenstein Monster, to find its creator. She closes her book and crosses the room, unaware that the tarantula is looking through the large window that faces the camera. The spider, whose gender we do not know, is looking straight into the room and appears to be looking at her; the centers of two of its eyes reflect light, making it resemble a two-eyed voyeur. When Steve turns out the light and starts to take off her robe and get into bed, the spider becomes agitated, as if excited to kill, or sexually excited (no matter how unlikely the attraction between species, for this is about the confrontation between a monster and a woman, a ritual union with its own conventions). Its excitement could also be a vehicle for the audience's feelings about the dangerous, sexy scene, because for the audience this is the moment of greatest excitement, the males presumably excited by the sight of the undressing woman, the females presumably alarmed by the woman's increased vulnerability now that she is undressing, and both of them identifying with the woman as a threatened being and feeling scared by the danger—or thrilled by it—now that the monster is so close to her, literally at her window. The tarantula also becomes violent because one point of the scene is simply to merge sex and horror, to juxtapose an active monster with a woman's undressing in a bedroom.[1] The spider begins to destroy the house, crushing the place and tearing through the roof. Steve runs out of the bedroom, still in her robe, and soon is in the arms of the hero, Dr Matt Hastings (John Agar). In short order the tarantula, one of many monsters that have destroyed their creators, kills Deemer. The question is, why would a spider spy on a half-dressed woman in her bedroom? Why is the moment when she gets into bed the moment when the monster sees her most clearly as a victim? The answer is that the monster at the bedroom window is an image with a history that has influenced and in fact determined this scene—in which the monster behaves according to form, the bed provides the key link between sex and horror, and the window is an interface.

The Cabinet of Dr. Caligari

The earliest example of this scene comes from one of the earliest horror features,[2] *The Cabinet of Dr. Caligari* (Robert Wiene, 1919, released 1920, Germany). The movie's narrator is a young man named Francis (Friedrich Feher). Dr Caligari (Werner Krauss), a mad psychiatrist, has a carnival exhibit whose centerpiece is Cesare (Conrad Veidt), who is actually one of his patients. Cesare is a somnambulist, but Caligari can awaken him. Cesare predicts exactly when Francis's friend Alan (Hans Heinrich von Twardowsky), a member of the audience, will die—before dawn—and soon we see in their shadows on the wall (a very influential shot—and entirely unlike those for which *Caligari* is better known, in which the shadows were painted and the sets were expressionist) Cesare's killing Alan with a long knife. Though he is not a full-fledged slasher nor a self-motivated serial killer, Cesare is at the head of a long list of movie villains who kill with a knife and who, like the psychologically disturbed murderers in *M* (Fritz Lang, 1931, Germany) and *Psycho*, are compelled to repeat their crimes. In *Caligari*, much is made of the fact that all the crimes are similar—as real psychopaths who kill usually have one preferred or compulsory way of killing. One night Caligari sends Cesare out to murder again, and the victim is Jane (Lil Dagover), whom Francis loves—but Cesare carries her off instead of killing her. In the chase that follows, Cesare drops Jane and soon dies of exhaustion.

Francis pursues Caligari to the asylum where it turns out Caligari is in charge. Francis convinces three of the other doctors to help him, and they discover in the director's office a book on somnambulism with a chapter called "The Cabinet of Dr. Caligari" that describes the original Caligari and "a series of foul murders committed under almost identical circumstances." They also find a diary in which the doctor decides to "become Caligari" in order to discover whether a somnambulist could be made to commit deeds that in his waking state would be repugnant to him, especially murder. The doctor is exposed and put in a straitjacket, and Francis is vindicated. As is well known, this story was given a frame in spite of the objections of the writers,[3] and in that opening and closing frame Francis tells the story to a stranger. Francis turns out to be crazy, his story a fantasy about his benevolent doctor and two other inmates of the asylum, Cesare and Jane. Thus *Caligari* is the first horror film, and one of the first films of any kind, to have an unreliable narrator—an important advance in the history of narrative complexity in the cinema and a useful device when a later horror film would want to render its events ambiguous or false. Francis loses control when he sees the man who he thinks is Caligari and is locked up (an ending that looks forward to the post-*Carrie* films in which the threat returns), but the doctor says he now knows how to cure him. The closing part of the frame narrative makes it clear that what we have been watching for most of the film is a mindscreen[1] and a misleading one, for Cesare is alive at the end, and he died in the tale.

In the abduction scene, Jane is asleep when Cesare appears at her bedroom window. The expressionist window is longer than a door and divided into panes that have no glass. Cesare tears out the bottom half of the high window, the skeleton of the panes, and throws it away, then steps through the man-sized gap in the window frame. As he walks from the window to the bed, he raises his knife, but as he is about to attack, he appears to be struck by Jane's beauty. He touches her hair, only she wakes up and screams, so he grabs her (Figure 4) and then carries her toward the window, her white nightgown and the white bedclothes momentarily stuck together and dragging after her like a bridal train. Her cry is heard by two men in the next room and they run in just after Cesare has borne the now unconscious Jane out the window. Jane's father comes into the room and collapses on the bed.

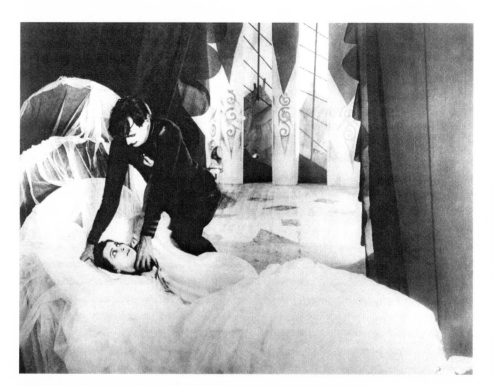

Figure 4. *The Cabinet of Dr. Caligari*: Cesare attacks Jane in her bed.

This establishes the basic scene: a woman who is in her bedroom, perhaps asleep, is confronted by a horror, usually a monster, whose access is through a window. She may be taken away, and others—observers and loved ones whose function is to validate the horror, to link the event to the everyday world—may rush into the room. The window opens outward onto the night and its creatures. It opens inward onto a site of privacy and vulnerability; the bedroom is a place for sleep, dreams and sex. The window is an interface between the world of horror and the worlds of normal activity and of dreaming, which itself can open one up to the impossible. Jane may be merely sleeping or having a nice dream, but there is a nightmare in the room, coming toward her from the night framed by the window. The window is one of the sites of horror, in the same scene with the bed on which it is possible to embrace a lover or have a nightmare. The window is also presented, in some films, as comparable to the frame of the movie— its proscenium—that allows horror to enter the consciousness of the audience, to bring nightmare into our cinematic dreams as if the theatre were a comfortable bedroom, to intrude into our private imaginative space. Even without the reflexive aspect, the scene accomplishes this interpenetration of worlds, this access and intrusion, for the characters. In almost all versions of this scene, the window is prominent. In *Tarantula* the window is large and near the center of the frame; in *Caligari* it is just to the right of the central background, and in a few close, diamond-shaped iris shots, when Cesare is breaking in, it nearly fills the view.

The window that frames the monster against the night can, then, be thought of as an image of the horror film. The frame that contains the monster can be considered an image of narrative structure, a contained tale, as well as of consciousness (for example, the horror may be mentally projected into or perceived within the window's space, like an objectified fear or a dream; consciousness is also implicit when we are aware of the dreamer or the narrator). The bedroom is a place made unsafe by nightmare or desire, a personal and subjective space that has been opened to horror, an image of the mind of the horror viewer. The movement through the window is an intrusion into the no-longer-safe bedroom or outward into the dangerous world of the realized imagination.

Nosferatu

At the climax of *Nosferatu*, Ellen Hutter (Greta Schroeder) deliberately makes herself vulnerable to the vampire, Count Orlok (Max Schreck). *Caligari* had an artificial mise-en-scène that needed to be shot entirely in a studio, but *Nosferatu* took the camera outdoors, in some cases to real sets, and used many more cinematic devices, becoming a film of horror expressed both artificially and in nature, of the touch of the supernatural on the natural world and mortal beings; nevertheless, this climactic sequence was shot in a studio. Ellen, wearing a white nightgown, is sleeping in bed when she feels the presence of the vampire, who stands at his own window. She wakes in alarm, as if from a nightmare, and sees her husband, Hutter (Gustav von Wangenheim), asleep in a chair. The vampire, reaching through the empty panes of the window of the large, decrepit building where he lives, just across the way from the Hutters, seems to urge her to open her own window. First as if in a trance, then deliberately, she opens the large bedroom window that faces the camera and that at this moment occupies more than half of the frame. The bed is across the room from the window, and in the foreground of many of the shots in this sequence. She sees Orlok in his window, which almost fills the screen (Figure 5); he leaves it, on the way to her, and opens his gate. She wakes her husband and tells him to get the professor (a Van Helsing type); this will leave her alone for long enough. For Ellen has read the *Book of the Vampire*, and she knows that the curse can be broken only when a woman who is pure of heart voluntarily sacrifices herself to the monster and keeps it with her, letting it drink her blood till daybreak destroys it. When her husband leaves, Ellen goes to the window, then turns as she hears the vampire behind her. We see his deformed shadow as it moves up the stairs and reaches for her door (reminiscent of but more stylized than the shot of shadows when Alan is murdered in *Caligari*). She backs toward the bed and gets on it. Soon he is drinking her blood in the dark, with the bed in the foreground and the window still open behind them. The cock crows, and Orlok realizes he has stayed too long. He gets up and moves in front of the window, dissolving as the sunlight hits him. Hutter returns with the professor just as Ellen dies.

The vampire summons her when she is in bed, he drinks her blood while she lies on the bed and she dies in her husband's arms on the bed. The prominent window in her bedroom signifies her openness to the vampire, her willingness to sacrifice herself, and faces another window that frames the vampire. The window also admits the sunlight that

Figure 5. *Nosferatu*: The vampire at his own window.

destroys Orlok; thus the window is a vehicle for his destruction and for Ellen's sacrifice, luring the vampire in and then burning it away. Rather than break into the bedroom and abduct the woman, the monster kills her and is himself destroyed before the observers rush in. Allowing for the censors' hiding it, there is a suggestion of rape in the image of a male's breaking into a bedroom and abducting or killing a female, and there is a strong sexual side to the figure of the vampire in general, whose intercourse is bloody and who often takes a victim in bed, like a nightmare of violation come true, which is one way to read the climax of *Nosferatu*.

In *Häxan* (Benjamin Christensen, 1922, Sweden) the Devil appears at the bedroom window of a woman who is asleep with her husband, at which point she begins to have a lascivious dream and moistens her lips. The Devil wakes her by knocking on the open shutter, comes through the window, and embraces her at her bedside while the man continues to sleep. More than the earlier bedroom-window scenes, this one explicitly links dreaming and sex in the presence of the monster.

Frankenstein

The bedroom-window scene in *Frankenstein* is similar to the one in *Caligari*. Elizabeth (Mae Clarke), who is to marry Henry Frankenstein that day, is in her bridal gown, pacing in the bedroom and holding her bouquet; her outfit has a very long train. She has been locked in there for her own protection while the men search for the Monster (Boris Karloff). She does not see or hear the Monster as he opens and steps through the large window that is just to the right of center in the background. At the moment she is looking away, and then she sits with her back to the window, holding the bouquet as if in a bridal portrait. When the Monster confronts Elizabeth in the novel, he murders her, and some echo of that threat is intended in this scene. Silently the Monster walks toward her (Figure 6), much as Cesare came in through the window and approached Jane's bed. Elizabeth gets up and walks to the door, then finally turns and sees him. He begins to chase her around the room. Henry hears her screaming, and people rush to the rescue but are delayed by the locked door. When we next see the interior of the bedroom, the Monster is going out the window—leaving because he had been interrupted—and the room is in disarray. Elizabeth is lying on the bed, and Henry has to step over her train, which evokes the image of Jane's bedclothes, to get to her.

Though the Monster would sooner kill Elizabeth than rape her, the scene is played in part as if she has escaped being raped, for the place the Monster leaves her is on a bed. She has been awake, not dreaming. To the extent that Frankenstein and the Monster are linked, this interrupted scene is the Monster's wedding to Elizabeth, an antiwedding complete with a fully decked-out bride. The Monster is a perverse groom, but there are many stories, poems, ballads and movies in which a woman is attracted to a demon lover. Often she is torn between a monster and a human lover, perhaps expressing her desire for both of them—the desire for the monster, in many cases, unconscious (unconscious in a film like *The Wolf Man* but quite conscious in *Twilight* [Catherine Hardwicke, 2008, US] and its sequels). This scene's principal goal is to make us fear for Elizabeth, the bride threatened by a monster. It is unusual that the scene takes place in daylight.

Figure 6. *Frankenstein*: The Monster approaches Elizabeth in a locked bedroom.

King Kong

Back in the night, in the original *King Kong* (1933), Kong has escaped from the Broadway theatre and is climbing a tall building, evidently a hotel, looking for Ann Darrow (Fay Wray). He looks through one window into a room where a woman lies on a bed, sleeping (Figure 7). We see Kong through the frame of the window. Kong reaches his hand in through another window,[5] grabs the woman in her bed and pulls her outside. Kong examines her, decides she is the wrong woman and drops her to her death.[6] Then he continues to climb. Ann and her fiancé, John "Jack" Driscoll (Bruce Cabot), come into a hotel room, talking about Kong. She sits on the bed, and he kneels before her. Kong's escape, Ann says, was "like a horrible dream." They are taking refuge from the streets, finding a quiet place where Ann will be safe, not intending anything sexual. Nevertheless, the bed is the item of furniture in the room that gets the most use in this scene, and the hotel room with a couple in it is an implicitly sexual site. Kong appears at one of the two windows in the room; the shot is composed so that the large window with Kong's head in it, to the left of center, faces the camera, and in the lower right of the image is the bed with Ann and Jack. Kong crashes his arm through the other window, then pulls back for another look through the first window. In the latter shot (Figure 8) the window frame is just inside the movie frame so that the window fills the screen and Kong fills the window.

Figure 7. *King Kong*: Kong looks at a sleeping woman through the window of her hotel room.
From the library of the Academy of Motion Picture Arts and Sciences.

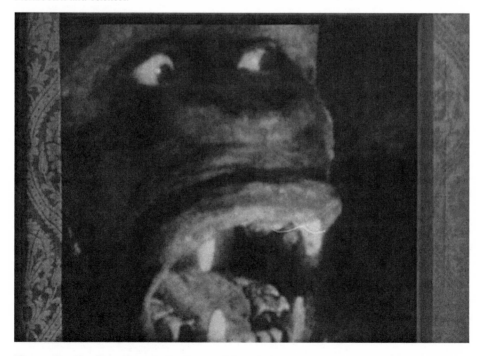

Figure 8. *King Kong*: Kong in the frame of the window.
From the library of the Academy of Motion Picture Arts and Sciences.

Kong knocks Jack out, then reaches for the bed Ann is lying on and pulls it toward him. Ann screams. Kong picks her up off the bed and pulls her through the open frame of the window. He dangles her far above the crowd while she screams and fights. Recognizing her, Kong begins to climb again with her in his fist. Jack gets up, looks out the window, then runs out of the room after them.

Here we see a woman taken into the night by a monster, another abduction from bed, after she has been talking about an event that resembled a horrible dream. The woman in the first bedroom is sleeping, with something like a nightmare in her window. Kong is the subject of Ann's living, waking nightmare, and he comes at her directly through the window. Unlike Cesare, he does not have to take a while to get from the window to the woman; the scene is played for action, not for suspense. When Kong's head fills the window frame, and Cooper and Schoedsack let that frame fill our frame, the horror film asserts both its power to frighten and its artificiality; it reflexively asserts its frame. With that shot, *King Kong* declares itself a scary *movie*. That same shot also lets us look full-screen at the literal frame of wood and drapery (not just the figurative frame), the window that gives us access to the horror and gives it access to us. It is the effectiveness with which the bedroom-window scene conveys this double access—along with its fusion of sexuality and horror, its evocation of the nightmare and the versatility of its framing devices—that accounts for its recurring so often.

The Mummy's Tomb and Others

There are three monster-at-the-bedroom-window scenes in *The Mummy's Tomb* (Harold Young, 1942, US), one of them shot in a way unlike the others. That first scene is shot from inside the bedroom, with the unseen window behind the camera and off to the side. What we see is a couple in their two beds as the shadow of the Mummy, Kharis (Lon Chaney, Jr), crosses the wall behind them (Figure 9). The woman wakes up when the shadow passes over her face. Then she gets her husband up, and they go to look out the window, which we finally see.

The other scenes are more conventional. Kharis has been sent by an Egyptian priest (Turhan Bey as Mehemet Bey) to kill the remaining members of an expedition that violated a tomb 30 years ago—and their blood relations. The expedition was led by Stephen Banning (Dick Foran), who lives in Massachusetts and has a son, John (John Hubbard); John's fiancée is Isobel (Elyse Knox). Stephen, now an old man, goes to his room and gets ready for bed. Outside, Kharis sees the light go on in Stephen's second-story window and begins to climb a ladder-like trellis to the balcony. Wearing a robe, Stephen opens the balcony doors, which consist mostly of window panes. The window/doorway is to screen left and does not face the camera; Kharis comes through it and strangles Stephen. John and another man run up the stairs as Kharis escapes via the balcony (we don't see him leave the room) and they find Stephen dead. Not only women are endangered or perish in bedroom-window scenes.

Later in the movie, the priest has Kharis bring him Isobel. Isobel has been trying on her wedding dress (it's a fitting; the wedding is to be held the next day). She is wearing a nightgown when her mother puts her to bed, but our memory of her in the wedding

Figure 9. *The Mummy's Tomb*: A woman sees Kharis through her bedroom window.
© 1942 Universal Pictures Co., Inc. All rights reserved. From the library of the Academy of Motion
Picture Arts and Sciences.

dress is fresh. She goes happily to sleep while Kharis approaches her window and opens
it. She is asleep when the Mummy's shadow appears on the wall and moves toward her.
As he reaches for her, she wakes up and screams. He grabs her. Much as in *Caligari*, a
woman in the next room hears the screams and runs into the bedroom. She is just in time
to see the monster carry Isobel out the window. The window is large and center-screen
but shot slightly from the side; it also has a lot of drapery, and there is just enough room
to see Isobel and Kharis among the folds. We never see the bed and the window in the
same shot, but they are certainly in the same room. The three scenes accomplish one
scare, one murder and one abduction, all with essentially the same terms: a monster, a
bed and a window.

Lest we think that these scenes recur only in the classical horror film, consider *Friday
the 13th Part 2* (Steve Miner, 1981, US), where the sexual aspect of the bedroom is made
explicit and where variations on the scene and its elements appear repeatedly. Early in
the film we see a voyeuristic old coot (Walt Gorney as Crazy Ralph), the first two films'
version of the One Who Knows, looking through a bedroom window. We see him from
outside the building, which is a twist on the usual setup. Inside, a couple is doing some
heavy necking. While the lovers (one of whom is Ginny, played by Amy Steel—the main
character and eventual survivor) continue to embrace, Crazy Ralph is choked to death

by Jason (Warrington Gillette) with a chain, which provides the necessary horror outside the window. After the killing, the next shot shows Ginny the next morning, alone in bed in front of the window. Later we see Ginny trapped in a bathroom (not a bedroom). She moves to close the window one last inch, but Jason breaks it, and we see his head and arm in the window frame as she runs out. Near the end, there is a scene in which her boyfriend (John Furey as Paul) carries the wounded Ginny into a room and sets her on a bed with a window behind it. Just when they relax, thinking the worst is over, Jason bursts entirely through the window and grabs Ginny.

Finally, *The Company of Wolves* (Neil Jordan, 1984, UK) turns an erotically charged dream into a realized horror. In that film, co-adapted by Angela Carter from her story of the same name,[7] a teenager named Rosaleen (Sarah Patterson) has a series of dreams that lasts almost as long as the movie. This is not kept as a surprise; there are many shots of her sleeping. The film asks us to imagine what it would be like to live in a world in which all the folklore about werewolves is real, as if her dream were a fairy tale. When Rosaleen dreams that she has become a character like Red Riding Hood and meets a werewolf who wins her heart, she turns into a wolf and runs away with him. Rosaleen gives herself an erotic dream whose central image is the wolf, an apparently safe immersion in folklore—but a pack of wolves runs through the barriers of the dream and into the real world, gathering outside her bedroom door. It is dangerous to play with horror, even in dreams, even in art. In the final shots, a large wolf breaks through the window of her bedroom, clearly intending not to seduce her but to eat her, the ultimate image of the bedroom window as a frame for dreaming and for the nightmare that may come through it, as the window is broken and left open by the reality of a horror the dream has made accessible.

Back to the Tarantula

One reason the tarantula appears to be attracted to Steve, then, is that sex is built into the confrontation between the monster and the woman in the bedroom. This does not usually depend on any potential or literal romantic consummation—although desire may be implied on the part of some monsters, even if it is confused with the desire to kill. (In *Häxan*, on the other hand, the desire the Devil and woman feel for each other is physically consummated.) Jane, in *Caligari*, is dragged out of her bed and through the window by a murderer who is attracted to her, and Kong is of course romantically attached to Ann. While no sex or attachment is involved at the end of *Friday the 13th Part 2*, the male Jason still grabs the female Ginny on a bed. In *Frankenstein* and *The Mummy's Tomb*, the young women are preparing to get married, and like Jane they wear white to bed, or while they are lying on a bed, the symbolic outfit of the virgin bride. The bed may also be a site of horror, as it is for Ellen in *Nosferatu* or for the women who are grabbed from their beds in *King Kong*, a place where a monster from the night has power. The tarantula approaches Steve in her bedroom because that is how the filmmakers see her as most attractive and endangered, in their general quest to find a strong conjunction of sex and horror—and because the scene is a given if not an imperative. The spider gets excited because it is part of a long line of monsters that become excited when they find women in bed or become part of a symbolic romance. It also approaches Steve in her bedroom because that is a place where people relax and undress, their lowered guard making it more frightening and dangerous when they are threatened. In addition, the monster comes from the dark like the nightmare Deemer said it was.

As this scene develops across the history of the horror film, the meaning of the bed becomes intricate, and it is presented as a site for sex, for death, for abduction and for dreaming or vision. Watching it, horror comes into our private imaginative space much as the monster enters the private room. The window lets a character look out at the monster, but it also allows the monster to get in; it provides the audience with the sight of horror and the feeling, shared with the character, of vulnerability. When the window is large and faces the camera, it can remind us of the movie screen. The monster appears in the bedroom window as the horror film appears on the screen and as the nightmare appears in the mind. The window is a vehicle for horror and an emblem of the genre.

3

FEAR IN A FRAME

Dreams and Reflexivity in *Vampyr*

When dreams appear in horror films, they often show the dreamer and the viewer what is really going on in the waking world. In *Vampyr* a man dreams of a skeletal hand with a bottle of poison (Figure 10) and wakes in time to stop the vampire's victim from taking poison from the bottle in her hand (Figure 11). The dream and reality shots are similar, showing that the dream was an image of the truth, even if it was stylized. Dreams may offer privileged access to the mysteries and forces behind the story's events and can show them in their real forms or in forms that are more stylized or disguised. Like the dreams in *Vampyr*, they often appear to unleash evil and show its power but may finally be forces for good, revealing what the dreamer needs to know. The skeleton's hand in *Vampyr* is a warning about a real event but also a symbolic form for the hand of the victim, for the death the poison will bring her and for the more general force of death that reigns with the vampire. It shows the presence of death behind the mortal scene, which can reveal itself in a dream or in a movie as a whole. In many films, especially reflexive ones, framed narratives such as memories, dreams and tales (like those in *Dead of Night*) call attention, often simply by their framing, to the larger narrative structures in which they are contained. As we have seen, the world of horror can sometimes be found in a delimited space, like a window frame or a nightmare, but has access to what in terms of the fiction is the real world. Another dream from *Vampyr* and the one that provides a narrative frame for *Dead of Night* will clearly show these reflexive tendencies and the power of a contained structure.

As one of the most unsettling and atmospheric of all horror films, *Vampyr* is the story of a night during which a traveler helps a family threatened by a vampire. The links between nightmares and this movie are strong, not only because of the reflexive coffin-window sequence in its long dream, but also because the whole film is set in a world of shadows, reversals and uncanny events that could best be sustained in a dream. At many points, what we are looking at is defamiliarized, such as when a door opens inside a door.[1] As Dreyer said in an interview while the film was being produced:

> Imagine that we are sitting in a very ordinary room. Suddenly we are told that there is a corpse behind the door. Instantly, the room we are sitting in is completely altered. Everything in it has taken on another look. The light, the atmosphere have changed, though they are physically the same. This is because *we* have changed and the objects *are* as we conceive them. This is the effect I wanted to produce in *Vampyr*.[2]

Figure 10. *Vampyr*: A dream of poison…

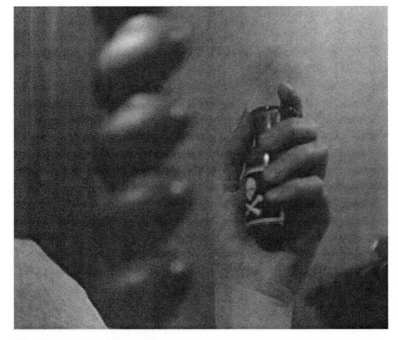

Figure 11. *Vampyr*: …and the reality.

Attempting to convey this other look, the sets, lighting, camerawork and effects of *Vampyr* render paradoxical and troubling the spaces in which the events take place.[3] This is a film that makes vampires, death and damnation truly frightening, and that has complete control of tone and atmosphere, while relaying a conception of evil that may be so vivid and forceful because the director believed in God. It has a much more oppressive, threatening and enigmatic supernatural mood than most vampire films—notably the 1931 *Dracula*, which served as a kind of negative inspiration.

The dreams in *Vampyr* are brought on by loss of blood, tying them into the symbolic structure of this vampire film. Losing blood opens one to the domain of such dreams or visions, and the terms of the vampire's world.

Vampyr is based loosely on two stories from J. Sheridan Le Fanu's *In a Glass Darkly*: "Carmilla," from which Dreyer took the idea of a female vampire with a female victim, and "The Room in the Dragon Volant," from which he took the trance state, induced in the story by a drug, that leaves a victim completely aware of what is going on but unable to move. *Vampyr* was made in German, French and English versions and has many alternate titles, one of which is *The Dream of Allan Grey*. In the English version and in much of the critical literature, the main character is called David, but we will call him Allan, based on the cast list and intertitles of the restored German version.[4] Allan is played by the film's producer, Baron Nicolas de Gunzburg, and in the script (by Dreyer and Christen Jul) he is called Nicolas.[5] In the movie no one ever calls him by name.

Allan Grey is an adventurer in search of unusual experiences, especially supernatural ones. He often finds that the border between the real and the otherworldly is ambiguous. The action takes place in a single night during which the supernatural exercises great power. Allan checks into an inn in the village of Courtempierre and then is visited by Bernard (Maurice Schutz), the elderly owner of a nearby manor—only Bernard is not exactly there. Somehow his spiritual appeal has reached Allan. After a change in the lighting (an unmotivated shift that announces the metaphysical ambiguity of the rest of the scene), Bernard walks into Allan's locked room and leaves him a book. It is this film's *Book of the Vampire*, and Bernard writes a note on the paper in which it is wrapped saying that it is to be opened after his death. The scene is played like a dream but is not a dream, even if Allan is in bed, because the book remains after Bernard has left. We have seen something impossible, yet have to believe that it happened, without being able to call it a dream, as a condition of following the story.

This fantastic visitation disturbs Allan, and he goes with the book to seek out the old man's home, arriving just in time to see him killed—by a rifleman shown only as an upside-down shadow. There are many shadows in *Vampyr*, some of which are shown without bodies or move in reverse. Most of the in-camera special effects are dedicated to filming these shadows and to giving the night air the quality of a grainy, whitish fog. The latter is said to have begun as an error, when cinematographer Rudolph Maté let a light shine into the lens, but it was adopted as a consistent effect. Dreyer did not set out to frighten us with ordinary shadows and dark night scenes. Instead he scared and disturbed us with unconventional uses of light and shadow, such as the weird light carved out of a blackness that reshapes the screen, as in Figure 12, and a shadow that joins its shadowless body when it sits beside him on a bench.

Figure 12. *Vampyr.* Light and dark reshape the frame. The central shadow is cast by a man with an artificial leg.

The old man has two daughters, Gisèle and Léone. Léone is the victim of the vampire, a blind old woman named Marguerite Chopin (Henriette Gérard).[6] There is no sexual component to her vampirism. The vampire's mortal helper is the local doctor. Léone's fear of being damned is convincing. One of the servants, Joseph (Albert Bras), reads the *Book of the Vampire*—here called *The Strange History of Vampires*—after Allan has begun reading it himself. Once it has given general information about vampires, laying out for the audience (in overlong inserts) the version of the myth and the ritual this movie will follow, the book addresses the immediate situation, naming Marguerite Chopin as the one most likely to be the vampire who once terrorized Courtempierre.

When the vampire is first seen, she brings a dancing crowd of shadows to silence. She has white hair and wears black. Then, in her room, she gives a small bottle of poison to the doctor, who is Léone's physician, so that Léone will kill herself and be damned. While Allan is reading the *Strange History*, Léone is outside, where the old woman preys on her. The book, a too-perfect text, mentions a village doctor who sold his soul to the Devil and became a vampire's accomplice just at the moment the doctor arrives to treat Léone.

The doctor convinces Allan to give Léone some of his blood, and the transfusion leaves him weak. In a scene that captures the dizziness and disorientation that may follow a loss of blood, Allan tells the doctor he is "losing blood," but the doctor assures him his blood is "right here," in the next room. Lost blood, inseparable from the fiends that drain it, is the central danger in this movie; its loss leads to death (and sometimes to vision) and declares the power of the monster. While Allan is dozing, Joseph reads how to kill a vampire. Allan then has a dream about the skeleton and the bottle of poison, while in the next room Léone's hand goes through much the same action as the skeleton's had gone through.[7] Allan is awakened by Joseph in time to take the bottle from Leone's lips and run after the doctor, who had seen the start of her suicide attempt and not interfered. This is a place and a night world in which nightmares tell the truth. *Vampyr* demonstrates that nightmares and horror films can be complementary modes of narration, for they are shown here to cover the same dark material in related ways. By calling attention to its inner framing and to the importance of vision within it (the long dream is especially about what Allan sees), a dream may make the viewer think of it as a kind of movie.

Faint from running and loss of blood, Allan falls, then stops to rest on a bench near a graveyard and falls asleep. His double-exposed dreaming self gets up and leaves his body on the bench. (This device of the split-off phantom had been used in earlier films, such as *Sherlock Jr.* [Buster Keaton, 1924, US].) He goes to a building where he finds a coffin with himself inside it. There is a locked room where he sees Gisèle is being kept, tied to a bed. The doctor comes to visit her, inadvertently showing Allan where the keys are. Allan's observing dream-self goes to hide under the floor while Allan's body is sealed in the coffin; then the dreaming intelligence and the camera switch to the body.

The coffin lid has a window whose shape is rectangular but taller than the movie screen. The camera, taking the corpse's point of view, looks straight up through the window whose sides we see. We then get a framed view of the man with an artificial leg, using his drill as the lid is screwed tight, and of the vampire looking down at him with her candle (Figure 13)—one of the most unsettling moments in the movie because she is otherwise blind. It is the kind of "error" that makes things interesting. This scene plays on our fears of death, claustrophobia, paralysis, being buried alive and encountering evil without being able to do anything about it. Allan is fully conscious and seen as a solid figure, but he is unable to move. This is the trance state adapted from Le Fanu's story, which also puts its immobile hero in a coffin, but not in a dream. As viewers, we share Allan's look through the coffin window, whose border soon disappears, which leaves us looking through the movie screen, straight up at the doctor and then at the trees, the buildings on the way to the church and graveyard, the sky. This literally entombs us in the theatre, making the movie the horror and the focus of fear. At the peak of a nightmare, *Vampyr* gives us the horror film's most reflexive moment. The window in the coffin lid becomes the window of the screen and our window into a dream vision. We are in the trance of the horror film, facing another version of the bedroom window, and we are so unable to protect ourselves or the characters from it and so unable to affect what happens in it that we might as well be paralyzed by a dream, like Allan, or a drug, like the hero of "Dragon Volant."

The coffin is sometimes shown from above so that we can see Allan's stiff, open-eyed face through the window, and to establish the point of view of the upward shots that don't contain the window's frame, where the glass of the window and the glass of the lens are figuratively one, and where the window and screen are also one. We look up through the screen at sights that will lead to death, and the reverse angle allows us to identify

Figure 13. *Vampyr*: The vampire looks down through the coffin window.

with the character's self-consciousness, his awareness of seeing although he appears to be dead. There is also the consideration that this dream might be as accurate as the last one, increasing the fear and suspense in the sequence. As the coffin reaches the cemetery where Allan is to be buried, the bearers pass the sleeping Allan, and when he wakes, released from the dream, the procession vanishes.

Allan and Joseph open the grave of the vampire and stake her with an iron rod, nailing her to the earth. They save her soul and free Léone from her influence, so that when Léone dies, she is not damned. (It is clearer in the script than in the film that she dies.) In a shot taken so that we can't make out whether it's real or not,[8] Allan takes the keys from the hiding place he discovered in the dream and frees Gisèle. This ambiguity brings into the waking world the equivocal reality of the dream, making the world more dreamlike at the same time that it substantiates the dream.

The doctor runs into a mill, accidentally locking the mesh door behind him. While Allan and Gisèle make their way to a river and a boat, then walk together in the dawn, Joseph starts the mill and leaves. The flour rains down on the doctor until it suffocates him.[9] In the last shot, the gears of the mill stop by themselves. Only God is around to effect this *deus ex machina*, to stop the mill now that the doctor is dead. Except for the shots of sunlight, the formulaic romantic resolution has little force. The real power of the ending comes when God wins, in a strong shot that declares that the reign of evil and the current need to destroy it are over.

For Allan, the darkest parts of the night have come from losing blood and having dreams of death. He turns them to good advantage, saving both Léone and Gisèle by using information he learns in the dreams, and he manages to avoid death, or his vision of death, by waking up. The dreams' images of death threaten to turn real in the physical world. They are warnings about the death and danger that confront Allan and the others—full of vital information, so that they have a benevolent side, while they are also direct expressions of evil. The dreams are keys to the whole of *Vampyr*. The long dream in particular delivers a narrative of being surrounded by horrors and nearly becoming their victim, as the film does. Both of them bury the viewer alive in the theatre, and that seated viewer may not be moving much, nearly as frozen as Allan, as the coffin window's rectangular frame is replaced by the rectangle of the screen. Here the horror film becomes frightening on its own, in that it has become a horror object, not just a fantasy containing horrors. *Vampyr* scares us not only with its content, but with itself. Yet within this horror is a force that acts for good and determines the ending. The vision of horror can save one from evil in this movie, and that applies ideally to the whole picture, as well as to the moments of paradoxical vision within it.

Narrative Structure in *Dead of Night*

A limited structure can encapsulate a horror that is central to a movie while referring reflexively to the movie as a whole, as the image of a victim in the viewfinder of the killer's camera, an iconic example of fear in a frame, does in *Peeping Tom*, to which we will return (but see Figure 17). In *Dead of Night* the principal dream is almost as long as the movie, but it is still a limited structure that is the key to the terrifying whole, while remaining an enigmatic and frightening thing in its own right. What one fears most is the dream itself, not just because of what it reveals but because of the invariable way it repeats.

As *Dead of Night* opens, architect Walter Craig (Mervyn Johns) drives up to the country home of his new client, Eliot Foley (Roland Culver), where he is to spend the weekend. Craig is very familiar with the place, and with the things his host and the other guests are about to say, though he has never been there before. He has had a recurring dream in which all the things that are now happening to him take place. Craig tells the others about this dream, which he cannot remember in its entirety, and says that for some reason he knows it is a nightmare, that at the end he will lose his free will and be in the grip of a force that drives him toward "something unspeakably evil," something still unknown. He remembers parts of the dream as events unfold that match those in the dream, and other parts before they happen. One of the guests suggests that they may all just be characters in Craig's dream and that they will vanish when he wakes up, a reflexive note doubtless inspired by *Through the Looking-Glass*. A psychiatrist, Dr Van Straaten (Frederick Valk), takes a scientific approach to dreams and does not believe they can foretell the future, as Craig's seems to have done. The doctor finds an explanation for every uncanny event the guests go on to relate, for to make Craig feel more comfortable, they tell stories of their own encounters with the supernatural and the inexplicable—one of which, "The Hearse Driver," is about the value of paying attention to a warning that comes in a vision or dream. Another, "The Haunted Mirror," is about an elaborately

framed mirror that shows a room in which a murder took place, a vision that affects the
living on the other side of the frame, as many framed horrors do. But nothing can stop
the catastrophe, and the nightmare Craig feared is realized. The lighting turns dark as
Craig gives into a compulsion to kill the doctor, and the scenes from the stories the guests
have told, now freed from the narrative frames that separated them, join in a threatening
montage until Craig finally is strangled by the ventriloquist's dummy from one of the
inner stories (Figure 14) as the image shrinks into a growing field of black.

Figure 14. *Dead of Night*: The dummy strangles the dreamer.

The scene dissolves to a bedroom, and Craig wakes up. He has had the dream again, and forgotten it again. Eliot Foley, whom he doesn't know, phones to invite him to spend a weekend in the country. This is apparently a real event, not part of any dream, and it implies that the following events really take place. Craig agrees to go to Foley's house, and then we see him drive up, meet Foley, and walk toward the house in exactly the same shots that we saw at the beginning of the film.[10] We do not know whether the dream, with its inevitable events, has started again or whether this is the real-world event at last, because it would look the same either way. No matter how much Craig tries to escape, there is no escape, whether he is dreaming or finally visiting. The dream or event replays itself without a change, precisely as if it were a film that is starting over. *Dead of Night* is a narrative trap. The film has shown a dream for most of its length and may be showing another at the end. Whether the dream and the film start over the same way, or the dream and reality prove identical, another reflexive link is forged here between the nightmare and the horror film. The repeated film—the ending of *Dead of Night*—signifying either the never-ending loop of the repeating nightmare, or the fulfilled action of fate after a prophetic dream, has become a horror object.

The Unfilmable in *Peeping Tom*

Peeping Tom (script by Leo Marks[11]) is a systematically reflexive intertwining of horror and film, from the viewfinder near its head to the projector that runs out near its tail. Its subject is not just fear but the filming of it, and it often makes us see filming as perverse. Mark Lewis (Carl Boehm) knows that he is crazy and that what he is doing is wrong, but he still does it, compelled by the need to work out what happened to him as a child, when his biologist father, Professor Lewis (played by director Powell), systematically and repeatedly frightened him for research purposes. Professor Lewis had been an expert on fear and the nervous system, especially the fears of children, and had used Mark as a test subject while he was growing up. The professor shot films and recorded tapes of his waking Mark in the middle of the night to frighten him—for example, with a lizard. He also shot other parts of Mark's life, wanting a complete record of a growing child. Mark never had any privacy, and his fears were studied. Now that Mark is an adult and his father is dead, the house is still wired for sound, and Mark, as the quiet landlord who lives upstairs, listens in on his tenants. He has become a filmmaker and a voyeur (voyeurism is presented partly as a neurosis that would draw one to filmmaking), sometimes peeping in through windows or baldly staring at lovers on the street and often looking at the world through a viewfinder. He is not the only voyeur in the film, however. There is a news shop that sells pornographic "views" to respectable-looking men, and Mark's sideline is to shoot those pictures, a task he performs with no erotic interest, although one day he is fascinated by the eyes of a model whose face is disfigured. Mark watches the films from his childhood, including a home movie he made when his father gave him a movie camera as a present. When he was a child, filming his father was one way to respond to and counter all the filming the father had done of him. Filming puts Mark in control. He gets a job in the film industry as a camera assistant. He devises his own way to spy on the fears of other people, as his voyeurism becomes sadistic like his father's—though his is more violent and has an original twist.

Mark wants to film his victims' faces in the moment of ultimate fear, when they see their own terror as Mark begins to kill them. They see their faces as they are reflected by the special apparatus Mark uses: a 16mm camera that shoots through the base of a bowl-shaped reflector, which reflects the victim's image as the camera approaches, and that is mounted on a tripod, one of whose legs can be unsheathed to reveal a knife. The knife pierces the victim's throat at the same time as the reflector surrounds her face, when the camera is at its closest. The reflector is essential to show the victim her own face, however distorted (Figure 15), because the most frightening thing Mark can imagine is to see one's own fear and be fully conscious of it, and to heighten and spy on *that* fear—to see that meta-fear so intimately that one would be nearly inside the victim's experience—would be an improvement on his father's spying, a sophisticated enhancement of the violation. The faces of his dead victims do in fact show an unusual degree of fear, as the police observe. The film Mark shoots during and in relation to the killings is part of what he refers to as a documentary he is making. In effect, he is finishing the factual film (actually a series of films connected only by their subject) begun by his father, for it is all one project dedicated to the photographing of fear.

The trouble, however, is that the shot Mark has devised cannot be taken, because at the moment when the face is inside the reflector, the victim's head blocks the light, and the film exposes only black. This is *Peeping Tom*'s graceful and compassionate way of saying that some things must remain private. The film uses the unshowable, uncapturable shot to communicate in darkness the horror of being surrounded by one's own fear at the moment of being murdered. An unshootable film becomes a sign that ultimate horror must be imagined, cannot be directly conveyed and should not be spied on. Mark's mad

Figure 15. *Peeping Tom*: Helen's view of her face in the distorting reflector.

attempts to frighten each victim to a unique extreme as well as violate her space make the killings worse. No more than Mark's apparatus can *Peeping Tom* capture the ineffable horror of the victim's awareness of her own agony, fear and death, and that is one reason the movie turns reflexive: to examine a self-conscious attempt to film horror, making that frightening in itself, and to make peace (as a civilized picture, while Mark's is insane) with the limits beyond which horror cannot be filmed. The unshowable horror, once Mark has described it, grips the viewer's imagination beyond what the film is able to contain. Its horror is transcendent.

Hoping that next time there will be enough light, Mark kills a number of women. The logical conclusion to his documentary is for him to use the apparatus on himself. He was, after all, the documentary's original subject. He realizes this and has rehearsed it, and this is how he actually dies, controlling the situation and being the victim at the same time, with the same actions, able to see for himself what is in the reflector (Figure 16)— but at the critical moment he closes his eyes.[12] In this respect the film is merciful to him, allowing him to escape the apex of the punishment and the immersion in horror he has arranged for himself by playing old tapes and turning on the projector to accompany his suicide. The film ends with a reddish-brown light on Mark's screen that signifies not only blood and (because of its resemblance to tail leader) conclusion, but also privacy, for it is like the red light that keeps anyone from entering a darkroom or a soundstage that is being used. Just before we see this light, the screen goes dark, and we hear a tape in which Mark bids his father good night and asks him to hold his hand, a hope for a relationship, love and freedom from fear that it is entirely beyond the capacity of the father to provide.

The potential for love does come to Mark in the person of one of his tenants, Helen (Anna Massey), whom he is careful never to let his 16mm camera "see" so that she will

Figure 16. *Peeping Tom*: The suicide setup. The knife can be seen at the end of the tripod leg.

never be in danger. When she does discover what is in his films, turning on the projector when she is alone in his room, it is as if she were looking into Bluebeard's forbidden chamber, as many people in horror films do. Helen's mother, Mrs Stephens (Maxine Audley), is blind and has an instinctive understanding of Mark, for she fears him and she does not need to see the movies to know they contain something frightful and sick. Her pointed cane is a parallel to his knife-tipped tripod leg. Mark controls vision, but one who can function without seeing has greater power than he. "Scoptophilia...the morbid urge to gaze"—as it is called in the movie by a psychiatrist who says that Mark "has his father's eyes" (a wonderful pun)—is the root of Mark's obsessive spying and filming. Although considered a sick and unredeemable film when it came out, *Peeping Tom* has a firm moral center. It shows compassion for Mark and for his victims, most fully attacking only the father whose own "urge to gaze" was responsible for Mark's madness. Its reflexivity renders especially horrific both its inner films and the look through Mark's viewfinder (Figure 17)—even, by implication, the look through the camera that shot *Peeping Tom*.

Those inner films, shot by Mark and his father, are miniature sites of the film's central emotional evil, a failure to care about the victim while arousing and spying on his or her fear. Mark's cold murderousness and that of his camera are linked. The inner films are not dreams, though Mark is usually asleep just before his father tortures him. Rather they are contained horrors, and within the fiction of *Peeping Tom*, they are short documentaries. When the murder films turn black as the reflector blocks the light, they address the limits of apprehending and conveying horror, the point beyond which the movie and the imagination cannot go; they are core statements of Mark's dilemma in miniature. As limited narratives, with Mark's camera their

Figure 17. *Peeping Tom*: The victim seen through the killer's viewfinder.

limited narrator, they stand out as emblems. Like the inner tales told in many horror films, they encapsulate, frame, delimit and extend from those limits the horror of the whole.

The Mummy's Tale

In *The Mummy* (1932) Imhotep, the Mummy (Boris Karloff), tells Helen (Zita Johann), the reincarnation of a princess, the story of the love they felt for each other in ancient Egypt and how they died. He tells her the story in front of a pool (Figure 18) in which we and she see the images of the past. The rim of the pool becomes a visual frame for the story as well as a narrative frame. When the tale has been told and he releases his control of her mind, she says she feels that she has had a dream. (In fact, he has awakened dead memories by reminding her of their history when she is in a trance.) He says that sometimes "one sees strange fantasies in the water, but they pass like dreams." This limited tale, which feels like a dream to Helen but feels reliable to us, shows the viewer the Mummy's history and motivation—the start, concealed until now, of the movie's real story. In the pool it appears in a virtual window of narration, a look into another world framed consistently by the pool's edge, and it intrudes into what once was Helen's ordinary life, taking it over.

Figure 18. *The Mummy*: The Mummy's pool.

A look at *The Mummy*, *Vampyr*, *Dead of Night* and *Peeping Tom* gives an idea of the complex uses and the continuing importance to the genre of the inner narrative, the dream and the inner frame. As dreams in horror films usually show the truth or a version of it (as in *Vampyr*) and are read, like tales and memories, as being dreamed or related, audiences gratefully pay attention to their frames to sort out levels of reality and narrativity—as in *Dead of Night* or *A Nightmare on Elm Street* (Wes Craven, 1984, US). There are instances, however, in which a horror image or scene refuses the frame the filmmakers put around it, when it cannot be contained. As we shall see later, some documentary horrors refuse the frame of fiction even when they are included in a fiction film. And in filming the autopsies in *The Act of Seeing With One's Own Eyes* (Stan Brakhage, 1971, US), Brakhage made the most literal of all framing issues—that is, determining to put the horror within the framing viewfinder of the camera and on frames of celluloid—a struggle with emotional and cinematic limits.

The horror film often calls attention to the ways it manages to include its difficult, unpleasant and even metaphysical subjects, and it may do this so systematically that the film turns reflexive, though of course there are other reasons and means for reflexivity to emerge. Sometimes a film will place itself in the creative tradition of the genre, deliberately referencing earlier movies, which is one kind of reflexivity (authorial self-consciousness), and sometimes it will present itself as a semi-autonomous horror object, frightening not just in its content but in itself, which is another kind (systemic self-consciousness).[13] Reflexivity may further contain and constrain the horror, acting as another, more systemic frame than the conventional narrative ones, such as putting a scene within a tale or a dream—or showing it through reversed binoculars and a closed window, which distances and silences the climactic tortures in *Salò*. The contained is, of course, tightly focused and may be more powerful than the same information expressed or shown directly. (Consider the levels of narration that contain and convey "the horror" in Conrad's "Heart of Darkness.") When a film appears to be aware of itself as a film, it presents itself (sometimes along with its story) as a fact confronting the audience. The reflexive film may emphasize the dangerous nature of going to horror movies, as in the previously mentioned *He Knows You're Alone* and *Demons*, as well as the danger of the key to the picture's primary horror. Such films make us think about the genre's or the movie's understanding of itself and the nature of our confrontation with the emotions and images of horror, a confrontation that can happen in the face of a spectacle or a suggestion, a memory or a dream, a mummy breaking violently through a window to abduct a woman or a mummy showing his tale in a screen-like pool to reveal the truth and draw the woman more subtly into his world.

Categories

Another way to frame horror is to organize it. As horror's primary elements are fear and revulsion, either might provide a key to the genre's structure. Thus the genre could be organized according to the kinds of fear the films arouse—as previously mentioned, the fear of the unknown, the fear of the self and the fear of others—or according to the nature of the horror object, the revolting monster or monstrous figure that expresses the horror.

The trouble with setting up categories based on fear is that fear of the dark and fear of death—key elements of the fear of the unknown—are found in almost all the films. Characters are always being led into or victimized in the darkness, and death is an ever-present threat as well as a key element of a movie's spectacle.

Consider the fear of the dark; consider black. Within the black-and-white horror film, there is nothing so rich and suggestive as a well-prepared area of black, a shadow in which one can barely make out what is happening or in which one can see nothing. We can fill that black with everything we fear, or we can let it characterize as dark and dangerous what can be glimpsed in it, what remains hidden in it or what emerges from it. Of course shadows are effective in the color film too, and *The Shining* (Stanley Kubrick, 1980, US/UK) has demonstrated that a horror film can be set more in the light than in the dark and still be visually unnerving. But most horror movies take advantage of the dark so as to set a mood or hide a threat. They count on our fear of the dark, whether or not we felt it mostly in childhood (a childhood the genre may momentarily revive), to make a scene feel full of danger. They set a great many scenes at night, making the black and the indefinite their background, and treating the night itself as frightening. They take advantage of the fact that they are shown in the dark, and they make some of their images out of the dim light and darkness that many people fear. With shadows before us and black around us, the theatre becomes a dark place when showing a horror film.

In *Cloverfield* there is a scene in which the monster's gigantic bug-like parasites drop onto the characters from the ceiling of an empty subway tunnel. The characters have decided to walk down that tunnel—the only way out—and except for a line of dim ceiling lights, the tunnel is lit only by the white light on the video camera that one of them is operating—an example of what might be called *embattled light*: light struggling against the surrounding darkness to show what it can, a cinematic trope that is basic to the horror film. They have been walking in the dark for a long time before they are alarmed by a large group of rats running away from something the characters can't yet see. Then they hear something they can't identify—two effective stimulators of fear that leave the nature of the threat unknown. Once they see the parasites (with the camera's greenish night-vision light), they have to fight and run, while using the camera's limited light to see what is attacking them and find a place to hide. This harrowing scene demonstrates that space, darkness and interrupted or limited vision can be charged with fear, both the object of fear and the fear felt by those who face it, the characters and the audience. The fear that the monster will get us, which underlies so many horror films, is enhanced by the darkness, the unknown space, in which it *can* get us.

But such a darkness, whether literal or metaphoric, is part of practically every horror movie, as said before. The fear of the unknown is a basic premise in horror, though not in science fiction. And while there are films that concentrate on the fear of death and the unknown (*Frankenstein*) and films that concentrate on the fear of the self (*Cat People*), there are so many films about the fear of others that they would need to be subdivided according to a different system. It makes more sense to start with that other system.

The genre, the largest category, is the horror film. It may be subdivided into its primary subgenres: horror films about monsters, horror films about supernatural monsters and horror films about monstrous humans. (Another way to describe a monster movie is to say that the central horror figure or horror object, the expresser of the horror, is a monster.) From there one moves to the sub-subgenres, which identify the specific kind of monster or horror object the film is about. Thus the supernatural monster movie may be subdivided into the vampire film, the ghost film, the zombie film and others, and *Dracula* would be a horror/supernatural-monster/vampire movie, while *Friday the 13th* would be a horror/human/slasher movie. In this way each film is organized by its central, defining horror whether it is a monster or a monstrous human.

The three subgenres have the advantage of being comprehensive and open to the invention of new horror objects, that is, of new sub-subgenres. An organization based on monsters carries fear with it, for monsters are intended to inspire fear. The only limitation is that there are some movies—*The Exterminating Angel* has already been given as an example—in which there is no monster. Instead there is an undefined agency or a pure force whose effects are felt but that remains disembodied. Such a power behaves like a monster, providing a focus for the movie and its sense of threat, but it is not visible and not characterized. These films must be called supernatural monster movies about nameless forces.

We can now move from an overview of the genre and a consideration of some of the things one might want to know before tackling it, to a taxonomy of the horror film as a whole. A summary of that taxonomy can be found as this book's Table of Contents (Part II). Each sub-subgenre is illustrated by at least one movie, and the order of the sub-subgenres is determined chronologically—to the greatest extent possible—by the earliest film of importance in the sub-subgenre. Thus within the human monsters category, the psychopathic killer films, which are taken to date from *Psycho*, come after the mad doctor films, which were at their height in the 1930s. Within sub-subgenres, the films are usually discussed chronologically so that one can follow the development of that monster. Topics are taken up as the films suggest them, and many are then interwoven in continuing arguments, but the only general argument the reader will find in Part II (which is really a demonstration) is that the core of a horror movie, and the first thing to consider, is the particular horror it incarnates and expresses, and how it does so. It is a simple argument that opens up the genre.

Part II

SUBGENRES: THE BOOK OF MONSTERS

4

MONSTERS

Monsters gather, concentrate and express horror as if they were focusing it.

What we ordinarily call a monster does not depend on the supernatural to exist. It is a dangerous and repulsive creature, perhaps deformed, perhaps gigantic, perhaps composed of the parts of different animals or plants, an aberration, not human or no longer simply human, a thing. The monster is physical, not metaphysical, and it can die. Often it requires unusual conditions for its creation or intrusion, and just as often it can be destroyed only in a special way. But it must be destroyed. As Ludwig Frankenstein (Sir Cedric Hardwicke) says of the Monster in *The Ghost of Frankenstein* (Erle C. Kenton, 1942, US), uttering what could be the motto of all monster movies, "While it lives, no one is safe." When the monster has been killed, the typical monster movie is over. It is *the* cause of the problems that motivate the plot, even if sometimes it may also stand for other threats, as Godzilla is both a gigantic monster and an image of the dangers of radiation, war and nuclear testing.

A monster's destructiveness and repulsiveness may be a matter of its physical form. We fear a monster because of its awful appearance and its power, and because of the terrible things it can do to us or to those with whom we identify or sympathize. It is dreadful to look upon. It could eat us or step on us or tear us apart or imitate us, for there are many kinds of monsters, from pods to giant ants. In this chapter we will consider gigantic creatures as well as tiny ones, transforming and composite monsters, rocks, animals, plants, parasites, body parts, creatures from deep in the earth or under the sea, both versions of the Thing and many others.

Transforming Monsters: *Dr. Jekyll and Mr. Hyde* and *The Thing*

Although supernatural transformations are better known (such as of an immortal count into a bat), there are numerous films in which a person transforms into another being, or phase of being, without the involvement of any supernatural agency. In *Sssssss* (Bernard Kowalski, 1973, US) a mad doctor administers a serum to his assistant, who gradually turns into a cobra-man (a composite monster) and then into a cobra. The unsupernatural transformation is often accomplished through the use of a potion or serum. It is not just that transformation is a device used in these films: the transformed being, which often comprises two selves between which it can change, is a variety of monster.

Nor does the metamorphosing creature need to be, or to have been, human. Carpenter's *The Thing* (John Carpenter, 1982, US) offers an extraterrestrial monster that can take the form of any organism and can freely change from one to another. It is the fact that no one can tell who or what it is that makes the Thing scary, dangerous and unnatural. Transformation and imitation are at the core of its horrific nature.

The transforming monster in Méliès's *The Haunted Castle* (Georges Méliès, 1897, France), one of the very first horror films[1] (whose title declares that it is dealing with a supernatural, haunting entity, not strictly the kind of monster under discussion here), changes from a chair to a hooded figure to a skeleton to a knight in armor to a devil and more.

The concept and the story for *Strange Case of Dr. Jekyll and Mr. Hyde* came to Robert Louis Stevenson in a dream. Edward Hyde, who is younger than Henry Jekyll and looks like a different person, sins with glee and at one point tramples a child in a frenzy. People regard him with a "hitherto unknown disgust, loathing and fear"; he is a horror by definition. He gives "an impression of deformity without any nameable malformation."[2] People are repulsed by him because they have an instinctive preference for good over evil, "and Edward Hyde, alone in the ranks of mankind, was pure evil."[3] Jekyll is an integrated person who has always lived a double life, in the sense that he has sometimes indulged in degenerate pastimes and at other times been a hard and brilliant worker. Jekyll is not all good, as the movies would have him. In the experiment he sets out to separate his good and evil selves, but it doesn't work; one self ends up with Jekyll's normal "composite"[4] personality, and the other is all evil. In the book there is no love story.[5] Hyde is a monster from the lab, for it is in his lab that Jekyll devises, mixes and drinks the potion that transforms him. Taking the potion to become Hyde turns into an addiction, until Hyde begins to take over. Unable to control the return of Hyde, into whom Jekyll—much to his horror—is transforming spontaneously, Jekyll uses the last of the drug to maintain his identity long enough to write a document that explains everything, then changes involuntarily into Hyde, who kills himself to evade capture. In the book, unlike what happens in almost all of the Jekyll-and-Hyde movies, the corpse remains that of Hyde, not changing back to Jekyll as if he were a dead werewolf or the antihero of *The Invisible Man* (James Whale, 1933, US).

As *Dr. Jekyll and Mr. Hyde*, the short novel was adapted for the movies many times, beginning in 1909. One of the first surviving versions was released in 1912 and starred James Cruze. One of the four 1920 versions (John S. Robertson, 1920, US) starred John Barrymore as Jekyll and Hyde.[6] The best-known versions are those starring Barrymore, Fredric March (Rouben Mamoulian, 1931, wide release 1932, US) and Spencer Tracy (Victor Fleming, 1941, US). All of these dramatize Hyde's life of sin, which Stevenson had for the most part left to the reader's imagination, and they usually do it by inventing a female character to whom Hyde is attracted and whom he abuses. They also invent a love story for Jekyll, and sometimes they let the subplots cross, for instance by having Jekyll be attracted to a woman but Hyde act it out. They all have crucial laboratory scenes featuring the mixing and drinking of the potion. The transformations happen on camera (in the 1912 film via a cut and in 1920 via a dissolve) and are the visual highpoints of the movies. One theme the movies and the novel share, along with the fears of the dark side, of the self and of transformation, is that it is a dangerous mistake to experiment with human nature, which has been correctly constituted as it is and ought not to be divided. There is no religious context for this judgment in the book, but there is in some of the films, where it is argued that Jekyll is trespassing on forbidden territory, playing with matters he is meant to leave alone. That links him with the movies' version of Frankenstein[7] and the more general figure of the overreaching mad scientist. All these versions drop the issue of Jekyll's double life before he conducted the experiment, and all of them reduce the split between Jekyll and Hyde to one between good and evil.

In the Barrymore version, when Jekyll cannot stop turning into Hyde in spite of the fact that he is not taking the drug, it is, reads a title, "outraged Nature" taking her "revenge"; it has "sent upon him the creeping horror that was his other self." Just after that intertitle, Jekyll dreams of a giant spider that crawls onto his bed, and wakes up as Hyde. It is also significant that in the Barrymore version Hyde has a lower-class mistress whom he treats badly and later abandons, and whom Jekyll finds attractive; in the later films she becomes the character Ivy. In the 1912 version, which is a short, Hyde kills himself much as in the book. At the end of the Barrymore version, after Hyde has made advances towards Jekyll's fiancée—the climactic meeting of the monster and the woman, which goes back to *Caligari* and to the novel *Frankenstein*—Hyde poisons himself, and when he is dead, he turns back into Jekyll through a dissolve (the origin of those final transformations of the Invisible Man and the Wolf Man); it is played like the lifting of a spell. A close shot of the face of Dr Jekyll provides the resolution, showing the monster is dead. There is no hope for a romantic relationship, however, for the hero is dead too. The fiancée sits forlorn by Jekyll's body.

The 1931 version opens with a subjective-camera or POV sequence in which we see things as Jekyll does. This sets up the picture's central theme of identity. Subjective camera is also used during the first transformation sequence, along with a series of mindscreens. Jekyll believes that if the good and evil in our natures were separated, the good could aspire to great heights and perform great deeds without interference, while the bad would fulfill its own desires and presumably pose no trouble. This is naïve; Jekyll needs to gain experience, and the genre will see that he does. When he begins his experiments, Jekyll is already engaged to Muriel (Rose Hobart), but he also has desires for a lower-class woman, Ivy (Miriam Hopkins), whom Hyde makes his mistress. Complicating the plot, Ivy goes to Jekyll for help against Hyde. Jekyll then transforms while on the way to an engagement party for himself and Muriel, and kills Ivy. To change back, Hyde has to get Jekyll's friend, Dr Lanyon (as in the book), to secure the chemicals from Jekyll's lab. Jekyll prays, asking forgiveness for trespassing on God's "domain" and going "further than man should go." He breaks up with Muriel, telling her he is damned and hoping God will accept this as his "penance," but another involuntary transformation comes, and soon he is threatening Muriel as Hyde. He also kills her father with Jekyll's cane. The police chase Hyde to Jekyll's lab (where he meets them as Jekyll but transforms back into Hyde) and shoot him. Dead, he changes back into Jekyll.

In the 1941 version, this love triangle—or quadrangle—among Jekyll/Hyde, Ivy (Ingrid Bergman) and the fiancée, Beatrix (Lana Turner), is maintained. The film opens in a church, where Jekyll and Beatrix are attending the service. The clergyman is praising Queen Victoria for her moral reign, and looking forward to a time when all evil is wiped out by the forces of good. This sets up rather baldly the moral and religious backdrop against which Jekyll's drama will be played. When Jekyll defends his theories at a dinner party, he speaks in terms of the good and evil parts of the soul, not of the identity or personality, and it is suggested by the clergyman, who is one of the guests, that he ought to leave these matters to the creator of the soul. Later Dr Lanyon tells Jekyll he has "committed the supreme blasphemy." At the end, when the dead Hyde changes back into Jekyll, church music plays. Except for the different handling of the religious scenes (though they ultimately have the same point) and the absence of experimental camerawork, the 1941 *Dr. Jekyll and Mr. Hyde* is very similar to its predecessor. The 1941 version could be called a remake even though the films were made by different studios. There is no basis for any of these relationships in Stevenson's original. As far as Hollywood was concerned, the women (and the fiancée's father) had become part of the story. Rather than going back to Stevenson, the pictures were influencing each other, creating their own tradition of Jekyll and Hyde with its own key scenes, like the final transformation, and its icons like the vial of smoky potion.

The split in *The Leech Woman* (Edward Dein, 1960, US) is not between good and evil but between young and old. A middle-aged woman (June Talbot, played by Coleen Gray) transforms into a younger, then eventually older, version of herself. At middle age, before she becomes a split monster, she is a depressed alcoholic with a nasty husband, Dr Paul Talbot (Phillip Terry). She is ten years older than he, and he never loved her anyway, but now he finds her repulsive. He does everything he can to make her feel bad about her age. Without love, she feels her life has no meaning. Thanks to Paul's attitude, it also has no meaning without beauty. As a doctor, he specializes in making women look younger. A very old woman, Malla (Estelle Hemsley), comes to Paul's office and offers him the secret of rejuvenation if he will help her return to the faraway land of her tribe. She leaves him a sample of the exotic drug that has allowed her to live over 150 years but says that when mixed with another substance, a practice sometimes followed by her people, it can actually reverse aging. Paul follows Malla to Africa to see for himself, and he convinces June to come too—rather than divorce him, which she was just about to do. The drug, Naipe, is a powder derived from an orchid that grows only in Malla's homeland. Mixed with pineal hormone taken (with a special hooked ring) from a man's head—a process that kills the man—the powder becomes a potion. The woman who drinks it becomes young again, but only for a day or two. Her tribe allows all the old women before they die a chance to be young and to make love as they used to. This is to make up for their lot of "contempt and neglect" as old women who, Malla says, cannot enjoy the dignified old age that awaits men.

Malla, who has transformed into a beautiful young woman after the ceremony in which a man has been sacrificed, tells Paul and June and their guide that they will die in the morning. But she gives June (to whom she had said, when they first met, "You are the one in my dreams of blood") the chance to go through the Naipe ritual, and June chooses Paul to be the sacrifice. It is fitting that he die, especially to make his wife beautiful, and even better that he can't enjoy the results. After a lucky escape and a night with the guide, after which she turns old, June kills the guide to get the packet of powder and the hooked ring he had stolen from the tribe. When the potion wears off, she becomes older than she was in the first place, and this alarms her to the point that she is willing to continue killing. As with Jekyll's later transformations into Hyde, the change into another version of herself is out of her control. It is part of the appeal of transformation as a horror element that it has a mind and a schedule of its own, and that to give it any power is to give it too much. June passes herself off as her own niece and shows romantic interest in her young lawyer, Neil (Grant Williams), creating a love triangle with his fiancée, Sally (Gloria Talbott). June and Neil are the monster and the boy; he is not carried off and passive, but he is in the role of the monster's chosen romantic partner. When June kills Sally and uses Sally's hormone, she becomes much older and throws herself out of a window as she ages to death. It turns out, then, that the hormone must be from a male. There is evidently a sexual component to the potion and to the transformation. Like Paul, most of June's victims are selected for their negative traits, such as trying to rob old ladies—that is, the older June. But Sally is good, as is the guide, and it is for Sally's death, and also because June has become a monster, that June must die.

She must also die because that is what usually happens to a woman after her time under the influence of the drug. The Naipe ritual should be performed only once. Thus there is a natural course even for the unnatural, age-reversing potion, and June must succumb to it. She dies of extreme old age and the fall, a fitting punishment for repeating the ritual—and for trying to escape the death that the ritual and life demand, killing to recapture her youth. But what finally undoes her, is her turning to a woman for what the ritual demands she get from a man. *The Leech Woman* rejects a lesbian solution to June's problem (there was no radical feminist movement yet), which in context is presented as unnatural—that is, as another unnatural solution when what is needed is submission to nature, letting oneself age and die. But there is no returning to the innocent if flawed world of Jekyll or the original June, to nature and to integrated being, after the split has taken place.[8] Once that split or the ability to transform has taken hold, the only solution these movies offer the transforming monster—whether it is a human or the Thing—is death.

Constructed Monsters: *Frankenstein*

The Frankenstein Monster, a living character made of the unliving and thus from the start violating our categories of being, is a figure of the dead as well as a killer, yet he often engages our sympathy, both in the novel and in the 1931 *Frankenstein* and its sequels. With apologies to fans of the Hammer series—in which the doctor reappears but there is always a new monster—it is worth spending some time on the Universal series because it introduces or provides the most influential examples of so many elements and icons used in other films, and because it is built around such a compelling monster. Although Dracula and Imhotep, like many other monsters, have full consciousness, the Frankenstein Monster is a creature whose growing self-awareness, whose knowledge that he is a monster—solitary and hoping to find a companion—is a central issue and a compelling dramatic development, at least in the first four pictures. The sequels are *Bride of Frankenstein* (1935), *Son of Frankenstein* (Rowland V. Lee, 1939, US), *The Ghost of Frankenstein* (1942), *Frankenstein Meets the Wolf Man* (Roy William Neill, 1943, US),

House of Frankenstein (Erle C. Kenton, 1944, US), and *House of Dracula* (Erle C. Kenton, 1945, US). These films were followed by *Bud Abbott and Lou Costello Meet Frankenstein* (Charles T. Barton, 1948, US), which dropped what had been a continuous storyline. The novel, Mary Wollstonecraft Shelley's *Frankenstein; or, The Modern Prometheus*, was first published in 1818, and while the movies never gave it a faithful adaptation, Universal did use many of its aspects, elements and themes, such as the Monster's relationship with its creator, its developing consciousness and its being made from "lifeless matter," much of which came from dead bodies.[9] The Universal pictures also brought many new elements, such as fire (which the Monster uses in the novel but hates and fears in the movies), the laboratory where a great ray linked to "the secret of Creation" is gathered from the lightning (there is no information in the novel on how the Monster was given life), and the mad scientist's hunchbacked assistant. The Monster is mortal in the novel, and he does kill Elizabeth as well as a little boy, William, the hero's brother, but he does not go around randomly killing, as in most of the film sequels (in the first movie he sets out to kill with intent, little Maria aside, closing in eventually on his creator), and he is not indestructible. Above all, the Monster in the novel is articulate, while he can speak only in *Bride*—and to a lesser extent in *Ghost*, where he speaks as Ygor (Bela Lugosi) thanks to a brain transplant that blinds him and whose consequences were dropped from the later films.[10]

The novel's hero, Victor Frankenstein (renamed Henry in the Universal series), is Promethean in that he creates man, as Prometheus did according to one version of the legend, and in that he suffers for his creative act, particularly when the Monster kills those he loves. Elizabeth is murdered on her wedding night in revenge for Victor's refusal to make the Monster a bride (he tears her up just before she is completed, afraid of making another monster and starting a race), and while Elizabeth lies dead on the bed, Victor sees the Monster through the bedroom window, the archetype of the scene we have been pursuing.[11] Although he is a Promethean creator, Victor fails to nurture his creation, which comes into the world *tabula rasa* and is educated by the behavior of those who fear and attack it; there is no criminal brain. An important theme in the novel is that Victor and the Monster are linked. They are even mistaken for each other when the Monster kills Victor's closest friend, Henry. After all these deaths, Victor pursues the Monster to the Arctic, where he tells his story to an explorer, Robert Walton, who writes the whole thing down in letters to his sister. The Monster's own first-person story comes at the center of the novel and is hemmed in by the narrative layers of Victor's tale and Walton's letters, which offer it insulation and protection and let the fantastic come through in its own terms.

The Monster's plan is to make Victor as isolated and wretched as himself, to link them in misery. The more the Monster is perceived as a conscious, self-aware being with readable if not sympathetic motives, the more he is seen to be as human as his creator, even if he represents the dangerous, destructive side of the overreaching creative act. The novel is primarily about the tragedy of Frankenstein and the Monster's education and growing consciousness. After Victor dies on Walton's boat, the Monster comes aboard, validating the story, and says that he will burn himself to death. The Monster does commit suicide in *Bride*, though for a different reason, and of course there are many other points of overlap and difference between the novel and the movies, evident just from what has been briefly mentioned here.

In the Edison Company's version of *Frankenstein* (J. Searle Dawley, 1910, US) the Monster (Charles Ogle) exists partly as a function of Frankenstein's (Augustus Phillips) thoughts.[12] The theme of the link between Frankenstein and the Monster is emphasized, first in the cross-cut shots in which the Monster forms in a vat while Frankenstein looks on, and then in the scene in which Frankenstein sees the Monster reflected in a mirror instead of himself.

Frankenstein (1931) shows in certain scenes, as well as in the design of some of its lighting and sets, that it was influenced by the German horror film. There is notable overlap with the bedroom-window scene in *Caligari*, for example, even if that scene may itself have been influenced by the bedroom-window scene in the novel *Frankenstein*. Universal's Monster may have taken his stiff walk from the strong but heavy creature in *The Golem: How He Came Into the World* (Carl Boese and Paul Wegener, 1920, Germany; Wegener and Henrik Galeen had made an earlier version in 1914), who is made from clay, as God is said to have made man from earth, and is played by co-director Wegener. The Golem—created by the astrologer and magician Rabbi Loew (Albert Steinrück) and animated by a magic word[13] contained in an amulet on his chest—stomps sturdily around, but when he carries the rabbi's fainted daughter, he does it far more gracefully and strongly than Cesare, using both his arms and creating the iconic image of the monster carrying the unconscious woman, an image that recurs in countless horror movies. When we see the woman in this position, we do not know whether she is expressing an unconscious desire to be carried off by the monster or has simply fainted and become a vulnerable figure who needs to be rescued. Many films insist on the latter but, perhaps unconsciously, imply the former.

Anticipating Frankenstein's assistant, Rabbi Loew has an assistant who makes a mistake, animating the Golem when it has become dangerous to do so. Like the Frankenstein Monster, the Golem is a constructed monster, one put together. There is also a scene with a little girl who removes the amulet and immobilizes the Golem that may have influenced the scene in Whale's *Frankenstein* with little Maria (Marilyn Harris).

That film opens with a warning from its producer, Universal's Carl Laemmle, Jr, that the picture may prove too horrifying for some. The warning is conveyed by Edward Van Sloan, the voice of authority in many of these pictures, who had played Dr Van Helsing in *Dracula*, played Dr Waldman in *Frankenstein* and was soon to play Dr Muller in *The Mummy*. The introduction changes the terms of the story by introducing the question of religion, which is not a significant theme in the novel.[14] We are told that this is the story of a man who wanted to play God, "to create a man after his own image without reckoning upon God." The film proper, set in Germany, begins with a funeral that immediately introduces the theme of death, observed by the grave-robbing Henry Frankenstein—who now has a friend named Victor and is the son of a baron—and his hunchbacked assistant, Fritz (Dwight Frye). From the grave-robbing to the postmortem operations and the hints of necrophilia—even just the brain wheeled into the operating room on a cart in *Ghost*—all the Frankenstein films focus on the creepy and repellent aspects of death.

The assistant may find his source in *The Golem*, and his being a hunchback here may go back to folklore, but another possible source for this character is the Faust legend, in some versions of which Faust has an apprentice who is usually a comic figure or a lower-class reflection of Faust, although he is not a hunchback. In Goethe's *Faust Part II* the assistant, Wagner, is in Faust's lab with Mephistopheles when the homunculus is created ("a man is being made").[15] Fritz thus may link Frankenstein (and later mad scientists) with the tradition of the tragic figure who seeks the extremes of knowledge. Because he is a hunchback, Fritz also creates an association between Frankenstein's work and deformity, even birth defects. The doctor's hunchbacked assistant becomes a recurring figure in the series, ending with the female one in *House of Dracula* (Jane Adams as Nina) who is a sympathetic and skilled researcher—unlike Fritz, who makes the mistake that leads to the Monster's being given a deformed, "criminal" brain and whose favorite tool is a torch. Only in *House of Frankenstein* does the hunchback (J. Carrol Naish as Daniel) turn against the doctor, in a powerful moment that leads, however, directly to the Monster's killing him. Ygor is not a hunchback but is in the tradition with his rock-hard broken neck. Fritz is the Monster's tormentor, but Ygor is his friend. Each of these assistants is killed, as if he or she were a minor monster or a sacrificial victim that had to be disposed of for the story to be resolved.

When it is given life in the lab, the Monster raises its hand and forearm. "It's alive!" Henry yells—and then says a line cut by the censors from the original release prints: "In the name of God, now I know what it feels like to be God!" His audience consists of Elizabeth, Victor and Dr Waldman, who fear that Henry is mad—and he is, in fact, well on his way to becoming a prototype of the mad scientist. Dr Waldman is convinced that the creature is "a monster" and that "only evil can come of it." Reluctant to call the creature a monster, Henry decides to show Waldman what happens when it first sees light. Understanding his gesture, the Monster sits down at Henry's command. When Henry opens a skylight and lets in the sun, the Monster slowly looks up, then stands and raises his arms to the light, trying to reach it. (Light, which makes images in concert with its opposite, the dark, is the hero of the horror mise-en-scène, as light and dark are often the key to the horror film's metaphysics of good and evil.) When the skylight is closed, the Monster is seen at his most innocent and sympathetic, gesturing with open hands for the return of the light. Then Fritz rushes noisily in with a torch. Even before he associates it with pain, the Monster is afraid of fire; thus he is seen at least in part as a kind of beast, not a user of fire like a person or like Shelley's Monster. Still, his reaction to light and then to fire—with an innocence that may be independent of the criminal brain—is the beginning of a major theme in the first two movies and a continuing theme in the next two. The development of the Monster's consciousness, which is related to his education in the ways of a hostile world, also poses the films' basic question: what if death or a thing derived artificially from death became conscious?

In his cell, the Monster is tormented by Fritz. Finally the Monster kills him, and then kills Dr Waldman when the latter is trying to dissect him. Harsh treatment and the criminal brain combine to make the Monster a destroyer. While Henry goes home, the Monster heads for the hills where he meets little Maria, a girl whose father has left her to play by herself. Maria shows the Monster how to play a game, throwing flowers onto the surface of the lake, where they float. The first time she hands him a flower, he smells it and smiles happily. When he runs out of flowers, he uses Maria, but she doesn't float. The shots in which the Monster throws her into the water and then runs distraught through the forest—important because this is the only time he shows remorse, an emotion he shares with Shelley's Monster—were cut by the censors. Compared with the murder of the child in the novel, this is a crime by an innocent. It increases our pity for the Monster along with our fear of him. We can begin to see the Monster as a tragic figure, even though that theme is not pursued until *Bride*.

The Monster makes his way to the Frankenstein mansion—in the first two movies and in the novel, the Monster seeks out his creator—and turns up on the day Henry is to marry Elizabeth. In preparation for the wedding, Baron Frankenstein makes a toast that must have inspired many sequels: "Here's health to a son of the house of Frankenstein... Here's a jolly good health to young Frankenstein." After the Monster intrudes on Elizabeth in the bedroom, Henry postpones the wedding. As we shall see, many honeymoons and marriages are interrupted in horror films, usually to allow one or both of the partners to go through a period or phase of horror that leaves them more experienced, more mature and a better couple.

Maria's father brings her body into the village, and an angry crowd gathers. The crowd has torches. They carry fire through the night like a tribe, a major influence on the vengeful mobs in the Frankenstein sequels and many other films. They were anticipated in 1925 by the torch-bearing crowd at the end of *The Phantom of the Opera* (Rupert Julian, 1925, revised 1929, US). Henry confronts the Monster in a windmill. For a moment they stand on either side of a turning wheel, and we see Frankenstein and the Monster in the same screen position in alternating shots. This is as close as this movie comes to equating them (even if it also sets them in opposition), but they will be linked more explicitly in *Bride*—and in *Son* via Henry's son, Wolf (Basil Rathbone), who is declared by Ygor to be the Monster's brother, as both are sons of Frankenstein. After the Monster throws Henry off the windmill, the crowd sets fire to it, and the Monster is burned alive. This is an unwilling death, not at all like the planned suicide in the novel, even if in both cases fire—an ancient means of purification—is what allows the destruction of the Monster and the righting of the world. It is the most painful and frightening way the film's Monster could die. Thus if we fear and hate the Monster, he comes to a satisfyingly bad end. To the extent that we feel sympathy for him, his end is terrible. Henry survives, and the baron looks forward to having grandchildren.

Nevertheless there was a sequel that opened up all this closure. The title of *Bride of Frankenstein* refers to Elizabeth (this time played by Valerie Hobson), whose honeymoon is delayed until after the end of the picture. But Universal, realizing that the Monster had come to be called Frankenstein throughout world popular culture,[16] had it both ways and made this the story both of the Frankensteins' marriage and of the Monster's search for a bride. Again the director was James Whale, but this time he would let his taste for bizarre dark comedy find fuller expression.

Bride of Frankenstein opens with a scene in which Mary Shelley (played by Elsa Lanchester, who also played the Monster's bride, as if Mary had projected herself into that role), Percy Shelley and Lord Byron talk about *Frankenstein* during a storm.

Then Mary decides to tell her companions how the story really ended. The publishers who have rejected her book, she says, have failed to perceive that her tale conveyed a moral lesson: "the punishment that befell a mortal man who dared to emulate God." That has evidently become the theme of the early films, their understanding of what Frankenstein did—or perhaps it was the producers' way to get these movies past the censors, targeting in advance what may at the time have been their most offensive aspect. The Monster (played again by Karloff, who played it for the last time in *Son*) is still mortal—a bullet can wound him—and his apparent death in the previous picture is explained away, setting a pattern for all the Frankenstein sequels: he fell through the burning windmill to the water below it. Among those at the burned-out mill is Minnie (Una O'Connor), one of Frankenstein's servants who later finds the right words to describe the Monster, declaring him "a nightmare in the daylight." Frankenstein (played again by Colin Clive) is taken home and people fear he is dead. He is laid out on a table like the Monster, with whom he is repeatedly coupled in this picture, starting when his arm moves and Minnie screams, "He's alive!" There is a later scene when the Monster tells Henry to sit down and makes the same gesture Henry had made when issuing that command (when the Monster was first to see light), and Henry sits the same way the Monster had, in the same screen position.

After he has recovered and his father has died, Henry is visited by a former professor, the comically diabolical Dr Pretorius (Ernest Thesiger). Pretorius is a scientist who does not mind being called mad. He wants Henry to work with him at making life. He displays the small, anatomically perfect humans he has grown but says he hasn't solved the problem of size, which Henry did. Pretorius wants to make a female of the same species as Frankenstein's Monster—to create a race (which Victor was afraid to do in the novel). Though Pretorius does not say so, it is clear that the first generation of this race will be made by men without the aid of women, not to mention of God. By the end of the film, Henry will have chosen marriage to a woman over a boys' project in a lab.

The Monster's education and growing self-awareness are dramatized more in *Bride* than in any other Frankenstein film. Sometimes he sees himself as a horror, as we see him, which creates a double perspective, a doubled look. Wandering in the woods, the Monster finds a pond at the base of a waterfall and drinks. Then, like an anti-Narcissus, he sees his reflection. It repulses him, and he dashes the image away. It is possible but not certain that he realizes he is seeing himself—that in this scene, horror faces and becomes conscious of itself. (When a similar scene occurs in *Son*—the Monster compares himself to Wolf in a mirror—his recognition of himself is definite.) The Monster is pursued by a crowd of townspeople and captured. When he is tied up, he looks almost crucified, which casts him as an innocent sacrifice and increases our sympathy for him. He escapes back to the woods, where he hears a violin being played by a blind hermit (O. P. Heggie). This matches the point in the novel where the Monster learns to speak and read, though the scenes in the movie, it must be admitted, are better. The Monster already understands what is said to him; he makes that clear to the hermit. When the hermit prays, giving thanks to God for bringing him a friend (the beginning of the crucial "friend" theme in this film and the series), the Monster cries and comforts the old man, and a crucifix on the wall glows after the rest of the scene has faded out. This emphasizes the spiritual and emotional value of friendship and picks up the image of the nearly crucified Monster, the sacrificial victim—for as we saw with the hunchbacks, and could remark of the victims in slasher films, many horror movies are ritualistic structures with defined sacrifices. Soon the hermit has taught him the words "bread," "drink," "smoke," "alone" and "friend," as well as "good" and "bad." The Monster thinks alone is bad and friend is good, fire is bad and music is good. Two hunters come into the cottage and recognize the Monster, and one of them says, "He isn't human. Frankenstein made him out of dead bodies." This gives the Monster the information that in the novel comes from Frankenstein's notes.

The Monster then goes to a graveyard where he meets Pretorius. The Monster tells him that he loves the dead and hates the living, his most self-conscious statement until the climax. One reason we feel an unusual degree of sympathy for the Monster in *Bride*, even if he remains a frightening killer, is that he can put his feelings into words. Pretorius tells the Monster that he will make a friend for him, a woman, from the dead. The Monster's search for a friend dominates this picture and is important in *Son* and *Ghost*, where the friends are Ygor and a little girl. It is in the sequels after *Ghost* that the friendship theme and the theme of the Monster's developing consciousness are dropped, and the Monster becomes a bit player in his own stories, moving through a series of rechargings and fights that turn ever more formulaic and brief while the Wolf Man, Larry Talbot (Lon Chaney, Jr), becomes a significant character in the series, as he tries to find a Frankenstein-like doctor who can bring him a real death. (At the end of *House of Dracula*, such a doctor actually heals him.) The friendship theme picks up the novel's emphasis on the Monster's singularity and his desire for a female companion of his own species.

Henry and Elizabeth are about to go on their honeymoon when Pretorius has the Monster kidnap Elizabeth, so as to force Henry to complete the work. Elizabeth is in her bedroom, sitting at her dressing table, when the Monster opens the window and comes in, grabs her, then takes her away. Minnie arrives in time to see him carry her out the window. This scene builds on the scene of the Monster's coming through the window to threaten Elizabeth in the 1931 *Frankenstein*, but lets the abduction take place as in *Caligari*, tightening the reference to the German film. The honeymoon will have to come later.

Pretorius has an assistant, Karl (Dwight Frye), who keeps Elizabeth tied up in a cave near Frankenstein's old mountain laboratory, where the bride is finally constructed. The brain, which is perfect, has been grown. The heart comes from a very recent murder, and we see it beating in the lab. The lab sequence is an extravagance of low-key lighting and tilted, off-angle shots. At the height of the storm, the Monster finds Karl on the roof, managing the kites that are out to collect the lightning. Karl tries to hold him off with a torch but fails, and the Monster tosses away the torch (a power he rarely has) and hurls Karl down to his death. At that moment lightning hits one of the kites. Thus death is part of the animation of the new monster.

Brought to life and pronounced by Pretorius "the bride of Frankenstein," the bride rejects her proposed mate. Her new-made brain has an unschooled reaction to the Monster—showing that he is inherently terrifying, as well as ugly—and she screams. "She hate me, like others," the Monster says. Elizabeth, who has somehow escaped, is at the locked laboratory door when the Monster discovers the lever that, when lowered, will blow up the whole place. The Monster, who is impressed by Elizabeth's refusal to leave without Henry, convinces Henry to save himself and his wife, but he tells Pretorius to remain with him and the bride. "We belong dead," the Monster says, then pulls the lever. The Monster has been growing in tragic self-awareness throughout the picture, and he knows well what it means to be alone and to be dead. Henry and Elizabeth escape and are shown together in a tight view at the end (the satisfactory conclusion of the ritual). Now they are a couple who are no longer pursued by the horrors against which they have proved themselves, and their honeymoon—in effect their marriage—can begin.

In *Son*, the last of the films to use any expressionist lighting or big sets, the Monster has become indestructible. Ygor says that Frankenstein made the Monster to live "for always." There is no explanation for why he cannot speak, and no reference is made to his ever having been able to. When Wolf jolts the Monster in the lab, he doesn't need lightning. He has discovered that the great ray actually was cosmic rays. Still, lightning will work; there is a strong scene early in *Ghost* when the Monster regains his strength by exposing himself to it directly. Much like the other films in the series, *Son* has a conservative happy ending in which social harmony is restored, the threat to the family is destroyed and the forbidden work is abandoned.

In *Ghost* the Monster (Lon Chaney, Jr) is given the brain of Ygor by Wolf's younger brother, Ludwig, who at one point takes advice from the titular ghost of his father. Ygor tells the Monster he will die for his friend, but what he intends is to combine his evil intelligence with the Monster's invulnerable body. The Monster wants the brain of an innocent young girl, Cloestine (Janet Ann Gallow), who is still alive—that is his decision about the future of his consciousness—but Ludwig's intention is to use the brain of a scientist the Monster killed, undoing the problems Henry introduced with his use of a criminal's brain by replacing the Monster's brain with a better one, giving him a different mind. Here the evolution of consciousness is reduced to the physical, primitive notion of literally switching brains. But an evil scientist who was promised power by Ygor intervenes and determines which brain is used. It turns out that Ygor and the Monster have different blood types, and the Monster goes blind after he has delivered a few lines in Ygor's voice. The friends prove incompatible. Beyond that, the Monster is denied the option of an innocence transplant from the little girl.

From *Frankenstein Meets the Wolf Man* through *House of Dracula*—though he is treated differently in some later films not made at Universal[17]—the Monster does not reveal a developing inner life. There are no moments of self-recognition, let alone of wanting to have an innocent brain. But self-knowledge and isolation, even if not verbally expressed, are part of the Monster's essential pain, and it is a loss for the late sequels that he does not appear to feel them. He is revived at the climax of each film, but does little or nothing before then, and he is quickly destroyed by water (*Frankenstein Meets the Wolf Man*), earth (the quicksand in *House of Frankenstein*) and fire (*House of Dracula*), after *Ghost* had ended with a shot of the sky. Each prime element is given the final shot in these four movies, as if the natural world were proving itself victorious over the aberration of nature that is the Monster, a creature who knows, when his self-awareness is at its peak, that he belongs dead. A killer made from the dead, he advances toward death (his own and others') in spite of occasional moments that feature light or friendship. That is the consistent route he takes, the route laid out for him by his origin and his nature. He is fundamental.

Composite Monsters: *Island of Lost Souls* and *The Fly*

One of the early uses of "monster" in English refers to an imaginary creature made up of the parts of two or more animals, one of which might be human.[18] It can also refer to a malformed fetus, usually born dead and resembling several animals, or a mix between human and animal. Ancient mythology includes such composite creatures as the sphinx and the centaur. Film gives us the *Creature from the Black Lagoon* (Jack Arnold, 1954, US), where the Gill Man, whose species has survived since the Devonian Age, has the characteristics of a man and a fish, and *The Fly* (Kurt Neumann, 1958, US), where a man has the head and arm of a fly, and a fly has the head and arm of a man—or the remake of *The Fly* (David Cronenberg, 1986, Canada/US), where the man and the fly are completely integrated on a molecular level. These creatures raise the question of the definition of man, the species, which stands—as it is said in *The Creature Walks Among Us* (John Sherwood, 1956, US)—"between the jungle and the stars." The horror of the monster, the challenge to human nature and the threat of a new category of life are found together in the dangerous mix.

It is part of the horror film's job to tell us about our nature. The genre is charged with the investigation of all forms of life, from the natural to the unnatural, with a special interest in human nature, which it continually defines and redefines in relation to other kinds and ways of being. It proposes a fable of who we are, often showing the image of our condition and our potential in a monster or in those who oppose it.

A composite creature, a combination of animal forms, the fruit of anything from mythology or surgery to genetic anomaly, disturbs our sense of the orderly classification of species—of the way things ought to be, much as the Frankenstein Monster displays life and death at once. These monsters are not human, yet they are not entirely some other animal. One of their most human characteristics is that they may find people sexually attractive. The Creature from the Black Lagoon (played by Ricou Browning in the water and Ben Chapman on land) is practically a romantic, so intensely does he concentrate on the only woman in each of the three films.[19] When he carries the unconscious Kay (Julia Adams) into his grotto in *Black Lagoon*, it is expected, iconic (Figure 19). Yet we do not consider them a human couple but see them as "the monster and the girl," as the phrase went. With his gills and dormant lungs, with his webs and claw-like fingers, with his arms and legs and fins, the Creature is a fork in the road between marine and land life: the point at which his species stopped evolving millions of years ago.

Composites can be especially dangerous, for they may have the intelligence of humans or something like it. Cronenberg's man-fly has all of his former intelligence along with an insect-like selfishness that perverts it. The Creature from the Black Lagoon has cunning and the ability to plan; he is almost a human opponent.

Island of Lost Souls (Erle C. Kenton, 1932, US) has creatures that describe themselves as "Not men, not beasts" but "things." The film was loosely based on H. G. Wells's novel *The Island of Dr. Moreau*—"loosely" because it added women to the story and changed the ending—but Wells had much the same monsters, and he had "the Law" and "the House of Pain." Dr Moreau (Charles Laughton), a mad scientist who respects no moral or physical boundaries, takes animals into his laboratory, the House of Pain,

Figure 19. *Creature from the Black Lagoon*: "The monster and the girl"; the Creature carries the unconscious woman into his lair.

and, after somehow altering their germ plasm, vivisects them. Sometimes (in the novel, often) he grafts several animals together—parts of a dog and a bear, for instance—and works on the results, cutting the animals into human form. It is horrible, and so are the screams. His assistant is a disgraced, drunken doctor, Montgomery (Arthur Hohl), who had probably been doing abortions, another forbidden operation, back in civilization. The humanoid beasts, the only inhabitants of the island aside from those in Moreau's compound, have a village where they recite to each other the Law that Moreau has conditioned into them: "not to run on all fours," for example. ("What is the Law?" Moreau ritually demands, cracking his whip. "Not to spill blood," says the leader, the Sayer of the Law [Bela Lugosi], "that is the Law. Are we not men?" "Are we not men?" the monsters chant in unison.) The Law keeps the monsters in line, and so does the ritual reminder, "His is the House of Pain."

Moreau has only two problems: the "stubborn beast flesh" keeps growing back—making it necessary to take the monsters back to the House of Pain—and he has a nosy, shipwrecked observer, Edward Parker (Richard Arlen). Before being abandoned on Moreau's island, Edward had telegrammed his fiancée, Ruth (Leila Hyams), when to expect him at the port where they were planning to marry. She and a local captain (Donahue, played by Paul Hurst) go to Moreau's island. In the meantime Moreau has decided to experiment with Edward, to see whether his prized creation, Lota, the Panther

Woman (Kathleen Burke), who looks entirely human, will be attracted to a human male. She is. As mentioned before, neither she nor Ruth is in the novel. The movie has made sex, particularly the prospect of sex between species, an important element of the confrontation between human and monster. Explaining his experiments to Edward, Moreau asks, under creepy lighting, "Do you know what it means to feel like God?" This desire seems to be what was most feared about mad scientists and doctors in the 1930s and 40s, though they were still playing God much later, as in *The Human Centipede (First Sequence)* (Tom Six, 2009, Netherlands), where a mad scientist cuts and stitches three people into a composite organism.

When Ruth and Donahue arrive, one of the monsters, the violent Ouran (Hans Steinke), is attracted to her. After a scene in which Ruth gets partly undressed for bed, Ouran pries away the bars on her bedroom window and comes through the opening as Ruth screams (this example of the bedroom-window scene is clearly about sex). Later, on Moreau's orders, Ouran strangles Donahue. Then Ouran tells the Sayer of the Law, "Law no more"—because Moreau told him to spill blood.

The beast-men confront Moreau at his house, where he asks whether they have forgotten the House of Pain. The Sayer of the Law says, "You made us in the House of Pain. You made us things! Not men, not beasts. Part men, part beast—Things!"—and the monsters advance on the camera in one chilling shot after another. The monsters pursue Moreau into the House of Pain and cut him to pieces. Edward, Ruth and Montgomery escape, and Lota, the film's ritual sacrifice, is killed protecting them from Ouran. Fire consumes all of Moreau's work (the work of a mad scientist doesn't last). The final shot fades out on Edward and Ruth, as Montgomery rows their boat away from the fiery island. Now, having passed through the horror phase of their relationship, which in this case has forced them to deal with the nature of life, and to undergo trials and perils proving themselves right for each other, they can marry.

Moreau is a mad scientist, and this could be called a mad-scientist picture, but its primary horror is centered in the monsters, composite "things" that clearly manifest, in their own terms, the threat that Moreau represents to the spontaneous course of evolution and to biology itself.

Giants: *King Kong* and *Them!*

Giants are unnaturally large people, animals or even plants (the beanstalk), conceived almost entirely for their size. A tarantula the size of a house is a gigantic animal, and so is a black widow the size of a washing machine, as in the short *Larger than Life* (Ellory Elkayem, 1998, New Zealand). Because they are naturally large, dinosaurs are big animals, not giants. Except for Godzilla, who is an oversized, gigantic dinosaur with some of the characteristics of a dragon, they appear in most films at their natural size, which is enough. King Kong is a giant, but his dinosaur companions are not.

The unnamed monster in *Cloverfield* is a 500-foot-tall member of an unknown species, who, like Godzilla, is able to destroy a city by walking through it, and is even more capable than King Kong of challenging Manhattan. This giant's principal characteristics are its destructiveness and its size. In addition, it sheds parasites resembling giant lice.

We see the monster in glimpses as it is caught by the video camera of a young man (T. J. Miller as Hud) who started out documenting a party. The less we see of the monster and the more we see and hear of its effects on the city, the more imposing and frightening it becomes ("Whatever it is, it's winning," one man says). *Cloverfield* demonstrates that the spectacle of a gigantic monster needn't dominate the screen to be effective. What it has to dominate is the situation, transfiguring ordinary life by its presence. We see one skyscraper leaning against another and imagine the force and the figure that toppled it. Although the revelation is delayed as long as possible, the filmmakers decided that the monster finally needed to be seen as a whole. The last image Hud takes (this is before and as the monster kills him) looks upward at the complete creature. Then the camera falls, showing us the head of the dead Hud—an echo of the shot of the dead cameraman that concludes the inner documentary in *Cannibal Holocaust*, which clearly was an influence here, along with the similarly influenced *The Blair Witch Project*. These are all films in which the characters advance into dangerous territory while documenting their journey on film or video, thus generating most or all of the movie. The film also demonstrates that it is not necessary to explain the monster[20] or to destroy it[21]; even without such formulaic elements and without a resolution (there is a partial explanation, but it's hard to find), *Cloverfield* remains a complete horror movie.

Some giants are found in folklore and ancient literature, from Homer's Cyclops to the biblical Goliath, and they often have normal human characteristics except for their size—or normal characteristics exaggerated by size, as strength in a huge arm becomes huge strength. But in horror films there comes with great size the potential and even the imperative to do great harm. Sometimes a person will suffer a mental change of some kind—often connected with what caused him or her to become a giant in the first place—that makes him or her do harm when gigantic (*The Amazing Colossal Man* [Bert I. Gordon, 1957, US]). Sometimes he or she will not change in personality but will be much more effective when he or she acts (*Attack of the 50 Foot Woman* [Nathan Juran as Nathan Hertz, 1958, US]). The mad scientist in *Dr. Cyclops* (Ernest B. Schoedsack, 1940, US) is consistently a ruthless murderer, but once he has shrunk his opponents and appears to them as a giant, his potential to do harm is increased, even if he does not become crazier than he already is.

Except for his attraction to tiny women, Kong behaves as an ape would in similar circumstances—when attacked, for instance, or when wanting to get to high ground. It is just that his size enables him to take on bigger opponents and structures, and of course makes him stand out. When he is angry, he is willfully destructive—wrecking a village and eating people—and when he is calm, he remains formidable. He is a big creature but not an evil one.

Of all the inhuman creatures attracted to human women, Kong is the most famous, perhaps because he puts so much energy into his pursuit of Ann but also because we understand his feelings. Thanks to Willis O'Brien's stop-motion animation, Kong is highly expressive, from the thinking in his eyes to the ripples in his fur. Like Cesare, he bears a woman away into the night—but like the Creature from the Black Lagoon, he carries her to his home, intending to keep her. Unlike either of them, he toys with her dress and sniffs his finger. Romance is perhaps not the right word for this pairing of

"Beauty and the Beast," as showman Carl Denham (Robert Armstrong) calls them. It is more the familiar pairing of "the monster and the girl": the monster, in this case male, reaching for or carrying the female whose beauty and vulnerability are significant for the audience, touching their own sense of vulnerability and their own desire, both of which they fear and both of which they find exciting. There is a sexual current running through the majority of horror films, and it often finds expression by bringing a monster and a woman together. When a monster abducts or shows romantic interest in a woman (as in those beautiful scenes when the Creature from the Black Lagoon swims below Kay), sexual desire is out of control and the normal process of reproduction is threatened. If there were intercourse between the Creature and Kay, it would be an extreme form of exogamy. That may be one reason there is a love story in almost every horror film, whether or not there is also a threatened coupling between a human and a monster: because sex is a crucial aspect of our nature that must be reaffirmed every time our survival is threatened. The whole of human nature is sounded by the horror film, but there is a repeated emphasis on those parts of our nature that seem to be in doubt or in danger, as well as on those that are our strengths. Set against monsters and monstrous drives, we continually assert our humanity. It is possible to identify the junction of sex and horror with the trauma of puberty, but there remain many cases, as we have seen, in which adult sexuality (which does in fact often stand in for adolescent sexuality) is threatened by horror or must go through a horror phase: where the woman, for instance, must *almost* become the bride of Kong.

Godzilla has the less-romantic motivation of the average monster: to destroy. All monsters have motivations—simple ones like hunger (the giant ants who want sugar—and to reproduce—in *Them!* [Gordon Douglas, 1954, US]) or complex ones like the Frankenstein Monster's wanting the little girl's brain—but most are simply out to wreck or kill what is in their way. Giants can do tremendous damage just by moving. Godzilla tramples Tokyo as much as he sets fire to it. It is the monster's progress and motivation, and of course the human resistance to them, that determine the action of the film. In *Tarantula* Deemer dies because the spider, like Frankenstein's Monster, has come back to find and kill its creator—that's unless the spider's showing up at Deemer's house is a coincidence with symbolic overtones. The motivations of human or humanoid giants are easier to consider. The 50-foot woman wants her cheating husband to stay with her, and when she is big enough to tear off the roof of the tavern where he is dancing with his mistress, she can drop a beam on the mistress and carry him off.

King Kong was not the first movie about a monster from the natural world. It owes a great deal to *The Lost World* (Harry Hoyt, 1925, US). Kong is a naturally occurring monster, as no lab had any part in making him. But there are many giants in the movies that appear because of some unnatural cause, or some natural force that is now out of control, such as radiation. The giant octopus in *It Came from Beneath the Sea* (Robert Gordon, 1955, US) had lived a long time in its deep native waters before nuclear testing made it radioactive, which warned away its food, so that it had to make its way to the surface to find something else to eat, mainly people. Radiation had many effects in the movies, but some things it enlarged. Thanks to the success of *Them!*, many of the things that became gigantic were bugs.

The ants in *Them!* are mutations caused by "lingering radiation" from the testing of the first atomic bomb. To the extent that the monster was created by science or can be explained by science, the scientist who believes in the monster—in this case Dr Medford (Edmund Gwenn)—becomes a standard figure in the science fiction horror film,[22] his ancestor being none other than Dr Van Helsing. In some cases, however, the authoritative figures are dispensed with: in *Night of the Living Dead* the nearest thing to a confirming authority is the television.

There are two scientists in *Them!*: Dr Medford's daughter is Dr Pat Medford (Joan Welson). Pat sometimes serves as the woman in distress—she screams when she sees the first onscreen ant, which is very near her—but she is also competent, a good scientist and not a feminine stereotype, which can also be said of the female scientist in *It Came from Beneath the Sea* (Dr Lesley Joyce, played by Faith Domergue), a "new breed of woman" who is a world authority on marine biology and who decides to stay single and keep her job—but is open to a relationship—when the hero proposes to her at the end. The scientists in *Them!* are helping policeman Ben Peterson (James Whitmore) and an FBI agent. In Washington, Dr Medford shows the country's real authority figures a documentary that informs them about ants and their behavior—the equivalent in this picture of the *Book of the Vampire*. There is a similar 16mm movie with the same function in *Tarantula*. Medford explains that the giant ants are as savage and well-organized as conventional ones (they have become no worse than ordinary ants, though their size makes them more destructive), which means they could wipe out humanity. In Los Angeles, where a nest has hatched in the storm drains beneath the city, Peterson rescues two boys—the hope of the future, in place of any romantic couple[23]—but dies. The last ants are destroyed—the very last ones by primitive, reliable fire—and Medford ends the picture with a speculation, almost a warning, about the unknown things we may encounter in the atomic age. The norm has been restored only to be called into question; we don't know what waits for us in the new world.

Giant bugs and lizards, creatures that are usually small, make us like Gulliver in Brobdingnag, where things are huge and display their worst features. They are a threat to the norm and to our role in it. The power structure has been reversed, and it is we who are underfoot. We become like helpless children—or resourceful ones, trying to figure out how to conquer the giants. The giants may remind us of our first impressions of adults, whom little children find very tall. Our weapons become insufficient, and we have to make new toys. Now that such small creatures are big enough to kill us, we must destroy every one of them to preserve and vindicate our position as the dominant species.

In *Tarantula* Dr Matt Hastings asks an agricultural researcher what would happen if "circumstances magnified" a tarantula "in size and strength, took it out of its primitive world and turned it loose in ours." The researcher tells him to "expect something that's fiercer, more cruel and deadly than anything that ever walked the earth." Making the spider bigger makes it worse.

Little People: *The Devil-Doll*

These are films in which tiny people are the monsters—or where tiny people are plunged into horror, as in *The Incredible Shrinking Man* (Jack Arnold, 1957, US), adapted by Richard Matheson from his novel *The Shrinking Man*. They are anything but giants but are equally removed from the norm. A spider in the cellar is a gigantic enemy to the shrinking man, who has, like many giants, been the victim of radiation or an unknown force.

One of the earliest examples of this sub-subgenre is *The Devil-Doll* (Tod Browning, 1936, US). Escaped convict Paul Lavond (Lionel Barrymore) runs a doll shop in Paris with his crippled assistant, Malita (Rafaela Ottiano). Using techniques invented by Malita's late husband, Lavond and Malita shrink and physically perfect people. The resulting beings, who are less than a foot tall, have no independent minds (it is as if they were dolls, and they can be placed with the victims as dolls). That makes it possible to control them, simply by concentrating on what one wants them to do, and Lavond wants them to help him get even with the men who framed him—by having the dolls stab them with tiny knives dipped in poison, for example. After Lavond has carried out most of his revenge and the dolls have been destroyed, there remains only the memory of the little people who could climb up a bedspread and stab a sleeping man, leaving him paralyzed forever, or could hide under a chair with a more lethal poison on the little knife while a clock ticked down to the appointed time of a victim's death.

Animals: *Murders in the Rue Morgue*, *The Birds* and *Jurassic Park*

Animals that are of natural size—from dinosaurs to tigers and scorpions—can be as formidable as the more fantastic giants, whether there are hundreds of them, as in *The Birds*, or only one, as in *Jaws* (Steven Spielberg, 1975, US). Some animals have always inspired fear, and the dangerous animal is an image anyone can access, often from experience. In films, domestic animals can be good at sniffing out monsters; they have crossed over from the wilderness side to the hearth side and are our partners—unless they become like the rabid dog in *Cujo* (Lewis Teague, 1983, US) and turn against us.

The dinosaur is one image of the monster that all people share. We know what dinosaurs looked like and that they were real; we have seen their skeletons up close. The picture and the fearfulness of the dinosaur are ready to hand. In terms of order, present-day dinosaurs upset our sense of time. But something, even radioactivity (as in *Lost Continent* [Sam Newfield, 1951, US]), has made it possible for them to survive unevolved into our time. On *King Kong*'s Skull Island, they are just there; no science fiction premise is necessary. But even with a science fiction premise, as in *Jurassic Park* (Steven Spielberg, 1993, US), dinosaurs are archetypal monsters.

One of the first feature films to show dinosaurs in action was the 1925 *The Lost World*, based on the novel by Sir Arthur Conan Doyle. To prove that the dinosaurs he has seen in the Lost World, which is in the uncharted Amazon, are real, Professor Challenger (Wallace Beery) organizes an expedition back to the Amazon, where he captures a brontosaurus that he brings back to London. But when the dinosaur is being unloaded, it gets loose, running amok in the London streets—the ancestor of Kong in New York (Willis O'Brien did the stop-motion animation for both pictures)—until it reaches the water and begins to swim home. In this sub-subgenre, there are cases where the animal does not have to be killed as long as it is expelled from our world (there are also, as we shall see, cases where the animals win). This relatively generous attitude shows up again in *The Lost World: Jurassic Park* (Steven Spielberg, 1997, US),[24] which ends on an island where the dinosaurs are thriving, and asserts the hope that people will let them alone.

Jurassic Park, based on the novel by Michael Crichton, had the most convincing dinosaur effects yet achieved. It is the story of a high-tech businessman, John Hammond (Richard Attenborough), who hires scientists to resurrect dinosaurs from their DNA, planning to put them on exhibit on a remote island. Hammond arranges for two paleontologists (Dr Alan Grant, played by Sam Neill, and Dr Ellie Sattler, played by Laura Dern), along with chaos theorist Dr Ian Malcolm (Jeff Goldblum), to inspect and approve of his work before the park opens. Hammond even lets his two grandchildren, Lex (Ariana Richards) and Tim (Joseph Mazzello), join the tour. It is established early on that Alan does not like children, nor does he want to have any. To be ready to have children, Alan has to grow up some, and he accomplishes that in the course of his horror adventure, mainly by taking care of Tim and Lex. The way the dinosaurs have been created, that science fiction premise, forces the audience to think about reproduction, a norm that is being outraged by all this genetic engineering. Once the dinosaurs have been grown, they can lay eggs, but sterile ones; the only major control on the animals is that Hammond has had no males created. Ian says the project shows a great lack of humility before nature. In the horror film, that's a red flag.

Things soon get out of hand. The dinosaurs find a way to reproduce. Some of them change sex, taking advantage of a quirk in their DNA mix, and the eggs hatch, which means that life itself objects to all the artificiality and manipulation. The electronics in the park fail, sabotaged by a greedy villain who appropriately gets killed by a dinosaur. It happens very often that a monster disposes of a character who ought not to live or who needs to be punished, as if the monster were an agent of morality within the plot. At the end it is made clear that the park will not be opening, and it is suggested that the dinosaurs will die without being given their regular enzyme supplement. As for Alan, he is finally ready to be a father, and Ellie sees it. This is a variation, but not an extreme one, on the familiar closing sequence in which sexual continuity is assured and the monster is destroyed.[25] *Jurassic Park* is a fable about growing up and having children, as well as about the hubris and danger of violating the rules that concern natural reproduction and of assuming that monsters can be controlled. It celebrates the dinosaurs' laying fertile eggs. The characters, especially Hammond, have learned to be more humble in the face of nature, more respectful of what it can do. As it so often does, the horror film here draws a conservative conclusion after having explored the alternatives.

Even animals that belong in the present can be considerable threats. Poe's "The Murders in the Rue Morgue" concerns an orangutan who gets loose from the sailor who owns him and kills two women—he disposes of a mother with a razor and her daughter by strangling—and then tries to hide the bodies so he will not be punished, throwing the older woman out the fourth-story window and thrusting the younger one, Camille L'Espanaye, up the chimney. Florey's *Murders in the Rue Morgue* (Robert Florey, 1932, US) changes the orangutan to a gorilla, Erik. It can serve as an example of the many pictures that partner a gorilla with a young woman. Erik's master is Dr Mirakle (Bela Lugosi), a carnival showman who is also a mad scientist, a kind of Caligari. He wants to prove the kinship between apes and humans by injecting some of Erik's blood into a young woman.

The trouble is that the women always die, and he blames this on their being sinful, their blood impure. Camille (Sidney Fox) is targeted by Mirakle for his experiment. At the climax, after Erik has stuffed not Camille but her mother up the chimney and later strangled Mirakle—who was about to inject Camille, whom he has found sufficiently pure, with Erik's blood—Erik carries an unconscious Camille across high rooftops, where he is shot by Camille's boyfriend, Pierre (Leon Waycoff).

Camille is set up to be the bride of the gorilla—a bit like the heroine of *Bride of the Gorilla* (Curt Siodmak, 1951, US), which is about a murderer (Raymond Burr) who thinks he has been turned into a gorilla by a curse and the lure of the jungle—and Erik does carry her away twice, once to Mirakle's lab and once up to the roofs, but she is saved by and for her human lover. Erik is attracted to a human female, tries to protect her and carries her off so that she can be with him in some monster's dream of romance. In this he acts out the presumed desires and fears of the audience. All we know about Camille's desires is that she is frightened and repulsed by the gorilla and that at the climax she is not just passive but has fainted. If she were conscious, her desire would be to save herself and get away from the gorilla. Caring about her, we fear for her—and perhaps also for her pure blood, for we do not want to see her blood mixed with that of the animal, whether through an injection or through the intercourse it symbolizes. Sexually, this movie says, the species belong apart.[26]

Jaws, based on the novel by Peter Benchley, opens with an excellent first-victim scene in which a young woman is eaten by something underneath the water while she is skinny-dipping. The scene ably conveys that we are, especially when naked, completely vulnerable to the creature, whatever it is. The monster does not show up on camera until halfway through the film; before then, it is conveyed in terms of its effects and its gaze. The camera often shows us what the fish sees, such as waving, swimming legs from below. When the shark does appear on camera, it is fast, and we usually see only part of it. This careful buildup, gradually establishing the nature and presence of the shark, is one of the chief accomplishments of the picture. Spielberg showed all this restraint, using the mechanical shark so rarely and using purely cinematic means to build the horror, because he was forced to. As he said in an interview,[27] the shark didn't work very well much of the time, and they had to do without it for many scenes.

The main character, Martin Brody (Roy Scheider), is the chief of police on an island in New England. He is afraid of going in the water, but he ends up on a boat hunting the shark, accompanied by the hardened shark hunter Quint (Robert Shaw) and shark expert Matt Hooper (Richard Dreyfuss). At the start of the climax, the shark eats Quint. A close view of the shark's biting a victim on camera has been withheld till, and for, this vividly violent moment. As the boat sinks, Brody is left to confront the monster alone—a showdown for which the film has been preparing all along. He throws a tank of compressed air into its mouth, then shoots the tank, using his native, landlubber tool to blow up the animal—that is, reinforcing and being true to his own nature by using a gun to kill a fish. Brody and Hooper (who missed the showdown) rig something up and start kicking for shore; Brody says that he used to be afraid of the water. He has overcome his fear as well as saved the community through this extreme confrontation with the shark on the water. There are times when horror can heal.

In *Cujo*, the threat is a good-natured St Bernard that has gone rabid. The little boy (Danny Pintauro as Tad) survives the encounter in the movie, but not in Stephen King's book (this change was suggested to the filmmakers by King[28]). Cujo is a good example of how an ordinary animal can become dangerous enough to become the central monster of a movie. The suffering animal is more than a pure threat; we feel for it. It forces the characters to deal with their personal problems and the danger it poses, bringing the clarifying energy of horror to a family that is on the verge of falling apart.

When animals whose normal size is not very large attack a group of humans—or all humanity as represented by the characters—they often do great damage because of their numbers. They can be organized by a directing intelligence—in *Willard* (Daniel Mann, 1971, US) the army of rats is controlled by their human trainer, Willard (Bruce Davison), and then by Ben, a rat with the qualities of a general—but it is more frightening and more unusual when they act as a group without any person or single chief animal telling them what to do. Then they have their own intelligence and motives and are not, say, symbolizing or acting out Willard's desire for revenge on his boss, but instead are turning against humans by themselves.

It is never explained why the birds in Hitchcock's film decide to attack people. There is no science fiction premise, no ecological explanation. Except for the coordinated attacks, they behave like ordinary birds. It is their unexplained and unpredictable destructiveness—the frightening element here, beneath which is the more general fear that nature can turn against us—with which the characters have to deal. That is the essential situation taken from Daphne Du Maurier's short story, "The Birds," and all that was taken from it; the characters and setting were changed completely for the movie. For one thing, it was made into a love story, following the rarely violated movie conventions that there can be no horror without romance and no monster that is not a threat. Women often represent the vulnerable aspects of the males and the females in the audience, including the aspects allowed by conventional roles—expressing that of fear in a scream. (Men in horror films scream in pain more often than fear, yet most males in the audience can feel the scream of the woman as part of their own response to fear.) *The Birds* is unconventional for the period in that although it has a successful romantic resolution, the birds do win and are likely to continue doing so. Beyond the fact that most of the main characters survive, there is no happy ending. What we have instead is one of the first open endings in the modern horror film (which dates from *Psycho*).

The Birds is a subtle and precise film. In one masterful sequence, a woman goes to the home of a friend to discuss why their chickens aren't eating, but he doesn't answer the door. In the kitchen she sees that the hanging teacups have been broken, an understated indication that violence has taken place. In the bedroom a quiet shot, virtually a still life, shows a gull smashed into the window, an original treatment of the bedroom-window intrusion scene and an example of horror beauty. Then she sees her dead friend in a series of quick shots that reveal his gory eye sockets.

Many less elegant films have dealt with the onslaughts of animals, some behaving according to type but in the wrong place (*Piranha* [Joe Dante, 1978, US]), some aggravated by human activity (*Squirm* [Jeff Lieberman, 1976, US] and *Kingdom of the Spiders*

[John "Bud" Cardos, 1977, US]), some directed by humans (*Willard*) and some with their own reasons to want humanity gone (*Frogs* [George McCowan, 1971, US]).

In *Frogs*, one of the first ecological horror films, pollution and pesticides have become unendurable to the lower animals, and the frogs have organized the snakes and other creatures to wipe out people and lay waste to their houses—notably the estate of Jason Crockett (Ray Milland), where the action is set. Crockett is a rich, arrogant man who believes that people control the planet. His opponent is a nature photographer and scientist who tries to convince Crockett to abandon his rigid plans for a birthday party and to get away, for people have been getting picked off one by one as they stupidly or for some good reason have gone off by themselves. This going off alone is a well-worn plot device in the horror film, usually employed because the victim could not be killed if he or she were not alone, because a death alone is more frightening, or because the death must be kept hidden for a while from the other characters. Those who do leave find that the animals' revolt has spread beyond the island. Crockett is left alone to face the frogs and vermin, who kill him. Many of the hordes of rats, frogs, piranha and birds, unlike the giants and the larger animals, win their battles with humanity, partly because they are too numerous to destroy and partly because rats, cockroaches and others have a history of surviving all efforts to control or eradicate them.

Body Parts: *The Beast with Five Fingers*

Brains in tanks, X-ray eyes and hands that can move on their own are only a few of the horrors possible when one isolates part of the body and gives it a special power: a power based in its nature (as it is natural for the eye to see and the hand to grasp) but perverted to destructiveness, as the X-ray eyes can see too much (in *X*, also known as *The Man with the X-Ray Eyes* [Roger Corman, 1963, US]) and the severed hand can strangle.

There is a disembodied hand with a signet ring in *The Beast with Five Fingers* (Robert Florey, 1946, US); it has been cut from the corpse of Francis Ingram (Victor Francen). The question about the hand is whether it is conscious and can move around by itself. If it can, it is being motivated by the ghost of Ingram. If it cannot, its movements are being hallucinated by Ingram's mad hanger-on, Hilary (Peter Lorre). While the latter turns out to be the case and everything is explained at the end, the picture takes its power from the scenes in which we see the hand playing the piano on its own (Ingram was a concert pianist who lost the use of one arm as the result of a stroke, and he put all his will to live and perform into his functioning hand) or strangling its enemies or looking for its ring.[29]

In *Donovan's Brain* (Felix Feist, 1953, US), based on the novel by Curt Siodmak, Dr Cory (Lew Ayres) keeps alive in an electrified, nutrient-filled tank the brain of a loathsome businessman, Donovan, who died in a plane crash. The brain, which is the audiovisual center of the film (beeping through the equipment attached to it and darkly pulsing in its tank), becomes strong and telepathic. Its evil personality and will control Cory until it is destroyed.

The Tingler (William Castle, 1959, US) is about an imaginary body part that is usually microscopic but becomes large and grips the spine when a person is afraid. It can cause a spinal tingle or can become big and strong enough to crack vertebrae. If a person screams, the tingler returns to its original, unthreatening form. At the climax, a tingler gets loose in the theatre (first a theatre within the fiction and then the one in which we are sitting). Castle wired a good number of the seats in the theatres that first showed this picture so that some of the patrons would get mild shocks in their lower backs during this sequence as if they were being attacked by the tingler, and some of them did scream.

Monsters from Outer Space: *The Thing From Another World* and *Alien*

Science fiction deals with the unknown, but the science fiction horror film often does so in a frightened manner, making the unknown, as Steve says in a scene in *Tarantula*, "creepy." Matt and Steve are driving in the desert when they stop by a hill covered with large rocks. Speaking of the desert when seen from the air, Matt says it looks "like something from another life. Serene, quiet, yet strangely evil, as if it were hiding its secret from man." "You make it sound so...so creepy," she says, and he replies, "The unknown always is." Of course it is not always creepy in science fiction but is usually a positive lure like that of an undiscovered world, a new technology or an expansion of human potential. But the unknown is mostly a threat in the horror film, as we can see when the rocks start to fall around Matt and Steve, a rockslide that they do not realize is caused by the tarantula—the unknown now made physical, behind the hill. Steve says she's "had enough of the unknown" for one afternoon, but she does not realize that she nearly had more of it, that she has been threatened not only by the desert, but also by the monster that sums up in its body and menace all the unknown, frightening aspects of the largely unexplored landscape.

Science fiction is regularly confused with horror, and it is not always possible to keep them distinct. It is not correct to say that a film with a monster in it is a horror film and one with a rocket ship in it is science fiction, for many films have both. There are numerous monsters that owe their existence to scientific experiments or technological developments or that come from outer space or are found there. Most of the pictures about them have a science fiction premise, and some are outright science fiction films, but some of them, like *Frankenstein*, are horror films. If there is a strong science fiction premise *and* if the burden of the picture turns out to be to induce horror, the film fits into the crossover or shared subgenre of science fiction horror (which is positioned between the genres of science fiction and horror; it is not only a sub-subgenre of horror). Prime examples of science fiction horror include *Tarantula* and *Alien* (Ridley Scott, 1979, US/UK), a monster movie set in outer space in a ship that is often dark or dimly lit. Some of these pictures are primarily about the monster, no matter where it comes from. The more their intention is only to horrify and the more their doctors and scientists say "There are things man is not meant to know," the less they are like science fiction. For there are things we are meant to know, and science fiction is open to them. *The Thing From Another World* (Christian Nyby, 1951, US; produced by Howard Hawks), also called *The Thing*, a monster movie that is also a science fiction horror movie, ends with the warning, "Keep watching the skies!" while the penultimate line of *Brainstorm* (Douglas Trumbull, 1983, US), a science fiction film, is the celebratory "Look at the stars!"

Genres are not determined exclusively by plot elements. Attitudes toward plot elements are also important. That horror is afraid of the unknown while science fiction is interested in it is a difference in attitude, and it can be clearly seen if we compare two pictures made during the same year under similar conditions (in 1951 in American studios during the Cold War), one of which is science fiction (*The Day the Earth Stood Still* [Robert Wise, 1951, US]), one horror (*The Thing From Another World*), and both of which have nearly the same plot elements, notably flying saucers with intelligent pilots and a complex of military, scientific and civilian characters who must deal with the pilot and his destructive potential. One element that is quite different is that the pilot in *The Thing* is a monster, while the pilot in *The Day* is not.

The Day the Earth Stood Still[30] is the story of a spaceman, Klaatu (Michael Rennie), who sets down his flying saucer in Washington, D.C., to put Earth on notice: anything resembling nuclear violence will be punished by the obliteration of the planet, courtesy of a race of interstellar robot police. The military wants to destroy the spaceman; the scientists are willing to listen to him. The central scientist, Dr Bernhardt (Sam Jaffe), is a kooky but open-minded and serious person. Although it is suggested that Earthlings understand violence better than most kinds of communication, they do respond to a nonviolent demonstration of Klaatu's power, and he does manage to deliver his message, perhaps at the cost of his life. The film is in favor of open-minded communication, personal integrity (seen particularly in the female lead, Helen, played by Patricia Neal), nonviolence and science.

The Thing From Another World—loosely based on John W. Campbell, Jr's "Who Goes There?," a story whose premise of a shape-shifting monster was not used until John Carpenter's *The Thing*—is about a military team sent to an arctic station to investigate what turns out to be the crash of a flying saucer. The saucer's unnamed pilot, the Thing (James Arness), is a bloodsucking vegetable that is described as intelligent but spends most of its time making noise and killing—though its plans to survive, eat and reproduce are not unintelligent, and it does command an advanced interstellar technology. The most misguided character is a scientist, Dr Carrington (Robert Cornthwaite), who wants to communicate with the Thing rather than destroy it and who admires the alien race for its lack of sexual emotion. The Thing, however, has no interest in the scientist. The human community,[31] from which the scientist wishes to exclude himself, led by the efficient, hard-headed and sexually experienced Captain Pat Hendry (Kenneth Tobey), manages to electrocute the vegetable monster. Pat's girlfriend is the efficient and intelligent Nikki (Margaret Sheridan), and his comic counterpart is the sometimes ineffective reporter Scotty (Douglas Spencer), who never can get a photo of the Thing. The film is in favor of that friendly, witty, sexy and professionally effective—in other words, Hawksian—community and opposed to the Grendel that lurks outside the station.

This is how the oppositions between these two movies stack up:

1. *Scientists vs. the Military*. In both films the military and the scientists are in conflict with each other. The military sees the alien as a threatening invader to be defended against and, if necessary or possible, destroyed. The scientists see the alien as a visitor with superior knowledge, to be learned from and, if possible, joined. In *The Thing* the military is right, and the scientist is an obsessive visionary who gets in the way of what obviously needs to

be done. In *The Day* the scientists are right, and the military is almost responsible for the end of the world.

2. *Intelligence vs. Violence.* The Thing is nonverbal and destructive; Klaatu is articulate and would prefer to be nonviolent. The military, which meets violence with violence, is correct in *The Thing* and wrong in *The Day* because of the nature of the alien in each movie, but the alien has its nature because of each genre's implicit attitude toward the unknown. The curious scientist is a positive force in *The Day* and a negative force in *The Thing* for the same reasons.

3. *Opening vs. Closing.* Both horror and science fiction open our sense of the possible (mummies can walk, Martians can land) and sometimes open the community to new forces. Until *Carrie* and the open-ended films that followed it, most horror films were oriented not toward any permanent opening but toward a closing down of what had been opened and the restoration of the status quo, though the open ending of the contemporary horror film still urges us to batten down the hatches and try to protect ourselves—in other words to close up. *The Day* is about humanity's opportunity to join an interstellar political system; it opens the community's boundaries and leaves them open. *The Thing* is about the expulsion of an intruder and ends with the warning to watch the skies in case more monsters show up; the community is opened against its will and attempts to reclose. What the horrified community often learns from the opening is to be on guard.

4. *The Inhuman vs. the Human.* Science fiction is open to the potential value of the inhuman. We can learn from it, take a trip with it (*Close Encounters of the Third Kind* [Steven Spielberg, 1977, US]) and include it in a larger sense of what is. In horror, we often shrink from that larger sense. Horror is fascinated by transmutations between human and inhuman (werewolves, for example), but the inhuman characteristics usually mandate destruction.

5. *Communication vs. Silence.* This links most of the above. The Thing doesn't talk; Klaatu does. To put it another way, Romero's living dead are at first completely nonverbal, while the climax *of Close Encounters* comes when Earthlings are given a primer in an interstellar language. What one can talk with, one has the potential to deal with. Communication between species is vital in *The Day*, absurd in *The Thing*. (This distinction still holds. *Super 8* reveals itself as science fiction the minute the hero manages to communicate with the monster, and that goes on to motivate a happy ending.) The opened community can be curious about and learn from the outsiders, while the closed community talks only among itself. Horror emphasizes the dread of knowing, the danger of curiosity, while science fiction emphasizes the danger and irresponsibility of the closed mind. There are many cases in which science fiction appeals to consciousness, horror to the unconscious.

When a given film includes scientists, space travel *and* a monster, as does *This Island Earth* (Joseph M. Newman, 1955, US), the first thing to determine is the attitude toward the question of discovery: whether the unknown primarily inspires fear or wonder. In the case of *This Island Earth*, where the science and technology are compelling and the bug-eyed monster is onscreen for only a few minutes, the film would be recognized as science fiction. It is unlike science fiction—and like horror's attempt to close what horror has opened and destroy what ruptured the norm—only in that no remnant of the extraterrestrial science is allowed to survive. In *The Fly* (1958), the vital elements are that the scientist and his creation are intimately interrelated and that the white-headed fly is destroyed rather than saved. The technology is important to account for the monster, not to open up a story about teleportation. *The Fly* is either a horror film or a science fiction horror film, consigning to monstrosity and terror everything that the scientist has discovered and saying that the scientist's work is "frightening" and "like playing God." (Actually *The Fly* tries to have it both ways. The inspector says the whole story reminds him of "science fiction," and science is presented as an attractive and positive force[32] in one scene at the end, when the scientist's son says he would like to be an "explorer" like his father.) In *Forbidden Planet* (Fred M. Wilcox, 1956, US), which might at first appear a perfect example of genre crossover (science fiction horror), the Krel science, the brain booster, Robbie the Robot, the ray guns and the images of humans traveling in a flying saucer all outweigh, as genre-specific elements, the "monster from the id"—a monster that the father-scientist, Dr Morbius (Walter Pidgeon), unleashes in the absence of conscious control. It is a monster that would, on its own, fit perfectly into the repertoire of the horror film. The moral of the story of the Krel monster and Morbius's decision to destroy the planet also fit explicitly into a horror worldview, but it seems important that the robot (as one aspect of Krel science, though built by a human) is integrated into the human crew and that the human race is presented as being on a positive evolutionary course. It is also significant that Dr Morbius, by becoming conscious of his accountability for the actions of his unconscious, denies the Krel monster and releases himself and his daughter from their Oedipal nightmare. (He cannot deny the monster without first accepting that it is *his* monster.) In other words, the balance shifts toward consciousness and a positive future. *Forbidden Planet* is science fiction, a science fiction film with horror elements and with a science fiction attitude toward those and its other elements. *It! The Terror from Beyond Space* (Edward L. Cahn, 1958, US), widely recognized as an influence on *Alien*, takes a horror-film attitude toward space travel and monsters, ending with a warning never to go back to Mars ("Another name for Mars is Death"); it is a horror film with science fiction elements. *Invaders from Mars* (William Cameron Menzies, 1953, US) is a science fiction horror film that takes a Martian invasion as its science fiction premise while it gets down to business, scaring the audience with victims who disappear into holes in the sand, parents and authority figures who change their natures and a world of safe people and places that have become unsafe, especially for the boy, David (Jimmy Hunt), whose point of view the film adopts—and setting all of it in a dream that comes true. Dreaming is not an important element in science fiction, but it appears regularly in horror. The fears that *Invaders from Mars* deals with include those of losing one's parents, not being believed, transforming into someone else, being controlled by a foreign object (the implant) and being conquered. These fears outweigh the exciting lure of the stars that David watches in the night sky and are confirmed when the Martian ship lands again, this time not in a dream, but for real. There may be Martians in straight science fiction films, but the ones in *It!* and *Invaders from Mars* get the horror treatment.

Science fiction and horror films usually portray scientists differently. In the science fiction film and in some science fiction horror films, such as *Them!*, they tend to be sane and are eventually proved correct. Even Professor Deemer in the science fiction horror film *Tarantula* is not crazy, although he does put his project ahead of everything else, much as Dr Carrington in *The Thing*, suffering from stress but not from madness, puts the search for knowledge ahead of all other considerations and loses sight of conventional priorities. In the horror film, where the mad scientist is a recurring figure, a scientist or researcher usually goes too far and may be overcome by the demands and results of his or her obsessive, dangerous project. The mad scientist does not have to be certifiable, like Dr Gogol (Peter Lorre) in *Mad Love*, but it helps. A more common sign taken for madness is the scientist's losing touch with or operating outside of established limits, such as those of relationship, of civilized behavior, of acceptable risk and of humanity (the accusation of playing God), limits that all are violated by the scientist who kills or shrinks those who stand in the way of his research in *Dr. Cyclops*. In the science fiction horror movie *Fiend Without a Face* (Arthur Crabtree, 1958, UK), an obsessed scientist creates what are supposed to be materialized thoughts but end up being invisible nervous systems, flying brains that strangle people with their spinal columns and then, like "mental vampires," suck out the victims' brains through two holes in the skull. The technology that led to this scientific breakthrough is not valuable and not preserved, and it offers a warning against the uncontrolled use of atomic power. Instead of dangerous but finally path breaking science we have, in true horror fashion, a scientist unable to control the monsters he created, who must be killed by them.

The monster that lurks in outer space in *Alien*, of which we know nothing at first, changes its form several times in the course of the picture and to that extent remains an unknown. We are always discovering how it looks and what it now can do. The design and action of the first stage of the creature draw on our fears of the spider, snake and claw as well as of being seized and smothered by something too fast and strong to guard against. In the first picture, the only way to kill the Alien is to expel it from an airlock. Its acid blood, should one be able to wound it, would eat through the walls of a ship in space. In *Aliens* (James Cameron, 1986, US/ UK), which simplifies a lot of this, the creatures can be shot with futuristic rifles, and the acid is less of a problem because most of the action is set on the ground. It is always a threat in these films—the other sequels are *Alien³* (David Fincher, 1992, US) and *Alien: Resurrection* (Jean-Pierre Jeunet, 1997, US)—that an Alien will reach Earth.

The ship in *Alien*, the *Nostromo*,[33] has a working-class crew, and the film has a working-class theme. The ship is run primarily by its computer, Mother, and Mother answers to the corporation (called "the company") that has sent this mining ship into space. The company seizes the opportunity to collect an Alien, a specimen it can study to improve the weapons it makes and perhaps reproduce to serve as a fighter. It decides the crew is expendable and directs them to answer a distress call from an alien ship on a poisonous planet. That ship, on which everyone is long dead, had been taken over by Aliens who left their eggs. A first-stage Alien attacks crew member Kane (John Hurt) when he touches the egg that contains it—building on our fear that he *will* touch that egg. The alien then grows inside him, and eventually bursts out of his chest, calling up fears of crazy childbirth, of having one's body go wrong and of being destroyed from within by an unsuspected Other. The adult Alien activates our fears of being trapped by a malevolent creature with big teeth in a dark and confined space. The Alien is protected by two machines,

Mother and Ash (Ian Holm), the science officer, who turns out to be a robot. As a robot and as a scientist, Ash is an extreme manifestation or logical extension of Carrington, the unemotional scientist in *The Thing*, who is lacking in some human qualities and is devoted to saving the monster. Ash admires the Alien for its structural perfection, which is matched only by its hostility, and for what he calls "its purity." When only Ellen Ripley (Sigourney Weaver) is left alive, she gets into the space shuttle, launches it and blows up the ship—and Mother in the process.[34] But the alien turns out to be in the shuttle, and she has to scramble to eject it into space. When she is changing into her spacesuit to do this, she becomes the standard figure of the half-dressed woman threatened by the monster, as in *Tarantula*, and the adult Alien's phallic design increases the sexuality of the threat. (She is not exploited this way in the sequels, and in *Aliens* her primary opponent is female.) Then Ripley and the cat, the survivors, turn in for a long suspended-animation nap, giving a tense picture a calm resolution.

Ripley is a strong character who thinks fast and gets things done, the best-known monster fighter of the late twentieth century. She is wary and efficient, good with equipment and guns and good in a crisis. It takes all her skill and resolve to get rid of the one Alien. There are many Aliens in the sequels, which makes for more action but less concentration and economy. *Alien* is a fear machine, while much of *Aliens* is a war movie. The risk *Aliens* ran was that a horde of Aliens would not stand out dramatically, so a Queen Alien was invented for the picture, bigger than the others and sufficiently powerful to be a fitting opponent for the hero. In all the sequels Ripley is the hero.

A sequel repeats what are considered the important parts of the original, from its tone to its particulars, with variations. Thus *Aliens* has its own human-looking robot (Lance Henriksen as Bishop), but he is a good guy. At the climax of both pictures there is a countdown, with pulsing horns and sound effects, to the explosion of a nuclear reactor. The company is again duplicitous. As she had saved the cat in *Alien*, Ripley finds and protects a little girl, Newt (Carrie Henn), and this becomes a moving relationship, the heart of the picture, which is essentially about mothering. The fear of being unable to take care of one's child plays a role here. The first stage of the Alien is now conjectured to implant an "embryo" that grows into the chestburster. Regardless of gender, the victim, Ripley says, is "impregnated." The final battle has Ripley in a loader that allows her to take on the Queen and eventually expel her out the airlock. She calls the Queen a bitch. This is the second bad parent Ripley has had to deal with—the first was Mother, also referred to as a bitch—and in destroying her and saving Newt, Ripley demonstrates the almost mythic power of the good mother.

From the beginning of *Aliens*, Ripley suffers from bad dreams, in which she often has a chestburster inside her. Newt has bad dreams too, and when Ripley suggests that Newt imitate her doll, who doesn't have bad dreams, Newt points out that the doll doesn't have bad dreams "because she's a piece of plastic." By the end of the picture they both are freed from their nightmares, which have been purged along with the Aliens, by dealing with fear and surviving an experience of horror. That is one of the primary functions of fear and horror in the genre: to empower one to survive them. Ripley, Newt, a soldier and the robot escape in a ship that puts them into what looks like a safe, resolved sleep. The torn-apart robot rather sappily tells Ripley that she has done well "for a human," but that is the point. She has been tested by another species and has shown what in the human race is worth preserving.

In *Alien³* Ripley kills herself to avoid giving birth to a Queen Alien, but in *Alien: Resurrection*, when she is reborn as a clone, her DNA and that of the embryonic Queen have been mixed. The films have been about mothering since *Aliens*, and in *Resurrection* Ripley mothers herself. Ripley is no longer a pure representative of victorious humanity. Instead it is a part-Alien clone, Ripley, and a robot, Call (Winona Ryder), who carry the day. The *Alien* movies set the best of humanity against the worst the stars have to offer, and they show that we have to lose part of ourselves in the fight, because it is a serious one. If the Aliens ever reach Earth, as at the open ending of *Resurrection* it seems they finally will, they will arrive in the person of this new Ripley, who is to some extent an unknown being as well as a composite monster created by science fiction technology. *Alien* is on the horror side of science fiction horror, while *Alien: Resurrection*, which is more speculative than scary, leans more to the science fiction side.

Monsters from the Lab: "You Made Us Things!"

This is the category that is most likely to overlap with other sub-subgenres, for the laboratory may be a dominant set in a science fiction film as well as in a horror film, run by scientists either mad or sane, and may be used to create any kind of monster.

There is no characteristic monster—that is, one that expresses a lab-like quality. The lab itself links the scientist with the sorcerer and alchemist and is a place to meddle with nature, which is dangerous. There are many kinds of monsters made in labs, from the Frankenstein Monster to the "things" of Dr Moreau, the fly, evil computers and Mr Hyde.

Monsters from Underwater: *It Came from Beneath the Sea*

As the ocean is the place where life was formed, it is likely to produce new organisms now and again, and to hide very old ones. That at least is a common attitude toward it in horror movies and in tales of sea monsters.

The ocean can generate and conceal anything in its depths, from the giant octopus of *It Came from Beneath the Sea*, which is appropriately killed underwater, to the more natural great white shark of *Jaws*. Lakes and rivers become dangerous in *Piranha* and *Creature from the Black Lagoon*. Bridges, the water and the sewer hide the amphibious monster in *The Host* (Bong Joon-Ho, 2006, South Korea). There is room in the water for things to grow to great size or great numbers without being detected; their stories begin when they become threats to humanity, whether the people are on boats or in coastal cities. The water is a natural cover, a hiding place and a source for the monster. Though it may have a placid surface, the water radiates danger and concealed horror.

As Godzilla does, a life form can emerge from the water and return to it.[35] The monsters in *Humanoids from the Deep* (Barbara Peeters, 1980, US), mutations that feel the need to mate with humans as part of their evolutionary drive, erupt onto the coastline where they kill men and rape women, then dive back into the water. What is unusual about this picture is that the rapes are made explicit, increasing the sense of horror at the monsters' carrying off the women, who usually are conscious: a strong reversal of the image of the fainted woman in the arms of the only implicitly sexual monster.

Plants: *Invasion of the Body Snatchers*

Nature can make some outrageous demands, as when the plant with a taste for blood in *The Little Shop of Horrors* (Roger Corman, 1960, US) insists that the hero, Seymour (Jonathan Haze), feed people to it. The tone of the picture is comic, but the plant's insistence is deadly: "Feed me," it says, because it can talk, "feed me more." Seymour works in a skid-row flower shop. Interested in flowers, Seymour has been raising a strange plant he developed (the seeds he bought came from an unknown farm, and he crossed a seedling with a Venus flytrap) that turns out to thrive only on fresh blood. There is no reason to call it extraterrestrial. When it is put on display in the shop, it attracts customers as it grows larger. It grows because Seymour can't get any more blood out of his fingers and finds victims for the plant to eat. Eventually, new flowers appear that contain the victims' faces and minds—an idea that could have been taken from John Collier's short story "Green Thoughts." Climbing into the plant with a knife, Seymour says he will feed it as it's never been fed before. Soon Seymour's face pops up in a new bud. This comic version of a mad scientist has appropriately been destroyed by and become part of his own monster.

In the remake, *Little Shop of Horrors* (Frank Oz, 1986, US), which was based on a musical that was based on the original movie, the monster is given more expressive movements and a larger vocabulary; it is also changed into "a mean green mother from outer space." *Little Shop of Horrors* is a good-time musical in which a couple who are meant to be together confront a monster and survive. The original is a tragicomedy in which everything is a put-on except the relation between the creator and the monster.

The Venus flytrap has long been presented in films as an image of the ruthless, carnivorous plant. A fly-eating plant fascinates Dr Gogol in *Mad Love* and inspires him as he prepares to trap his own victim. The plants that consume people in *Voodoo Island* (Reginald LeBorg, 1957, US) and elsewhere are fantastic extensions of the world's true carnivorous plants, and they are usually presented as hungry and relentless. In *The Day of the Triffids* (Stephen Sekely, 1962, UK), based on the novel by John Wyndham, the ambulatory plants that come from the stars are highly motivated and hostile. Plants choke and consume people and grow under their skin as well as lure them with the sound of cell phones in *The Ruins* (Carter Smith, 2008, US/Germany/Australia), based on the novel by Scott Smith, which had a more uncompromising conclusion. Plants can eat us, invade us, even replace us, and beyond that they play an important role in potions that can transform us.

The plants whose seeds come from outer space and land in a farmer's field, the pods in *Invasion of the Body Snatchers* (Don Siegel, 1956, US), based on Jack Finney's novel *The Body Snatchers*, have no emotions. They coldly destroy and replace people. Their coming from outer space and growing into vines with pods, out of which the doubles burst and grow, is the science fiction premise, but what dominates the picture and makes it more of a horror film is the way the monsters replace the normal world with a frightening one of their own in which anyone can be or soon will be a monster—and the way natural sleep is made an unnaturally deadly threat. All the pods, which are vegetable monsters, think alike and have no emotions. In part they are a parody of 1950s conformists. To the extent that they think alike and are cold, they have also been read as a symbol for communism as 1950s Hollywood portrayed it. But mainly they are plants. They are frightening and soulless in their own right, in addition to any 1950s' social context (for although it has been argued otherwise, not every horror film expresses or concerns a current social anxiety), as aliens who take the place of humans but are essentially different from us, lacking the ability to love. Each is only an extraterrestrial in a shell that looks like us and contains our memories. It is authenticity that is at stake here, put in terms of personal identity, emotion and the vegetable double, which is the monster.

As is well known, the framing scenes in which Dr Miles Bennell (Kevin McCarthy) tells his story to doctors who think he is crazy and then find out that he is right were added at the last minute. The picture was originally supposed to end as Miles runs in highway traffic, yelling "You're next!" at the drivers and the audience. It was not, as written, supposed to have a closed and reassuring ending but was meant to present a problem that was ongoing, in which a fine and loving person (Dana Wynter as Becky Driscoll) could fall asleep, have her mind pass into the pod that had grown to replace her and wake as a heartless being—with the real Becky dead. Here sleep leads not to a dream but to a real-world nightmare. Human values and emotion itself are threatened by the monsters, along with everything that distinguishes us from the pods. Perhaps the movie proved so on target and disturbing that to leave it open-ended was considered too unsettling. With or without the framing scenes, however, *Invasion of the Body Snatchers* is a film in praise of humanity, of what makes us not vegetable but human. It makes us treasure love as we watch love be destroyed.

Minerals: *The Monolith Monsters*

It is hard to dramatize a rock. *The Monolith Monsters* (John Sherwood, 1957, US) does its best. A huge meteorite crashes in the desert, leaving smooth black rocks all over the landscape around the crater. Some people pick up these rocks and take them home, for various reasons exposing them to water (a little girl washes her rock). But when they are wet, the rocks react and grow until they tumble over from their own height and weight. Anyone who touches an active, growing rock has the silicon drained from his or her body and turns hard as stone. That makes rock hardness a property of humans, not just of minerals, giving the horror a human face. It rains just after the hero (Grant Williams as Dave) and his former professor have figured out the effect of water on the rocks, and the monoliths rise and crash forward, moving toward the town. The monoliths have the persistence and destructiveness of a monster, and they come from outer space. It turns out that as they can be stimulated by something as common as water, they can be stopped by something as common as salt, another mineral and thus a fitting means of opposing them—appropriate to the monster's nature and related to it. Through salt water, earthly nature is vindicated and becomes part of what destroys this aberration of nature.

There is a hitherto unknown element in *The Magnetic Monster* (Curt Siodmak, 1953, US), dangerous for its extreme magnetism and frightening for the way it continually doubles in size and in its demand for energy, which could destroy the Earth. Both of these mineral monster films are science fiction horror with an emphasis on science fiction, while in *Invasion of the Body Snatchers* and *The Blob* the emphasis is on horror.

Amorphous Monsters: *The Blob*

At one extreme of monster design is the formless creature, seen most memorably in *The Blob* (Irvin S. Yeaworth, Jr, 1958, US). An amorphous thing that can roll or flow, that can be divided and rejoin itself, that absorbs people and grows larger from their mass as it turns red from their blood, it comes from outer space, arriving in a meteorite as a small clear mass. The first victim, an old man (Olin Howlin), prods it onto a stick, then watches the snotty glob move down the stick under the force of gravity (Figure 20). When the old man reverses the stick, instead of falling downward the mass moves *up*, making it clear that it is alive. It leaps at his hand and covers it, causing great pain as it begins to digest the hand. This is one of the greatest of all first-victim scenes, the best since the one in *The Mummy*. The old man is found and taken to a doctor by the heroes, Steve (Steve McQueen) and his girlfriend, Jane (Aneta Corseaut). The blob absorbs the old man entirely and becomes larger than it was before. Steve and Jane do their best to notify the authorities, but only one policeman, Dave (Earl Rowe), a friend of teenagers, believes them. The other police and Jane's parents (her father is the principal of the high school, a double authority figure) think the story is a teenage prank. Steve's dad trusts him and is portrayed as a good father.

The Blob was clearly influenced by *Rebel Without a Cause* (Nicholas Ray, 1955, US), in which the American family of the 1950s is shown to have many unhealthy characteristics,

Figure 20. *The Blob*: The first victim.

including that of ignoring teenagers' feelings and insights. There is a problem in town, as big as juvenile delinquency and inadequate parenting, and only some of the teenagers know about it: the problem that monsters are real. "How do you get people to protect themselves from something they don't believe in?" Steve asks, a recurring question in the genre however differently it is phrased. The blob becomes public knowledge when it oozes through the windows of the projection booth at the downtown movie theatre, which is showing a midnight spook show. It makes an appropriate and reflexive entrance as the real monster at a show of illusory monsters. After that, gorged with patrons, it is too big to deny. The most teen-hating policeman admits that he was wrong and becomes a force for the good. Thus awareness of the blob, shown eventually by the police and the citizens, and bravery in the face of it, shown especially by Steve and Jane, serve as healing forces within the community, getting the adults to respect their children more than they did before and unifying them against the blob. It is as a community that they gather enough fire extinguishers[36] to freeze the blob—its only weakness turns out to be susceptibility to cold—and ship it off to the Arctic, where it will stay until the Arctic thaws, or not.

"The End" turns into a question mark in the film's famously open ending. It is impossible to return entirely to what Steve calls "good old yesterday" now that the monster has become evident and real, and now that it has changed the terms of their existence from romance and play to life and death. An essentially indestructible creature that is insatiable as pure appetite itself, the blob engulfs and dissolves its victims in its desire to find more food and become larger, a never-ending project. It can only be arrested in its progress, at its current huge size, and banished: a problem that has been dealt with but that may, like a neurosis one has tried to suppress or a social issue that has not been adequately dealt with, arise again.

An amorphous monster that can be poured into any form, even a pint container, is central in *The Stuff* (Larry Cohen, 1985, US), a satire about consumerism and health food. Called "the stuff" by an advertising genius, it is a natural product that comes not from outer space but from the earth, bubbling up out of the ground near a mine. It is irresistibly good and apparently good for you. It looks like yogurt or vanilla ice cream. The problem is that when people eat it, they become addicted to it, and when they have stuffed themselves with it, it controls them. When enough of the stuff accumulates in a person, he or she vomits it out and starts over, leaving an independently moving stuff creature. The stuff compels people to eat more of it and thereby gets processed in some way it needs. One of the main characters is a boy (Jason, played by Scott Bloom) whose family won't believe that he saw the stuff moving after a carton spilled in the refrigerator and who do everything to force him to eat it. The other main characters are the woman who thought up the ad campaign (Nicole, played by Andrea Marcovicci) and an industrial spy (Mo, played by Michael Moriarty); they eventually become a couple, and they take care of Jason after he runs away from home. With help, the three of them defeat the stuff and the people who have been controlled by it.

The slogan for the stuff is "Enough is never enough." This is a product that forces the consumer to consume it and then consumes the consumer. It is an extreme model of capitalism and addiction. It can move and kill, and its goal is to be eaten and accumulated—and to destroy its enemies—so that it can get on to the next stage of its evolution and gain control; it aims for "a new order." At the end, when the heroes have destroyed the quarry where the stuff is taken from a great pool in the earth, when people have burned or cooked what is in their homes and stores and when the villains[37] who marketed the product but never touched it themselves have been forced to eat the stuff, a rare case of it is shown being sold like cocaine.

Child Monsters: *It's Alive*, *The Brood* and *The Funhouse*

The children considered here are young monsters, not strictly human and not supernatural (for some of the others, see Demons, Ghosts, Mad Killers and Families in the upcoming chapters). In *Village of the Damned* they are partly creatures from outer space. In *The Boys from Brazil* (Franklin J. Schaffner, 1978, UK/US) they are clones of Hitler. In *The Brood* (David Cronenberg, 1979, Canada) they are incarnated rage. In *It's Alive* (Larry Cohen, 1974, US) they are mutant killer babies. The baby in *Grace* (Paul Solet, 2009, Canada/US), a simpler and more upsetting movie than most of these, looks normal but will drink only human blood, preferably her mother's.

"It's Alive" is a line from *Frankenstein* (1931), and it is only because of his symbolic link with the Frankenstein Monster[38] that the unnamed infant in Cohen's movie is able to find his way home without help. His principal motive, aside from killing whomever he considers a threat, is to find his parents and enjoy their love. The problem is that he is a murderous monster with big teeth and claws as well as unnatural strength and mobility. When he was born, he killed the delivery team. The father, Frank (John Ryan), and the mother, Lenore (Sharon Farrell), are terrified of their child at first, but gradually they come to love it. When Lenore hides the child in the basement and feeds it gallons of milk, Frank fears she is unbalanced. But when Frank, who has been trying to kill his son all along, suddenly feels compassion for the infant and tries to save it from the police, the audience is on his side and the film finds its payoff, which is a moment of tenderness. The baby is killed by the police anyway, but the film ends by letting us know that another baby, with the same characteristics, has been born in another city. It is suggested but not definitively stated that the mutations are being caused by pesticides in the diet and pollution in the environment.

The ending is open and features a return of the monster. Whatever problem the babies represent has not been solved. It may be pollution, or it may be a problem in the institution of the family. Throughout this film and the sequels—*It Lives Again* (Larry Cohen, 1978, US) and *It's Alive III: Island of the Alive* (Cohen, 1987, US)—parents look forward to having perfect babies that will improve their lives but are disappointed when they give birth to monsters that are killed by the authorities. Clearly the babies are a threat to social order—judging by who responds to the threat—and they are also presented as a threat to the dominance of our species. The series ends when a man and woman—married and up until now estranged—decide to raise one of the mutants, their grandchild, in what they will seriously attempt to make a happy family. This merging of the monstrous and the ordinary allows for a resolution, the only one that includes the possibility that the family, as an institution, can accept what is different, what it has utterly rejected, and change. This resolution also presumes that the couple will stay clear of the bad guys, the authorities who want to kill the mutant babies. Thus the authorities and their social order lose, which is presented here as a good thing. The emotional theme of the trilogy is love between parents and children, and love for the child wins the battle in all three movies, whether or not the child survives.

Children can be little monsters. We all remember when other children were our equals, and some of them were rotten people. The child in the viewer can recognize as an old enemy—or as a figure to emulate in fantasy—the dangerous child. The parent in the viewer can fear that his or her child could be terrible in some unsuspected way.

The child need not look like a monster to be one: *The Godsend* (Gabrielle Beaumont, 1980, UK) is the story of a beautiful little girl whose mother has the characteristics of a cuckoo. The mother has her baby in the house of Kate (Cyd Hayman) and Alan (Malcolm Stoddard), then abandons the child, whom Kate and Alan adopt and name Bonnie (Wilhelmina Green). Bonnie kills all four of Kate and Alan's children, as a young cuckoo may eject the other eggs or baby birds from the nest. The mother of this child has the ability to change into a bird (indicated by several aerial shots and some of the dialogue). She is not human, no matter how she looks, and Bonnie will surely grow into another like her.

As *Children of the Damned* (Anton Leader, 1963, UK), the sequel to *Village of the Damned*, makes clear, frightened people can make bad decisions as they batten down the hatches against the unknown—in this case, mutations, which are sometimes presented as the face of the future. In movies, we often put our anxiety about the future into figures of children, who are the future. Just as plainly, we use children to express our anxieties about the family and about such issues as intimacy, emotional honesty and trust, which are expected but not always found in the parent–child bond; consider *Peeping Tom*.

In *The Brood*, where issues of bonding and trust are central and where it is hard to tell whether a mother or her "brood" is the chief horror, a father (Frank, played by Art Hindle) tries to take care of his daughter, Candice (Cindy Hinds), who is in either psychological or physical danger for most of the picture. The mother, Nola (Samantha Eggar), is under the care of Dr Raglan (Oliver Reed), a psychiatrist who leads the new field of "psychoplasmics," in which patients express anger at old or current situations by developing growths on their skin—or inside them, where for a few patients this turns out to be the start of cancer. Nola, who is living at Raglan's compound so she can have full-time therapy, is very angry at her formerly abusive mother and others. Instead of a small growth, whenever Nola is angry she grows a fetus outside her abdomen; when born, each child becomes a deformed dwarf. Frank suppresses the urge to vomit when he sees Nola bite the fetal sac and then lick the blood off the baby. It is a strong, revolting moment in which Nola becomes a monster of motherhood, an aspect of her that many other critics have recognized.[39] Psychically, Nola sends these "children of her rage" out into the world to kill those she hates. Typically, the monster dwarfs leap on a victim and bash in his or her brains with whatever is handy. (This is rather like the behavior of the baby in *It's Alive*, who leaps onto a victim, then bites and tears at the neck.) These child monsters live in a building on the compound, and Nola takes care of them.

The climax comes when the brood threatens Candice. While Raglan, who as a scientist is obsessive and too sure of himself, tries to get Candice away from the brood, Frank has to keep Nola calm so that the children do not become aroused. This doesn't work, and the monsters terrify Candice and kill Raglan, another mad scientist destroyed by his work. Frank strangles Nola to quiet the brood. Without her to motivate them, the dwarfs die or soon will. At the end of the film, with Nola and her brood destroyed along with the obsessed scientist, we see Frank and Candice together in his car. But this is not the start of a fresh new life, for Candice has two bumps on her skin, the sign of her mother's affliction. Considering all she has gone through, this is not a merely formulaic gesture but makes psychological sense. In the future she will express—indeed, already is expressing—her own rage and victimization psychoplasmically. The horror has been passed on to the next generation, much as a history of child abuse can repeat in the next generation (and does in this picture). Thanks to Nola and her doctor, the family has become a horror show, and the only good thing that survives the apparent closing of the show is the love between the father and daughter.

The father in *The Funhouse* (Tobe Hooper, 1981, US), an unnamed carnival barker played by Kevin Conway, swears that he does not hate the sound of his son's voice. The voice is terrible, part gibbering whimper and part scream. Two of his children, both of whom suffered birth defects, are with him in the sideshow. One is a dead baby on exhibit in a bottle, and the other (the Monster, played by Wayne Doba) roams the carnival and helps out in the funhouse, wearing a Frankenstein mask so he will fit in. Both children have split faces, a family resemblance. The Monster, who may be in his early twenties and who is highly sexually motivated, is hideous (makeup by Rick Baker) and not very bright. The barker and his son are family; when the son kills somebody, the barker covers it up. The barker expects his monstrous child to be a comfort and support to him in his old age. This horror family is contrasted with the failed bourgeois family of the heroine, Amy (Elizabeth Berridge), whose parents drink, do little more than watch TV, and cannot be relied on. (Such comparisons also show up in horror films about monstrous human families, such as *The Hills Have Eyes*.) Amy's brother, Joey (Shawn Carson), is not disturbed, but he is a handful. Joey begins the film by imitating both *Psycho* and *Halloween*, wearing a mask that leaves the camera looking through eyeholes and sneaking up on his sister in the shower with a rubber knife. Joey is obsessed with movie monsters and likes to scare people. It is the 1980s, and he is from the then-new generation of self-aware horror audiences.

Just before Amy leaves the house to go on a first date with Buzz (Cooper Huckabee) and two of her friends, Liz (Largo Woodruff) and Richie (Miles Chapin), the television her parents are watching shows Dr Pretorius as he says "The bride of Frankenstein." At the climax of the picture, Amy will nearly become the romantic victim of the Monster who hides behind the mask of the Frankenstein Monster. A reflexive film from the start, *The Funhouse* creates a world of horrors that is itself like a funhouse. Everywhere one turns there is another scary image and another reference.

The conventions of the dumb-teenager horror film are used to put the characters in increasing danger. They do a stupid thing by deciding to stay in the funhouse after it has closed, and Richie does a very stupid thing by stealing some money he finds there. Richie also gets stoned (it is never good to relax one's vigilance in a horror film, and one will be punished for it). If Richie deserves the death that finds him in the funhouse—especially because he has decided to play with horror—Buzz does not. Buzz dies as a plot convenience so that Amy will be left alone with the Monster, but he goes out like a hero, killing the now murderous barker. Liz (who is presented early in the film as promiscuous and, in conventional terms, is punished for that) is killed by the Monster when she tries to seduce and stab him.

That leaves only Amy and the unmasked Monster alive in the funhouse—in its basement, where all the machinery is that runs the carts and the pop-up shocks. The Monster and the funhouse share the same energy, and they are shown to be bonded together when Amy kills the Monster by trapping him in the machinery whose great geared wheels grind him to death and break down. The funhouse cannot survive without the monstrous child, symbolically its animating spirit. Amy, the "final girl"[40]—the last combatant—leaves the funhouse alone while a big female doll, identified in the credits with the director, laughs at her. She can truly escape only when this reflexive film ends, for it declares itself a funhouse at every turn.

Monstrous children are, in general, protected by their parents or other family members—as in *Basket Case* (Frank Henenlotter, 1982, US), the story of a young man's devotion to his mutant killer brother. Such films declare that blood is thicker than water, and bloody.

Parasites: *Shivers*

The working title of Cronenberg's *Shivers* (David Cronenberg, 1975, Canada) was *The Parasite Murders* (it was released in the US as *They Came from Within*). This picture concerns a mad scientist who develops something between a parasite and a gland, whose effect is to make people lose all civilized characteristics and indulge in wild orgies. The idea is to undo the modern world and all its shortcomings,[41] forcing people, who are too rational, back to a presumably more fulfilling level and putting them more in touch with the energies of "the flesh," as Cronenberg called it in many of his early movies. Driven by the hormones excreted by the squirmy parasite-glands, people become less rational and lose self-control. They vomit the parasites into victims while kissing them or pass the germs for the parasites as a venereal disease. Out in the open, outside of bodies, the parasites bite people, and the painful bite soon leads to a flock of parasites inside the victim, which are vomited out and begin the cycle again. In short, these ugly, nasty things have no trouble generating more of themselves, and in the course of the picture they win.

Parasites cannot live on their own. A parasite needs a host, and a fictional parasite can interact and combine with its host in many original ways. *Shivers* plays with the fear that people could be hormonally rewired, that something horrifying could merge with them, take them over and make them extensions of itself.

The hero of *Shivers*, Roger St Luc (Paul Hampton), is the doctor for a modern, supposedly self-sufficient high-rise building that includes businesses and many apartments and that is located on an island near Montreal. The water and the eventually sabotaged garage doors allow the place to be isolated long enough for the parasites to spread to everyone. One of the fears this film stimulates is that of being unable to leave a terrible place, and another is that of having one's home be invaded or somehow turn dangerous and unfamiliar. Roger's nurse, with whom he is romantically involved, is Forsythe (Lynn Lowry). One of the tenants, Annabelle (Cathy Graham), is the experimental subject in which the scientist, Emil Hobbes (Fred Doederlein), grew the first parasites. She has spread the parasites venereally to several of the other tenants,[12] notably Nick (Alan Migicovsky), an emotional bully with a long-suffering wife, Janine (Susan Petrie). Much of this film is about the fear of venereal disease, of rape and of sex itself. In a set of revolting scenes, the lustful Nick vomits blood and pushes the lumpy parasites around in his abdomen. It is through Nick that we see the slow progress and pathology of the parasite, though with other victims—those who are bitten by a parasite or ingest one—the onset is more rapid. It is especially disgusting when Nick slowly licks the blood off his lips after a creature crawls out of his mouth.

Janine has a friend, Betts (Barbara Steele). A parasite swims up her vagina when she is in the bathtub, and when she has recovered, Betts infects Janine, who has just avoided being raped by her husband. Forsythe is raped in the basement garage. Roger's friend and Hobbes's co-researcher, Rollo (Joel Silver), is attacked by Nick's parasites and then murdered by Nick while the audience is hoping he will stop looking around and *get out of there*—an audience reaction horror films strive to provoke. With a parasite in her system, Forsythe tells Roger about a sexy dream she had, in which she had been told that everything is erotic, including dying, and that disease is "the love of two alien kinds of creature for each other." Finally Roger is trapped in a swimming pool with Forsythe and forced to kiss her; he swallows a parasite that slides up her throat. This is a horror climax with a difference, for it marks the meeting of hero and heroine and monster but destroys the hero at the hands of the heroine and shows the triumph of the monster. In the closing sequence, the garage doors open and the infected people drive out, presumably to infect others, as casually as if they were merely going to work. In the first car we see Roger and Forsythe, then Betts and Janine in the second. All the couples are happy. The ending follows logically from the situation and from the nature of the monsters.

If we did not see the disgusting, freely moving parasites, *Shivers* might be considered a film about the fear of diseased people, and in many respects it is a tale of the infected. But disease here is caused by and incarnated in powerful, active monsters. As parasites, they not only symbolize but also effect the damage that can be done by a foreign organism that can bond with us and change our nature, making us over for its own purposes and killing us as we were.

Machines: *The Car*

A car is a mindless vehicle. It is unnatural for it to have intentions, to direct itself. The car in *Christine* (John Carpenter, 1983, US), based on the novel by Stephen King, is conscious from the beginning and, as the song tells us on the soundtrack, "bad to the bone." A Plymouth, it is appropriately a red Fury. Christine, the car, has a radio that plays only oldies, songs from the time it was manufactured. It can drive and repair itself, it is a willful killer and it develops a jealous crush on its socially awkward teenage owner. Eventually Christine is crushed into a block. After a wonderful fakeout in which old rock comes from a portable radio rather than from Christine's, the camera scrutinizes the steel block to find out whether Christine's radio is going to start up again and prove the monster alive, and the music does start—but it could be just the music that goes with the closing credits, beginning a second or two early. The ambiguity is intentional, as *Christine* comes from the time in the history of the horror film when the open ending was well established and its conventions could be played with.

The novel *Christine* may have been influenced by the movie *The Car* (Elliot Silverstein, 1977, US), in which a malevolent automobile drives itself, mowing down bicyclists and a hitchhiker before it goes after others. Its opponents are the police. As Oedipus appropriately punished himself for his skills as a detective by blinding himself and as ambitious villains are brought down by their ambitions, a monster is best destroyed in its own terms, by a force that is like it, related to it or diametrically opposed to it. The opposite of internal combustion is external combustion, and the car must somehow drive itself to its destruction—so the police lure the car off a cliff and blow it up.

Another machine that can be made conscious and willful for purposes of horror is the computer, as in *Demon Seed* (Donald Cammell, 1977, US), where a computer goes mad (if it can be conscious, it can be crazy) and tries to isolate and impregnate a woman. Still another is the computer-driven robot, as in *The Terminator* (James Cameron, 1984, UK/US). With technical advances have come films about lethal cell phones and Web sites.

Monsters from Underground: *The Descent*

There are creatures that live far beneath the earth's surface, as in *The Mole People* (Virgil Vogel, 1956, US), in the tunnels of abandoned mines, as in *The Boogens* (James L. Conway, 1981, US) or deep underground in caves, like the humanoids in *The Descent* (Neil Marshall, 2005, UK). There are gigantic wormlike creatures that can drag people and animals underground to eat them or can erupt to the surface (*Tremors*, Ron Underwood, 1990, US), not to mention the conventional worms of *Squirm*.

The earth has dark caves and tunnels that can conceal lurking creatures, other threats or something one wants to hide. Some items, like buried treasure and embalmed mummies, are preserved there; otherwise, things are buried to decay or to be consumed by worms and vermin. The earth is the place where we put the dead and where we grow food. It is the location of the underworld, the mythical Land of the Dead. It goes through an annual cycle of death and rebirth, from the death of vegetation in the winter to its coming to life in the spring.[43] Spring often demands a ritual of blood, a sacrifice. Blood runs into the earth to give it life, and life comes back. Heroes are made to challenge the earth with their blood. Most of us resist being enclosed by it forever, let alone being buried alive.

The Mole People tells of a Sumerian city that sank into the depths of the earth as the result of volcanic activity and still managed to function as a Sumerian city. In a fitting end, what has lived underground is buried.

The Boogens is about monsters who live in a mine. They have big fangy mouths and long sharp tentacles. They come up from the bowels of the mine when it is reopened. Now they can reach anywhere in the mine and, thanks to the tunnels that lead to all the cellars, any house in town. They make the house a vulnerable place with the cellar as its weakest point. At the end the mine opening is blown up, and again, the monsters from underground are buried.

The monsters in *The Descent* have been underground for untold generations. They are blind, but they can hear acutely, and what they hear, they kill with their teeth and nails. They may once have been humans or may have split off from a common ancestor. They are white, as they never see the sun, and they are naked as animals but have no hair. There are males and females. They growl and squeal, and it's possible that lets them communicate. They are subhuman creatures of the dark, as threatening as the huge black system of caves. They appear from nowhere and kill fast. Sometimes they hunt outside, but primarily they are suited for life inside the Earth. The heroes, however, are just tourists from the surface: six highly competent young women in an uncharted cave, who expect at first to be able to get out. But it is underground everywhere, and that is the horror they can't escape: the dark, precipitous, claustrophobic underworld and its violent inhabitants, a hell. Sarah (Shauna Macdonald), the last survivor we know about, appears to get out at the finish, but that is just a dream. At the very end she has a torch but is closed in by the dark and will surely be the prey of the monsters.[44]

There are many considerations that can make a monster artistically successful, apart from the crucial importance of its presentation, its design and the degree to which it is frightening. (As *The Giant Claw* [Fred F. Sears, 1957, US] demonstrates, if the design is lacking the film has no chance to be frightening or to be an effective horror artwork.) Some of the most interesting monsters have character and consciousness, like King Kong, the Creature from the Black Lagoon and the Frankenstein Monster. We can see them make decisions for reasons. Some of them are humanoid or partly human, and some of them, like the creatures in *Island of Lost Souls*, can conceptualize their condition ("You made us things!"). But there is also great power in the nonhuman monster that intrudes on known reality and whose consciousness is never explored, like the giant tarantula. A great monster, such as a pod, built intriguingly on a universal fear, can frighten anybody. The best monsters resonate with what we fear, reject or find darkly compelling.

The monster is a pure antagonist. The genre has always set humans against monsters and defined us in relation to them. Even if some of them look like us, they are not us but the worst we can imagine. Human nature is threatened by monsters and seeks to control or exterminate them as well as to find strength in its own self-knowledge, the definition that the confrontation with the monster provokes. Even if some of them earn our understanding, like Kong, they must be removed from our world if normal or nearly normal conditions are to be restored—not that they always will be restored. Monsters have powers that are inseparable from their natures, which we must come to understand before we can defeat them, and are equally inseparable from the fears they are designed to evoke. We rise to destroy them.

5

SUPERNATURAL MONSTERS

All those who have come back from the dead are supernatural monsters, but they are not the whole story. There are other kinds of supernaturally or metaphysically empowered beings that have not died, like demons that possess the innocent or werewolves that answer to the moon. The laws of nature include that what lives must die and that while an organism may grow and mature, it may not change species[1]—for example, from a human into a wolf. Supernatural beings defy these laws and others. Their very existence renders the world an unsettling, unsettled and otherworldly place: the principal difference between supernatural films and films with natural-world monsters that take place in a knowable world. To believe in a supernatural figure is superstitious, but it can also be religious, like a belief in Satan. The supernatural entity, good or evil, is an unknown about which we make conjectures. In his book on supernatural horror, Lovecraft called the fear of the unknown the oldest of human emotions.[2]

We may fear the supernatural in general, particularly because we do not understand it. More specifically we may fear supernatural beings, such as demons; supernaturally animated or reanimated people, such as ghosts and zombies; supernatural curses, such as those that afflict werewolves; mortals who are said to have supernatural powers, such as witches, and more. The supernatural itself can be unnerving because it presents us with a metaphysical realm in which knowns are replaced with unknowns, and because it can open the way for mysterious, powerful forces and beings to get at us.

Evil—which is a serious, founding concept in the horror film—is often associated with these forces and beings, though it rarely is identified with unsupernatural monsters (but can be with humans). Like Dracula, the Devil is dedicated to evil and to enlarging its role in the world; he is energized by it. A werewolf who doesn't want to be one may strike us not as evil but as the victim of evil forces. Godzilla is not evil. A ghost, a mummy or a witch may or may not be evil. In most horror films, evil is presented as a force in the universe, comparable and opposed to the force of good (a dualism, often expressed in movies as a struggle between darkness and embattled light, that goes back at least to Zoroastrianism), as well as an individual condition. It may be linked with the Devil or be independent. It may be called evil or, like many horrors, nameless, an energy or condition that goes beyond the power of language to express.

Demons and the Devil: *Faust* and *The Evil Dead*

A devil makes one of his earliest film appearances in Méliès's *The Haunted Castle* (1897), where it repeatedly changes form. Like other supernatural figures, the Devil in early films was an occasion for special effects. Beyond that, Satan, as the leader of all devils (lesser devils are also called demons), Prince of Darkness, Lord of the Flies, center of absolute evil and fallen angel determined to vanquish God, has long been a reliable thrill and a vivid threat, good's adversary. Outside the Judeo-Christian and Islamic traditions, one finds demons but not Satan.

Satan makes an appearance in *Häxan, Rosemary's Baby* and other films but is also known for sending high-ranking devils as his emissaries. Mephistopheles (a figure derived from the Faust literature of the sixteenth century, when the historical Faust lived, but not found in the ancient folklore of devils) offers youth, pleasure and power to the knowledge-hungry Faust, notably in the silent *Faust* (F. W. Murnau, 1926, Germany).

Early in Murnau's film a huge Mephistopheles, or Mephisto (Emil Jannings), spreads his wings above the town, and a plague breaks out. It is his inability to defeat this plague, using all the science and faith he can muster, that turns Faust (Gösta Ekmann) away from his former piety and toward a Satanic solution. When Faust is burning his books, he saves one that tells him how to summon "the Lord of Darkness." An angel has offered Satan the Earth (Satan appears to be confused with Mephistopheles here, making a devil *the* Devil for purposes of this picture) if he can "destroy what is divine in Faust." The power that eventually defeats evil, though Faust perishes in its affirmation, is love. Love and self-sacrifice are often presented as effective against the demonic, as in *The Exorcist* (William Friedkin, 1973, US), adapted by William Peter Blatty from his novel.

Mephistopheles (Robert De Niro) also appears in *Angel Heart* (Alan Parker, 1987, US/Canada/UK), though he calls himself Lucifer (another name of the Devil) because it is less cumbersome. His project is to track down a soul that has been sold to him but appears to have gone missing. The detective (Mickey Rourke) who is hired and occasionally possessed by Lucifer finds that his own soul is the one being sought.

Satan and his emissaries are often interested in buying souls, in making bargains for them and offering contracts. As in Murnau's *Faust*, the contract is usually the central visual symbol of the deal. Up front or implicitly, the contract promises damnation. But there may also be something in the contract that works further against the human who signs it—often a matter of an imperfectly thought-out bargain—even before the person dies and goes to join the damned. Selling one's soul to the Devil for a set of wishes and having the wishes frustrated by the Devil, who really can't help himself from finding the flaws in them, is the subject of the inspired comedy *Bedazzled* (Stanley Donen, 1967, UK), written by Peter Cook, in which Peter Cook plays the Devil (George) and Dudley Moore plays Stanley, a quiet fellow who sells his soul for the love of Margaret (Eleanor Bron), who works as a waitress at the hamburger joint where Stanley is a cook. At the end, Stanley has been set free. The Devil's reign may be temporary or somehow limited by the forces of good, and so may that of the lesser devils, like the demon Pazuzu[3] in *The Exorcist*. One exception is *The Omen* (Richard Donner, 1976, UK/US), written by David Seltzer, where Satan wins a battle with the forces of God and good, making a safe place in the world for his son. (A couple of sequels later, Satan loses.)

A human spirit that has consigned itself to evil may possess a person. This is the case in *The Possession of Joel Delaney* (Waris Hussein, 1972, US), in which, after his death, the spirit of Tonio Perez, a lower-class young man who was a killer when he was alive, takes over the body of his friend, Joel (Perry King). Soon Joel's behavior is embarrassing and frightening his upper-class sister, Norah (Shirley MacLaine), who is the target of much of the picture's satire. The lower class erupts fully into Norah's world, and into her character, when the now-murderous Joel is killed by the police and Tonio's spirit transfers itself into Norah, who becomes the convincing image of everything she has feared and hated. In *Child's Play* (Tom Holland, 1988, US) a doll is possessed by the spirit of a criminal. But it is more common for possession to be accomplished by outright demons, not by the evil spirits of the dead.

There is much suggestion at work in the spectacle-laden *The Exorcist*, particularly in its prologue, set in Northern Iraq, in which Father Merrin (Max von Sydow) finds a small sculpture of the demon Pazuzu, then seeks out a large statue of it. Like the rest of this picture, the prologue is as realistic as the subject matter allows. The fact that many inexplicable things are presented the way they might really happen accounts for a good deal of the film's impact. The principal story is set in Washington, D.C., in and around a house in Georgetown. Chris MacNeil (Ellen Burstyn) is a divorced movie star; her daughter, who is 12, is Regan (Linda Blair). When Regan begins behaving drastically and obscenely out of character, Chris exhausts medical solutions before she asks a Jesuit priest (Jason Miller as Damien Karras) to perform an exorcism. When the exorcism is approved, Merrin is called in as the exorcist, and Karras, who fears he has lost his faith, becomes his assistant. At one point during the exorcism the demon appears, looking like the statue in the prologue, and Merrin recognizes it.

After Merrin dies, Karras becomes the exorcist. He grabs Regan and tells the demon to take him instead, to come into him. The demon obliges, and Karras's eyes and face change as he becomes possessed. But he fights back and returns to his former look for the second before he throws himself out the window of Regan's bedroom to his death. Having found his faith, he has triumphed over evil through sheer spiritual power and self-sacrifice and has freed Regan, who comes back to herself. What has been demonstrated is that evil is powerful and that good, seen primarily in the devoted efforts of the exorcists (not particularly in the ritual) and in Regan's true nature, can conquer it. Regan's life and Karras's faith are what are principally at stake here, and the self-sacrifice at the climax saves them both. It is a Christian solution.

One of the most relentless films about demonic possession is *The Evil Dead* (1983). Its gimmick is that people who are possessed can be destroyed only by being dismembered. The five young characters are possessed by demons that live in the woods where they have come to spend a weekend in a cabin. The cabin belonged to a professor who left an old book—a forbidden text called *Book of the Dead*, bound in human skin and written in human blood—and a tape recorder in the cellar. On the tape, which the young people play for fun, the professor explains about the demons and how they can be "recalled to active life" by reading some of the incantations in the *Book of the Dead*. He reads his phonetic transcription of the crucial passage aloud, which raised the demons when he made the tape and raises them again when the tape is played. The evil dead are "enduring creatures," sometimes dormant but "never truly dead," that are given license, by the incantations, to possess the living. The tape is, as previously mentioned, this picture's *Book of the Vampire*, with the professor as the One Who Knows. It is on the tape, for example, that the professor explains he has to dismember his possessed wife, providing the clue that may help some of them survive.

But none of them survives. The only character who makes it through the night, Ash (Bruce Campbell), is taken by a demon in the picture's final shot as the camera rushes up to him. (The sequels allow him to survive.) The camera often adopts the point of view of a demon, tilting and tearing around the cabin or through the woods with the speed of a forest spirit. We never see this demon, though it may be invisible; it is always behind the camera.

The demons in *Hellraiser* (Clive Barker, 1987, UK), adapted by Barker from his short novel *The Hellbound Heart*, are formidable and creatively conceived. Since we get time to know them, especially the one who speaks, Pinhead (Doug Bradley; in this picture he is simply called the Lead Cenobite), we are able to appreciate both their threatening nature and their sense of style, which are inseparable. The Cenobites are dedicated to going past limits, especially sensual ones but also moral ones. The Cenobites offer those who solve a magic puzzle box to open the way to their world an experience that combines and goes beyond the heights of pleasure and pain. Normally, no one who summons them ever escapes back to the natural world.

Frank (Sean Chapman) buys the puzzle box and returns to an unused room in his empty family home to solve it, and when he does, the Cenobites pull him to pieces, using hooks on chains. His brother, Larry (Andrew Robinson), and Larry's second wife, Julia (Clare Higgins), move into the house. Julia once had an intense affair with Frank and still longs for him. When Larry cuts his hand on a nail, his blood falls on the floor of the unused room. Frank partially regenerates from the blood. There is a fine moment of horror, one that Arthur Machen would have appreciated, when Julia is in the room and the unknown thing moves toward her in the dark, then calls her by name. Frank convinces Julia to get him more blood so that he can grow back the rest of his body and they can be together, and she brings him men to kill. Soon he has all his bones and more flesh but no skin (as a monster Frank is played by Oliver Smith). He is a bloody horror, and to some extent he represents sex, for he has great sexual power over Julia even when he is raw and repulsive. The excess of horror leads, in this picture's rigorous style, to beauty, to such intense images as Frank's red, skinless face and his body generated from blood. In the final scene, the box is offered to a new customer; the dealer asks, "What is your pleasure?" The search for pleasure beyond the limits of normal experience is what opens the doors to horror in this picture even as Julia and Frank's adultery and their willingness to do anything to regenerate Frank opens the doors to evil. *Hellraiser* is a movie about desire and what happens when it is taken far beyond conventional limits. The demons bring out the worst in people, but the worst is already there, the part of human nature that has created figures who represent its evil, figures as ancient as Satan and as updated as the Cenobites, demons and devils that set traps for souls as the puzzle box was set before Frank and the contract before Faust.

Doubles: *The Student of Prague*

A double can be one's twin, reflection, projection: another self. As a monster, it can be the unacknowledged part of one's nature given will and form, a psychological or fantastic Other. It can be "the other one," divided from the protagonist who is presented as the primary identity, or it can be both of them, the dual figure. (The unsupernatural doubles that kill their originals in *Invasion of the Body Snatchers* and *The Stepford Wives* [Bryan Forbes, 1975, US], from the novel by Ira Levin, are nonhuman replacements for the lost, dead originals, deeply Other but still doubles.) It can be a pair of humans, or one can be a spirit. The double can be, as in Poe's story "William Wilson," a nemesis, an equivocally independent being and a person whose character is the opposite of one's own (the unscrupulous narrator is hounded by a man who has the same name, is the same age and gradually comes to look more like him, and this double behaves like a conscience, showing up to frustrate the narrator's immoral schemes, until the narrator kills him in a duel and realizes that he has murdered himself). We see a reversed twin in the mirror every day but would find our identity compromised in a frightening, impossible manner if the reflection were to move and act on its own—as in both versions of *The Student of Prague*, where the central horror is a reflection given independence through magic power.

In Stellan Rye and Paul Wegener's short feature *The Student of Prague* (1913, Germany, remade in 1926 by Henrik Galeen[4]), the double is the fundamental threat. The student, Balduin (Paul Wegener), who is the best fencer in Prague and has friends but no money, makes a deal with a sorcerer, Scapinelli (John Gottowt). It might seem as if Balduin were signing a deal with the Devil, but the contract is strictly between Balduin and Scapinelli, and there is no explicitly Satanic imagery present—except that the contract is written on a scroll, and in Murnau's *Faust* Mephistopheles also puts the contract on a scroll. It is possible that *The Student of Prague* is drawing on pre-cinematic Satanic imagery to associate Scapinelli with the Devil while leaving him a sorcerer. The contract specifies that in exchange for a great deal of gold, which the sorcerer comically pours out of a small bag, Scapinelli may take anything he wishes from the student's room, for any purpose. He takes the young man's reflection from the mirror. The reflection is Balduin's second self, comparable to his soul. Lacking a reflection, Balduin is a freak, and beyond that he is pursued by an Other in the person of the double, who always looks and dresses as he first did in the mirror. The reflection becomes another Balduin—an evil one. Crucially, there is a duel to which Balduin is late. Balduin had given his word of honor that he would not kill his opponent, but the double shows up on time and does kill the man. Balduin is left without honor or friends. He tries to escape the double and finds him everywhere. Finally he shoots the double—who vanishes when shot, then can be seen again in the mirror. Then Balduin feels the same wound himself and dies. Thus they have been brought back together, which is where they belonged. Scapinelli appears from thin air, tears up the contract and scatters the pieces over Balduin's body. Once Balduin made his bargain with the sorcerer, he submitted to and may be said to have entered the terms of horror, and they could not be resolved without his death.

From the beginning, Balduin is out of his depth. The loss of a reflection seems trivial at first but is catastrophic, and the final reconciliation—his seeing the reflection in the mirror just before he succumbs to the bullet wound—comes only at the point of death. The wizard took advantage of the foolish student's limited sense of values, for Balduin thought money was more important than anything he had, anything the sorcerer could want. Thus the audience is frightened into realizing the importance of wholeness and integration and of leaving black magic alone, along with the danger of putting money above everything. That is how the horror film teaches its lessons: by scaring us. It shows us the frightful consequences of doing or encountering what the story and its thematic structure consider wrong.

It is a problem when one is not whole without the uncontrollable Other who is paradoxically a part of oneself, a problem seen in "William Wilson," in Dostoevsky's *The Double* and in *The Student of Prague*, but also in films about unsupernatural doubles, notably the dead boy (Martin Udvarnoky as Holland) kept alive in his brother's mind in *The Other* (Robert Mulligan, 1972, US) and the identical-twin gynecologists (Jeremy Irons as the Mantle twins) in *Dead Ringers* (David Cronenberg, 1988, Canada/US). It can be just as damning or destructive when the double is a real person, like either one of the Mantle twins, or used to be a real person, like Holland, as it is when the double is an impossible mirroring and fracturing of personal identity, a figure that springs from the glass to take up its own existence.

Vampires: *Nosferatu* and *Dracula*

Vampires are after blood. Blood is the ocean inside us, and it is meant to stay inside. When it is outside, its red is the oldest sign of danger and damage. We feel our heart pump it and our lungs give it air; we see the veins pulse. Without it we lose strength and eventually life. To watch our blood run out is to watch life leave us, and the bleeding may flood us with alarm and fear before it leaves us too faint to fight. We may also feel strong or rewarded by the bleeding of prey or an enemy. For many vampires, the neck is blood's sensuous fortress (Figure 21).

The strength of the vampire, as Dr Van Helsing (Edward Van Sloan) explains in the 1931 *Dracula*, is that people will not believe in him. That is how much vampires contradict the laws of nature; they reverse everything, lying immobile in the daytime, living—or doing something like it—when they should be simply dead, sucking blood instead of milk. They live on blood because, as Dracula himself (Bela Lugosi) explains to Renfield (Dwight Frye), "The blood is the life."[5] The way to defeat the vampire is to believe that it exists, with all its seemingly impossible powers and parasitical desires, and confront it on its own terms, the terms of blood and death—for example, a stake through the heart.

Blood is not sex, though the vampire can come to a victim in bed. The vampire might also be seen as a figure for the nightmare, which comes to one in bed. When dealing with a vampire, it is dangerous to sleep. It is the fact that there are two "people" in the bedroom, engaged in blood intercourse, that gives a sexual aspect to the nocturnal visit, along with the way the vampire may appear to be kissing the victim's neck, the way the vampire may seduce the victim into an intimate surrender, and the fact that there is a history in the vampire film—and in Bram Stoker's novel—of deliberately associating vampirism with sex; this became more overt after the success of the 1979 *Dracula* (John Badham, 1979, US/UK). It is because of the sexual aspects of vampirism that there is a homophobic taboo against male-on-male

Figure 21. *Dracula*: The vampire and the neck.

vampirism in many of the movies (one exception is *Nosferatu*) and in most of Stoker's *Dracula*. The most common combinations are a male vampire with a female victim and a female vampire with a male, female or child victim.

A vampire may be an evil person who died in an extreme state of sin and came under the power of the Devil, or it may be the victim of another vampire. There are different rules in different stories and traditions, for traditions about the vampire go back to the ancient world.[6] One rule about vampires that almost never changes is that the vampire must at some point return to its grave or to a coffin containing the earth in which it was buried.[7] In its perverse desire for eternal life and for the blood that sustains it, the vampire has become not eternally alive but eternally undead, damned forever and doomed to an unchanging future (for which in some of the movies, such as Herzog's *Nosferatu: Phantom of the Night* [Werner Herzog, 1979, Germany], it has been pitied). When it is given a final, ritually correct death, the vampire finds peace, though this isn't shown often in the movies, before it crumbles to dust.

A creature of inversion, it lives in the night. It casts no reflection in a mirror, perhaps because of the legendary purity of silver. It can command the dead as well as the rat and the wolf.[8] It has the strength of many men. With enough blood, a vampire can appear younger. It usually ingests blood by biting the victim on the neck, leaving two tiny unwholesome wounds. A mortal vampire can drain strength and life from someone as if drawing blood; an example can be found in Bergman's *Persona* (Ingmar Bergman, 1966, Sweden), in one of whose climactic dreams the patient (Liv Ullmann) who silently sucks up others' experience is forced by the nurse (Bibi Andersson) to drink her blood forthrightly.

In most of the movies and in Stoker's novel, vampires can change form at will—most famously into bats[9]—except when they are lying in their coffins. Dracula can dress, speak and behave like a gentleman, but he can also change into a wolf or a mist. An aristocrat, he dresses—in the movies and in the Deane/Balderston play, discussed below, but not in the novel—in the manner of the society he has come to England to join, contaminate and conquer. In contrast, Count Orlok in *Nosferatu*, who can walk through walls but cannot change his form, is designed as a loathsome creature with rat-like teeth and clawlike hands who would not be out of place in the grave or a nightmare (Figure 22).

Stoker's novel has never been faithfully adapted, but the makers of *Nosferatu*—the 1922 film that most forcefully established the sub-subgenre—at least had the excuse that they were trying to conceal the source to which they didn't have the rights.[10] They changed all the names, changed the ending so that the threatened wife sacrifices herself instead of being saved by a group of men, created *The Book of the Vampire* and invented the rule that sunlight can kill a vampire.[11] The film bears the subtitle *A Symphony of Horror*, and it presents and interrelates emotional states as if they were music, now striking a chord

Figure 22. *Nosferatu*: The monster on deck.
© 1922 Friedrich Wilhelm Murnau-Stiftung. All rights reserved. From the library of the Academy of Motion Picture Arts and Sciences.

of tension or dread, now interweaving the tragic love theme. Narrated by a researcher in the first person, *Nosferatu*[12] is a chronicle of a plague that offers, after long thought, an explanation for it. (The script was by Henrik Galeen.) Orlok is associated with rats throughout the picture, and it is he that brings the rats as well as the plague of vampirism to the German city of Wisborg in 1838. In Orlok, vampirism is seen as a contagion, an unclean horror. The earth in his coffins is "cursed dirt from the fields of The Black Death."[13] On the other hand, Hutter's wife, Ellen, is associated from the start with open windows and living flowers. Hutter's boss, the real estate agent Knock (Alexander Granach), corresponds with Orlok in an unknown language based on completely unfamiliar symbols, which sets them in their own secret, separate world. When Knock sends Hutter to Transylvania to sell the count a house in their town, just across from the one he shares with Ellen, Hutter finds the *Book of the Vampire*[14] in an inn, and what he reads, though he doesn't take it seriously at first, provides the audience with information. Orlok's letter and the *Book of the Vampire* are the textual poles of this movie, the evil one unreadable except by an occult audience and the other one urgently clear.

When Orlok's coach picks up Hutter to take him to the castle, the fast-motion photography, and especially the normal-motion shot that is shown in negative, separate the coach from the natural world. The negative shot is one example of approaching horror as a cinematic problem—how to envision and communicate the difference it makes in the world—and offering a purely cinematic solution, a transformation and reversal of the values of the world that could be effected on and by film. (The cinematographer was Fritz Arno Wagner.) Soon Hutter is urgently consulting the *Book of the Vampire*, and Ellen is spiritually protecting him; the link between her and the vampire is strong. For example, when Orlok walks into Hutter's room, filling the arched doorway with his openly threatening presence, Ellen has a sleepwalking episode and calls out to Hutter, and at that moment the vampire, the one who hears her or feels her power, pulls back from Hutter and leaves the room.

Orlok makes his way to Wisborg by sea, Hutter by land. Ellen reads the *Book of the Vampire*, though Hutter asks her not to, and learns the way to destroy the vampire, which is for a sinless woman[15] to give freely of her blood and keep the vampire with her past the first crowing of the cock. As discussed before, this is what she does, luring the vampire into her bedroom and sacrificing her blood to expose him to the daylight. The sun pours through the large open window (reversing and capping the entry of evil allowed by Ellen when she opened the window) and kills Orlok, and that ends the plague. It is the mortal woman's self-sacrificing courage and purity that attract and defeat the monster, the way she is his supernatural and moral opposite. This opposition between her essential good and his essential evil is put in a resonant image when the shadow of Orlok's hand closes over Ellen's heart. She also represents the clarity and force of the book whose advice she is following, as opposed to the private language of the demonic. Orlok is especially frightening in the still scene in which we see his head and hand hovering over Ellen's neck as she lies in bed and he drinks her blood (Figure 23); it is the fact that no one moves that is most unsettling, that most decisively establishes the chilling tone. In this primarily dark shot, lit by one small lamp at the far side of the frame (just past the open window), the vampire is truly a creature of the night. There are no wielded crucifixes in *Nosferatu*,

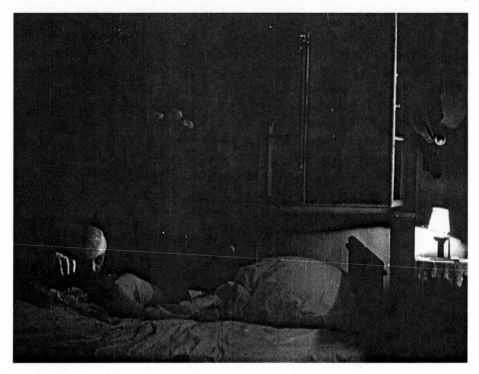

Figure 23. *Nosferatu*: Sucking blood at night.

no missing reflections, just the raw essentials of the coffins filled with earth, the teeth, the wounds and the blood. What opposes Orlok successfully is the power of the spirit as it is focused in one heroic woman.

Dracula, however, is opposed by a strong group of men, each of whom is religious to some degree, while the woman, Mina, works with them and provides their spiritual focus. That is, at least, how it is in Stoker's 1897 novel. (Earlier vampire fictions include John Polidori's "The Vampyre: A Tale" [1820], James Malcolm Rymer's *Varney the Vampyre; Or, the Feast of Blood* [1845–47], and Joseph Sheridan Le Fanu's "Carmilla" [1872]). In the novel *Dracula*, Jonathan Harker is the solicitor who is sent by his boss to Transylvania to give Count Dracula the papers for Carfax, the estate Dracula has purchased in a suburb of London, and Mina Murray is the woman who becomes Jonathan's wife after he escapes from Dracula's castle and the three vampires—women whose "deliberate voluptuousness" is "both thrilling and repulsive"[16]—to whom Dracula left him. Mina's friend is Lucy Westenra, who is pursued by several suitors: Dr John Seward, who runs a private lunatic asylum near Carfax; Arthur Holmwood, later Lord Godalming, whose proposal she accepts; and a Texan named Quincey Morris. Renfield is an inmate in Seward's asylum, later a slave of Dracula. Jonathan, Mina, Seward and the others are guided by Dr Abraham Van Helsing, a heroic[17] older man with experience of both science and the occult who once was Dr Seward's teacher. Both Van Helsing and

Mina have strong Christian beliefs. These characters are both repeated and changed in the movies.

In the novel, most of the major characters keep journals and write letters that record their separate experiences with the vampire. They begin to have a complete sense of what is going on only when the journals are typed by Mina, then read in relation to each other.[18] The superbly constructed novel consists of the collated journals and related documents and thus represents in itself both a human achievement—its collectivity and mortal perspective the opposite of Dracula's—and the solution to Dracula's tyranny, which is to share information and act together with full knowledge, including the knowledge of ritual. Dracula, however, keeps no journal, as if he were foreign to or, in his eternity, beyond the mortal practice of writing.[19] In his relative silence he is, compared to the journals, an antitext.[20]

Crucifixes, garlic and mirrors are anathema to Dracula in Stoker's novel, but he can move about in the daylight. Lucy is killed by Dracula and turns into a vampire who attacks children. Feeling terrible about what they have to do, the men[21] destroy her, driving a stake[22] through her heart, cutting off her head and filling her mouth with garlic. Thus Lucy is ritually, metaphysically and literally transformed from an example of what R. H. W. Dillard would call the failure of death[23] into a figure who is properly dead and completely saved. The heroes are the human community[24] united against evil and the unnatural.[25]

Dracula sets out to make Mina his bride and has her drink blood from his sliced-open breast. The heroes follow Dracula back to Transylvania, where they destroy him as he is arriving at his castle. Quincey dies in the effort (affirming the power of self-sacrifice as opposed to the selfishness and parasitism of the vampire), but Mina is saved (affirming the power of Christianity over the demonic and confirming the superstition that its victims are freed when a vampire is destroyed), and she and Jonathan go on to have a child (affirming the continuity of life and natural birth as opposed to the blood-driven reproduction of the undead).

It is a vivid novel with a palpable sense of evil. But on the way to the screen, *Dracula* suffered the same fate as *Frankenstein*: being adapted from a play. Hamilton Deane had written the play *Dracula* in 1924. In 1927 the American version opened; it starred Bela Lugosi and Edward Van Sloan and was called *Dracula: The Vampire Play*, and the co-author, or rewriter, was John L. Balderston. As Deane's solo version had done, the American version reduced the novel's plot considerably, cramming most of the action into a few rooms.[26] It also gave us the suave count in evening clothes rather than the imperious, tall, pale, sharp-toothed and often repulsive figure in the novel.[27] In both respects, the movie followed the lead of the Deane/Balderston play,[28] giving us both limited action (though it did restore a few—altered—scenes from the novel) and Lugosi and Van Sloan, who are its most resonant performers.

In the 1931 *Dracula*, which was made before the 1931 *Frankenstein*, it is Renfield who is sent to Transylvania to give Dracula the papers for Carfax Abbey, his property in London. This leaves little for "John" Harker (David Manners) to do in the movie other than to be the boyfriend of Mina (Helen Chandler) and Van Helsing's assistant. John is there only to be the norm (even Mina calls him "normal"), the alternative to the horror figure who would make her *his* bride. Nor is Mina the fully realized character she was in the novel, where she was the crucial copier (and, with Jonathan, the collator) of the texts and a brave and spiritual woman. Indeed, no one in this film keeps a journal, so there is nothing to collate, and the related idea that evil figures have their own language is dropped, at least in the vampire film, after *Nosferatu*. Mina's strongest moment in the movie comes when she is filled with vampiric and vamp-like energy and nearly bites her fiancé. Seward is now Mina's father but does nothing important except run the sanitarium, and there is no sign of Arthur or Quincey. The movie belongs not to the official hero and heroine but to Dracula, Van Helsing and Renfield. Lugosi makes a stylish count with his evening dress and opera cape. After the opening sequence with Jonathan Harker in his castle, Dracula makes only a few appearances in the novel, and the sharp teeth and red eyes are dominant in his pale face—pale unless he has been feeding. In the movie Lucy finds Dracula attractive. He speaks politely and conducts himself well, aiming to infiltrate the world of his victims. Lugosi nevertheless makes this revised vampire frightening and imposing. It is as Lugosi that Dracula becomes an iconic presence in world culture, a nearly universal symbol of undead evil wearing the formal mask of evening clothes that shows how evil can adapt to and hide within a society—or, from another point of view, shows the vampire's aristocratic decadence.

In one of the movie's strongest scenes, when Dracula raises his arm in a commanding gesture, his hand tensed like a claw and calls "Come here" to the strong-willed Van Helsing—almost controlling him—the two most powerful figures are joined, each of them bearing old knowledge. Van Helsing is connected to the rituals and superstitions that together with his religious faith will allow him to vanquish the vampire. Dracula is himself an old figure who was born and who died hundreds of years ago, bearing in himself the age-old quality, the extension into and continuity with the past, of the aristocracy. Both of them are foreign to the England where their encounter takes place, as their supernatural knowledge is foreign to the normal, unsuspecting world. The supernatural makes the rules, and it offers only supernatural solutions, such as the crucifix that Dracula cannot look at. Nature plays a role too, as the sun's daily rising forces Dracula back into his coffin.

In an elemental scene, Lucy is visited by Dracula in the form of a bat who comes through her bedroom window and hypnotizes her while she is reading in bed, then turns into human form and leans over her now sleeping body to bite her fatally. After a cut from a shot of the bat, the camera pans right from the sleeping Lucy to reveal the transformed Dracula, then pans left with him and moves forward as he approaches Lucy, closing in on her as he does.

When Dracula first bites Mina in her bed, it is shown from the perspective she'd have if awake. From the victim's point of view, we see Dracula widen his mouth and move, in close-up, down to and just below the camera into a fade-out. He has been moving closer to his victims all along, and Mina is revealed through camerawork (the cinematographer was Karl Freund) to be the most important victim. She remembers the event as a dream.

The defense of Mina—who has a demon lover and a conventional one at both sides, each with his distinct pull on her—is organized and primarily carried out by Van Helsing.

Taking a clue from *Nosferatu*, the 1931 *Dracula* stipulates that a vampire must stay in its coffin by day. It is important how the rules change in the films, for the films build up their own traditions.

At the end, John and Mina walk up a huge stone staircase after Van Helsing has, with a little help from John, destroyed Dracula by driving a stake through his heart (this occurs off-camera) and Mina has been freed from Dracula's control. John and Mina walk into the sunlight, which edges the steps, to the tune of church bells—striking a note both religious and matrimonial. (As we shall see in other supernatural movies, the surviving couple often demonstrates spiritual purity as well as romantic resolution.) The monster is dead, the couple has survived, the old supernatural tales and superstitions have been reaffirmed, and Christianity, as represented by the cross, has triumphed over evil. This affirmation of both superstition and Christianity is not inconsistent, for superstition leads one to suspect the existence of the supernatural monster, while religion (in a great many movies) gives one effective tools to conquer it.

In the next major vampire movie, *Vampyr* (1932), my candidate for the greatest horror film, the power of religion is affirmed throughout, and the vampire is part of an evil night-world that looks different from and plays by different rules than the day-lit world.

One significant change in the cinematic treatment of vampirism comes in *Son of Dracula* (Robert Siodmak, 1943, US), where, for her own reasons, the female victim decisively wants to be a vampire. That desire would show up again in *Dracula* (1979) and still later in the *Twilight* films.

In the 1979 *Dracula*, released two decades after the Hammer Dracula films began to emphasize the sexual elements of the vampire picture, Dracula himself (Frank Langella) becomes extremely seductive. This *Dracula* returns to the Deane and Balderston play (in a revival of which Langella had recently made a sexy impression), but it also makes up a great deal of its own material. The names of Lucy and Mina have been switched as in the play, with Lucy (Kate Nelligan) the heroine and Mina (Jan Francis) the daughter of Van Helsing (Laurence Olivier). Dracula is soft-spoken and virile, and his hypnotic gestures are understated. Lucy is drawn to him of her own will, and they have a unique kiss scene that leaves her throat intact.

Two bedroom-window scenes indicate how sexualized the encounter between vampire and victim has become in this influential picture. When Dracula appears at Mina's bedroom window and scratches at it like a bat, she is afraid at first but, giving in to his hypnotic control (played as if she were surrendering to his magnetism), opens her nightdress to bare her throat as he approaches the bed. When Dracula comes to Lucy's door-sized bedroom window, he makes it open by itself and walks in, knowing he will be welcome. Without using hypnosis, he exposes Lucy's throat, then picks her up and carries her to the bed (it makes a great difference here that the carried woman is conscious and expresses desire), where they kiss before he demands her blood. A red light fills the screen behind them, bloody and erotic. Then he makes her drink his blood so that she will be his bride after death, and she doesn't need convincing.

Martin (George A. Romero, 1978, US) asks how it would be for a vampire if there weren't any "magic," any supernatural element to vampirism, any transforming into bats, any throat-piercingly long canines, any hypnotic control. Martin (John Amplas) is a young man—or an 84-year-old vampire still in his relative youth—who is frustrated that people will not just lie down and allow him to drink their blood. So he uses needles to inject drugs that put them to sleep and razor blades that let him open their veins. Martin has an old cousin, Cuda (Lincoln Maazel), who is convinced that Martin is a vampire. Martin behaves like a vampire for whom there is no magic but also like a deranged human who thinks he is a vampire. When Cuda drives a stake through Martin's heart, it may be the triumph of madness—Cuda's—or it may be a good way to kill a vampire (but then, it would kill anybody).

Religion plays no role at all in three interesting films: *The Hunger* (Tony Scott, 1983, US), *Lifeforce* (Tobe Hooper, 1985, UK), and *Near Dark* (Kathryn Bigelow, 1987, US). *Lifeforce* offers a secular explanation for vampires, which is that they are not creatures of the Devil but come from outer space, and have left their traces behind them in folklore. They drain the life force out of their victims—in folklore, blood is a ready symbol for what they do take—and they are highly sexualized. In *Near Dark*, where the vampires don't need to lie in coffins and don't transform, the greatest enemy of the roaming group of vampires is sunlight, which makes them catch fire. *The Hunger* gives the rules a twist and specifies that the vampire's lover does not live eternally, or at least does not enjoy eternal health, but after a long while suddenly deteriorates and ages until it is too infirm to move. It becomes its real age but cannot die. The normal action of time is the vampire's enemy here, while the usual situation is that the vampire has made some kind of agreement with eternity and has nothing to fear from time. Christianity poses no obstacle, nor does daylight. The vampires sleep normally in a normal bed, and nobody turns into a bat. Catherine Deneuve plays the vampire, who is thousands of years old, and David Bowie plays her vampire lover, who is only hundreds of years old. Stylishness and sensuality (and Bowie's suffering) constitute the appeal of the vampires in *The Hunger*.

Let the Right One In (Tomas Alfredson, 2008, Sweden) is the story of a 12-year-old boy, Oskar (Kåre Hedebrant), who makes friends with a vampire who died at 12 and appears to be a 12-year-old girl, Eli (Lina Leandersson). One very brief genital shot implies that Eli was castrated.[29] Eli offers and demands both protection and loyalty. At the end, Oskar becomes her protector. This happens after she has killed some of the bullies who oppress Oskar at school and has also killed the man (Per Ragnar as Håkan) who appears to be her father but is really her protector and provider (bringing her, in a jug, blood from victims whose throats he has cut), but who has become useless to her. However violent and bloody, the film is tender and captivating as it shows this developing relationship. Oskar's final commitment to being Eli's best and only friend is presented not as a fate he is crazy to choose—nor as an ordeal like Håkan's, though it could turn into that as he grows older and she does not—but as the satisfactory resolution of their feelings for each other. All is right in this horror world, for now.

Like some mummies, vampires can bring mortals the prospect of supernatural romance. This distinguishes them from the other undead, such as the notably unromantic zombies, and makes their versions of eternity—or of a very long time spent with an undying lover—both attractive and repulsive. The disturbing, romantic component of vampirism (revived in *Twilight*, where the vampire—Robert Pattinson as Edward—is cool, young, serious, powerful, devoted, protective and Byronic) remains consistently important, an element of the vampire film that appears almost as regularly as the coffins, the special powers and the one indispensable element, the only one that always shows up: blood.

Witches: *Häxan* and *Suspiria*

Witches and sorcerers are not supernatural beings, but they are said to consort with them and take power from them. They exercise supernatural power.

The witch and wizard are humans who have, according to many old stories, made deals with the Devil so that they can perform magic. Some have sold their souls, some have engaged in intercourse with devils and many have found it important to commune with other witches and wizards, as well as devils, at the Witch's Sabbath. They have great skills with herbs and use them to make many kinds of potions and ointments. A potion could cure a headache (dispel a demon) or act as an aphrodisiac (make someone fall in love), while "the witch's ointment" was said to induce visions of flying.[30] Most real witches were pagan herbalists who did no harm, but for hundreds of years witches and those convicted of being witches (which could be anyone who confessed under torture) were burned alive. Stories about evil witches may have soothed the consciences of those who condemned so many.

There were movies about witchcraft, most of them about witches rather than sorcerers, before *The Student of Prague*. Georges Méliès made *The Witch* in 1906, a short in which a witch, who at one point flies on her broom beneath the moon, vows vengeance on a troubadour who has cheated her and frightens him by making ghosts and other phantoms appear in a graveyard.[31] In the early films, witches were often used as figures whose powers would justify special effects, as devils did; this lasted long after Méliès and was prominent in the Harry Potter films (2001–2011).

The usual horror film about witchcraft presents it as a fact with supernatural backing. In a film like *Rosemary's Baby* there are witches, and they are not just herbalists but are very effectively in league with the Devil. In some of the films, however, a more sophisticated approach leaves open the question of whether witches really have supernatural ties and powers, and concentrates on the feelings about witchcraft held by those who believe in it; such a film is *Day of Wrath* (Carl Dreyer, 1943, Denmark). There are also pictures that celebrate magic as an occasion for fully creative filmmaking in which anything can happen, such as the amazing *Shadows of Forgotten Ancestors* (Sergei Paradjanov, 1964, USSR).

In the silent period, the most ambitious feature-length film about witchcraft was *Häxan* (1922) or *The Witch*, a Swedish documentary that included some dramatized scenes. (A sound version released in 1968 is called *Witchcraft Through the Ages*.) *Häxan* took for its starting point the historical fact that witches existed, but as persecuted and often skillful women—or women who were merely denounced and confessed under torture but did not practice witchcraft—around whom a vast supernatural lore had developed since ancient times. Examining woodcuts and engravings as well as other sources, it surveyed the portrayals of witches and sorcerers and their trafficking with devils, thus putting much of the venerable imagery of witchcraft on film for the first time. Dramatic scenes with representative characters, woven into the documentary, realized some of these images and many others on sets, creating an iconography for film: the cauldron being stirred on the fire, the bundles of sticks, the bones, the dead man's hand, the bottles and potions, the barrels of witch's brew, the toads and snakes and other ingredients, the cat, the broomstick, the Witch's Sabbath, the intimacies with demons and the Devil himself, the magic (we see witches both perform and imagine wonders), the judges and the hooded executioner of the Inquisition, the torture sessions and instruments, the confession (which in this case allows the film to portray many fantastic images of witchcraft and demonology, such as witches flying through the air on brooms, putting a dead baby into a cauldron to brew it with toads, or kissing the Devil's ass), the denunciation of others, the stake.

Häxan argues that many people, particularly in the Middle Ages, accepted witchcraft as an explanation for some of the things they did not understand, from the mystical to the medical. The film works its way to the present, where 1920s' psychology recognizes certain traits formerly associated with witches and spells to be treatable symptoms of hysteria, compulsion and so on.

As people have imagined her, the witch brings evil and manipulates baffling power. She is a sign of something wrong within society, as if the town were spiritually out of balance or out of favor, and she must be burned if the town is to be freed from dark supernatural influences and returned to its normal ways under the protection of God. Thus the stake is surrounded by a crowd, and the values of the official culture are upheld by the judges as well as by the mob. But this simple world and its simple fix are complicated and morally undermined if witches are mortals without supernatural powers and if the Devil is not behind them. The troubling ambiguity created when one does not know whether witches are supernaturally endowed gives *Day of Wrath* much of its effect.

Day of Wrath is about people who believe that witches exist and have unnatural powers sustained by spiritual evil. The question is whether the movie believes this. Rather than make a film with a superior modern attitude toward the subject, Dreyer made a film that, as many have noted, seems to come directly out of its period (Denmark in the year 1623) and to share its assumptions. The story concerns Anne (Lisbeth Movin), whose mother was a witch, whose old friend is burned as a witch (Figure 24), and who eventually confesses to being a witch. She is in love with Martin (Preben Lerdoff), the son of her elderly husband, Absalon (Thorkild Roose). One night the husband is walking home from a friend's deathbed in a storm, and he feels Death brush by him like a wind at just the moment Anne confides to Martin that she has been wondering how it would be if Absalon were dead. That may be a coincidence or it may be a matter of cause and effect; the film doesn't say. But the sequence makes Anne's witchcraft seem real, even if other scenes point the other way.

In the film's moving final scene, Anne confesses. She has apparently come to believe that she is a witch and that she bewitched Martin into loving her and killed Absalon by wishing him dead.[32] *Day of Wrath*, whose title refers to Judgment Day, shows the limits of human judgment. It objectively presents a culture that believes in witchcraft, within which Anne finds her doom by following her human, fallible nature in search of love. We do not know whether she is condemned unfairly; that is much of what makes *Day of Wrath* such a powerful and sophisticated picture. In Anne's confession, *Day of Wrath*

Figure 24. *Day of Wrath*: Tied to a ladder, a witch is thrown onto the fire.

shows how a person comes to consider herself endowed with supernatural power—how a witch is made. It also shows the frustrating limits of the judges' knowledge. Religion advances against witchcraft in the story of *Day of Wrath*, but the film leaves open the question of whether this is a legitimate spiritual victory of good over evil, or the triumph of ignorance over immoral but not supernatural behavior. Thanks to its refraining from making final transcendental statements, *Day of Wrath* shows better than any other film what it means to believe in witchcraft.

Sorcerers and "witch cults" definitely exist, and demonology is a valid pursuit in *Night of the Demon* (Jacques Tourneur, 1957, UK), released in the US as *Curse of the Demon* and based on M. R. James's short story "Casting the Runes." In the course of the picture the skeptical hero battles a deadly sorcerer and becomes more wary of the supernatural ("Maybe it's better not to know"). Part of the resolution of many supernatural pictures involves letting the supernatural remain unknown. Most monsters are fully known, fully described and realized by the time they are destroyed, but a supernatural monster or force might not and perhaps must not have all its mystery explained.

"As a doctor, I have complete faith in science," says Dr Gorobec (John Richardson) in *The Mask of the Demon* (Mario Bava, 1960, Italy), released in the US as *Black Sunday* and in the UK as *Revenge of the Vampire*. Characters who share this doctor's conviction are usually educated by the events of the supernatural-monster movie, as he is, and come to agree with the supernatural explanations. The information in old books and manuscripts is more reliable than conventional scientific information, for it comes from the sciences practiced by alchemists and wizards. The student of old, sometimes occult texts is usually a substantial authority figure in supernatural movies.

In *The Mask of the Demon*, where the witch (Asa, played by Barbara Steele) and her consort, Javutich (Arturo Dominici), are also vampires, the executioners have the fires lit at the start of the movie. (They are not vampires of Stoker's variety,[33] but they do thrive on blood and leave undead victims.) Asa curses the chief judge, her brother, saying that her image will reappear in his descendants and that she will take revenge on him through his own house. A mask with long nails inside it is hammered onto her face so that she will always bear "the Mask of Satan." This violent, frightening and ritualized moment sets the scale for the film and even for the generations of Italian horror films it influenced,[34] letting us know that it (and they) will reach for rich effects and will be violent and hard to take. When Asa and Javutich are being burned, rain puts out the fires; thus they are dead but not completely destroyed. (Aside from complete immolation, a religious character in this movie learns from an old inscription, the only way to destroy a witch is to pierce her through the left eye.) When Asa comes back to life 200 years later, as a witch who is both erotic and repulsive, she goes after the descendant who resembles her (Katia, also played by Steele), through whom she intends to be fully reborn. The nail holes in her seductive face are horrific. They disappear once she has drunk enough blood. At the climax she almost drains Katia of all her vital energy (not her blood) before she is, finally, completely burned.

Katia and Gorobec are the romantic couple. The surviving lovers are, as usual, the sign of rightness, fertility and continuity in a world that is no longer threatened—or isn't threatened at the moment. In the supernatural subgenre they have an additional burden, also found in *Dracula*, which is to signify spiritual health, something that is emphasized through the cross that Katia always wears and that the plot doesn't allow us to miss.

Dario Argento, who was influenced by Bava, became Italy's leading horror director in the 1970s. His witchcraft films are tense, atmospheric and filled with panels and other shapes drenched in deep color, especially colored light surrounded by black or near-darkness. Along with the insistent music and the probing, often swiftly moving camera, these colors are heightened and unsettling. A panel of dark red and a wash of dark blue may be the only light for a corridor in an old house. His first two witch films, *Suspiria* (Dario Argento, 1977, Italy) and *Inferno* (Argento, 1980, Italy)—part of a trilogy that remained unfinished for decades[35]—deal with the Three Mothers, three sister witches who live in large, specially designed buildings in different cities. The building in New York, the central setting of *Inferno*, is the home of the Mother of Darkness.

According to *Inferno*, the others are in Rome, home of the Mother of Tears, and in Freiburg, Germany (the setting of *Suspiria*), home of the Mother of Sighs. The story of the witches is found in an old book, *The Three Mothers*, written by the alchemist who designed their houses. In *Inferno* it is important for the characters to find, read and believe this book and discover the truth about the old building, even though this may lead to their deaths. The black-gloved hands of the killer—who is killing those who have the book, mostly with a knife—are played by Argento, as in all his films that have such killers.

The intense colors and camera movements in *Inferno* build on those of *Suspiria*. The music, by Goblin, has a nagging, serial quality and is played loudly. The rest of the movie's effective assault on the audience comes from the color, the tension and the violence. Set in Freiburg, where the witch's house is a renowned school of ballet, *Suspiria* is the story of an American, Suzy Banyon (Jessica Harper), who goes there to study. An elderly expert on witches whom Suzy consults calls them "malefic, negative, and destructive" and says they have "tremendous powers. They can change the course of events and people's lives, but only to do harm... Their goal is to accumulate great personal wealth, but that can only be achieved by injury to others. They can cause suffering, sickness and even the death of those who for whatever reason have offended them." The students who discover that the teachers are part of a coven consequently suffer extreme, stylized deaths before Suzy kills the nearly immortal head witch.

At one point one student, Sara (Stefania Casini), asks, "Suzy, do you know anything about *witches?*" The last word is whispered, with an echo, and the screen goes dark while the line is said. That unmotivated lighting change—the fade-out on Sara's face as she says "Suzy"—is the kind of directness, an almost musical declaration of tone, that makes *Suspiria* a heightened poem of horror. The director is always present in this film, using lights to change the colors and the psychological values of sets, notably in the long, brilliant sequence in which Sara is chased down hallways and murdered in a pit of razor wire. (The cinematographer was Luciano Tovoli.)

The script was by Argento and Daria Nicolodi. Nicolodi had drawn on memories of her childhood for the first draft, of hearing from her grandmother how, when she was a little girl, she had gone to study piano at an academy where they actually taught black magic. In an interview[36] Nicolodi said that in writing *Suspiria* she had been influenced by *Alice in Wonderland*, "Bluebeard" and "Snow White." Argento spent some time looking at children's books as well as thinking about the history of witchcraft.

Many children have taken their images of witches and sorcerers from the witch in *Snow White and the Seven Dwarfs* (Walt Disney, 1937, US) and the sorcerer with the apprentice in *Fantasia* (Disney, 1940, US) as well as from the old tales of witchcraft that are often reserved for the young. The most influential, indelible witch on film is Margaret Hamilton's Wicked Witch of the West in *The Wizard of Oz*, even though that is not a horror movie.

In *The Blair Witch Project* (1999)[37] the witch is never seen, let alone burned. She is known mostly through the effects that her signs and her magic have on the main characters, Heather (Heather Donahue), Josh (Josh Leonard) and Mike (Michael Williams). These three film students set out, under Heather's direction, with a 16mm camera and a video camera as well as a tape recorder, to make a documentary about a Maryland witch.

They never come back, but their footage is found a year later (a plot device and narrative frame previously used in *Cannibal Holocaust*, as noted before). The 16mm footage is in black and white, and the video is in color, making it easy to keep track of who is shooting what. The fact that the footage is motivated, that someone within the story's world is shooting it instead of having the action be observed by an omniscient, invisible camera, is intended to increase our belief in what we are seeing, as if the footage had documentary authenticity. The tension and confusion increase as the filmmakers get lost in the woods, particularly when they spend one day walking due south and find that they have, impossibly, gone in a circle.

One of the scariest and simplest scenes comes when Heather finds a bundle of sticks and string tied with a ribbon outside their tent and realizes that the witch has designs on them, in fact a hold. At other times the witch leaves little piles of rocks or larger constructions made mostly of wood, and all of them are enigmatic and eerie, belonging to no known iconography. They seem to be part of the way the witch casts spells. As the witch can arrange pieces of the natural world into supernatural signs, making a malevolent language out of nature, nature itself becomes frightening in this movie. The woods are a threat not only because the characters are lost, but also because they are being pursued by a witch to whose power the woods may answer.

Josh disappears, and Mike and Heather eventually find themselves at the witch's cabin. They run through the house and up the stairs, then down. Heather loses track of Mike, and we see his camera drop, then stop. At the bottom of the stairs, in an image as enigmatic as any of the witch's signs, Heather sees Mike in a strange position, standing in the corner of the basement, not moving and not answering when she calls his name. Heather is hit from behind, and she and the camera fall to the floor. The movie ends when the camera stops. Evil wins in this picture; the characters fall into its grip and can't find their way out. The logic of the unhappy ending is rigorous and satisfying. It is not that we want to see the witch triumph but that no one can stop her. Our sympathies are with the victims, but they are in a trap of horror that has been solidly built, and we admire its solidity even as we are frightened by it. We get a good scare without a resolution, which can be a pleasure if encountered within the frame of the horror film. This picture gives us a witch who truly commands black magic, a figure not to be approached with the sympathy one might feel for the real victims of the witch trials.

Ghosts: *The Uninvited* and *Ringu*

The undead are those who have died and come back, not to life but to a state hard to identify as living or dead, usually in their own bodies. They include vampires, zombies and mummies. Ghosts are distinguished from the rest of the undead because they are disembodied and immaterial, and because they have gone through death into another phase of existence reserved for the spirits of the dead. They have not been reanimated but have continued to exist after death. For all these figures, real and final death, the norm, may be presented as a release that is preferable to an eternity of compulsively repeated behavior, such as eating the living (thus many characters who are about to die in the zombie films made after *Night of the Living Dead* ask to be shot in the head if they revive, so they can be killed completely and won't turn into monsters), but there are many undead, like Imhotep in *The Mummy*, who fiercely resist their destruction and are not shown finding peace when it comes. Ghosts, which many people fear to encounter, give a form to the fear of death, the fear of an unknown doom that may wait after death, the fear of an immutable curse and the fear of an eternal lack of resolution: of having to deal forever with the worst issues and emotions in one's life, of being unable to affect one's life now that it is over and of never passing on to the rest of the afterlife, perhaps missing out on Heaven. Caught between the worlds of the living and the dead, the ghost must find resolution if it is to achieve the oblivion of death or the rewards of the afterlife, whichever waits for the soul—but the ghost movie is, of course, biased toward the existence of an afterlife.

Trapped on Earth, often because of an outrage requiring vengeance or a still-active issue suffered in life, ghosts usually haunt the places they used to live—or, as in *Ringu*, the objects to which they have become linked. A haunted house may be cleaned if the ghost occupying it is appeased or exorcised, and this coming to terms with the ghost or with the curse is often what provides the dramatic resolution of the ghost movie. There are, however, haunted houses that themselves are conscious, like Shirley Jackson's Hill House, which is "not sane,"[38] and the Overlook Hotel in Stephen King's *The Shining*, and to deal with them it may not be enough to pacify a single spirit. Such houses themselves are the central threats while the ghosts are their tenants. Not every "old dark house" is haunted—the one in *The Old Dark House* (James Whale, 1932, US) conceals a living madman, and the one in *The Beyond* (Lucio Fulci, 1981, Italy) has in its basement an entrance to Hell—but many of them are, and sometimes it seems as if every haunted house, aside from the hotel in Kubrick's *The Shining* and the bright new home in *Poltergeist* (Tobe Hooper, 1982, US), is an old dark one designed to scare.

Movie ghosts determine when they may be seen by ordinary people or certain people. Otherwise it may take a psychic to perceive them. They usually manifest or express themselves at night. They are sometimes presented as figures whose reality cannot be absolutely established, like the ghosts in Henry James's "The Turn of the Screw" (adapted as *The Innocents* [Jack Clayton, 1961, US/UK]). Many ghost movies, such as *House on Haunted Hill* (William Castle, 1958, US), explain that most of the figures we thought were ghosts were not, while vampire movies always insist on the reality of the vampire.

Ghosts are investigated as paranormal phenomena and feared as supernatural entities. Those who advertise their presence by making noises and moving objects around, which helps when invisible characters are to be tracked in a movie, are called poltergeists. Direct views of ghosts are often transparent. A double-exposed image was originally called a phantom, and double-exposure was used often in the early films to present ghosts. Later, more sophisticated effects still strove to present figures that could be seen and sometimes seen through, a disturbance in the light that indicated the presence of an immaterial being. Beyond that, many audible and visible events, both spooky and corny, have been thought up to indicate that ghosts are present.

There are two kinds of ghost movies: those that accept the existence of ghosts (an early example of which is the short *Mary Jane's Mishap* [G. A. Smith, 1903, UK], in which a ghost comes out of her grave, holding the jug of paraffin that led to her death, though one could go far back into literature for other ghosts that are treated as real, such as Banquo in *Macbeth*) and those that explain the ghostly phenomena away as the acts of living people, usually villains. The latter are mysteries with the trappings of ghost movies, not movies about the supernatural—they use a bait-and-switch technique that dates back to the Gothic novel—and one of the most typical and influential of them is the silent feature *The Cat and the Canary* (Paul Leni, 1927, US), which will be taken up shortly. Most of these unsupernatural films fool us almost up to the end. One example is the silent short *Au secours!* or *Help!* (Abel Gance, 1923, France).

In *Au secours!* comedian Max Linder plays a newlywed named Max who is challenged by members of his club to spend an hour in a haunted castle. The owner bets he can't do it. When he gets there, Max meets all sorts and sizes of ghosts and other disturbing figures. Thanks to a special effect that repeatedly makes the frame about half its normal height and then full height, the main room squashes and stretches itself as he hangs onto the chandelier—an early example of the problematizing of space in the horror film; another comes when the room changes several times to negative and back. Just before the hour is up, Max receives a phone call from his bride, who is being menaced in her bedroom by a deformed man. She wants Max to come home at once, and he hits the alarm bell, calling for help. The deformed man looks at his watch, takes off his mask and laughs because he, the owner of the castle, has won the bet. Then the owner, who makes these bets to cover the expenses of the unrentable (because supposedly haunted) castle, pays off his assistants, for all the ghosts were living people. The earlier the film, the more likely that "ghost" and "haunt" will be in quotation marks in any description of its supernatural content—unless it is one of the adaptations of *A Christmas Carol*, the first of which was made in 1908. Still, *Au secours!* offers one way after another to portray ghosts and their manifestations, as well as to make the nature of space in a haunted house volatile and paradoxical. The ghosts are explained away, but not because *Au secours!* is a comedy. Neither *The Cat and the Canary* nor *Mark of the Vampire* (Tod Browning, 1935, US), in which a troupe of actors play not ghosts but vampires, is a comedy, and each is unwilling to let its supernatural horrors stand, while *Topper* (Norman Z. McLeod, 1937, US) is a comedy that lets its ghosts be real.

The Cat and the Canary, based on the play by John Willard, advances the tools of the ghost movie while denying that its ghosts are real. The as-if ghost is presented in scenes that have to work as ghost scenes, even if they will be given a credible explanation later. The same is true of the other weird figures that appear in this old dark house but are not supposed to be ghosts. There are many secret passageways that allow tricks to be pulled. An intertitle informs us that Cyrus West's greedy relatives gathered around him "like a cat around a canary," and it turns out that the heroine who is supposed to inherit from the late Cyrus, Annabelle (Laura La Plante), becomes the next canary. One greedy relative wants her declared insane—and she would be, if she insists that she can see ghosts—so that he can inherit in her stead (it is a condition of the will that the inheritor be declared sane). He therefore sets about making frightening things happen to Annabelle or in her presence, though we do not find out he was responsible until the end.

The Canterville Ghost (Jules Dassin, 1944, US) offers an example of what is meant by an unresolved issue with which a ghost must deal in the afterlife. Sir Simon de Canterville

(Charles Laughton) runs away from a duel, in which he is standing in for a kinsman, and hides in his father's house where he is walled up alive for dishonoring the family. His father curses him, saying he will haunt the castle until he finds a kinsman to do a brave deed on his behalf, like the one he failed to perform. The problem is that, generation after generation, the Cantervilles are cowards. Eventually the Cantervilles cure themselves of their cowardice and end the curse on the family ghost in the same terms and by the same actions. In other words, when a living Canterville finally does something brave to protect others, which is what the curse demanded and is also a positive development for the man, the ghost is freed and disappears, surrounded by light. In the background of the ghost movie there is usually something that needs to be dealt with, something old and hidden and perhaps evil, and a ghost arises to manifest the evil or the problem. That happens in *Poltergeist* as much as in *The Canterville Ghost*.

In *The Uninvited* (1944), based on the novel by Dorothy Macardle, a large seaside house is haunted by two ghosts: Mary, who is presumed to be the mother of Stella (Gail Russell), and Carmel, who actually is Stella's mother. The house has been bought by a brother and sister (Ray Milland as Roderick and Ruth Hussey as Pamela) from the previous owner, Commander Beech (Donald Crisp), whose daughter is Stella, whose wife was Mary, and whose model (he used to be a painter) was Carmel. Beech has forbidden Stella to go to the house where she spent her first three years until Mary died, but she wants to go there to feel close to her mother. It takes a while to figure out that there are two ghosts (and which is which), one of whom, Carmel, makes her presence evident with a strong scent of mimosa and a benevolent mood—though she is heard crying piteously almost every night—while the other, Mary, can be seen as a moving light and brings with her a dark mood that can induce depression or self-destruction. Most of the time we think the evil one is Carmel and that Mary is trying to protect Stella, though the reverse is the case. (In other words, the mystery component of the story is successful. Trying to find out the reason a ghost is present is often carried out and constructed as a mystery.) The ghost with the scent of mimosa reveals the truth, coming into a room and turning the pages of a journal to the entry that reveals that Carmel had a child.

At the climax, when Roderick confronts the semitransparent Mary at the top of the great staircase in the dark, holding only a few candles, the twisting light (resembling a windblown cape that changes in size) and the out-of-focus upper body and face are unsettling and threatening because we have not seen Mary this closely before or long enough to make out that there is a face in the light, because she is still unclear and powerfully understated, a silent figure of moving, unfocused light in the darkness, and because it has finally been established that she is evil. In an advance over earlier ghost pictures, *The Uninvited* made the ghosts' presence evident while showing little or nothing of them on camera. The mood Mary induces is noticed by the living characters as clearly as Carmel's scent.

Some ghosts are benevolent, like Carmel or like Irena (Simone Simon) in Lewton's *The Curse of the Cat People* (Robert Wise and Gunther Von Fritsch, 1944, US), a film that plays largely on one's fears, especially in childhood, of strangers and of being disliked and misunderstood as well as on the fear of being a bad parent. After Irena's death at the end of *Cat People*, Oliver (Kent Smith) marries Alice (Jane Randolph), and they move from the big city to Tarrytown, where they give birth to a sensitive, dreamy, imaginative daughter, Amy (Ann Carter). Amy sometimes does not recognize the difference between imagination and reality, and her parents, especially her father, often accuse her of lying, though she never lies. Amy's parents are responsible for some of this, for they make up stories they assume she will realize are made up, such as that a certain tree is a magic mailbox. When Amy puts the invitations to her birthday party in that tree, nobody shows up. Oliver dislikes Amy's tendency to believe in the imaginary because he thinks his first wife had the same problem—by now he is sure Irena only imagined she was one of the cat people—and both he and Alice are afraid that Irena is somehow extending her influence over the child. In fact she is, but her influence is good. The ghost of Irena, whom only Amy can see, becomes Amy's only friend (her "imaginary friend," one would have said at the time), and they play together in the huge back yard, where Irena can play tricks with the light and make everything beautiful.

One day Amy had been walking by an old dark house inhabited by two women of whom the local children are afraid, an old actress named Julia (Julia Dean) and her daughter, Barbara (Elizabeth Russell). Julia had given her a ring—a wishing ring, she said, for people are always filling Amy's head with fantasies. Wishing on the ring, Amy had gotten the only thing she wanted: a friend, Irena, who appears first as a change in the wind and the light in the garden, then as a singing shadow in the bedroom at night and finally as a kind of fairy princess. At the climax, afraid of Barbara, Amy calls for her friend, and a transparent Irena appears, superimposed over Barbara. Seeing Irena in Barbara's place (though what we see is Barbara), Amy goes to the woman, calling her "My friend," and hugs her. Barbara puts her hands around Amy's neck, preparing to strangle her, when for the last time Amy calls her "My friend." The insistent words and loving tone reach Barbara, and she takes her hands away. It is one of the strongest moments of the power of love in the horror film, significantly and effectively nonviolent, whether Irena is truly present at the climax or is conjured up in the mind of a frightened girl.

The curse of the cat people is to have a strong imagination (or, for the *Cat People* movies can be read in two ways, to be in a supernatural situation in which those with conventional minds will not believe); it may be to be an artist. Others may consider one a liar or a fool, and their attempts to help may not improve the situation but only isolate one further in imagination, belief and magical thinking. Irena is both an imaginary playmate and a real one, for Irena is too much herself, too recognizable as the character from the earlier movie, for Amy to have made her up from a photograph found in a drawer. Lewton's films rarely present unequivocally supernatural figures but let their characters coast on the edge of understanding in a world that readily ceases to become comprehensible by purely conventional means, an uncertainty that allows his films to suggest more than they declare.

In *Ugetsu* (Kenji Mizoguchi, 1953, Japan) the ghosts are unequivocally real and can appear physically solid, though they can also be disembodied spirits. In one of its two intertwined stories, a potter, Genjuro (Masayuki Mori), has a love affair with a woman (Machiko Kyo as Lady Wakasa) who turns out to be a ghost, while his wife Miyagi (Kinuyo

Tanaka) is murderously attacked on the road, unbeknownst to him. The film also tells the story of a couple whose experiences are purely mortal. It is the balance of the ghost story with the realistic story that makes the supernatural aspects so effective, for they come to be part of a vision of a whole that is both natural and supernatural, a complete physical and spiritual world.

Kwaidan (Masaki Kobayashi, 1964, released 1965, Japan), based on a book of ghost stories by Lafcadio Hearn, reflects the influence of *Ugetsu* (it is interesting to compare the scenes in which men meet the ghosts of their wives), but each of its four ghost stories, wonderfully scored by Tôru Takemitsu and designed by Shigemasa Toda, offers its own memorable approach to horror: "The Black Hair" in its frightening use of darkness and its treatment of guilt and revenge, "The Woman of the Snow" in its gorgeously artificial skies and sets, "Hoichi the Earless" in its painted and theatrical battle and its bloody ear scene, and "In a Cup of Tea" in its metaphysical cleverness. Years later, the most influential Japanese ghost movie would be *Ringu*.

One of the most controversial adaptations of any horror novel is Kubrick's *The Shining*. Even if one acknowledges that the picture succeeds in its own terms, it leaves out what many have felt is the crucial point of the book, as if Kubrick either didn't get it or dismissed it. He may have considered it a needless pulp element that the Overlook Hotel wants Jack to kill Danny so that Danny and his shining (a psychic ability that includes seeing the future and the traces of the past as well as communicating telepathically) will become part of the hotel, vastly increasing its power. Kubrick does make it clear, as King does, that the hotel shines, that the spirits of those who die in the hotel remain there, that it has a will and that it can make ghosts (or alcohol) materialize—in which form the ghosts are not just visions, but also beings who can, for example, squeeze Danny's neck and leave marks. But Kubrick does not make it clear why the hotel is doing all this, why it wants Danny (Danny Lloyd) and his mother, Wendy (Shelley Duvall), killed, beyond that it enjoys violence. It seems that Jack (Jack Nicholson) succumbs to the impulse to slaughter his family simply because the hotel is an evil place that has a terrible influence on him. Kubrick may have felt that the father who tries to kill his family, not the ghost hotel, was the key horror figure and that the film got to Jack's craziness better by pursuing a simpler plot line. He may also have felt that the hotel was malevolent enough as he had it. Certainly the central fear the movie deals with is that a parent will turn insanely violent and try to kill members of the family.

Kubrick's ending shows that Jack has joined the ghosts that haunt the Overlook; we see him in a 1921 photograph on the wall of the hotel. This makes it seem as if the hotel has been after Jack all along, not Danny, and is glad to have him in its timeless grip, just as it would have enjoyed the spectacle of the murders. The film does a good job of showing how Jack gradually loses control of himself and comes under the influence of the hotel, particularly in the scenes when the ghost bartender serves him real drinks after he has abstained for a long time. Jack's madness is brilliantly conveyed when Wendy sees the manuscript he has been typing and reads nothing but "All work and no play makes Jack a dull boy" on page after page. An example of great psychological horror, it is the most effective moment in the picture. The alcoholic, insane father on a rampage becomes the climactic horror because, both as a novel and as a movie, *The Shining*—at its heart—is a horror story about the family. In this respect and this respect alone, Kubrick did not miss the point. One understands the film by determining what it has chosen as its monster—the father, not the hotel.

As at the climax of *The Uninvited*, ghosts often appear in *Poltergeist* as figures of light.[39] They are also known by the objects they move when they are invisible. But there is a more powerful ghost behind all the lost souls manifesting as poltergeists in this movie, and it is consumed with rage and betrayal. This "terrible presence" is described as "the Beast." The house in which the bourgeois family lives—in fact, much of the housing development—was built over a cemetery, and the developer, Teague (James Karen), moved the tombstones but not the bodies. The first of two resolutions takes place when the ghosts, no longer stymied, move into the Light. Then—after coffins and corpses have erupted out of the ground, uncovering the outrage that has infuriated the Beast—the house is sucked into the great beyond, which, along with the exposure of the secret, apparently ends the curse.

The ghosts' first means of entering the family's life is the TV. Early in the movie the younger daughter, Carol Anne (Heather O'Rourke), can hear the ghosts talking through the static. Soon they have taken Carol Anne into their own dimension (pulling her into her scary closet when it has become a gateway), and her family can hear her through the static on the TV. The mother, Diane (JoBeth Williams), brings Carol Anne back by going through one supernatural gateway in the house and coming out another, an image of maternal power—and for Carol Anne of rebirth. At the very end we see the strong but exhausted family going into a motel room. Then the father, Steve (Craig T. Nelson), wheels the motel TV outside and slams the door on it, finally feeling safe. (The film begins with an image on a TV—the signoff of traditional or in this case natural programming, after which comes the static—and ends with a disconnected TV.) The ghosts go on to the phase of the afterlife where they belong, the evil that has been done to them is completely exposed, the house that could not be cleaned is destroyed and the universe is back in order. The family is not the playground for horror that it was in *The Shining*, but a loving and functional group that is together at the start and at the finish despite the terrors they have undergone. As much as it follows the classic formula of the ghost movie with its spirits who are angry about a secret but eventually find peace, *Poltergeist* is also original. It hits one horror peak when an investigator imagines tearing off his face and another when the son, Robbie (Oliver Robins), is practically eaten by the monstrous tree that breaks through his bedroom window.

After the great success of *The Shining* and *Poltergeist* in the early 1980s, the viability of the ghost movie depended on thinking up new aspects of the afterlife, new ways of detecting ghosts and new situations for ghosts to be in—such as being certain that the other people in their house are the ghosts, as in *The Others* (Alejandro Amenábar, 2001, Spain/US), or discovering the bizarre rules of the afterlife, as in the horror comedy *Beetle Juice* (Tim Burton, 1988, US)—as well as on thinking up new kinds of ghosts, like the spirit evoked by a videotape in *Ringu*. As in *The Others*, one intriguing situation was that of not knowing one was a ghost, and the film that offered what may be the most moving and clever dramatization of that condition was *The Sixth Sense* (M. Night Shyamalan, 1999, US). Never showing the disembodied ghost (which turns out to be a demon) but presenting evidence of what it does when the characters are sleeping and have left a video camera on, *Paranormal Activity* (Oren Peli, 2007, revised and released 2009, US) was most effective when a bedroom door moved by itself in the middle of the night.

Some ghosts can never accept the fact of death or forgive the way they died. *Ringu*, also called *Ring*, based on the novel by Koji Suzuki, is the tale of a ghost, Sadako (Rie Inou), who sends out hints about her death by means of a videotape that she has psychically imprinted and cursed. After playing the tape, which contains images from Sadako's mind, some of them relating to her death, one will die in exactly seven days. The only way to save one's self is to make a copy of the tape and play it for another, which starts the seven-day clock for that person. At the end of the movie the main character, a reporter named Reiko (Nanako Matsushima), saves her son, who has watched the tape, by making a copy to show to her father. As the resolution of a ghost movie this has an unusual cruelty. (Nevertheless, some ghost movies *are* cruel, like the gory *Two Thousand Maniacs!* [Herschell Gordon Lewis, 1964, US], whose Civil-War-era ghosts come back like bloodthirsty versions of the spirits in *Brigadoon*.) *Ringu* makes us fear ghosts, curses, unmarked tapes (innocently opened forbidden texts), water and what we might do to stop death from striking us or others.

Sadako, the central horror, who was both evil and psychically powerful when she was alive and remains so in death, has long black hair that always covers her face. She was drowned by her father in a well. At her most terrifying, Sadako crawls out of a TV, a color figure emerging from a grainy black-and-white image, to claim a victim (Hiroyuki Sanada as Ryuji). She hits him with a look frightening enough to kill—the one time we can see any part of her face as one of her eyes, looking grotesquely down at him, is momentarily revealed behind her hair.[40] A solution that would have worked in numerous other pictures (finding her body and revealing the truth about her death) is ineffective, and the rage of the ghost continues, extending itself with a reach like that of the media: the tapes whose magnetic fields can be influenced by her brainwaves and the TVs that take her image into the rooms of her victims. Like a ring, this supernatural curse has no end. It is passed on by those who discover the way to escape it, as reproducible as the image on a videotape.

In *Ju-on: The Grudge* (Takashi Shimizu, 2003, Japan) "ju-on" is defined as the curse of one who dies in the grip of extreme rage, a fatal curse that is concentrated in the place where that person lived. The house in the movie is haunted, and its present owners and visitors are beset, by the mother (Takako Fuji as Kayako) and her little boy (Yuya Ozeki as Toshio) who were murdered there. In one of *Ju-on*'s striking moments of fear and repulsion, a woman is washing her hair in the shower when she touches someone else's hand in her hair. In another horror moment that is powerfully cinematic, a different woman (Misaki Ito as Hitomi) is shown going up to her apartment in an elevator with glass doors. She does not realize, because she is looking in the wrong direction, that she is passing a floor, shown in black and white, where the ghost boy is waiting. She passes that floor over and over until she arrives at her destination, a floor that like the rest of the film is in color.[41] That boy or someone like him is always waiting in a ghost movie, literally or equivocally present in our world and beyond the world we know, on its own floor on the other side of the elevator door.

Zombies: *White Zombie* and *Night of the Living Dead*

There are two kinds of zombies: mindless slaves and eaters of human flesh. The former are found primarily in Haiti, where voodoo priests and secret societies can condemn a person to zombification, particularly a person whose behavior has violated important social rules. The latter are the creation of George A. Romero,[12] who introduced them in *Night of the Living Dead* (1968); they are not cannibals, strictly speaking, because they eat the living, not each other. In the movies, both kinds have returned from the dead, but they do not have the advanced faculties of vampires and other varieties of the living dead. Also unlike vampires, they are regularly found in groups. They shuffle or move slowly, their eyes are glassy and in most cases they cannot speak. Their motivations are simple: to follow orders, if they are slaves, or to find people and eat them. They do not have the manners of a vampire, the memory of a mummy or the continuity of personality of a ghost. They cannot be reasoned with and, short of destroying them in some special way, they cannot be stopped. Of all the living dead, they are the closest to dead. Except for their compulsions or the orders they obey, their brains are empty. The word "zombie" (or "zombi") is derived from the African "nzambi," which can refer to a god, a fetish or the spirit of a dead person.[43]

In his study *The Serpent and the Rainbow*, Wade Davis established that in Haiti those who become zombies are not brought back from the dead, but are given a poison that produces a state long indistinguishable from death ("long" because in the case of a genuinely dead person, putrefaction would set in after a while, whereas a zombie would not decay), with virtually undetectable reflexes, respiration and heartbeat. What is most undetectable is that the paralyzed victim is conscious, but is unable to tell those who are pronouncing him or her dead, and who go on to mourn and bury the body, that he or she is alive. After the victim has been buried, the *bokor*, a voodoo priest skilled in the uses of sorcery and black magic, unearths the person he drugged and administers another poison that wipes out the victim's memory and higher functions (in some cases no second poison is used, only magic). At that point the victim is given a new name and a simple job and begins life as a mindless slave. The drugs do not accomplish zombification entirely on their own; cultural and religious beliefs influence the victim's interpretation of what is happening to him or her during the burial and the reviving ceremony. The bokor may sell the victim or maintain control. There is no cure for these poisons, but in rare cases they can wear off.

The movies have shown little interest in anthropologically rigorous approaches to Haitian culture or religion. They have taken the concept of the zombie, the mindless walking dead, and run with it.[44] In *White Zombie* (Victor Halperin, 1932, US), set in Haiti, the heroine (Madge Bellamy as Madeline) appears to die but probably does not. She is saved by the killing of the sorcerer (Bela Lugosi as Murder Legendre) who controls her and his other slaves, men he raised from the dead who work in the sugar mills. When he is dead, the sorcerer's mental and magical connection with the zombie is broken, allowing Madeline to return from death, or a state resembling it. It is possible that Legendre put her into a deathlike trance, taking possession of her soul, but did not kill her before he raised her from her coffin as a slave—perhaps a sex slave. She is living with the man (Robert Frazer as Charles) who paid Legendre to make her a zombie and who is now racked with guilt and dissatisfaction. Madeline returns as a live woman to her husband, Neil (John Harron) momentarily when Legendre is unconscious, and then completely when Legendre has been killed by Charles. If she was dead, she has been freed into life. Their marriage had been unconsummated, as she collapsed and apparently died just after the service. The film does not make it clear whether Charles and Madeline were having sex, although it's likely they were, but whatever happened between them, it was part of what Madeline had to undergo, the horror phase of her relationship with Neil, the honeymoon interrupted by a period with or as a monster—a phase (and its value) upon which, as we have seen, many horror movies insist. They are released from the horror to begin life as a couple.

White Zombie opens with drum music, for drums are as important an aspect as voodoo dolls and rituals in the zombie movie. Of all the music in Val Lewton's *I Walked with a Zombie* (Jacques Tourneur, 1943, US), the drums are the most powerful, instantly evocative of the voodoo ceremonies, which begin after the night walk taken by the nurse (Frances Dee as Betsy) with her patient (Christine Gordon as Jessica) to the voodoo temple (here called the "homefort"), the drums beginning as they pass the crossroads guarded by the tall zombie (Darby Jones as Carrefour). The drums are in the homefort but can be heard as far away as Jessica's bedroom. A song is also used with unusual skill in a sequence set in a tavern in town. The singer (Sir Lancelot) sings an "old song" about the family, then breaks it off when he realizes one of the people he is singing about—Jessica's brother-in-law, Wesley (James Ellison)—is in the audience. Betsy had been interested in the song. After Wes passes out, the singer appears and completes the song, directing it straight at Betsy and adding a new verse that includes the "nurse." In this threatening scene, Betsy is confronted with a living folklore that grows to embrace her.

Assigned the title *I Walked with a Zombie* by the studio, Lewton decided to adapt *Jane Eyre* and set it on the island of St Sebastian in the West Indies.[45] There is a sculpture of St Sebastian, complete with arrows and prominent in the picture, which was the figurehead on a slave ship that brought many blacks to the island. Within the fiction the sculpture serves as a reminder of the sacrifices made for freedom and the fight against enslavement of any kind, but within the symbolic structure of the movie Sebastian is known for having been taken for dead and surviving the first of two attempts to execute him (the first time by shooting him with arrows); zombies are relevant to both these interpretations. Jessica's husband, Paul (Tom Conway), is the Byronic figure. His brother, Wes, is an alcoholic in love with Jessica. Their mother, Mrs Rand (Edith Barrett), doubles as a priestess in the voodoo temple and is the one responsible for turning Jessica into a zombie (once when Mrs Rand was authentically possessed and Jessica was about to run off with Wes, she asked the priest to zombify Jessica).[46] There is no point when Jessica actually dies, at least according to her doctor, but after a fever and a coma induced by voodoo she is presumed dead by Mrs Rand and begins to behave like a zombie, showing no emotion and never speaking, with such higher functions as free will burned out of her nervous system. She responds to the drums that beckon her, she is controlled as the doll representing her is controlled and she does not bleed when wounded in a ceremony. Jessica's being a zombie disturbs the voodoo community, and they play drums and use a voodoo doll to summon her. It is not clear to what extent Wes is driven by his own desire to free her from being a zombie or is himself controlled by this voodoo (the film has it both ways), but Wes stabs Jessica with an arrow from the statue of St Sebastian just when the doll is stabbed, then takes her body into the surf. Thus she dies a definite death, whether or not it is her first, and he drowns. A final voice-over says that Jessica was wicked and was "dead in her own life…dead in the selfishness of her spirit." It is never absolutely settled, then, whether Jessica died before she began acting like a zombie. As in *White Zombie*, the question is left open. As in *Cat People*, the point is to capture in art how it feels to be on the ambiguous side of things, how it feels not to know exactly with whom or what one is walking.

The zombies in *Zombies of Mora Tau* (Edward L. Cahn, 1957, US) are emphatically dead. They guard a sunken underwater treasure. Underwater zombies are also depicted in *Shock Waves* (Ken Wiederhorn, 1977, US) and in Fulci's *Zombie* (Lucio Fulci, 1979, Italy), also known as *Zombi 2*, *Zombie Flesh Eaters* and *Island of the Living Dead*.[17]

Romero's zombies, imitated around the world so that they have become a distinct species (*Night of the Living Dead* is the most influential horror film since *Psycho*) have nothing to do with voodoo. It is never established exactly what it is that makes the unburied dead rise, though it could have begun with some kind of radiation brought back from outer space. It could also be that Hell is full, to paraphrase a line from *Dawn of the Dead* (George A. Romero, 1978, released 1979, Italy/US). The other sequels, as of this writing, are *Day of the Dead* (Romero, 1985, US) and *Land of the Dead* (Romero, 2005, Canada/France/US). *Diary of the Dead* (Romero, 2007, US) is not a sequel but starts a new story with its own sequels. A bite from a zombie is inevitably fatal, and whoever dies becomes a zombie. They cannot be stopped unless they are burned or their brains are destroyed, for it is the brain that animates the dead body. By now everybody knows to shoot a zombie in the head. This kind of zombie eats its victim alive, though it will also consume parts taken from the very recently dead. The pain and violence involved are incredible—like being eaten by a wild animal, with the extra component of revulsion. Beyond the central horror of being eaten by the dead, there is also something disgusting about the biting and the hands-on butchery performed by the zombies in these films, those of Romero and Fulci and others, where zombies tear abdomens open with their hands and pull out the guts or rip off limbs to bite into them with their reeking teeth—when, in other words, one sees images of people reduced to the lowest moral and physical level.

The painful, frightening and repulsive are all vivid in Romero's movies about the living dead. They are among the most straightforward examples of horror, and unlike many of their imitators, they have a vision of human nature and society that insists on being attended to. For if many horror films set good against evil and us against them in the same terms, Romero's set good against evil (often a human battle) and us against a version of ourselves (the zombies). Society has rarely been presented with such force as a system in which people consume each other, even if we know some of them are supposed to be dead. Human nature becomes a battlefield for the struggle between consciousness and mindlessness, between civilization and the violent and instinctual parts of ourselves—or in the terms of *Night of the Living Dead*, between the upstairs, which has windows, and the cellar, which does not. The cellar is rigid, closed off, overdefined, instinctual and often called "the safest place"—but not so safe if one needs to get out and zombies are coming in through the only door. The living in Romero's films can behave very badly. In contrast with the zombies, they have free will and can be condemned for the things they do. It is being human that makes us able to be evil. The zombies, at least in *Night* and *Dawn*, have no moral force—although they begin to show moral awareness in *Day* and *Land*. They are horrors, but they have not chosen evil. They become the conditions of the world, the backdrop against which the moral and immoral actions of the living characters are judged.

Human nature is most effectively deployed between two characters in *Night*: Ben (Duane Jones), who happens to be black,[48] represents consciousness and Harry (Karl Hardman) represents the more primitive drives, especially self-preservation. Harry is selfish, self-important, hypercritical, cowardly and only superficially civilized. Always putting himself and what is his first—his territory, which is the cellar, and his wife (Marilyn Eastman as Helen) and daughter (Kyra Schon as Karen)—Harry is unable to commit to the community when well-coordinated group action by the living, most of which is directed by Ben, is needed.[49] The upstairs of the farmhouse that the characters are defending has doors and windows—ways to get in or out—as well as the "windows" of radio and TV and the monster-controlling fireplace, a source of torches. If the house were taken as a symbolic structure analogous to human nature and culture, the main floor would be the place of perception, communication and insight, of sight and the mind and the moral impulses (such as to help those who need help) along with the impulse to control the uncivilized, while the cellar would be the unconscious and the dark and the baser instincts, where there are no morals but only the determination to survive, and where the brutality of the outside may find a home (considering the ways the zombie daughter kills her mother with a trowel and eats her father's arm). The cellar has only one door in or out of it and no vision of the changing outside world, because the unconscious and its drives almost never change. The cellar that Harry calls "the safest place" and "the strongest place" does, in the end, prove the only safe place for Ben to hide once all the other characters are dead. It is ironic and typical of the politics of Romero's *Dead* films that death comes to Ben through a main-floor window when he is shot. Long before *Halloween*, *Night of the Living Dead* brought the unhappy open ending to the modern horror film, although as we have seen, it was partly anticipated in this respect by *The Birds*.

Most of society, from human relations to institutions, is judged and found wanting in the *Dead* movies, beginning with the patrol that shoots Ben and going on to embrace the entire culture that is often shown to be corrupt, sexist and racist. Harry is as rapacious and self-centered in human terms as the zombies outside. He is the part of us that the best of us is set against in these pictures, and his influence can be felt in several later characters as well as in the widely disseminated sense of human evil, of the culture that may not be worth saving, that runs through the films. There is no return to the norm in these movies. In sequel after sequel, the living lose ground.

Beginning with the farmhouse in *Night* and the mall in *Dawn*, the semi-defensible space is central to the *Dead* pictures. Zombies are always breaking through the boarded-up windows and barricaded doors, groping through any open space. The territory of the living must retain its integrity if people are to survive there, and at or near the endings of *Night*, *Dawn*, *Day* and *Land* the no longer defensible fortress is opened to zombie traffic.

The black-and-white cinematography of *Night* gives great power to the black: particularly the shadows and the enveloping night. Later zombie pictures were shot in color, beginning with *Let Sleeping Corpses Lie* (Jorge Grau, 1974, Spain/Italy; also released as *The Living Dead at Manchester Morgue*, *Breakfast at the Manchester Morgue* and *Don't Open the Window*; literally titled *Do Not Speak Ill of the Dead*) and continuing with *Dawn of the Dead* and *Zombie*.

Much of the violence in *Night* and its sequels is directed against zombies, and it shows humanity reduced to the single exercise of killing with whatever is available. The media are reliable in *Night* as they are not in the later pictures: the radio and TV provide necessary and valid information (the list of rescue stations becomes invalid only later, at the start of *Dawn*).[50]

The most repulsive moment comes when the zombies on the dark lawn, lit by the burning truck, eat the parts of the teenagers, Tom (Keith Wayne) and Judy (Judith Ridley). The imagery of this uncompromising, no-holds-barred scene, partly inspired by EC horror comics, was widely imitated.

In the beginning of a theme that runs throughout the *Dead* films, a zombie picks up a rock to break a window. In each of the sequels the zombies learn more about the use of tools as they begin to develop a more advanced existence.

For the record, the zombies aren't called zombies in this picture, but "ghouls" and "flesh eaters," nor does anyone take a bite out of a living victim on camera (that begins in *Dawn*). The working title of the film was *Night of the Flesh Eaters*. "Zombie" stuck to Romero's living dead when *Dawn of the Dead* was released in Europe, in a cut supervised by producer Dario Argento, as *Zombi*.

Dawn opens three weeks after *Night* as the heroine (Gaylen Ross as Fran) wakes from an unshown nightmare. The attack on the media begins right away, as WGON-TV, as in "gone," runs an outdated list of stations because the list is the only guarantee that people will keep watching. The culture begins to fall apart in *Dawn*, and the media's quarreling experts reflect this, but the problem is seen most clearly in an inner-city housing project that a group of soldiers has been assigned to attack. The building's African American and Hispanic occupants have been refusing to burn or decapitate their dead, wanting to wait for services and to honor the dignity there is in death, and they are socially targeted and shot by the soldiers as well as eaten by their loved ones.

Fran's boyfriend, Stephen (David Emge), steals a news helicopter and takes himself, Fran and two soldiers fresh from the assault on the housing project (Ken Foree as Peter, the strong, smart black man in this picture,[51] and Scott H. Reiniger as Roger) out of the city and to an isolated shopping mall, where they make a home. The mall is a ready symbol of consumerism, the primary target of this satiric sequel in which zombies consume people and people consume goods. Looking at a milling crowd of zombies who could almost be shoppers, Peter observes, "They're us, that's all."

By the end of *Dawn*, the TV displays only static. In *Day* there is no broadcasting at all, and in *Land* the only TV is closed-circuit and dominated by ads. *Diary*, for its part, gives credence only to independent video.

As *Dawn* closes, Fran and Peter, who are not a romantic couple, fly off in the helicopter into the titular dawn, their fuel low and their future uncertain. Fran is the pilot, and she is pregnant. (In the unpublished script, which was written by Romero as all the later

Dead films were—with John Russo and Romero collaborating on the script for *Night*—Peter shoots himself in the head as he had originally planned, and Fran raises her head into the helicopter blades, both of them making sure they will not come back after death. The script ends with the zombies' eating Fran on the roof of the mall.) It is an open ending but a somber one, a gesture of hope in an increasingly hopeless context.

For their extreme gore and violence, both *Dawn* and *Day* were released with self-imposed X ratings. Even with no sexual activity onscreen, both films needed to take this drastic measure to avoid censorship. The *Dead* films have very little sexual energy and no sexual plot developments except for Fran's pregnancy. There is never a sexually bonded surviving couple, though a man and a woman may be among those who get away at the end. There is no intercutting of scenes of sex and horror, which are normally thought to enhance each other. The crisis of living death is so all-pervasive that there is little interest in creating life or in making a sexual claim to life. Romero makes other movies' insistence on interweaving sex and death seem optimistic.

Day of the Dead begins with a dream that we do see, as Sarah (Lori Cardille) imagines herself in a small white room with a calendar on one wall, marking down the days to Halloween. As zombie hands thrust through the wall, she wakes up in a helicopter—as if in a jump cut from the end of *Dawn*—piloted by a black man (Terry Alexander as John) who sees the underground base the living characters are inhabiting, which includes a vast holding area full of goods and records from pre-zombie times, as a museum of futility, "a 14-mile tombstone." As a repository, the base is an expansion of the mall in *Dawn*, but it is also a place where a group of scientists, at first guarded and assisted by a group of soldiers, is trying to find a cure for the plague.

The top soldier, Rhodes (Joe Pilato), takes over the base and puts the scientists under his command. He becomes the Harry in this grim picture, his cruelty, rigidity, stupidity and desperation enhanced by authority. One of the scientists, the mad one, Logan (Richard Liberty), is training a captured zombie, Bub (Howard Sherman), to follow commands and to speak—and rewarding him with body parts taken from dead soldiers. The battle between scientists and soldiers ends when Sarah, John and the radio operator take the helicopter and flee the base for an apparently safe island, while the soldiers in the overrun base are devoured. When Bub shoots and salutes Rhodes (who then gets eaten), it is clear that he has a memory, an emotional life, a dawning moral consciousness and a sense of irony.

On the island Sarah puts an X on her calendar so that it shows the correct date. This picks up from her opening dream. She is still dedicated to the human practice of keeping records, keeping track. (John had predicted that all her scientific results would be added to the piles of reports no one would read in the storage facility.) Thus the final shot of the calendar is a tribute to science and to the potential continuity of civilization.

During the long wait for the next picture, when it appeared the film would appear in the late 1990s, Romero granted an interview. He told *Fangoria* the new film would be "about the devouring of the old society":

The *Dead* movies always fit into the respective decades they were made in. The 60s were active, angry and much more overtly political. The 70s were "Spend, baby, the times are good." The 80s was the downfall of that and a collapse into darker territory.

The 90s version would basically be about people ignoring the problem. To me, that's what things are about now—somehow conning the people to look the other way. The zombies would be treated the way the homeless are treated.[52]

This is the key to the ways the *Dead* films correspond to their times and choose their social and political targets, as each movie both reflects and addresses its decade. *Land* turned out to address the 2000s (as did *Diary*) as well as the 1990s.

In *Land of the Dead*, which takes on the class system and the economy—along with the running theme of the development of the zombies—Romero's primary target is how some people can ignore real and pressing conditions, trying to isolate themselves from the lowest class, which the zombies represent here, as well as from the real members of the lower class, who live in slums. The zombies are excluded from the city by fences and rivers, and the poor are excluded from the fancy condos that are being offered to the elite. The housing project (Fiddler's Green) that is being set up in a remodeled tower, and in fact the city, are run by Kaufman (Dennis Hopper), a selfish capitalist and another Harry. Fiddler's Green resembles both a high-class residential skyscraper and an enclosed mall and reminds one of the building, as well as the ads for it, in *Shivers*.

The dead evolve in *Land*, showing emotion for each other, the ability to unite for a common goal and a relatively advanced ability to use tools. They are led by a thinking and feeling zombie who is functionally similar to Bub although he has not undergone any conditioning or training. He is a former gas-station owner named Big Daddy (Eugene Clark), who is the lead black in this picture and who is introduced as an example of how the zombies, who used to be us, are trying to be us again. We see Big Daddy responding to the bell at his gas station and going to the pump, then doing something that resembles talking to other zombies. (It is said early on that both the zombies and the humans are "pretending to be alive.") At the beginning of the film, a commentator worries what would happen "if these creatures ever develop the power to think, to reason, even in the most primitive ways," and that is the trajectory Big Daddy follows as he develops an outraged sense of justice and compassion and leads an army of zombies on the fortified city, eventually breaking all the way into Fiddler's Green. What is surprising is that the zombies, not just talented ones like Bub and Big Daddy, engage our sympathy and our rooting interest. For the first time in the series we feel sorry when some of them are destroyed. Our introduction to the zombies comes in a moonlit churchyard, where some are playing music in a gazebo. The scene is an homage to horror art and an example of horror beauty.

There are significant variations and extensions of the themes, actions and images of the earlier films. After Big Daddy discovers how to use a gun, he teaches another zombie to shoot it. Once they are on the move, many of the zombies use tools and weapons. When Kaufman's nemesis and former assistant, Cholo (John Leguizamo)—fired because he wanted to move into Fiddler's Green and is a working-class Hispanic—is bitten, we expect him to follow the pattern and ask to be shot in the head, but instead Cholo says he doesn't want to be shot. Making it clear that he would be interested in experiencing the change and linking the zombies to the lowest urban class, he says, "I always wanted to see how the other half lives." For the first time in the series, the undead are called zombies (by Kaufman). When Kaufman is trapped while trying to drive away from the overrun city, Big Daddy, who remembers how to use a pump and is glad to find gas in the one next to where Kaufman is parked, soaks the car and goes off to get fire, of which he is the first zombie not to be afraid, returning to blow up the car along with Kaufman. Although he is about to be bitten by the deceased Cholo, the upper-class villain is actually killed by the working-class hero, a zombie—much as Rhodes was shot by Bub, but this time it is clear that the villain and the zombie are at the poles of a sociopolitical structure.

After Romero, zombies came back hungry. Internationally, the films are consistent in having zombies return from the dead with limited functions and contagious bites, determined to eat people and in most cases vulnerable to head wounds. Some of the Italian pictures chalk up the onslaught of the living dead to the action of a virus—as in *Virus* (Bruno Mattei, 1980, Italy; also known as *Hell of the Living Dead*, *Night of the Zombies* and *Zombie Creeping Flesh*)—that may have been designed as a bacteriological weapon. In *Virus* the intention is to make Third World populations devour each other.[53] But there are many other causes. *Let Sleeping Corpses Lie*, a Spanish–Italian co-production, is ecologically oriented. Its zombies are animated by a machine that sends some kind of force or vibration into the ground that is designed to rid farms of insects and parasites (it works on their nervous systems, driving them mad so that they attack each other) but is also able to activate the recently dead, an effect not anticipated by the Ministry of Agriculture, which is conducting the expanding experiment. *Let Sleeping Corpses Lie* is the first picture to show zombies ripping open and devouring the living on camera and, as previously mentioned, in color. Fulci's *Zombie*,[54] set in the Antilles, establishes that voodoo is causing the problem, which also affects the buried dead, and some pictures followed that up. At the end of most zombie movies, including Romero's, the undead are spreading without check.

Mummies: *The Mummy's Ghost*

The god Osiris was the first mummy[55] and was often portrayed in mummy wrappings. According to Plutarch, when he was an earthly king, Osiris taught the Egyptians to grow crops, gave them laws and religion and even taught them to make beer. When he traveled outside Egypt, he brought the knowledge of agriculture with him. He had two brothers, Horus and Set, and two sisters, Isis and Nephthys; Isis was his wife. Set murdered Osiris by sealing him alive in a coffin, but Isis found the coffin and brought it back. On her travels, Isis gave birth to a son (she conceived by flying over the dead Osiris's body as a hawk), the younger Horus. When her child died from the sting of a scorpion, Isis asked for help from Ra, the sun god, who sent Thoth (called Hermes in Greek mythology) to teach her a spell. Reciting the spell, she raised Horus from the dead. Then Set found the coffin and cut Osiris's body into 14 pieces and scattered them across Egypt. Isis searched for the pieces and found all of them except the genitals,[56] of which she made a sculpture. Each piece was buried as if it were the entire body of Osiris. That is how Plutarch related the myth, but Frazer went on to include a "native Egyptian" version in which Isis and Nephthys gathered the parts of Osiris's body and—with the help of Anubis, Thoth and Horus—assembled them, then wrapped the body and performed over it the rites that became tradition. That was the first mummy, and Isis waved her wings over it and revived it in the Underworld, where Osiris became king. His names included Lord of the Underworld and Ruler of the Dead. As a god of the corn, of wheat and barley, his coming back to life was celebrated when the crops annually returned to life. Wrapped as a mummy like Osiris and having the same rites performed, the dead could be assured of coming to life in the Underworld.

Shortly after Howard Carter discovered the tomb of King Tutankhamen in 1922 and opened the burial chamber in 1923, the myth of the mummy's curse, effective against the violators of tombs, was born. Carter's patron and partner, George Molyneux Herbert, Earl of Carnarvon, died from complications of a mosquito bite in 1923, two months after the opening of the chamber. The mummy itself was found in 1924. Tut's tomb and the death of Carnarvon were recent news when Universal released *The Mummy* in 1932 and set its opening in Egypt in 1921 and the rest of its story in the early 1930s.

Mummies have always been capable of being resurrected, but not in the world of the living. They remind us of things that come back from the dead, like the wheat. But an undead mummy, set loose among mortals, is a figure of death as well as of unnatural life. It is death come awake and bearing death with it, determined to carry out a plan or enforce a curse. It is the force of the past and of unresolved compulsion.

Directed by Karl Freund from a script by John Balderston, *The Mummy* is similar to *Dracula* (1931), to which both men had contributed, in the way it sets up a love triangle among the supernatural being, a woman and her human lover, overseen by an older man who knows and respects the old ways. The mummy is Imhotep, played by Boris Karloff (makeup by Jack Pierce, who had done Universal's Dracula and Frankenstein and would later do the Wolf Man). Imhotep was buried alive for sacrilegiously attempting to use the Scroll of Thoth to revive his dead lover, the princess Anckesenamon. The scroll contains the spell Isis used to revive Osiris from the dead (a change from its ancient function, which was to revive Horus). It was buried with Imhotep so that no one would ever use it again, a definitive example of a forbidden text. The Van Helsing figure, Dr Muller, is played by the actor who played Van Helsing, Edward Van Sloan. The young man, Frank Whemple, who is not as ineffectual as John Harker, is again played by David Manners, and his father, Sir Joseph Whemple, is played by Arthur Byron. The young woman, Helen Grosvenor, who has ancient Egyptian blood on her mother's side, is played by Zita Johann.

The curse is placed not on those who open Imhotep's tomb but on whoever opens the box containing the Scroll of Thoth. In 1921 Sir Joseph Whemple is stopped from opening the box by Dr Muller—who makes it clear how dangerous it is to open the box and accept its curse of death and eternal punishment—but instructs his assistant to open it after Muller is gone. Unfortunately, while Muller and Whemple are outside, the assistant feels he cannot wait to open the treasure. He finds the scroll and reads the spell under his breath. This revives the mummy (whose organs were not removed when he was buried alive, so that he has all his working parts, and from whose sarcophagus the spells to protect his soul on its journey into the afterlife were scratched out, so that he has not left this world), who slowly opens his eyes and lets his hands drop from the wrappings, then takes the scroll and leaves the assistant a laughing madman. It is the best first-victim scene in the classic horror film.[57] When Whemple and Muller return and find the mummy gone, the assistant explains, "He went for a little walk" and adds, "You should have seen his face!" The context for his reviving is set by Dr Muller, who believes that the gods of Egypt still live and that the old spells retain their potency.

In 1932 Imhotep visits a dig, introduces himself to Frank as Ardath Bey and provides the location of the tomb of Anckesenamon. His skin is dry but could pass for that of an old man. It is both amusing and informative that he doesn't like to be touched. Imhotep wants access to Anckesenamon's mummy so he can read the scroll over it and bring her back to life, to make her undead as he is. But after he has met Helen, who is the reincarnation of his beloved princess, he decides to kill and revive her rather than raise the mummy, for she has the soul of Anckesenamon that her mummy lacks. As he puts it, they can share an eternity of love if she will undergo a few moments of horror—yet an eternity of love with an undead creature is itself a horror. Helen feels that half of her is an ancient princess and half is a modern woman. As one part of her is attracted to the mummy and his transcendentally romantic offer as well as aware of the pain and horror he underwent for her, the other part is attracted to Frank. She appeals to Isis, who teaches her the ancient words that successfully entreat the goddess to destroy the mummy; she speaks as Anckesenamon to do this. As he is dying, Imhotep ages until he is nothing but bones. Then, under Muller's guidance, Frank draws Helen's soul back to the present. The ancient mummy and the pull of Helen's past are both vanquished, and the modern couple can live freely in a modern world.

Imhotep represents undeath as well as undying love, which is mixed up with his compulsive desire to see through to its proper conclusion a project to which he has been dedicated for thousands of years. There is no stopping him except by appeal to the forces that animate him; he can be destroyed only by a supernatural power. Imhotep can speak, and his words carry a threatening but polite edge. Thus he can plead his case with Helen instead of just picking her up and carrying her off. He can also defy Muller in a drawing room as articulately as Dracula (in the Mummy films of the 1940s Kharis was silent). A creature of desire and sacrilege, he goes after what he wants—like Kharis, he is almost impossible to stop or evade—but we feel that he loves his would-be bride as Dracula does not. Vampires and mummies are the romantics of the supernatural subgenre, but with a difference.[58] While Dracula wants a bride to be his companion and in some cases his beloved, one in a series of lovers, Imhotep loves only Anckesenamon and has done so for 3,700 years.

The Mummy is a cosmic romance stretched across vast time. It brings the past—Imhotep and the reincarnated spirit of Anckesenamon—into the present where they do not belong, where they can remain and, undead, love each other forever only if horror wins the day. We may find ourselves rooting for this couple—Imhotep and Anckesenamon, not exactly Imhotep and Helen—more than for other couplings of monsters and humans because they share a love that has lasted through the centuries, because he can reach her even through her new mind and body when he summons her spirit, and because what motivated Imhotep in the first place, back in ancient Egypt, was his love for the dying Anckesenamon and his hubristic desire to undo her death. That this love leads him to plan and perform horrors turns the whole romance dark. He becomes Helen's demon lover, the dead thing she must escape. She has to fight to be Helen, and she has to go into her past self to do this, fully becoming Anckesenamon if she is ever to be fully Helen again. Submitting to the horror offers her an opportunity for integration and healing after it has introduced a split. (This healing after a split can happen in horror films, in spite of what happens to Dr Jekyll.) Anckesenamon is not exorcised but goes back to playing her regular anonymous role in Helen's psyche. But the mummy and the evil it represents are blasted by the gods and rejected by the present. The scroll whose discovery led to all of this is burned by the power of Isis, closing the forbidden text forever as the mummy and its power are undone, vindicating the pharaoh who buried the scroll and reinforcing the tenets and curses of the old religion. The last shot moves down from the burning scroll to the skeleton that was Imhotep, emphasizing not the couple (shown in the previous shot) but the forbidden text and the monster—and what Isis has done to punish sacrilege and unholy desire.

The Mummy's Hand (Christy Cabanne, 1940, US) used much of the ancient Egyptian story from The Mummy but made many well-known changes. Imhotep is renamed Kharis, and Anckesenamon is renamed Ananka. Kharis had tried to bring Ananka back from the dead through the use of tana leaves, not the Scroll of Thoth. His tongue was cut out before he was buried alive so that his curses would not offend the gods, and the "forbidden" tana leaves were buried with him so that no one else would ever use them. A group of priests, dedicated to preserving the integrity of the tombs, moves Kharis's body to a tomb adjacent to Ananka's. The ironic curse placed against Kharis, for violating the rules of the ancient gods and trying to resurrect Ananka, is to reinforce their will and keep Ananka properly entombed. He is to guard her tomb for eternity. Those who attempt to defile her tomb will be in mortal danger and subject to an immortal curse; this ties the story back into that of Carter and Carnarvon. The priests sustain Kharis, for he "never really died,"[59] by giving him the fluid from three dissolved tana leaves every night during the cycle of the full moon. Should they want him to be able to move, they use nine leaves. All this is explained to the new high priest of Karnak (George Zucco as Andoheb) by his dying predecessor at the beginning of the picture, using footage from The Mummy with some new shots to deal with the change of actors and the change from scroll to leaves, which gives The Mummy's Hand the feel of a sequel, though it is also the beginning of a new series.[60]

While The Mummy kept out of tombs, The Mummy's Hand offers the full mise-en-scène of the Mummy picture: the tombs and caves, the torches and lanterns, the desert, the crucible in which the tana leaves are dissolved. There is also the wrapped walking Mummy (Tom Tyler as Kharis), a figure seen only briefly at the start of The Mummy. What drives the Mummy in this picture, though in the next two his motives are more complex, is his desire for tana fluid. If he could get more than the priests are willing to give him, he would become an uncontrollable monster. The priest in charge of Kharis selects his victims. The motive of the priest is simple: to kill all those who entered Ananka's tomb. Kharis is a simpler figure than Imhotep, still a figure of death and desire but less autonomous, though he does sometimes reveal a will of his own. Kharis is both controlled and served by the priests. He needs them to brew the tana fluid and, eventually, to transport him so he can pursue his victims in America. In almost every sequel, a priest expresses the side of Kharis that risks forbidden desire (which is always punished in the Mummy films), falling for the heroine and trying to make her and himself immortal with tana fluid.

Those who cross the desert to open Ananka's tomb are Steve Banning (Dick Foran), his sidekick Babe Jenson (Wallace Ford), Dr Petrie (Charles Trowbridge), the magician Solvani (Cecil Kellaway), and his daughter, Marta (Peggy Moran). The curse to which they become subject, which is repeated throughout the Kharis pictures with some rewording, is: "Who shall defile the temples of the ancient gods, a cruel and violent death shall be his fate, and never shall his soul find rest unto eternity." It should be noted that while Kharis and the priests are the enforcers of the curse, its power comes from the still-powerful ancient gods, and the gods must once have pronounced such a curse on Kharis, who suffered a cruel and violent death and whose soul never has found rest. The defilers open the tomb of Kharis when they are hoping to find that of Ananka.

The Mummy is almost always alone with his victim, and he usually kills by strangling with one hand. One leg and one arm are not functional yet. To move them he will need far more tana fluid, which he never gets. The dragging leg provides his characteristic walk. While it makes him slower, it contributes to the impression that nothing can stop him.

One night Kharis advances on the tents where the unbelievers are camped and carries off Marta. His not killing her indicates that the image of the monster's carrying the unconscious woman has become a ritualistic favorite. Kharis takes Marta to Andoheb, who ties her to an altar and tells her that he is going to make both of them immortal like Kharis. Babe shoots Andoheb. Then Babe and Steve stop Kharis from drinking the tana fluid Andoheb had prepared, and set him on fire. At the end, Steve and Marta are a couple. The riches from Ananka's tomb—and, we later discover, her sarcophagus—are going to America with them, and Steve has been vindicated with a job at the Scripps Museum. It's a very pro-American ending.

The curse against these characters motivated a sequel: *The Mummy's Tomb* came out two years later and was set 30 years after the events of the previous film. Marta and Steve had been happily married a long time when she died.[61] Their grown son is John Banning (John Hubbard), and his fiancée is Isobel Evans (Elyse Knox). Steve's sister is Jane Banning (Mary Gordon). Babe is played by Wallace Ford again, but his last name has been changed to Hanson. As he would be till the end of the series, Kharis is played by Lon Chaney, Jr, wearing his fully realized, iconic final makeup (again by Jack Pierce), which hides one of his eyes. The high priest is Andoheb (George Zucco), who survived his wounds. He indoctrinates the new high priest, Mehemet Bey (Turhan Bey), who accepts the responsibility of taking Kharis to Mapleton, Massachusetts and wiping out the Bannings and all their descendants along with any others who defiled Ananka's tomb. Andoheb prays that Mehemet Bey will not fall victim to temptation as he did. The priest's temptation has become an important part of the story, one that will be repeated here and in *The Mummy's Ghost* (Reginald LeBorg, 1943, released 1944, US).

The priest takes a job as caretaker of the Mapleton cemetery and sends Kharis out from the resting place of the dead (the equivalent of the tomb setting) to strangle Steve in his bedroom. The Mummy is incongruous in the New England woods as he walks through them to reach the Banning house, but that does not make him less frightening or uncanny. One point of this wartime film is to bring the Mummy and the priest (who is, for once, distinctly foreign-looking, though he doesn't look Egyptian) to America, to threaten the audience on its own turf. Kharis is shown to be charged with the formidable powers and curses of ancient Egypt, even when he is far from home. His foreignness in space and time—for he comes from the past as well as from Egypt—makes him a powerful unknown. Instead of being a fish out of water, he brings the water with him.

Kharis moves only during the full moon, a time that in horror movies has great power. He comes back as a threat with the periodicity of the full moon, returning like a destructive Osiris, like a force of nature but also like the force and domain of the supernatural. He walks straight through walls and fences, anything that is in his way, just as he will let nothing stop him from fulfilling his project.

After Steve, Kharis kills Jane and Babe. John takes a strip of wrapping Kharis left behind, snagged by a branch, to Professor Norman (Frank Reicher), who confirms that it and the mold on the victims' throats came from a mummy. The only one left to kill is John, who decides to get married before going to war (the film was made in 1942). One day the priest sees John with Isobel and feels the pull of temptation. The characteristics of the living Kharis, who was a high priest, have been split once again into the Mummy and the priest. The priest is the mortal who can speak, who performs rites, who can function in the normal world and who almost succeeds in his sacrilegious desire to live with a woman in an undead romance. All of these are traits Kharis had before he became a silent monster.

When the priest tells Kharis he is going to take a wife, become immortal with her and minister to Kharis through eternity, the Mummy is clearly displeased. Still he goes to collect Isobel as the priest directs. The priest tells Isobel, who is tied to a table, what he plans to do to her—an iconic scene, taken from *Hand* and repeated in *Ghost*. The priest is interrupted by a torch-bearing crowd and shot. They pursue Kharis, who has carried the unconscious Isobel to the Banning house, and burn him.

The threat to Mapleton is revived when it turns out that Kharis has survived and the priests become aware of it. If *The Mummy's Hand* dealt with opening the tomb in Egypt and *The Mummy's Tomb* pursued in America the consequences of opening it, *The Mummy's Ghost* drew the original Egyptian story—and *The Mummy*—back into play and let Kharis find the reincarnation of Ananka. Because Mehemet Bey failed, the high priest (Zucco again) must send a new priest (John Carradine as Yousef Bey) to America to find Kharis and take him home, along with the body of Ananka, which is in the Scripps Museum where Steve Banning brought it. The indoctrination gives this sequel the usual opportunity to summarize its predecessors but adds the new information that Ananka's soul was cursed too, for she was a priestess and her loving Kharis was forbidden, and it is important that she not be reincarnated so that her soul cannot seek salvation in a new body. Andoheb begins the story of Kharis, and Professor Norman finishes it in a lecture to his class. One of Norman's students introduces the reflexive aspect of this picture when he suggests that Kharis might have been "a man made up as a mummy, to keep the legend alive," but Norman assures him the creature was real. Throughout *The Mummy's Ghost* there are many references to and expectations concerning the ways things go in a Mummy movie, and they are systematically frustrated on the way to this picture's original conclusion. For this is one classic horror movie in which the monster gets the woman and the norm is not restored.

The woman he gets is Amina (Ramsay Ames). She works at the university where her boyfriend, Tom (Robert Lowery), is a student. She is of Egyptian descent and finds the mention of Egypt creepy. She reacts to it, every time, as if someone had mentioned sex, of which she appears also to be afraid. (If "sex" is substituted for "Egypt" in their dialogue, the scene still plays. For example, Tom says that every time he mentions Egypt, she freezes up.) Unaware that she is the reincarnation of Ananka, Amina does not know why ancient Egypt seems so threatening, but what Egypt finally means for her is death and forbidden love. It is the demon lover, here a force of sex and death at once, who will take her in the end, and she fears the lover long before she is aware that she has one. In *The Mummy's Ghost* there is a forbidden union of monster and woman that leads to their temporally and metaphysically syncing up, becoming at last two mummies. But if they are now free to seek their salvation, this doesn't last long, for just as Amina completes her transformation into Ananka, Kharis carries her into a swamp from which there is no escape. As they drown, the curse is intoned in a voice-over: for daring to love each other and defying the will of the ancient gods, they have been punished with a cruel and violent death. The gods appear to be in power—unless we feel that Kharis and Ananka have escaped them in a romantic apotheosis, in which case the curse has been evaded and is inappropriate, its intonation a contradiction. The couple of Amina and Tom is no more, and Tom's little dog, Peanuts, looks confused on the bank of the swamp into which Amina has disappeared. It is a stunning ending in which horror reaches out to claim Amina, aging her to Kharis's age, the age of Ananka, making her skin dry up and her hair go entirely white (it has been going white in streaks since she first saw Kharis—a device imitated in later movies). The ancient couple is reunited, and it may be satisfying in terms of their long attachment that they die, or pass into another phase of undeath, together. Amina's transformation is an extremely resonant horror moment—her being captured by the irresistible pull of Kharis, destiny and time, turning rigid and ancient in the moonlight, moving from a face we recognize to that of an impossibly old woman, a living mummy, as we cringe at her image, feeling pity, revulsion and fear. (The scene was inspired by one in *Lost Horizon* [Frank Capra, 1937, US], in which a woman suddenly ages when she leaves Shangri-La.) What happens to Amina by purely supernatural means as Kharis carries her is what Imhotep wanted to do to Helen.

That should have been the end of the series. It was ambitious and ambiguous, affirming the unpredictable and counter-formulaic in this supposedly formulaic genre, and it ended the story of Kharis and Ananka. But one more sequel came out, one that made little sense: *The Mummy's Curse* (Leslie Goodwins, 1944, released 1945, US). The swamp is now apparently in Louisiana[62] instead of Massachusetts. The mummy of Ananka (Virginia Christine) rises from the mud after a steam shovel exposes her. Cleaned up, she appears to be a young woman who has amnesia and has inexplicably lost the look of a mummy (nor does she resemble Amina). Kharis, uncovered by a bulldozer, comes back looking like himself. At the conclusion the mummies, both apparently dead, are shipped to the Scripps Museum, another American victory.

Ananka turns out to know a great deal about mummy wrappings and ancient Egyptian history. The knowledge seems to her like a dream. All the way back to Imhotep and his pool—through Amina, and the shadow of Kharis that crosses her face as she sleeps—the knowledge of ancient Egypt, the contact with reincarnation and the presence of the Mummy have been tied to dreaming. Dreaming and mummies were linked even in one of the earliest mummy films, the 1911 short *The Mummy*, in which a professor dreams that a mummy comes to life.[63]

What is most compelling about Kharis is his slow presence—the fact that he has shown up and is advancing on a victim or through a tomb—and behind that the concept of an undying killer who is also, tragically, a figure in rebellion against the gods, who has been doomed to enforce their will, an endlessly questing figure of night and the moon. Repetition is part of his strength—he always comes back with his full mythic power—and the similar sequels provide a resonant structure for his eternal return.[64]

Others Back from the Dead: *The Walking Dead*

There are other people who come back from the dead in physical form, like ghosts who have not left their bodies. They are undead but not zombies, for they have most of their basic functions. For one thing, they can usually speak. They remain supernatural creatures, animated by a change or exception in the laws of nature and the rules of death. Many of these films are about the need to accept death over living death.

In *The Ghoul* (T. Hayes Hunter, 1933, UK) an Egyptologist (Boris Karloff as Professor Morlant) comes back after death thanks to his faith, his will power, a sacred jewel and the power of the full moon, but he comes back as a killer, determined to find the person who stole the jewel from his corpse. The dead often come back as killers, though not always. In *The Walking Dead* (Michael Curtiz, 1936, US) a pianist, John Elman (Boris Karloff), who is framed and executed for a murder, then revived by a scientist (Edmund Gwenn as Dr Beaumont, who wants to know what Elman experienced after death), suffers from amnesia. Nevertheless, he finds his way to each of the men who framed him and, for only as long as each of those scenes lasts, not only remembers everything, but also knows more than he did when he was alive. The pianist behaves, as Beaumont puts it, "as if he were the instrument of some supernatural power," a force with aspects of an avenging angel and a clear sense of right and wrong. He knows immediately, without knowing how he knows, whether a person is his enemy, and his assessments are just. When he meets one of the villains and asks, "Why did you have me killed?" that person backs into a train or otherwise disposes of himself; the reanimated pianist is not actually a killer, though he is a vehicle for death.

"Death is better" is the motto of *Pet Sematary* (Mary Lambert, 1989, US), adapted by Stephen King from his novel. Those who are buried in an old forbidden burial ground (one that lies beyond the cemetery built by the children for their pets) come back possessed by the evil spirit of the place. To some extent like Elman, they bring the world of death back with them. A doctor (Louis Creed, played by Dale Midkiff) who has an unprofessional difficulty accepting death revives the family cat when it is run over, and it comes back a vicious monster of a cat. The same thing happens when he buries his son and finally his wife. Far better than Louis's desperate actions and the horror generated by an attempt to change the course of nature is the mild attitude of Elman in *The Walking Dead*, who feels comfortable hanging out in cemeteries until it is time to return to one forever.

Werewolves and Other Shape-Shifters: *The Wolf Man* and *Cat People*

The shape-shifter is the supernatural equivalent of the transforming monster, Jekyll and Hyde. The werewolf, or "man-wolf," is supernaturally afflicted but not undead. With the exception of Universal's Wolf Man, Larry Talbot (Lon Chaney, Jr), the werewolf, when killed, remains dead. The silver bullet and the pentagram were added to the werewolf legend by Hollywood, but werewolf legends go back to ancient times on their own, and the belief in the actual existence of werewolves and other shape-shifters was as prevalent in medieval times as the belief in witches—one of whose abilities was said to be that of changing into another form. A shape-shifter who transforms exclusively between a wolf and a human is a werewolf. In the witchcraft trials in Basel in the year 1407, many so-called werewolves were tortured and burned.[65] In sixteenth century France, tens of thousands of people were charged with being werewolves.[66]

Lycanthropy is named after King Lycaon of Arcadia, who in Ovid's version of the myth tried to feed human flesh to Zeus, who became so angry that he turned Lycaon into a wolf.[67] Lycanthropy is a mental disorder in which the afflicted person thinks he or she is a wolf, runs on all fours and satisfies an appetite for raw or living meat, but the word is also used to describe those who, according to folklore, have the actual power to transform into wolves.

Many researchers have tried to discover what human behavior could have accounted for the worldwide belief in shape-shifters and the widely held belief in werewolves.[68] Some murderers, including those who have kidnapped and eaten children,[69] and even some soldiers have behaved like bloodthirsty animals. The Old Norse berserkers, whose violent rampages gave rise to the word "berserk," wore bearskins into battle and felt that they took on the powers of the bear, though they may in reality be said to have contacted their inner beast. For thousands of years there have been people who have been seized with the desire to rend and devour living flesh.

Gilles de Rais, who wallowed in death, killed as many as eight hundred children and was executed in 1440.[70] At his trial he confessed that he had killed children

> or caused them to be killed, either by cutting their throats with daggers or knives, or by chopping off their heads with cleavers; or else I have had their skulls broken by hammers or sticks; sometimes I had their limbs hewn off one after another; at other times I have ripped them open, that I might examine their entrails and hearts; I have occasionally strangled them or put them to a slow death; and when the children were dead I had their bodies burned and reduced to ashes.[71]

A real-life compulsive killer with the means and power to satisfy his curiosity about the body and his fixation on death, he entered folklore as a werewolf.

The werewolf is a testament to a belief in an animal nature deep within us, an animal that can come to the surface and dominate our being. Unlike Mr Hyde, who is the product of a lab experiment, the werewolf is transformed supernaturally. Other shape-shifters, such as Native American skin-walkers, take on other forms because they have the supernatural power to do so, often for their own convenience—to run long distances as a wolf rather than as a human, for example, or to change into a bird and fly off. They are not necessarily cursed as the werewolf is but have a skill shared with the great magicians.

In most of the old stories werewolves have no tails, and their eyebrows meet. They can be male or female. Some are said to wear their skin reversed, with their hair on the inside. The talking wolf in "Little Red Riding Hood" is often considered a werewolf. They can transform under the influence of the full moon—may even be compelled to—but in some cases their shape-shifting is independent of the moon and can even occur in the daytime. The werewolf was often said to attack members of its own household first, and that bit of folklore gave rise to the movies' warning that the werewolf would try to kill the person it loves the most. Unlike a berserker going after his enemies, the movie werewolf, whether in the human or in the werewolf stage, is in a divided position, for indulging its appetites would go against the dictates of its consciousness and bring about the death of a beloved. The fear of sexual passion and its ability to bring chaos is part of the arsenal of anxiety inherent to puberty, and the werewolf does, as has been widely noted, grow hair and become subject to animalistic drives as if it were going through puberty. In *The Wolf Man* (1941) as well as in *Cat People* (1942), desire is dangerous. The monster is one's animal nature, out of control and making one behave like an animal. Where the werewolf of folklore usually delights in its power, the werewolf of the movies usually does not seek to become a beast (although in an early werewolf movie, *The Werewolf* [1913, US], a Native American deliberately transforms himself into a wolf[72]). It is characteristic of shape-shifter movies that the protagonist becomes the monster (as in puberty), and the monster's death is presented with a degree of sadness, sometimes a tragic nobility.

Movie werewolves come in two forms: those that look like wolves and may walk on two legs, as in *The Howling* (Joe Dante, 1981, US), or four legs, as in *An American Werewolf in London* (John Landis, 1981, UK/US), and those that go on two legs and look like people with wolflike attributes, as in *The Wolf Man*. Actually both kinds of werewolf are in *The Wolf Man*, for when Larry is bitten by Bela (Bela Lugosi), Bela looks like a wolf to Larry and, more importantly, to the camera.

A werewolf can be killed by normal bullets in *WereWolf of London* (Stuart Walker, 1935, US) and *An American Werewolf in London*, or by silver bullets and silver objects in *The Wolf Man* and *House of Frankenstein*. In *The Howling* a werewolf can be burned to death, but a silver bullet is more humane and reliable. In *WereWolf of London* and *The Wolf Man* a werewolf will try to kill the one he loves, but only in *The Wolf Man* will it see a pentagram in the palm of its next victim or bear the sign of the pentagram where it was bitten. In all these pictures the full moon brings on the transformation. This is not the case in every werewolf picture: *I Was a Teenage Werewolf* (Gene Fowler, Jr, 1957, US) has the teenager (Michael Landon as Tony) change in the afternoon when a school bell goes off right next to him. Because he is given injections and hypnotic sessions that take him back to a more primitive form of being, Tony's transformations have nothing to do with the moon and are not supernatural. Another werewolf movie that has no supernatural component and whose mad scientist administers drugs that transform a man (a timid man, while Tony is a violent one; either kind can be afflicted) is *The Werewolf* (Fred F. Sears, 1956, US), but these pictures are variations on the theme. In the movies most werewolves are supernatural, and the most common way to become a werewolf is to be bitten by one. In folklore there are many other ways, such as drinking the water left in a werewolf's footprint or being one of seven consecutive daughters.

WereWolf of London begins in Tibet, where botanist Dr Wilfred Glendon (Henry Hull) and his assistant are in search of a rare flower, that blooms only by moonlight and that grows only in a high valley, said to be filled with demons. Invisible things grab at them. The exhausted assistant can't keep climbing and feels that it's all like something in a dream—a sign that the rules of being are about to change and that the characters are entering a region where dreamlike things take place in reality. Glendon finds the plant, but so does a werewolf, who bites him. The werewolf is Dr Yogami (Warner Oland), also a botanist, and he comes to Glendon's London home to tell him about the flower[73] and werewolfery. It is Yogami who warns Glendon that a werewolf "instinctively seeks to kill the thing it loves best" and says that "the werewolf is neither man nor wolf, but a Satanic creature with the worst qualities of both." Glendon dismisses werewolfery as a "medieval unpleasantness."

Glendon doesn't share with his wife, Lisa (Valerie Hobson), any information about what is happening to him or how he feels, and when an old sweetheart of hers shows up (Lester Matthews as Paul), Glendon's jealousy, his fears for her safety that become directives and his absorption in his work, which is also an absorption in his affliction, drive her to confide in Paul and to miss her old times with him. (They are being set up as the surviving couple.) Glendon doesn't want to become a werewolf and doesn't want to attack Lisa, but he is condemned to all of that. When he advances on Lisa at the climax, she recognizes him and calls him by name.[74] He is shot and is glad to die. As virtually all werewolves in the movies would do after him, Glendon returns to his normal appearance when he dies, linking the transformations of the movie werewolf with those of Jekyll and Hyde, which they resemble in any case. Glendon begins by determining to ignore superstition, but superstition and its truths claim him, and he becomes their tragic incarnation. Horror is enacted in his person. His work includes an attempt to create artificial moonlight, but the real moon proves his undoing.

The Wolf Man opens with what looks like its own version of the *Book of the Vampire*, a psychology book with an entry on lycanthropy. The true source of reliable information, however, is the gypsy Maleva (Maria Ouspenskaya), the old One Who Knows; her son is Bela, the fortune teller. Sir John Talbot (Claude Rains), Larry's short, controlling father, believes that the only authority on spiritual matters is God. Sir John, who is an astronomer, calls all astronomers "amateurs; when it comes to the heavens, there's only one professional." The heavens include the stars Sir John studies and the moon that controls Larry, and only God can fully know them. Gwen (Evelyn Ankers), who works in her father's antique shop, sells Larry a cane with a silver handle in the shape of a wolf's head, explaining to him about werewolves, notably how a werewolf is marked with a pentagram and sees one in the palm of its next victim's hand. She also recites the poem for him, which everyone seems to know: "Even a man who is pure in heart / And says his prayers by night / May become a wolf when the wolfbane blooms / And the autumn moon is bright." (The script was by Curt Siodmak.) Gwen is the woman Larry falls for, and when he first approaches her, he behaves like a sexually aggressive "wolf," though no one calls him that. She is engaged to the gamekeeper on the Talbot estate, Frank (Patric Knowles), a man who believes in keeping animals (and perhaps sexual impulses) in line. She will, however, go out with Larry and a girlfriend, Jenny (Fay Helm), to get their fortunes told. Bela sees the pentagram in Jenny's palm and warns her to run. Then Bela turns into a wolf and kills her, but is himself killed by Larry with the silver-headed cane after biting him—and when Bela is dead, he turns back into a man. Larry feels guilty for killing a man but doesn't really believe he did. He goes to the crypt where Maleva is mourning her son and reciting a ritual passage, telling Bela that "tears run to a predestined end" and he can now find peace.

The link between Larry and Maleva is crucial, for she gives him the information he needs about his condition and becomes his protector, at one point helping him transform back into a man. She ties this man who has lived most of his adult life in America back to the old ways of Europe, introducing Larry to legends at least as old as the patriarchy into which Sir John wants to initiate him.[75] Maleva provides the female side of the background Larry is going to acquire and Sir John the male side. Maleva is also more compassionate than Sir John and almost comes to play the role of Larry's mother. The battle between Maleva and Sir John is between legends and paganism on the one hand and organized Christianity on the other, and it should be noted that Maleva wins, leaving Sir John wide-eyed and horrified at the fact that he killed a wolf and it turned into his son. The old ways and the old curses are very much in power at the end of *The Wolf Man*, as Sir John has unwillingly learned.

There is a surviving couple, Gwen and Frank, and although they are shown together in the final shot (right after a shot of the dead Larry), Gwen's mind is on Larry and the horror he embodied and suffered. She says "Larry," realizing that it was he who attacked her, and mourning him she buries her head in Frank's chest. She had begun to feel close to Larry—making them the movie's primary romantic couple, in spite of Frank and the fact that any relationship with Larry would be doomed—and was, in a recent scene, about to go away with him. In this version of the triangle of the monster, the woman and her normal lover, there is an unusually strong bond between the woman and the monster's human phase. Much as Gwen does, the audience sympathizes with Larry and fears him. He suffers a great deal on the way to a death which he sees as his only solution. His tears (and unlike most monsters, he and *Cat People*'s Irena have many) "run to a predestined end."

It is interesting to consider what we are seeing when we see the Wolf Man (Figure 25), for he is supposed to be the same kind of werewolf as Bela, who looked like an ordinary wolf. Perhaps we are seeing Larry as he imagines himself, a man who has become like a wolf and is subject to beastly drives, the equivalent of human compulsions and forbidden desires. To others he might look like a wolf. This may, of

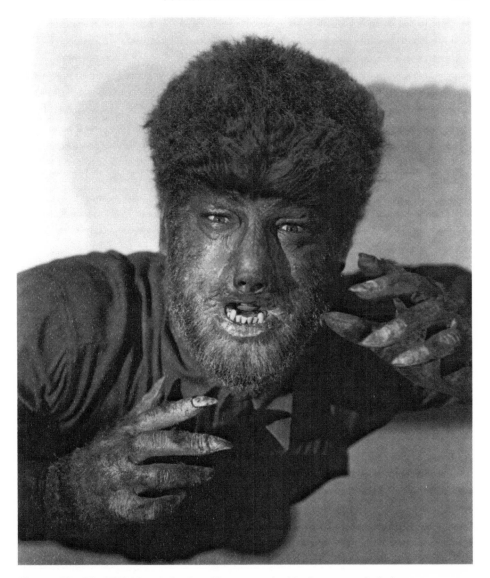

Figure 25. *The Wolf Man*: Animal and human, united in the monster's design.

course, be too psychological a reading of what may be just a stylistic enhancement of Larry's state. Like Glendon, Larry remains clothed after the transformation (which is shown with dissolves between successive makeups), walks on two legs and attacks both men and women; unlike Glendon, he never speaks during his Wolf Man phase but only growls and howls. His struggle is, as Sir John puts it, between "the good and evil in every man's soul; in this case, evil takes the shape of an animal." Chaney plays Larry as a calm and successfully aggressive man before he is bitten, but it is not hard to imagine that he has violence inside him.

The picture is steeped in fog, particularly when the Wolf Man is on the prowl. The final hunting party uses torches. At the climax Larry attacks Gwen and, as noted before, is killed by his father: an Oedipal nightmare in which the child is punished for his patricidal desires and emerging sexuality before he can completely act them out.[76] The film might be said to be enacting a Freudian dream, a mythic history of the attempted overthrow of the father, or a worst-case scenario of puberty. It begins just before Larry meets Gwen, and though she is engaged to another man, *The Wolf Man* is the tale of their courtship, climaxing when he tries to tear out her throat. It is a romance complicated by the monstrous.

Cat People is the story of a woman (Simone Simon as Irena) who fears that if she gives in to any sexual impulses, even jealousy, she will turn into a panther or some other large cat and kill the man who has excited her or the woman who has angered her. She is not a werewolf but a shape-shifter, and maybe not even that. Producer Lewton, director Tourneur and writer DeWitt Bodeen left it ambiguous whether Irena actually ever turns into a cat, but the front office at RKO insisted on putting in two shots that made it definite that she does. Even with these changes, the film still lives up to its intention not to be another *Wolf Man*. What we see of her cat form is a panther, not a panther woman, and we see very little of that. And there are no on-camera transformations. She has very sharp nails in her ordinary human form, as we see when she runs them down a couch and slits the fabric, and she needn't have transformed to tear up the bathrobe of her rival, Alice (Jane Randolph), in the swimming pool scene. Even so, that scene plays on our curiosity, and we're left wondering whether or not Irena turned into a cat while off-camera.

The picture focuses on the possibility that Irena is cursed the way she believes she is, how she feels about this and what she does about it. *Cat People* is about the possibly ungrounded fear of being a monster—the ambiguous territory Lewton set out to explore. It was a way to get to an essential aspect of horror without having to whip out the fangs and the big violence. Indeed Lewton's films often avoid violence when we expect to find it—as when the loud arrival of a bus climaxes Irena's pursuit of Alice—just as they avoid blatant explanations and conventional images. The low-key lighting dominant in his pictures (most of which were shot by Nicholas Musuraca) obscures certain horrific details while increasing the image's psychological richness and its atmospheric and emotional effectiveness.

Irena, who is from Serbia, was raised in a village where belief in the supernatural was strong. Evil practices had come to them through evil beings, most of whom the heroic King John had put to the sword. She has a sculpture of King John with a cat on his sword, and she explains to Oliver (Kent Smith) that the cat is a symbol of the evil, Satanic ways into which her people had fallen. King John's sword is similar to the cane of the psychiatrist, Dr Judd (Tom Conway), which conceals a sword. When Irena is wounded by Dr Judd's sword-cane, it is as if she has finally been impaled on King John's sword and found the destiny that waited for her as a cat woman. Both sword and cane are phallic symbols, suggesting that she feels a link between sex and death (the death not only of others, should she transform, but also of herself, for she is tragically determined to destroy the evil inside her even if all of her must die to accomplish that). Irena believes that the cat women in her village, who descended from witches, were turned into panthers when aroused and driven by their own evil to kill their partners. It is not that sex is evil in itself, but that it can unlock and is cognate to the evil inside her.

Irena has never been in love before meeting Oliver, so she has never tested what she fears, but she puts him off after they are married, and they never do consummate their marriage.

The film opens with Irena outside the panther cage at the zoo, drawing a sketch of an impaled panther. Soon Oliver comes over and manages to meet her. It ends with Oliver and Alice next to Irena's body outside the panther cage, where Oliver, realizing the truth, says, "She never lied to us." (This sets up the ironic ending of the sequel, where Oliver lies to his daughter about seeing Irena.) The period covered by the film is that of Irena's and Oliver's relationship from their first meeting to her death. While she is keeping Oliver at a safe distance, Irena repeatedly visits the panther at the zoo as if she were tempting that part of herself—or perhaps making sure that it is still caged. One time she throws the corpse of her pet bird to it (a bird that died of fright when she tried to touch it), and one time she finds the key left in the cage door (another phallic symbol, another link between death and what she sees as her panther nature and, in her dreams, the key to her problems) and steals it.

Irena is apparently not worried about turning into a cat if the target is Alice, of whom she has good reason to be jealous. One night Alice feels she is being followed. She looks up and behind her and sees tree branches waving as if an animal had jumped into them. Later, near there, muddy tracks are found, leading from where some sheep have been killed, that change from those of a big cat to those of a woman in heels. The shot of the tracks is followed by one of Irena, with Irena moving at the same pace and in the same direction as the camera had moved over the footprints. The cut between these shots, which are joined by our eye movement, suggests that Irena left the prints. We assume, without having seen it, that Irena was in her cat form when she pursued Alice and killed the sheep, and that she transformed as she was walking. (Her clothes appear to have metamorphosed with her. That is consistent throughout the picture.) This is as close as the movie, as planned, comes to confirming that Irena transforms.

It is when Irena confronts Oliver and Alice when they are working late at the office that we see her in panther form, and not just as a shadow. This was one of the scenes in which the front office insisted there be an actual panther on camera, giving the audience what they presumably wanted and in the process removing the possibility that Irena is delusional. Oliver holds the animal off with a T-square, which throws the shadow of a cross on the wall, and says, "In the name of God, leave us in peace." The threat disappears for the moment, making it clear that Irena answers to supernatural forces. She is exorcised like something evil, though she submits like a believer to the power of God. There is also an actual panther in the scene where Irena kills Dr Judd. Irena, who may already be dying from the wound given her by Dr Judd with his sword-cane, finishes herself off by using the stolen key to free the panther at the zoo. The cat knocks her down and kills her as it charges out of the cage, then is killed in traffic. This brings the panther and her together at last, physically and in death, fulfilling the promise of the opening scene and giving the whole a tight, circular structure. Although we have to accept that she transforms, it is also the worldview to which Irena holds that swamps her in horror and leads to her destruction.

In the years since *Cat People*, most films about supernatural shape-shifters have been about werewolves. Hammer's *The Curse of the Werewolf* (Terence Fisher, 1961, UK) took the unusual step of showing the growth from boyhood of a born werewolf (Oliver Reed as Leon), cursed to be one because he was born on Christmas and came of unfortunate parentage, not because he was bitten. *Ginger Snaps* (John Fawcett, 2000, Canada) concerned the love between sisters, one of whom (Ginger, played by Katharine Isabelle) is bitten by a werewolf—and, as she gradually transforms, grows a tail she tries to cut off—and the other of whom (Brigitte, played by Emily Perkins) deliberately infects herself with her sister's blood. Relating all this incurable blood-borne disease to AIDS, *Ginger Snaps* let the werewolf condition be transmitted to Ginger's boyfriend during intercourse. The werewolf in the *Twilight* sequels (Taylor Lautner as Jacob), particularly *Eclipse* (David Slade, 2010, US), is controlled, effective and at peace with his wolf–human duality. He shows how a werewolf can be both supernatural and integrated into nature.

Legendary Figures: *Candyman*

Within the *Friday the 13th* sequels there is a legend of Jason, a story of his origin and powers and proximity that is told around campfires and in bunkhouses. Many of the monsters discussed so far have legends attached to them, but the focus here is on beings whose energy comes specifically from legend, who are figures of folklore and augmented, unverified history before they are anything else.

The legend and its central figure need not predate the movie. *Candyman* (Bernard Rose, 1992, US), based on a short story by Clive Barker,[77] recounts the made-up legend of the Candyman (Tony Todd), a black artist who had his hand sawn off and then was smeared with honey so he could be stung to death by bees as punishment for loving a white woman. Now he has a hook in place of his lost hand, his body is filled with bees and he will appear—and in most cases kill the speaker with his hook—if a person says "Candyman" five times into a mirror. The ritual of saying his name indicates belief in the Candyman, and belief in his legend is what allows him to exist. He represents and is sustained by the power of legend. He tells Helen (Virginia Madsen), a researcher into folklore and urban legends who has summoned him, that he is nothing without the stories told about him by those who believe in his power and fear it. He kills so people will believe in him. He challenges Helen to believe in him and become his victim. He says at one point that he lives in people's dreams, which as we have seen are a recurring home for horror.

At the end her unfaithful husband, missing the dead Helen, says her name repeatedly into a mirror—as it happens, five times—and she appears and kills him with a hook. Helen, once a student of urban legends, becomes a figure of legend, the story of her death and her power "a tale to frighten children."

There is an actual ritual or game, "Bloody Mary," that is dared by young women in many parts of the world but particularly in North America and England.[78] If a person says "Bloody Mary" three times into a mirror, the dreadful Bloody Mary will appear. This superstition could well have influenced Barker and *Candyman*. To say the ritual words the ritual number of times is to take an extreme risk, for what one toys with believing may be true.

Nameless Forces: *Final Destination*

In *The Exterminating Angel* we never find out what force is causing the desperate guests to be unable to leave the party. Only the title suspects its existence and gives it a name.

In *Kalevet* or *Rabies* (Aharon Keshales and Navot Papushado, 2010, Israel) there is no explanation why, in a certain region, all car batteries die and everyone becomes a killer. There is a serial killer in the neighborhood, but he hardly matters. Those we assume will become his victims turn on each other, apparently under the spell of the place, though that is never mentioned.

In *Final Destination* (James Wong, 2000, US) and its first four sequels we never know for certain which force is demanding that people die when it is their appointed time. It could be death (which is suggested by a recurring character, a mortician who convinces the hero of this in the original movie, making that the most likely answer since he appears to be the One Who Knows), an unnamed power that enforces the order of the universe, a self-fulfilling pattern, fate or something else. It makes cause-and-effect, Rube-Goldberg-style accidents happen as if by themselves. It is incorporeal, invisible and silent. It is a supernatural force, but it would be hard to say what kind. That it might be death as a willful power is a good guess, but only a guess. The ordained order of deaths organizes the movie, and as an audience we generate some notion of what is behind it, although not what that force might look like if it took form, for it is not that kind of monster and never could have a form. We know it by what it does. We know just as much and as little about what makes the repetition in *Dead of Night* or the prophecies and cataclysm in *The Last Wave* happen.

One point made earlier in this book and of course by many others, from Edmund Burke forward, is that horror can tread on the inexpressible, the sublime, even the ineffable, which it often calls the nameless—that it has an affinity for the infinite. A limit-smashing experience of unnamable horror could come when a person in the grip of extreme horror passes out or goes mad, could be a point of incomprehension or could be transcendent. The nameless can stand at or lead to the expressive limit of the genre, a limit not easily transgressed.

Immortal Slashers: Michael, Jason and Freddy

The setting of the opening of *Madman* (Joe Giannone, 1982, US) is familiar: a campfire around which teenagers tell stories about Madman Marz (Paul Ehlers), who has only to be mentioned to be evoked. The story of Marz is supposed to be scary (it's not, and the movie is weak), but the fact that the story can bring its subject into active being is the actual threat in the present and a good idea. As in *Wes Craven's New Nightmare* (Wes Craven, 1994, US) or *Dead of Night*, horror may be the most successfully reflexive when it makes a horror story or film the central threat. Hearing that all one has to do is call his name, the teenagers promptly do so, which is one indication of why the teens in these movies are so often called dumb.

Not every slasher or slasher prototype is an immortal being beyond the reach of death—Norman Bates is mortal in *Psycho*, and so is Jason's mother in *Friday the 13th*—but some of the most famous and influential of them are. They can live after death in the world of dreams, as Freddy Krueger does, or repeatedly spring back from mortal wounds, as Jason Voorhees and Michael Myers do. They can inhabit and be activated by legend. Campfire tales are told about Jason. And Michael is linked to the supernatural energy and folklore as well as the festival of Halloween—the folklore because it is said in some traditions that the dead come back home at Halloween when the barriers between the natural and supernatural worlds are lowered, and the festival because it comes back every year with its full power and original energy, as the year itself does in many cultures where the new year is considered to erase history and restart time.[79]

Slashers kill with a great many weapons—never guns, which don't offer enough close-up, hands-on violence—but especially with long knives. Slashers are named for the slashing movements of arms and knives (extended to Freddy's finger blades and Jason's machete). In certain films the knives are phallic symbols, but sometimes, as Freud said of cigars, they are just knives. Many slashers hate sexual activity, especially when indulged in by horny teenagers, but they may also kill to satisfy their own sexually perverse psychological needs, as many serial killers do. They usually take their victims one by one, finding them when they are alone and most vulnerable.

Slashers are psychopaths regardless of whether they are undead, and some of them are psychotic. (As the terms are used here, psychopaths have a sociopathic lack of empathy or conscience, an indifference to the suffering of their victims and poor impulse control, while psychotics have suffered a delusional break from reality and a derangement of personality. Freddy is psychopathic, but Norman Bates is psychotic.) They are determined to kill, sometimes because they are settling a grudge or finishing off a defined set of victims. They are merciless, and most of them do not speak, expressing themselves through violence. The immortal ones are impelled by supernatural forces that allow them to overcome death—within a film, not just between a film and its sequel—and pursue their compulsive killing.

Some slashers, notably Michael and Jason, wear masks that give them a mythological edge, as if they have become pure forces of anonymous destruction, figures out of their own myths. Jason wears a hockey mask because it looks better than the bag he used to wear over his head. The audience is left, for most of the time, to imagine his ugliness behind the mask, which of course makes him more effectively ugly, but the audience also fears him because of the mask. The mask identifies him but also makes him faceless and implacable, a figure without the varying emotions that a face of flesh and blood would reveal. The slasher's mask may find its origin in the mother outfit worn by Norman Bates, which let him be a killer. It also is an outgrowth of the hiding of the slasher's face through camera position and through the use of POV shots from the killer's perspective, which was done in the interest of concealing the killer's identity—most of this inspired by the conjunction of Michael's

POV and mask at the start of *Halloween* and the ways Mrs Voorhees's identity is hidden in *Friday the 13th*. The mask can also be considered the inspiration for horror makeup in general. In the history of theatre in many countries, East and West, masks are dated earlier.

Slasher films are sometimes called "dead teenager movies," though not every victim is a teenager. Teenagers are selected because they are a large part of the target audience and because they may engage in premarital sex, and there is a strong link between sex and death in the slasher film. For having sex, teenagers are punished by being killed. Like the strangled dog in *Halloween*, they have a "hot date" with death. Many of the pictures are both puritanical and dedicated to showing a lot of flesh, as if sex and death belonged together. Both kill scenes and sex scenes are rewards, the exciting spectacles the target audience has come to see. One effect of joining sex and death scenes is to affirm a perverse desire to follow or accompany sexual excitement with the sight of blood, in fact with the sight of bloody murder. One excitement leads to and reinforces the other. On the more positive side, the association between sex and death may also go back to the ways people have used sex to create life and fight death. In either case the link reveals the slasher as an enemy of life, both as a killer and as one who usually hates sexual activity.

Halloween opens with the 6-year-old[80] Michael Myers putting on a Halloween mask and knifing to death his half-naked sister, Judith, who had just been making love with her boyfriend. Until his parents unmask him, all this is shown as Michael sees it, in what is meant to look like one continuous POV shot. Fifteen years later, Michael (Tony Moran; the masked Michael, also known as the Shape, is played by Nick Castle) escapes from the mental hospital where he has been since childhood—under the care of Dr Sam Loomis (Donald Pleasence), named after a character in *Psycho*, who considers him evil—and goes back to his home town and even to the vacant Myers house itself, arriving home on Halloween like a spirit in a folktale. He has come back to kill his other sister, Laurie Strode (Jamie Lee Curtis, whose mother, Janet Leigh, starred in *Psycho*), though the fact that she is his sister is established only in the version of *Halloween* broadcast on TV (1980) and in *Halloween II* (Rick Rosenthal, 1981, US). As far as the original *Halloween* is concerned, this latter-day Norman Bates is just back to kill people, especially teenagers, particularly three babysitters—Laurie, who has no sex life (the guys think she's too smart, and she's shy), and her two sexually active friends, Annie (Nancy Loomis) and Lynda (P J Soles). From the time he killed Judith, Michael has hated sex. A force of evil without a conscience, he never speaks. The power of repetition is an essential aspect of his compulsion to come home and kill again.

Whether or not it was the first slasher film—that was, according to some, *Black Christmas* (Bob Clark, 1974, Canada), while some name *Blood Feast* (1963)—*Halloween* was the one that was powerful and imitated enough to define the sub-subgenre. As a completely realized slasher film it presented a masked and silent psychopathic killer with a big knife and a fixation, a scene from the killer's point of view, a series of mostly young victims who are punished for having sex, a scene in which arranged bodies are discovered (probably inspired by a similar scene in *Black Christmas*) and a climactic sequence in which a lone female, the "final girl,"[81] fights the killer.

The fact that the last fighter, in many of these films the only survivor, is female can be traced to several causes in addition to those argued by Carol Clover. Primarily, in too many pictures women were having to be saved at the last minute by men. In line with the emerging feminist movement of the late 1960s and 1970s, it made women look more powerful to show them combating the killers themselves instead of fainting. Having a woman fight back also reduced a picture's impression of misogyny, considering the many female victims. In the woman's victory there is an affirmation of life (and of sexual power whether or not she is a virgin, for she may represent the ability to give birth as well as the desire to find sexual fulfillment, both of which she can do in the future). The woman who squares off with the slasher is in almost all cases a good, strong, resourceful, moral person (her morality often indicated by having her be a virgin) who has shown, at least up until this point, that she can survive. Her prototype is Ellen in *Nosferatu*, though Ellen dies. As it happens, in *Halloween* the final girl is saved at the last minute by a man, Dr Loomis, who unloads his revolver into Michael. In the influential open ending, Michael impossibly survives these wounds, disappearing from the ground where he fell.

In the discovery scene, when Laurie sees the corpses of her friends and realizes what has been going on, Lynda is stretched out on a bed with the tombstone of Judith Myers behind her head and a burning jack-o-lantern beside her. It is a spectacle that derives from an impulse to ritual, both Michael's and the movie's. As Laurie is overcome with horror, closet doors open by themselves, revealing first the body of Lynda's boyfriend, which falls swinging into the frame, and then Annie's body. The spectacle of Lynda on the bed reveals Michael's obsession with ritual, his sense of style and—thanks to the tombstone—his awareness of repetition. With the sacrificed woman and the jack-o-lantern he defines his own myth.

Michael targets Laurie again in *Halloween II*, in *Halloween H20: 20 Years Later* (Steve Miner, 1998, US) and in *Halloween: Resurrection* (Rick Rosenthal, 2002, US). He adopts many weapons, though he remains identified mostly with the butcher knife. He is unique in concentrating his murderous fixation on a female relative (the theme of coming home, which is crucial), and when the focus isn't Laurie, it is his niece, Jamie (played twice by Danielle Harris), in *Halloween 4: The Return of Michael Myers* (Dwight H. Little, 1988, US), *Halloween 5* (Dominique Othenin-Girard, 1989, US) and *Halloween: The Curse of Michael Myers* (Joe Chappelle, 1995, US). He remained a silent, unkillable slasher in the sequels but became far less the mythical figure he was in *Halloween*: the boogeyman.

Jason Voorhees's fixation is, like his mother's, on those who try to open Camp Crystal Lake, particularly the sexually active teenagers who are hired as counselors, but he will also kill anyone who crosses his path regardless of the victim's connection with the camp, and in that sense he is fixated on killing for its own sake. Because he is to some extent avenging his mother in the sequels, especially *Friday the 13th Part 2* (reversing and continuing the situation in the original, where the mother avenges the son), family is important to Jason, though not as consistently as it is to Michael.

In *Friday the 13th* Jason appears only at the end, as a deformed boy who is undead in the lake, but that scene is presented as a possible dream of the survivor, Alice (Adrienne King). Years ago, Jason had drowned while two counselors had been making love instead of acting as lifeguards, and for that his mother, Mrs Voorhees (Betsy Palmer), has decided to kill everyone who has any part in opening the camp this season. The camera adopts her POV (or in some sequences works in the third person—that is, with objective rather than subjective shots—without showing her face or much if any of her body) to conceal her identity, although this has the effect of repeatedly putting the audience in the position of the killer, encouraging voyeurism and sadism in the viewer as he or she is led to identify with the camera as it seeks victims—that is, sexual and violent spectacles. In the sequels, where everyone knows who the killer is, the identification between camera and killer is not entirely dropped, making it possible that this identification was intended all along.

Friday the 13th is not a supernatural horror film until it suggests at the end that Jason is not mortal, for Mrs Voorhees is a mortal slasher. (The supernatural takes hold more firmly when Jason appears as a man in *Friday the 13th Part 2*, a man who has somehow grown from that undead boy.) Mrs Voorhees imagines that she hears Jason's voice in her head, telling her to murder the victims: "Kill her, Mommy."[82]

Mrs Voorhees uses many weapons in her relentless mission to wipe out the counselors at Crystal Lake and the camp's new owner, all on Friday the 13th, Jason's birthday. People fall victim to hunting knives, arrows and axes, and Mrs Voorhees is decapitated by a machete, the weapon most closely associated with Jason in the sequels. The expanding arsenal of Michael, Mrs Voorhees, Jason and other slashers was a reflection of the central problem facing most of these filmmakers: having to think up new ways to kill people. The special-effects makeup for *Friday the 13th* was by Tom Savini, fresh from his work on *Dawn of the Dead* and *Maniac* (William Lustig, 1980, US), and his touch is evident in the scene when an arrow is pushed through the throat of counselor Jack (Kevin Bacon) from beneath the bed on which he is resting after making love (Figure 26). It was Savini who suggested to director-producer Sean Cunningham, after Savini had seen *Carrie*, that they should have a shock ending too and that the boy Jason (Ari Lehman) could jump out of the lake. This highly successful, audience-pleasing, jolting second ending—the zinger ending after one thought everything was over—was, as previously noted, widely imitated. Influenced by earlier films, it codified the device of the shocking open ending.

The thrill for the audience of *Friday the 13th* and its sequels lies in imagining ways of evading the killer and being horrified at the recurring spectacles of bloody murder as well as enjoying them, either sadistically or while cringing. We are on the side of the victims and the survivor, but the camera also lets us into the killer's perspective. That the killings are intended to convey pain rather than pleasure—emphasizing the pain of the victim rather than the pleasure taken by the killer—makes it possible that the implicit viewer is not a sadist, that the viewer is supposed to be frightened of the killer, on balance, more than to identify with him or her (and in a horror film we generally reject what we are afraid of). The scenes in which victims are spied on through windows encourage the double response of alarm, as we realize the character who has been spotted is in danger, and the desire to witness the character's death, along with the related double perspective of being seen (the identification with what is shown, the victim) and peering in (identification with the camera and the killer). One way to escape the sadistic element of these scenes is to identify with the victim; one way to escape the pain is to identify with the killer. Some viewers simply will not follow a film into extreme on-camera violence but will reject the picture and its subject positioning even if the latter is temporary. The emphasis on the killer's or monster's[83]

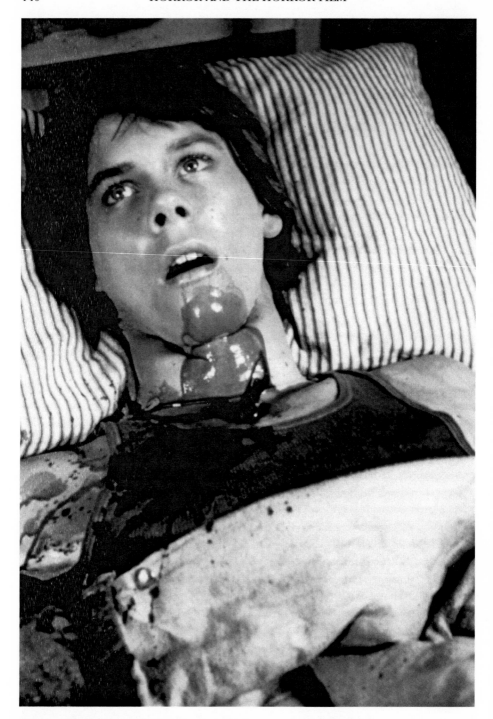

Figure 26. *Friday the 13th*: Relaxing in bed after sex, the slasher version.

perspective is nowhere so prominent as in the slasher film, which can be charged with encouraging sadomasochism as well as voyeurism. The slasher film's emphasis on scenes of bloody violence made killing in the horror film more vivid. The more sexy and exposed the body is, the filmmakers found, the more readily it can be meat.

Another effect of the violence and stimulation of the sex scenes and killing scenes is related to the release of adrenaline. The *Friday the 13th* pictures reportedly set out to offer one killing in every reel, leading to a string of adrenaline highs and periods of relaxation (whether one identifies with the victims or with the killer) that for some is the principal appeal of these films, the workout they put the audience through. The viewer can be physically thrilled, energized, excited and relaxed by the adrenaline ride.

Killing scenes in the slasher film are particularly valued for being inventive but also for delivering the goods, for being hard to take. Most earlier horror films implied violence and inspired fear and revulsion without showing extreme violence on the screen; *Blood Feast* is an obvious exception. It is the cinematic and narrative atmosphere around the violence, along with the depth of the emotional experience this combination evokes, that makes a film like *Halloween* so effective, regardless of how much or how little it shows— and *Halloween* is restrained in comparison to what followed it.

In *Friday the 13th* there is an unkempt old man who is clearly unbalanced even if he is right about the camp, Crazy Ralph (Walt Gorney), the One Who Knows. He warns the campers that there is a "death curse" on the place and that they're "all doomed" if they stay there. Much as in *Halloween*, there is a series of young victims, a killer who uses a knife (among other weapons), a delayed discovery, a significant use of subjective camera and a female survivor who combats the killer. The influence of Bava's *A Bay of Blood* (Mario Bava, 1971, Italy; also known as *Twitch of the Death Nerve*; literal title, *Ecology of Murder*) is clear, as a killer—several in Bava's film—does away with practically every character in the picture, one by one and in gruesome ways, beside a lake. One of the more cleverly conceived sex-and-death scenes in *Friday the 13th* shows a doomed couple making love, unaware of the corpse in the bunk above them. Alice, the survivor, is not presented specifically as a virgin, but she plays a game of strip Monopoly so well that she is the only one to keep all her clothes on. The film ends with a look at the trembling surface of the beautiful lake beneath which Jason is presumably alive. The ending is paradoxical and confusing in a fruitful and stimulating way, as are those of the first two sequels, for we do not know how Jason could be alive and spring on her—we assume he's undead, but his existence in any capacity is a shock—nor how Alice could have been pulled into the lake by Jason and survived long enough to be pulled from the lake by the police. At the conclusions of the first three *Friday the 13th* films, something impossible happens, and elision creates the impression that something is wrong, that our ordinary understanding of things has been ruptured.

Friday the 13th Part 2 and *Friday the 13th Part III* (Steve Miner, 1982. US), the latter released in 3D, are notable for their violence as well as their endings. *Part III* also introduces the hockey mask that became a permanent part of Jason's image, though his face is still concealed in *Part 2*. Parts 2 and 3 are the most inventive and interesting of the sequels, which might be called the Jason films, although there are good moments in part 4 (*Friday the 13th: The Final Chapter* [Joseph Zito, 1984, US]) and part 6 (*Jason*

Lives: Friday the 13th Part VI [Tom McLoughlin, 1986, US]). Several movies later, *Jason X* (Jim Isaac, 2002, US) takes him forward in time, launches him into outer space, and gives him a new body but does, at the end, return him to Crystal Lake. In his old form (responding to an attempt by Freddy Krueger, who finds him in Hell, to revive him in his legendary aspect), he then takes on another immortal slasher in *Freddy vs. Jason* (Ronny Yu, 2003, Canada/US/Italy); as in *Frankenstein Meets the Wolf Man*, since neither of them can die, neither can prevail. So by the time of *Freddy vs. Jason*, Jason had evolved in a circle—or the changes that had been introduced had been undone—so that he came back to the fully achieved form he had in *Part III*, complete with machete and mask, a figure whose transformations in sequels straining for new concepts had finally been abandoned. Jason had earned his image.

At the beginning of *Friday the 13th Part 2*, the suddenly adult Jason (Warrington Gillette), his face not shown by the camera, kills Alice in her home. Then he goes back to Crystal Lake to kill counselors (a different camp has opened on the same lake) carrying out his mother's project and ensuring the continuity of the series. (Shock open endings themselves encourage sequels.) The heroine and survivor, Ginny (Amy Steel), is not a virgin, though she is having her period and may gain from that some blood power against Jason. Ginny is majoring in Child Psychology, which lets her deal with Jason (who, she deduces, has the mind of a child fixated on the mother he saw be killed because she loved him) when she pretends to be his mother. She survives partly because she takes children's emotions seriously. Crazy Ralph again offers his warning of doom but is choked to death by Jason with a chain against a tree, outside the window of the bedroom where Ginny and her boyfriend, Paul (John Furey), are embracing.

Early in *Part 2*, around a campfire, Paul tells the story of Jason, beginning with the fact that his body was never recovered from the lake and suggesting that he lives as a demented creature in the surrounding woods. The story has the quality of a legend, but it turns out that Jason does live in the woods, in a shack. There he kills a policeman with a hammer (throughout the series his victims are not only teenagers and young adults). In a scene inspired by a similar one in *A Bay of Blood*, two lovers are impaled while they are having sex, nailed to the bed by a spear. A machete is used to kill a counselor in a wheelchair, and a butcher knife is used on the girlfriend who comes looking for him. It is when he is killing the latter that we see Jason has a white bag tied over his head, with one eyehole (like a camera), making it clear that it is part of his psychology to conceal his face.

Running to Jason's shack, Ginny finds an altar with Mrs Voorhees's head on it and realizes she was right about him. She imitates the mother to distract Jason. Then she and Paul hide in a room at the camp, but Jason—without his bag-mask—lunges through a window and grabs Ginny. When she comes to, Paul is missing. She asks the authorities where he is and gets no answer. We don't know what happened to Paul or to Jason or how Ginny survived, but we did see Jason seize Ginny much the way he seized Alice (there is an attempt to repeat the ending of the earlier film) when he bore her away into his territory, where impossible things happen. The big differences are that he breaks through a window and takes her from a building, not from a boat, and that there is no suggestion that her abduction is a dream. After Ginny asks where Paul is and is taken away, the film ends with an image of the altar. Placed in a circle around the head, the candles are still burning. This implies that the mother's spirit has continuing power or that Jason is still alive and lighting the candles.

In *Friday the 13th Part III* Jason (Richard Brooker) gets away from the camp, starting out by killing a couple who run a store (the man is punished, or selected as a victim by the picture, for his gluttony, the woman for her unpleasant personality). A group of teens, who are not counselors, visit the lake area for a vacation. Among them are Shelly (Larry Zerner), a jerk who thinks horror is a good joke and who is punished for not taking it seriously (he pretends he has been killed until he really is), and Chris (Dana Kimmell), who once had a run-in with Jason but survived—but she doesn't know how she survived and remembers only blacking out, then waking up in her own room. Being seized by Jason, if one is not killed, is an occasion for elision. There is something unexplained and perhaps inconceivable in what is left out, something that the movie may not be able to show. The teenagers stay in Chris's old house, which has a barn.

One of Chris's girlfriends is killed by an airborne shaft to the eye, fired from a spear gun. One couple is killed (individually) after making love, another after smoking dope. By the time Chris starts finding bodies—her boyfriend's when it is thrown in through the living-room window—everyone in the house has been killed, and Jason has found and put on the hockey mask. Chris fights Jason in the barn, and at one point she even hangs him and then sees him come back to life, which surprises her but not us. Finally she stops him with an ax blow to the head, then gets in a rowboat and pushes herself into the lake.

The impossible ending that follows is linked to the endings of the previous pictures by integrating this boat and the building in which Chris sees Jason through a window. Jason emerges from the house, bursting through a door. Then the door is whole, with no indication that Jason ever was there. Then Mrs Voorhees comes out of the lake and drags Chris from the boat. Chris survives the experience, again we don't know how, and she is carried off in a police car laughing and screaming, an echo of Ginny's being taken away at the end of *Part 2*. There is no trace of the "lady in the lake" that she told the police about, just as there had been no trace of Jason when Alice had been pulled from the lake. The last shots show Jason in the barn, apparently dead, and the enigmatic surface of the lake; this is not the sort of movie to leave a happy, fertile couple at the end. The device of the impossible ending was not pursued in the subsequent sequels. This elegant conclusion—which in a formal sense wrapped up the series as a trilogy—was the last of them, a paradoxical sequence in which the key elements of all three endings were brought together.

Like Michael (or Kharis, another silent, fixated, deathless killer whose face is covered, for immortal slashers are the mummies of their period), Jason never says a word. The talkative slasher is Freddy Krueger. Freddy (Robert Englund) killed 20 children before he was burned alive by a group of parents and now appears to the teenage children of those parents in their dreams, where he has the power to kill them. Craven's *A Nightmare on Elm Street* (1984) emphasizes nightmares as sites of horror and (as *Invasion of the Body Snatchers* did) shows the difficulty of staying awake when to sleep means to confront Freddy and risk death. It is eerie when the characters discover they are having the same dreams, dreams in which the same easily recognizable man appears, the man with claw-like blades on his gloved right hand. (He wears no mask but has a burned face.) It is with these razor-sharp blades, extensions of his fingers, that Freddy slashes and stabs.

In dreams he is invulnerable, but he can be pulled into our world. The movie claims that an object can be taken back with the dreamer when she or he wakes up. Freddy wants to kill the teenagers not because they are having sex—even though two of the victims (Tina, played by Amanda Wyss, and Rod, played by Nick Corri) do have sex—but to get even with their parents and because of the simple fact that they are alive. He gets pleasure from killing children.

The dreams are usually presented without introductory shots of the characters' falling asleep, making it seem for a while as if the dreamlike events are happening while the characters are awake. This departs from the conventional bracketing of a POV shot with shots of the person looking or of a dream or memory sequence with shots of the individual sleeping or remembering, though it actually duplicates what is found in the first British dream film, *Let Me Dream Again* (G. A. Smith, 1900, UK), which shows a dream in the first shot before it shows the dreamer waking in the second and final shot. Because in *A Nightmare on Elm Street* the orientation to the waking world is delayed until the end of the dream, when the character is shown waking up, the nightmare appears real until its own bizarreness gives it away. This keeps the picture alternating between narrative worlds. At any time reality can cut to a dream, and the nightmare can extend itself from the dreaming to the waking world. Instead of a bedroom window, this film offers the frame of a dream as an interface between the normal, daily world and the intrusive world of horror. Many of the horrors found in literature and film originated in nightmares, like Stevenson's Jekyll and Hyde, and are akin to them. Many horror films play like nightmares on movie screens.

What happens in the characters' dreams in *A Nightmare on Elm Street* is real enough to manifest in the real world. Thus when Tina or the heroine, Nancy (Heather Langenkamp), is slashed in her sleep, the wounds appear on her actual body. As the dream world and the waking world can be equally real in this picture, the whole movie can readily become a nightmare, fulfilling an inherent goal of the horror film.

The worlds are bridged in many cases by the wounds Freddy inflicts, as in Tina's case. Falling asleep gives Freddy the power to affect the sleeper even in the real-world territory of the bed, which is how Rod is tied up and hanged by a bed sheet while he is alone in a jail cell. The sheet answers to a force from dreams but acts in the physical realm and is itself a bridge between worlds. The bed, another bridge, becomes a site of danger in this film not because of sex but because it invites one to sleep. Characters also fall asleep elsewhere, as Nancy does in an English class; in a powerful transition, one quotation from *Hamlet* is replaced by another that turns ominous in tone and import as it speaks of "bad dreams."[84]

Nancy, who is "into survival" like a good final girl and who, unlike her alcoholic mother (Ronee Blakley as Marge), faces things, pulls Freddy's hat back from a dream. Unlike her policeman father (John Saxon as Lt Thompson), Nancy is open-minded enough to realize what is going on and deliberately goes to sleep so that she can pull Freddy himself out of her dream and defeat him in the real world. Nancy dispels Freddy by taking back all the energy she had given him by thinking about him and fearing him— a psychologically healthy approach to getting rid of the demons that may oppress one. After that comes the extra ending, in which everyone who had been killed is miraculously alive—Nancy had demanded them back from Freddy—but Freddy's influence is still felt. This muddled ending concludes well, however, with a view of some girls who are playing jump rope and singing an old song about Freddy, one we have heard before. His survival in folklore is more convincing and chilling than his springing tricks on the characters. The song emphasizes that "Freddy's coming for you," that you're going to "stay up late," that you'll "never sleep again."

Of the many sequels, the most interesting are *A Nightmare on Elm Street 3: Dream Warriors* (Chuck Russell, 1987, US) and *Wes Craven's New Nightmare*. In *Dream Warriors* the teenagers at a psychiatric hospital are being visited by Freddy (played again and throughout the series by Robert Englund) in their dreams. Nancy (played again by Langenkamp), now a psychologist, helps them by believing them. Freddy's origins are revealed by the ghost of the nun his mother became after she was gang-raped in an asylum. He is the "son of a hundred maniacs," and as he himself reveals, he takes his strength from children's souls. In the long climactic dream Freddy stabs Nancy with his razor fingers, killing her.

In *Wes Craven's New Nightmare*, Craven (Wes Craven) has been having a nightmare and writing a script about it—or rather, from it. He wants Heather Langenkamp (Heather Langenkamp) to play Nancy in a film to be made from that script, which is the film we are watching. The events in the script happen in real life as the script is being written. Craven himself doesn't know how it will turn out, as he is only dreaming it. Going through these scripted but real and terrible experiences is how Heather plays Nancy one last time. She asks for help from Robert Englund (Robert Englund) and John Saxon (John Saxon) as well as Craven. Craven tells Heather that he suspects that demons and ancient forces can be trapped by stories, that Freddy was snagged by the *Elm Street* series because it got at a truth about a destroyer who lives in dreams. Now that the stories are no longer being told (Freddy was killed in the previous film, *Freddy's Dead: The Final Nightmare* [Rachel Talalay, 1991, US]), he has been freed from the bounds of the story and wants to cross over into the real world, and the only way to stop him is to contain him in another movie, the one Craven is writing. Thus making a horror film becomes the solution to a horror. This completely reflexive movie has Freddy coming from the fantasy of film into the real world of the filmmakers, which itself turns out to be part of a film called *Wes Craven's New Nightmare*. The series that began with a movie that played like a nightmare and mixed the worlds of dream and reality ended with a movie that declared itself a filmed nightmare and brought the mythic slasher into the interwoven worlds of reality and art.

Immortal slashers just look human. Like other supernatural monsters, they are impossible but present, and they reach from beyond the grave or from the beyond itself to enlarge our fearful understanding of what violates the limits and rules of the known world.

6

HUMANS

People can behave like monsters. And human monsters can die.

Human aberrations, violators of deep moral codes, icons of disturbed psychology, perpetrators of atrocities, followers of certain cults, outragers of the body, mad scientists, mortal slashers, torturers, ghouls and cannibals have all been called human monsters, even if most of them have normal bodies. Though not a literal monster, a human can fulfill the role of a monster, which is to incarnate and focus the horror, and can function in the film's structure exactly as a monster would. Although it has often been said—most rigorously by Carroll—that horror requires an inhuman monster and that something impossible or fantastic has to be associated with it, it is clear that a picture like *The Texas Chain Saw Massacre* is a horror film, for it deliberately, atmospherically and painfully puts horrors on show, even if they are credible horrors performed by humans. It also contains such horror icons as Leatherface's mask—doubtless an influence, with *Halloween*, on *Friday the 13th Part III*, though the mask can be traced back at least to *The Cat and the Canary* and indicates *Texas Chain Saw*'s participation in the genre's traditions. The repulsive nature of such an icon is probed further when a mask is made from a freshly carved-off face in *The Texas Chainsaw Massacre 2* (Tobe Hooper, 1986, US). Some humans not only perpetrate horrors, but are horrors themselves. They are not supernatural entities in human form or allied with the spirits as witches are, and they cannot transform themselves like a Dr Jekyll. If they have powers, they are those a human might have, such as telepathy. Many of them are mad, and many are evil.

Demonstrating the worst aspects of human nature, monstrous characters attack the body and the spirit, performing atrocities that are both physical and, in their way of testing and passing limits, transcendent, going beyond our ordinary experience (even in a movie) of the bad, the painful, the merciless and the murderous. Horrors carried out or manifested by humans in films create a world that differs from ours, though sometimes only in the degree to which it is stylized, for there is extreme, cruel and bizarre violence in the real world too, violence that goes well beyond ordinary experience and can shake the foundations of our apprehension. We witness things we thought could not or should not exist. As real or figurative violence touches the level of the unspeakable, it becomes a vehicle for horror—not the only vehicle, but certainly a limit-smashing and troubling one. The world charged with human horror, even that of a family of sadistic, mortal, cannibal Texans, is as frightening as any world threatened by a werewolf or a giant spider.

Some criminals, even crazy ones, must be left to the crime film, but not all. What makes *Se7en* (David Fincher, 1995, US) or *The Silence of the Lambs* (Jonathan Demme, 1991, US; the first horror film to win the Oscar for best picture) different from conventional crime thrillers and from police procedurals is what the mad killer in each does to his victims, giving them gruesome, symbolic deaths in *Se7en* or sewing their skins into a suit in *The Silence of the Lambs*, as if he were the ghoul Ed Gein, who will be taken up later. In both cases there is something horrific and disturbing about the criminal's psychology and its compulsive expression. A related and general consideration is the degree to which the killer, psychopath or other threat becomes a figure of horror—evoking terror and repulsion (and sometimes even a transfigurative, uncanny, symbolic force, a kind of mythic energy) in himself or herself and in his or her actions, as Norman Bates and Leatherface do—rather than a mere criminal. There are horror crime films, then, like *Se7en*, that set out to horrify not just in selected sequences but as a whole, as the burden of what they have to say.

Those humans who have sometimes become horror figures include artists, believers, cannibals, families, ghouls, human anomalies, the infected, mad doctors and scientists, the mad in general, those with psychic and telekinetic powers, psychopathic killers, romantics, sadists, mortal slashers and torturers. The first of these to make a significant impression was the mad doctor, as Caligari.

Mad Scientists and Doctors: *Caligari* and *Mad Love*

Dr Caligari and Cesare are human threats, threats to the safety of the normal world into which they introduce an element of nightmarish and, for a time, inexplicable horror. Cesare is Caligari's slave and the one who carries out the killings.

The main difference between mad scientists and mad doctors is that the latter see patients. Cesare is also Caligari's patient, for the mad doctor or scientist usually has someone to experiment on, a human or an animal that becomes a kind of monster, like the assistant in *The Mad Ghoul* (James P. Hogan, 1943, US). Those scientists who create outright monsters, like Dr Moreau or the scientist in *Fiend Without a Face*, have been discussed along with their monsters. It remains to consider doctors and scientists whose special characteristic is their madness, especially those who experiment on and manipulate people in the interest of their often bizarre and usually obsessive concerns—projects that come to a bad end and usually are destroyed.

Caligari first becomes unbalanced not when he decides to imitate the medieval Caligari's experiment but when he decides that he must "become Caligari" to do so. He goes completely insane when the truth is exposed and he finds that Cesare is dead, which reduces him to life in a straitjacket, as he cannot sustain the exposure and the end of his power, nor maintain the mask of sanity. At the conclusion, however, as previously discussed, it is revealed that Dr Caligari is an inmate's fantasy and that the real doctor never was crazy.

In *Doctor X* (Michael Curtiz, 1932, US) and *The Invisible Man* (1933) the scientist's experimental subject is not a Cesare but himself; that is, in both films the mad scientist is the monster rather than simply creates it. In *Doctor X* the mad scientist (Preston Foster as Dr Wells) uses a substance, "synthetic flesh," that allows him to change his face into a monstrous one, replace his amputated hand and commit murder undetected, taking the live flesh he needs for further experiments from the victims he is driven to kill, all under the influence of the full moon. In *The Invisible Man* the formula for invisibility drives the scientist (Claude Rains as Griffin) mad. Griffin learns, as obsessive and overreaching scientists often do in horror films, that he has "meddled in things that man must leave alone." Horror-bound scientists in particular are given this warning, for they cross the boundaries that restrict us to ordinary knowledge and ordinary states of being. They eat the fruit of the tree that gives knowledge, that could make them like God, and if they learn to their sorrow the difference between good and evil, they also learn not to play God. Dr Morris (George Zucco) says in *The Mad Ghoul* that he is indifferent to good and evil and is interested only in the true and the false, but he soon uses his scientific discoveries for evil ends (turning his assistant, whom he considers a romantic rival, into a kind of zombie) and becomes more enmeshed in evil the more he proceeds, for in the horror film good and evil are part of the world the scientist investigates, even if he or she would prefer to consider it morally neutral. Since each of these scientists has become a murderer as well as a horror figure, each must die by the picture's end.

Mad Love suggests at its reflexive start,[1] after a hand has punched a hole through the window on which the credits appear (breaking open the interface and letting horror enter our world more directly), that it can be sick to enjoy the sadistic spectacles of the Grand Guignol, as Dr Gogol (Peter Lorre) does when he watches, night after night, the actress Yvonne Orlac (Frances Drake) be tortured. At first the movie urges us to maintain our knowledge of the difference between reality and illusion—for example, when it shows an apparently headless attendant checking Gogol's coat at the theatre—but once Gogol has become possessed by his obsessive desire to make Yvonne his own, he has difficulty telling the imaginary from the real, and we share some of that problem. One aspect of his "mad love" is that he believes a work of art can come to life, especially if one is romantically obsessed with it. He is too open to the apparent reality of representational art for his own good and seems to have few mental defenses against it. A wax statue of Yvonne, which Gogol buys from the theatre, is portrayed (when seen in close-up) by the real actress to encourage the audience to become confused about what is real, or at least to understand Gogol's confusion. But there is also something that is (within the fiction) not illusory about the horrors in this picture. Yvonne's husband, Stephen (Colin Clive), a pianist who loses his hands in a train accident—and onto whom Gogol grafts the hands of an executed knife-murderer—finds that his new hands cannot master the piano but throw knives very well, and that is no illusion. Stephen uses that talent to save Yvonne from Gogol at the end, throwing a knife into his back through the bar-crossed, glass-free window of a locked door. This sewing on of hands is ironic and reflexive, for the actor who played Henry Frankenstein only a few years before is now being put together from the parts of two men, one being a corpse: the knife-thrower, Rollo (Edward S. Brophy). Stephen's first reaction to the hands is that "they feel dead." Even after death, Rollo's hands do have a skill and impulse of their own, which gives this picture a supernatural component.

After the accident and the operation, when they are indebted to Gogol (they do not realize he has used Rollo's hands but think at first he has saved Stephen's) and Stephen has become a dual being, Stephen and Yvonne enter the horror phase of their relationship, a phase they must come to terms with and incorporate into their lives. For Yvonne this finally means playing the role of her own statue so as to buy time when she has become trapped in Gogol's house—where, like the Phantom of the Opera, he plays the organ for her and dreams of love triumphant. She must support Gogol's delusion that his love has made the statue come to life, as if he were Pygmalion. For Stephen it means throwing the knife to save Yvonne, accepting how Gogol has defined him.

Pretending to be a strapped-together Rollo (Figure 27) whose head Dr Gogol put back after he was guillotined and speaking in a whisper, Gogol convinces Stephen that Stephen murdered his cheap and vicious stepfather with Rollo's hands.[2] His aim is to drive the unstable Stephen mad, and to have Yvonne for himself. Gogol is, of course, the one who murdered the stepfather. Gogol has proved the prey of illusions—carrying on a conversation with his changing reflections in three mirrors, for instance—but this time he creates his own. In other scenes he quotes poetry and takes its words as instructions. When he is trying to decide what to do with the statue he believes has come to life, he remembers Oscar Wilde's "The Ballad of Reading Gaol"—"each man kills the thing he loves"—and decides to kill her. When he is wondering how to do it, he quotes and acts out the lines from Robert Browning's "Porphyria's Lover" about strangling a woman with her long hair, changing the hair color and the tense to make the poetry fit what we see onscreen. For Gogol, life follows art, and in the end he follows art into a mad world where love and power drive him crazy and he cannot separate illusion from reality.

Figure 27. *Mad Love*: Meeting the patient in disguise.

The Orlacs, on the other hand, accept reality. At the end Gogol is separated from their life (they embrace in one shot, and he dies alone in the next and final shot)—but Stephen will never be a pianist again, because some of the changes introduced by horror are permanent.

As *Island of Lost Souls* does, *Eyes Without a Face* (Georges Franju, 1959, France) touches our fear of the doctor's knife. In that sometimes repulsive, sometimes beautiful film, Dr Génessier (Pierre Brasseur) is interested in transplanting living tissue and organs. His assistant is Louise (Alida Valli), and his obsession is to give his daughter, Christiane (Edith Scob), who was disfigured in a car accident when he was driving, a new and beautiful face. He takes faces from other young women, but the grafts always fail.[3] Christiane wears a neutral, facelike mask that reveals only her eyes (hence the title), the only undamaged part of her face, and forces us to imagine how terrible she looks. Her blandly masked face strikes a recurring note of understated horror.

The horrors Génessier inflicts are less suggestive and more overt, as when he and Louise, having cut off a woman's face, use forceps to stretch it away from the head and briefly reveal the bloody mess that is left when the face is removed. It is a shot that strikes one in the gut with revulsion while it presents a terrifying image, a definitive horror moment that hurts.

Romantics: *The Phantom of the Opera*

Sometimes, like Dr Gogol, a romantic can get out of hand, demanding one's exclusive attention and that one become a part of his or her world—which in this genre is usually a horrific one. He or she might be crazy or might be a sensitive type bearing some distinguishing inner wound, a pain that can determine character. This kind of romantic is a figure not of Romanticism but of romance, and there is sometimes a danger in romance—even a fear, based on its unknowns—that one's lover could take matters to disturbing extremes, as does the soft-spoken but violently possessive woman in *Audition* (Takashi Miike, 1999, Japan).

The Phantom of the Opera (1925, revised 1929) starred Lon Chaney as Erik, a disfigured musician. Escaped from Devil's Island, where he had been exiled for being criminally insane, he makes his home in the cellars of the Paris opera house, where he is feared as the Phantom. He plays the organ and dreams of the singer he loves, Christine (Mary Philbin), whom he offers a great career if she will follow his directions. He appears to her at first as a shadow wearing the mask of a normal face. He has a "melodious" voice. She is inspired by the voice and attracted by the offer, which will require her to dedicate herself entirely to her work and her "Master," but she is also in love with Raoul (Norman Kerry). One night Erik takes her down below the opera house; the shots of the gondola moving through the old archways are especially atmospheric. He hopes that "that which is good within me, aroused by your purity, might plead for your love." While he is playing "Don Juan Triumphant" on the organ, she defies his warning and unmasks him (Figure 28), hoping to find the face of a mysterious romantic hero.

She cowers before him, terrified and repulsed by his face, which the audience sees and reacts to before she does (we need no mediator to be horrified by his face).

Figure 28. *The Phantom of the Opera*: The phantom unmasked.

The film is at its most powerful when it shows Erik unmasked, though he is also impressive in the masked ball sequence when he dresses as the Red Death and wears the mask of a skull. Chaney succeeds at making Erik both a frightening, imperious, dangerous figure and a tortured romantic. While Raoul is the good-looking good guy, he has no deep romantic drive beyond the conventional, and compared with the Phantom he has no hold on the screen.

Erik does not have the option, as the romantic hero does in *Beauty and the Beast* (Jean Cocteau, 1946, France), of turning into a handsome prince once the curse has been lifted and his term as a monster is done. He will always be a monster. His beautiful voice (which is how the intertitles describe it) points to an inner life that cannot defeat the outer shell, cannot become all that he is, for he is also the horrific figure we plainly see. As an extreme romantic who is also a human monster, he is a threat to conventional romance. His ideas of conjugal happiness are as creepy as his coffin-like bed or the cellars where he wants Christine to live. This familiar love triangle of the monster and the couple finds conventional resolution in the destruction of the monster, leaving Christine free for Raoul, her proper romantic partner. Erik is both the tragic romantic hero and the villain. His horror lies in the extreme (and morbid) nature of his romanticism and the fact that he is disfigured and crazy. Chaney played another frightening and limit-smashing lover whose obsessive desire led him to a bad end in *The Unknown* (Tod Browning, 1927, US).

May (Lucky McKee, 2002, US) shows that a romantic can come to a horrific happy ending. May (Angela Bettis), a shy young woman who was born with a lazy eye and who sews to make extra money, admits that she is weird. A romantic but a totally inexperienced one, she fantasizes about having a boyfriend and settles on Adam (Jeremy Sisto), particularly because he has beautiful hands. They almost become lovers, but he decides she is too weird. Adam had said he loved weird, and so does Polly (Anna Faris), the woman she turns to next, but May finds they do not truly love the weird and do not love her. Polly has an attractive back, and her new lover is a woman with beautiful legs. May decides that people have good aspects but are only good in part. She begins killing people, including Adam and Polly and Polly's friend with the legs, taking the parts she wants. "If you can't find a friend," she says, "make one." She sews the parts into a bisexual, human-sized doll as if she were assembling the Frankenstein Monster. She decides that the doll, which has an artificial head rather than the head of one of her victims, cannot see her, so she stabs out her eye—the one she had trained all her life, which marked her first isolation from others, now a romantic wound that defines her full entrance into horror—and puts it in place on the head, then lies down beside the perfect lover she has made. Then the doll slowly embraces her and rubs her face with Adam's hands the way she had wished Adam would do. It is a happy ending for May and an immersion in fulfilled romantic horror.

Human Anomalies: *Freaks*

There is no inoffensive term for the human anomalies commonly known as freaks. The oldest word for those suffering from extreme birth defects is "monster."[4] They include dwarfs, giants, hermaphrodites, Siamese twins, bearded women, those born without arms or legs and many others. For generations they were exhibited in sideshows. The response to a sideshow freak might vary from wonder to revulsion. One might resist identification with the human in the freak and see him or her as the Other, identify with the freak's anomaly and find it an image of one's hidden inner self,[5] feel pity, be glad to have escaped a birth defect oneself or even be frightened.

Freaks (1932) used no makeup or special effects to create its human anomalies, and early reviewers warned that the use of actual freaks might make it more difficult for audiences to "sympathize" with them.[6] That meant that in themselves they were repulsive and would not encourage identification or understanding as made-up actors would. The horror they manifested was felt to be too real. But it is the use of reality that makes *Freaks* so powerful and does in fact let us relate to its characters. It is inherently cinematic to show real freaks in this film, not conventional actors in makeup.

One reviewer wrote, "Saying that it is horrible is putting it mildly: it is revolting to the extent of turning one's stomach… Any one who considers this entertainment should be placed in the pathological ward in some hospital."[7]

All the characters in the film are circus folk. Following a written prologue added after the picture was first released, in which the film itself is described as a "highly unusual attraction," *Freaks* opens in a sideshow where a barker tells the story of a "living monstrosity" on exhibit, a woman we do not see till his tale is over. She had been a trapeze artist named Cleopatra (Olga Baclanova). Her beauty and normal size made her attractive to a rich dwarf named Hans (Harry Earles), who married her. At the wedding

Figure 29. *Freaks*: The wedding banquet and the goblet.

feast (Figure 29) the freaks chanted that Cleopatra was "one of us, one of us," but she refused the communal goblet, called the guests "freaks," and reassured herself of her normality in the arms of her lover, the strongman Hercules (Henry Victor). Cleopatra poisoned Hans, planning to inherit his fortune, but he figured out what she was doing and survived. Cleopatra and Hercules had violated "the code of the freaks" by trying to hurt Hans, and the freaks took their revenge during a rainstorm at night when the circus wagons were moving between towns. In one version of the film it is implied that they castrated Hercules.[8] Cleopatra—and here makeup and effects *were* used—was changed into a croaking composite monster with a feathered torso and arms that ended in bird feet. The world of the freaks has purged itself of its destructive elements, the evil normal characters (some of the normals are good), and has continued as a sideshow of natural horrors (in which Cleopatra is the unnatural one) and as a community that has defended itself. The freaks reject what to them is horrific and reclose the system. In this respect it is a normal classical horror movie with a difference, for the norm is a realm of what others may consider the horrific. Even so, these freaks are neither mad nor evil.

The film exploits freaks as spectacles while it encourages sympathy and admiration for them. A man without arms or legs who lights a cigarette demonstrates his impressive skill along with his congenial nature, but at the climax, when he wriggles through the rain with a knife in his teeth, he is memorably frightening. In the rainstorm, even the gentle pinhead crawling with her knife becomes a terror, as do the freaks advancing steadily on the wounded Hercules or running after Cleopatra. In the mud, the rain and the lightning, the freaks who crawl or run through the night are scary even if we are on their side. For the moment, they do look like human monsters.

Artists: *Mystery of the Wax Museum* and *In the Mouth of Madness*

Actors and magicians can be masters of deception, writers can create dangerous worlds and painters can be driven mad by the quest for perfection. A sculpture can hide a corpse just as a slasher movie soundtrack can contain a real scream of death, as in *Blow Out* (Brian De Palma, 1981, US), and as the red on a canvas can be blood, as in *Color Me Blood Red* (Herschell Gordon Lewis, 1965, released 1966, US). The art work can fool the viewer into thinking it is entirely real, as in *Mark of the Vampire*, where performers attempt to persuade a character and the audience that vampires are on the loose, or that it is entirely artificial, as in *House of Wax* (Andre de Toth, 1953, US), where the realistic sculptures conceal real bodies. The fictitious horrific artwork exploits the border between reality and artifice as the horror film often does, and the artist is the character who controls the degree to which his or her work is meant to generate the illusion of a horror or conceal the fact of one. Usually the horror artist is a danger to the other characters.

Mystery of the Wax Museum (Michael Curtiz, 1933, US) is the story of the gifted Ivan Igor (Lionel Atwill), whose wax figures have attracted artistic interest while the wax museum has been doing poor business, as Igor will not put in a chamber of horrors. When the realistic sculptures are shown in close-up, real actors stand in; this makes the sculptures appear as realistic as Yvonne's in *Mad Love*. Igor's partner sets fire to the museum for the insurance money, destroying all the sculptures and disfiguring Igor. Twelve years later Igor brings his newly restored wax museum from London to New York, where he is struck by the resemblance of his assistant's girlfriend (Fay Wray as Charlotte) to the best of the sculptures he had made, the beautiful figure of Marie Antoinette. Igor, who pretends to be confined to a wheelchair, has a wax mask that makes him look normal, while he allows people to see his deformed hands. He explains that his hands will not allow him to do more than give instructions to those who make the sculptures, when actually he is taking the shortcut of killing people who resemble his old sculptures and then encasing them in wax. As his accomplice confesses to the police, the whole place is a morgue. At the climax Igor reveals his secret to Charlotte, whom he is about to drench in boiling wax, and she smashes his false face. The police shoot Igor, who appropriately falls into the vat of wax. Igor's wax museum is a secret chamber of horrors, and the killer is an artist obsessed with his work, a figure not that different from a mad scientist.

The remake, *House of Wax*, added 3D to the presentation but made few changes.[9] The major difference is that the sculptor determines to feature a chamber of horrors in his new museum, something he had, before the fire, considered beneath contempt. As an artist, he is still obsessed with beauty and realism but has become more excited by frightening and violent displays.

How to Make a Monster (Herbert L. Strock, 1958, US) concerns a makeup artist (Robert H. Harris as Pete Drummond) whose specialty is monster movies. He repeatedly calls himself a creative artist. When the new studio heads decide to make teen musicals instead of horror films, Drummond makes up two actors as monsters, drugs and hypnotizes them and then sends them out to kill the executives. In a final fire, Drummond burns to death, and his career-long collection of masks and makeups is destroyed. It happens often in these pictures that the artist and his or her works are consumed together, as in the fire at the start of *Mystery of the Wax Museum*.[10]

Color Me Blood Red is about a painter (Don Joseph as Adam Sorg) who finds the red he needs by using his blood. Soon he is covered with cuts and decides to kill women to use their blood. His newly energized work wins critical acclaim. Where at first he had rubbed directly on the canvas with one razor-cut finger after another, he later drains one woman's blood into a clotted bowl and uses a paintbrush. He thinks he makes his victims immortal in art, a conviction shared by the artists in *Mystery of the Wax Museum* and *House of Wax*. When Sorg is shot by a young man who is saving a victim, he bleeds onto a blank canvas, creating his final piece. The owner of the gallery that exhibits Sorg's work burns what appears to be that canvas and says he is burning Sorg too. Again the horrific work and its creator are destroyed together.

Another obsessed painter becomes a gory murderer in *The Driller Killer* (Abel Ferrara, 1979, US). Reno (Abel Ferrara), a perfectionist like many of the artists discussed here, works on what may be his greatest painting while under a lot of stress. It is hard to concentrate in a rundown loft with a rock band practicing next door, not enough money and a live-in girlfriend (Carol, played by Carolyn Marz) who is unhappy.[11] The painting calls for fine brush strokes, for control, but Reno also feels like exploding in large gestures. He buys a battery belt that allows him to plug in a portable drill with which he kills derelicts he finds on the streets. To some extent these isolated men are symbols of his own spiritual isolation, a condition emphasized at the picture's start. His attacks with the drill, often carried out while straddling the victim, are homophobic. Here the mad artist and his violence are loud, dark, chaotic, nerve-racking horrors while the artwork, his painting, is controlled and uncontaminated.

In *Hour of the Wolf* (Ingmar Bergman, 1968, Sweden)—where what is frightening is the madness of the artist—a painter, Johan (Max von Sydow), draws the scary figures that appear to him and shows them to his wife, Alma (Liv Ullmann). The figures come in nightmares or from the night itself. What Johan sees in his madness is shown onscreen without any "dream" or "mad sequence" framing, and at several points the audience is unsure of how much of this is real, particularly because Alma, who is sane, often sees the same things. The figures are grotesques, as close as Bergman ever came to Fellini, and they live on the same island as Johan and Alma, if they live at all. They may be dreams become real, they may be entirely imaginary or they may be actual people. One of them comes in through a locked door as if he were a phantom but leaves a real gun on the table, with which Johan shoots Alma in the arm (an event confirmed by Alma much later, when she speaks with the filmmaker to whom she has given Johan's diary). Alma wonders whether she sees these figures because they are real or because love and long acquaintance have made her think and feel as her husband does. The film doesn't answer that question, but it takes the grotesques so far that we realize they cannot be ordinary mortals, for the face of the "Bird Man" can change from human to masklike, and a woman can take off her face along with her hat. Madness and its minions turn the artist's world into a dark labyrinth, and when Johan finally disappears without a trace, there is a hint that he has been swallowed by the world of his persecutors.

The labyrinth created by the popular horror writer Sutter Cane (Jürgen Prochnow) in Carpenter's *In the Mouth of Madness* (John Carpenter, 1995, US) is tightly reflexive. An insurance investigator, John Trent (Sam Neill), is sent by Cane's publisher to find the missing author and bring back his latest manuscript. Cane, who lives in a town that is not on the map except for in his fiction, believes his fiction is real. It turns out that Cane is in league with the Old Ones (dark beings inspired by the work of H. P. Lovecraft) and that the publication of his next book will help to bring about an age of evil. Already Cane's "less stable" readers are left disoriented and paranoid, even with memory loss, and when Trent reads Cane's novels, he has bad dreams. One of Cane's readers tries to kill Trent, coming at him through a restaurant window. The new book, *In the Mouth of Madness*, is published even though Trent tries to destroy the manuscript—the forbidden text—and an age of evil does begin. When a movie is made from the book, Trent goes to see it. His own picture is on the poster for this movie (just as it is on the genuine poster outside the real theatre), and the inner movie, whose footage is identical to Carpenter's, shows Trent's life as we have seen it. That life is his fate, a fate determined by Cane's writing.[12] He laughs hysterically, especially at assertions about what is real, then begins to cry, driven mad by the trap of art.

Believers: *The Black Cat, Blood Feast* and *The Wicker Man*

The leaders and followers of cults often become figures of horror. The aims of the cults and the desires of their leaders and members are usually presented as evil, as in the real world they sometimes are. They may sacrifice victims as part of their rituals. They may strike down those whom they believe the supernatural force to which they are dedicated wants them to destroy. Most cults do not directly employ supernatural power as a coven of witches and wizards might, but exercise human power in the light of their insights, as in Lewton's *The Seventh Victim* (Mark Robson, 1943, US). By implication, the movies usually set up the larger religions as safer, saner alternatives for conventional believers, but even they or their offshoots are sometimes shown—as in *Frailty* (Bill Paxton, 2002, US/Germany/Italy)—to have attracted their share of the disturbed and destructive.

In *The Black Cat* (Edgar G. Ulmer, 1934, US) Dr Vitus Werdegast (Bela Lugosi) meets a young couple (Jacqueline Wells as Joan and David Manners as Peter) on a train. They have just been married, for this is another story of an interrupted honeymoon. After getting off the train and surviving a car accident, the three (accompanied by Werdegast's servant) become guests of architect Hjalmar Poelzig (Boris Karloff). Poelzig is the leader of a Satanic cult that meets in his ultramodern house, which is built above the ruins of a fort where, during the war, Poelzig betrayed the thousands of men under his command, most of whom died. Werdegast wants the couple to be allowed to leave, but Poelzig wants to sacrifice Joan in a ceremony. They play chess for the couple, and Werdegast loses.

The architecturally impressive house and the bleak military region below both have an air of evil that extends into the future and the past. In the basement where a gun turret and chart room used to be, preserved behind glass, hangs the body of Werdegast's wife, Karen. When he is shown Karen's body, Werdegast attempts to kill Poelzig but stops when he sees a black cat. His fear of cats amuses Poelzig, who keeps a black cat (which he calls a symbol of evil) as a pet. Poelzig officiates at the cult's rites (Figure 30) until the ceremony is disrupted and Werdegast saves Joan. Werdegast starts to skin Poelzig on a rack, but Peter shoots Werdegast, thinking he means to harm Joan. Giving the couple time to escape, Werdegast blows up the house and the cult, along with Poelzig and himself, with the dynamite that had been placed throughout the old fortress. Poelzig, who is cruel and sophisticated, represents the horrors of World War I, on which his immoral new world is built, and of Satanism. His modernist, partly expressionist house suggests that he is the wave of the future. The cult is an extension of his personal evil, but it is also true that he is the key expression of the cult's evil.

Blood Feast (1963), the first gore film, is well known for its grisly, convincing effects and its terrible writing and acting. This low-budget film is in color, as most low-budget films of the period were not, and that makes the gore more vivid. It contributed significantly to the development of the slasher film (it shows one man, armed primarily with a machete, killing a series of young women) and can be considered one of its key prototypes.[13]

Figure 30. *The Black Cat*: A ceremony.

The horror figure, an Egyptian named Fuad Ramses (Mal Arnold), belongs to an ancient cult of which he appears to be the only surviving member. Were he not such an intent believer, he would be categorized simply as a mad killer. He is devoted to Ishtar and intends to revive her by holding a blood feast in her honor (where the food is prepared from different parts of numerous women), the like of which has not been seen for 5,000 years. He has written a book called *Ancient Weird Religious Rites*, and he selects his victims primarily from those who have ordered the book. In Ishtar's name he keeps a gold-painted, blue-draped mannequin in the back room of his exotic catering business. The only action it performs is to weep blood when he dies—a supernatural surprise.

Dorothy Fremont (Lyn Bolton) hires Ramses to cater a dinner party for her daughter, Suzette (Connie Mason), and Ramses decides to make this the occasion for the blood feast. The police (Thomas Wood [William Kerwin] as Pete and Scott H. Hall as Frank) are baffled and a bit slow. While Pete and Suzette fall in love—and attend a lecture on ancient Egyptian cults that explains most of what is going on, not that they realize it—Ramses kills a woman in her bathtub and then hacks off her leg with a machete, cuts off the top of a woman's head on the beach and takes the brain, tears out a woman's tongue and flays a woman for her blood to add to the sauce. He lays out and cooks the body parts in his institutional kitchen. All this is very bloody. At the party itself, he goes too far. Before serving Mrs Fremont's guests, Ramses tries to sacrifice Suzette in a dedication ceremony in the kitchen, but she is saved just in time, and Ramses is crushed to death in a garbage truck.

Fuad Ramses is the consummate threatening believer, a man driven by the demands of an ancient cult to construct a masterpiece of human sacrifice. The gore is both the literal result and the symbol of his mad violence, which is inspired by his cult project. Not just gore but gore inspired by religion is the center of the horror and the unifier of the picture. The gore is central to the cannibalistic feast and its preparation, and though cannibalism is a running theme of the picture, no human flesh is eaten in it, no blood drunk, no sauce sampled. Cannibalism and gore are included in the bloody cult and in what Ramses, as a believer, does and plans to do.

The Wicker Man (Robin Hardy, 1973, UK), written by Anthony Shaffer, is the story of a policeman, Sergeant Howie (Edward Woodward), who is a devout Christian and a virgin. He goes to an island in search of a missing girl, Rowan (Geraldine Cowper). He finds that the inhabitants are pagans. Their leader is Lord Summerisle (Christopher Lee), whose beliefs he considers blasphemous. The people are all far too sexually frank and liberal for Howie's taste and for his principles. He fears they plan to sacrifice Rowan in a pagan ceremony, but by pursuing her he falls into a trap, for he is the sacrificial victim they wanted all along, the key figure in their ritual. With some animals, he is burned alive inside the wicker statue of a giant. He dies as a Christian martyr.

The horror is in what the cult members, as a band of worshippers, gather to do: the May Day burning of the innocent fool in a fertility ritual that will appease the gods of nature and lead to the good harvest they were denied the previous year. ("It is I who will live again," Howie says in defiance, "not your damned apples!") The fire is painful, and the happy singing and dancing of the pagans, who are content with themselves and indifferent to the suffering of the sacrificed, is cruel.

Sadists and Torturers: *The Raven*, *Salò* and *Hostel*

Sadists inflict pain, all kinds of pain in all kinds of situations, because it gives them pleasure and satisfies desire. Torturers specialize. Torture, which may be used to extract information or confessions, has a long history in politics and religion. In that context, it is primarily coercive and may not have a psychological motivation. But there is also torture carried out for no motive beyond the torturer's pleasure, and its psychologically disturbed perpetrators are sadists. As an element of horror art, torture goes back at least to the Grand Guignol, the theatre of suffering and effects. *Salò or The 120 Days of Sodom* (1975) is based on one of the books that defined sadism, and it is deliberately repulsive as well as, in a damned way, beautiful; it offers for consumption human feces on fine silver before it moves on to matters of blood. *Saw* (James Wan, 2004, US/Australia) and *Hostel* (2005, released 2006) and their sequels are examples of what has been called "torture porn," with painfully violent onscreen actions and with the audience generally on the side of the victims but still excited by or at least focusing on the spectacles of torture and suffering, which are as intense as possible whether they and their instruments are stylized, like the elaborate machines and setups in the *Saw* series, or realistic, like the circular saw shoved into a woman's face in *Hostel Part II* (2007).

The *Raven* (Louis Friedlander, also known as Lew Landers, 1935, US) teamed Boris Karloff (Bateman) as a criminal on the run and Bela Lugosi (Dr Vollin) as a mad doctor obsessed with Poe. In his elaborate basement Vollin has a "museum of torture" that includes several devices described by Poe, including a knife-edged pendulum. Vollin is infatuated with Jean (Irene Ware), who is engaged to Jerry (Lester Matthews), a doctor who has recently become Vollin's assistant. Jean's father, Judge Thatcher (Samuel S. Hinds), is grateful to Vollin for saving Jean's life in an operation but wants Vollin not to pursue her romantically. Vollin feels "tortured" by his frustrated love and determines to "torture… those who have tortured" him; this will free him from his madness, leaving him able to do his work. He believes that Poe was tortured and driven mad in the same way by his love for the "lost Lenore" of "The Raven."

When Bateman comes to him demanding plastic surgery, Vollin makes him hideous, then cruelly laughs at him. Vollin promises to make him attractive after Bateman has tortured and murdered some people for him. Both men feel that a person who looks ugly may find it easier to do ugly things—a principle that has affected the design of many monsters. Vollin invites Jean, Jerry, Judge Thatcher and four others to a dinner party at his home, where they are to spend the weekend. That first night, Vollin has Bateman secure Judge Thatcher to a slab below the pendulum (Figure 31), subjecting him to the "torture of waiting" for the blade to reach his heart, and has him put Jean and Jerry into a locked room whose walls begin to come together. The latter is a "torture" that Vollin considers a parody of togetherness in marriage. "Yes," Vollin says as the walls approach each other and the pendulum swings, "I like to torture." But Bateman, who will not allow Jean to be killed, lets her and Jerry out of the contracting room even if Vollin shoots him for it. Before Bateman dies, he puts Vollin in the room where the walls crush him, destroying the torturer with his own device, a fitting end.

Figure 31. *The Raven*: The pendulum.

Salò sets its adaptation of the Marquis de Sade's *The 120 Days of Sodom* late in World War II, when Mussolini's final government was located in Salò in the north of Italy. Four fascist authority figures—the Duke (Paolo Bonacelli), the Monsignore (Giorgio Cataldi), His Excellency (Uberto P. Quintavalle) and the President (Aldo Valletti)—kidnap eight young men and eight young women and subject them to repulsive, humiliating torments that increase as the symbolic structure of the film descends a new version of the circles of Hell (the outer chamber, the circle of obsessions, the circle of shit and the circle of blood) until the victims are murdered in a final torture session. Three whores excite the sadists daily with erotic tales, and a pianist (Sonia Saviange) plays to set a controlled, light, civilized mood. When she sees at the climax that the young people are being killed, the pianist draws a line, much as Bateman had in regard to the plan to kill Jean, and silently kills herself, as previously mentioned. She offers a moral judgment on the carnage, which is refreshing in a film in which the villains get away with everything.

The victims are introduced to anal eroticism, used as sexual objects, made to eat feces, kept naked and threatened with death or dismemberment if they break the rules. In some places as red as the walls in an old whorehouse,[14] though most of its colors are subdued, the set is photographed in a cold manner, and the naked bodies are not eroticized. The viewer of this movie is not encouraged to become a sadist, though the movie fully realizes the sadistic vision. Fascism is made equally repellent; for example, one man defends the social hierarchy while another fills a piece of cake with nails for a captive to eat.

One boy hopes that one of the fascists will spare him because they have become lovers, but at the end no one is spared anything. Eyes are gouged out, penises and breasts are burned, tongues are cut out, scalps are cut off, nipples are branded. The torture killings, which were prepared for in story by a laughing whore, are shown through a pair of binoculars—at one point inverted—making the audience feel the violence more because it is kept small, framed and silent. The binoculars are directed through a window that reveals the horror, making the interior of the building (any part of which can be used as a virtual bedroom for perverse sexual acts) the realm of the voyeuristic sadist. The victims suffer realistically, though we can't hear them. The last one we see is about to vomit from pain. The binocular shots are a great example of the power of understatement to convey horror and pain, while they are also a Brechtian estrangement device. In their robes, the sadists dance with joy. The ending shows another side of the horror as two of the soldiers, who have helped the fascists, slow-dance together and talk about their girlfriends[15] as if it were simple to go back to the normal world, untouched by all they have done. No matter how immoral its events, *Salò* is a relentless film that refuses to play the easy emotional chords of sentimentality, pity, revenge, humanism and the triumph of justice while it shows how terrible fascism and sadism can be and how closely they can be related. It presents a damned world in which some people suffer and some have a good time causing their pain. *Salò* is the most moral and scathingly controlled of the sadist pictures.

Between 1985 and 1990, a series of violent and sometimes sadistic videos called *Guinea Pig* was produced in Japan. Each is less than an hour long and is characterized by extremely realistic special-effects makeup. Making independent videos allowed the artists to do things not permitted in movies or on TV. The first two videos pretended to be, or to reproduce, snuff films, and they nearly attained the effects and the simultaneously sociopathic and sadistic attitude necessary to sustain that illusion. (Some of the later *Guinea Pig* videos were comedies.) In the earliest video, *Guinea Pig: The Devil's Experiment* (Satoru Ogura, 1985, Japan), a woman is stalked by a group of men, tortured and killed. The next one, *Guinea Pig 2: Flower of Flesh and Blood* (Hideshi Hino, 1985, Japan), has two killers—one of whom is behind the camera that "documents" all this[16] and the other of whom is shown doing everything: abducting a woman, giving her a drug that reduces her bleeding and makes her enjoy the pain, and then slowly cutting her to pieces. The killers are aesthetes (suffering from "aesthetic paranoia," according to the introductory crawl), and the one who is on camera, who wears white makeup and a black samurai helmet, speaks about the beauty and the aesthetic integrity of what he is doing: the "blossoms" he is making of the woman's blood on her flesh, the "ideal of beauty" it represents when he cuts through her wrist, the "necklace of bright red flowers" that appears when he chops off her head. The most beautiful part of her body, he says as he takes one out and sucks it clean, is a woman's eye. Unlike most sadists, he is not interested in causing the woman pain, only in cutting her up and watching her blood flow. It is convenient for him that she does not struggle while he creates all this "beauty" but is silent, in what he presumes to be "a state of ecstasy." Unstylized and shot up close, the gore is presented as fascinating and exciting so that the inner video[17] shares the sick aesthetics of the killers. The complete video, *Flower of Flesh and Blood*, even with its judgmental explanatory titles, presents the bloody, drugged dismemberment for its own sake, encouraging the viewer either to squirm or to discover a compelling beauty in it at the ground zero of the wounded body. It is an experiment in declaring a beauty in horror, although it admits that the artist who perceives, controls and presents that beauty is insane.

In *Saw*, John Kramer (Tobin Bell), known to the police as the Jigsaw Killer or simply Jigsaw, abducts people who have, to his mind, committed moral crimes and puts them under pressure, trapping them in situations or mechanisms that will usually lead to their deaths in a set amount of time if they do not hurt themselves in some awful manner (or in some cases kill another person) to get free. Each torture device or situation is ironically related to the victim's moral failing or character flaw. In the sequels, which ran annually from *Saw II* (Darren Lynn Bousman, 2005, US/Canada) until *Saw 3D* or *Saw: The Final Chapter* (Kevin Greutert, 2010, US/Canada), it is revealed that Jigsaw has assistants whose conflicts intensify after his death.

Saw opens with two men (Leigh Whannell as Adam and Cary Elwes as Lawrence) who are in a large, isolated bathroom in which lies a dead body. One foot of each man is shackled and chained, and there are two hacksaws in the room. Tape recordings inform them that Lawrence must kill Adam (by sawing off his own foot to reach the gun in the corpse's hand) or see his family killed.[18] Lawrence's sin is adultery, and Adam's is not appreciating life. The killer of the family will be a third man Jigsaw is also controlling. There is a time limit. The torture culminates when Lawrence, who is a surgeon, saws through his leg (Figure 32), then shoots Adam and crawls out of the room.[19] Adam, not mortally wounded, is left to die in the bathroom after the "corpse" gets up—a terrific horror moment—and is seen to be Jigsaw. Part of Jigsaw's pleasure comes from observing his captives, and from the floor he has followed the entire event.

We have heard from Lawrence, who is familiar with the case, about some of Jigsaw's other torture devices and chambers. For example, a man who tried to kill himself by

Figure 32. *Saw*: Pain up close.

slashing his wrists wakes in a room full of razor wire. A tape informs him that he must find his way through the wire to the door before it is locked forever, and the question is how much he will cut himself to live. One of the victims, Amanda (Shawnee Smith), survives an encounter with a machine that would have torn off her jaw (as a videotape of Jigsaw informs her, in which a puppet with a mask-like face acts as narrator) if she had not retrieved the key to unlock it from her cellmate's stomach. To get that key, she had to kill him. A drug addict, she feels Jigsaw helped her. The tapes usually begin with Jigsaw's greeting the victim and saying "I want to play a game." For the victim the object of the game is to survive by following instructions, and as Amanda's case demonstrates, Jigsaw plays fairly. Given the terms he sets out for the game, it is possible to win.

Throughout the sequels, the tapes that announce the terms of the torturous tests, the games, remain central to the action and the dark, ironic mood. Some of the assistants do not play fairly, allowing victims no release. In *Saw II* Jigsaw says he is "testing the fabric of human nature," but such testing depends on a fair game. At the climax of *Saw V* (David Hackl, 2008, US/Canada) the walls of a locked room come together much as in *The Raven*, but they crush the hero. This scene is far more elaborate and bloody than the climax of the earlier film and of course has the opposite result, leaving the torturer safe. It is the original, unforgiving design of Jigsaw's devices and chambers that makes the tortures compelling in most of the films (the victims' mutilating themselves, as when Lawrence saws off his foot, is also part of the spectacle), and it is the cleverness of the best-designed traps and games that gives the stories their intrigue and coherence.[20]

In *Hostel* and *Hostel Part II*, as in the *Saw* films, the tortures are the central spectacles. Both series offer vividly graphic wounds and realistic sounds.

Few of Jigsaw's "test subjects" survive to appreciate life and make better decisions in the new way he had hoped they would, but in each of the *Hostel* films a victim manages to escape and avenge, at least in part, what has been done to himself or herself and his or her friends. The villains in the *Hostel* films are rich people out to enjoy the thrill of torturing a captive to death, and belong to a private Eastern European club that can be compared to a brothel for torture killing, an extreme instance of paying to use others' bodies. The victims whose stories we follow are men in the first film, then women in the second, all of whom are college age and are kidnapped after they check into a youth hostel. Some are implicitly punished for their sexual activity as in the slasher films—like the young woman in *Part II* who makes the reckless decision to go off with a potential boyfriend, or like the horny young men in the first film who are glad that the hostel is full of sexually available women—but some are simply abducted.

Hostel opens while a torture cell is being cleaned after use. A shot of blood being washed slowly through dirt and down a drain is beautiful and all but abstract. The three backpackers who disappear from the Slovakian hostel are Paxton (Jay Hernandez), Josh (Derek Richardson) and Oli (Eythor Gudjonsson). When Josh comes to, he finds himself chained to a chair in a locked, dingy room where a table is loaded with tools and instruments and where a sadist (a Dutch businessman, played by Jan Vlasák, whom the three had met on a train previously, and a character who, the audience finds, always wanted to be a surgeon) first takes a power drill to him, then—as part of giving him an apparent chance to walk away—slices his Achilles tendons. Later he kills Josh with a chest operation.

When Paxton is taken to the large factory-like building where the tortures take place, he asks a departing customer (played by horror director Takashi Miike), who takes him for a club member, what the place is like, and the customer warns him that he could spend all his money in there. When he is chained to a chair in a room when it's his turn, Paxton manages to kill his German torturer (Petr Janis), who has cut off two of Paxton's fingers with a chainsaw and inadvertently freed his hands. Making his escape, Paxton discovers Oli's body in a superbly grisly chamber where the victims' corpses are butchered before being cremated. He learns the gist of how the club operates by talking to an American customer (played by Rick Hoffman) who is on the way to his torture session. Working himself into a state of sadistic excitement, the customer compares torturing and killing someone to sex, expecting the torture to be much more memorable. In a stolen car, Paxton runs over the man and two women who conned him and his friends and set up their abduction. When he gets on a train, he finds by chance the Dutch businessman whom he saw carving up Josh and kills him in a station toilet—after cutting off two of his fingers—then rides out of the country. This bloody revenge and successful escape provide a satisfying sense of justice served (undone at the beginning of the sequel when Paxton is murdered by the club's agents), while the impression of a sick and violent side of human nature remains: our memory of the "Elite Hunting" club and its sadistic customers, who want the "rush" of doing anything to a person—anything as long as it ends in death—and having had it, go back for more. The victims are commodities as well as suffering beings. The club puts into practice the worst aspects of capitalism, which here include the premise that a person can, like a slave, be abducted and sold.

But capitalism has its good points in *Hostel Part II*, where having a lot of money allows the heroine to buy her way from victim to club member. This time it is three American college students, Beth (Lauren German), Lorna (Heather Matarazzo) and Whitney (Bijou Phillips), who take a break from their studies abroad to check into the same hostel. The woman responsible for conning them is Axelle (Vera Jordanova). The first victim is Lorna, who is abducted on an ill-advised date and hung naked above a tub in a large candlelit chamber, where a naked woman cuts her with a scythe—first teasingly, then all over, finally slicing her throat with a sickle—and bathes in her blood. In the sequel, more time is spent on the emotional makeup of the customers. Two of them have bid on Whitney and Beth, the Americans Todd (Richard Burgi) and Stuart (Roger Bart). Todd is excited about killing someone, while Stuart is less enthusiastic and even makes personal contact with Beth—but when they actually carry out the tortures, their positions are reversed. In the film's most morally powerful as well as gory scene, Todd is sickened when he sees the damage his power saw has done to Whitney's face. He tries to leave, but the club's contract stipulates that no one can leave without killing, so he is set upon by dogs. When he sees Todd's body, Stuart becomes violent and interrupts his session with Beth to kill Whitney, an experience that he feels does, as Todd had predicted, make him more of a man—a man who is finally ready to kill Beth. For a while he treats Beth as he would like to be "allowed" to treat his wife. Beth overpowers Stuart when he tries to rape her and summons the guards, who bring the club's owner. She says she wants to buy her way out of the place, and when it is explained that she has to kill someone, she castrates Stuart and leaves him to bleed to death (as castrated men almost always do in horror films). When she is free—and she is truly free and will be allowed to live, for unlike Paxton she has followed the rules of the club—she traps and decapitates Axelle. Beth is an admirable example of the powerful woman in the contemporary horror film. She is not just a victim who manages to survive, but a hero. With their male and female victims, the two symmetrical movies are a diptych, and both end with the exercise of violent justice by a strong hero who has survived an encounter with sadism, torture and the prospect of death. The *Hostel* films do not actually offer "torture porn" but instead reveal the moral and psychological weakness of the torturer, an approach that would be as forbidden in pornography as the portrayal of impotence.

Ghouls: *The Body Snatcher* and Ed Gein

Ghouls do their damage to the dead. They delight in the loathsome and morbid. They plunder graves, sometimes eating the flesh of the corpses or committing necrophilia. Obsessed with death and the dead, it is in cemeteries that they exercise their extremes of desire—unless they take the bodies home. There may be a fear of the living behind this, as a living lover has a will but a corpse does not. A corpse cannot object to being sexually violated or having its heart cut out or being eaten. But there is also a pull that death exerts as if it were a primary value for the ghoul, a state to be celebrated.

Ghouls are not simply imaginary creatures. In Paris in 1849, an officer named Bertrand confessed to a court-martial that he had felt compelled to violate the graves of many women, most often tearing the corpses apart with his hands and teeth or a spade. Sometimes he "rolled among the fragments."[21]

In some cases it is the fact, the state, of death that fascinates the psychopath, and digging up the dead can give him or her a sense of control over death, a special knowledge of it. But there are also cases where the corpse is a romantic or economic object.

In Edinburgh in 1827–28, William Burke and William Hare sold corpses to Dr Robert Knox, an anatomist. Body snatchers, also called Resurrectionists, were digging up corpses and selling them to doctors, but Burke and Hare decided to murder people instead, suffocating them in a way that left no marks of violence (ever since called "to burke") and then selling them to Knox. They were caught late in 1828 after killing at least 15 travelers and others they presumed would not be missed. Lewton's *The Body Snatcher*, set in Edinburgh in 1831 and based on the story "The Body-Snatcher" by Robert Louis Stevenson, is the tale of a fictitious assistant to Dr Knox, a Dr "Toddy" MacFarlane (Henry Daniell), and what happens when he takes on an assistant of his own, Donald Fettes (Russell Wade). MacFarlane must introduce Fettes to cab driver John Gray (Boris Karloff). Gray digs up fresh corpses and sells them to MacFarlane, who dissects the specimens with his medical students, since the school can't get enough bodies for its needs through official channels (the municipal council, which provides the corpses of paupers). Fettes feels morally compromised by his dealings with Gray, but MacFarlane does not; he values the time he spent with Knox and considers Gray a necessary evil. As grave robbers, both Gray and MacFarlane are ghouls. The emotional effect of having a son's corpse dug up is strongly conveyed by an old mother.

Things go wrong when Fettes demands Gray find a body quickly (so that MacFarlane can study its spine before operating on a little girl; the film is clearly in favor of anatomical research while it deplores grave robbing). On impulse, Gray kills and delivers a blind street singer. Later he burkes one of MacFarlane's servants, Joseph (Bela Lugosi), when Joseph blackmails him, and he brings the body to MacFarlane as a gift. Gray insists the doctor will never get rid of him. They fight, and MacFarlane kills Gray, then makes plans to dissect the evidence.

At the picture's memorable climax, Fettes and MacFarlane are heading home in a carriage during a rainstorm. Between them, in a bag, is the body of an old woman the doctor has insisted they dig up. MacFarlane becomes convinced the body in the bag, which he imagines is calling to him, is Gray, and he tells Fettes to get out and get the lantern to shine on the corpse. Once the bag is opened so that only the doctor can see the face (preserving the ambiguity of the supernatural, as in most Lewton films), the light reveals the face of Gray. The doctor's shout alarms the horses, and they take off, leaving Fettes behind. As the lightning flashes, we see that the corpse really is Gray, being jostled by the horses so that his naked body is leaning against MacFarlane and even reaching for him; the intermittently bright image is ghastly. After the first shot, the ones following of Gray are not POV shots but also show the doctor (though the scene could still be read as subjective, as showing how MacFarlane imagines and experiences it). Gray may appear as a figment of MacFarlane's conscience, but the possibility that he actually shows up to take vengeance and to enforce the bond between himself and MacFarlane is more thrilling—and more instructive for what it reveals about horror—because it can't be happening yet *is* happening, and because it has the force of moral truth even if it can't be true. The fantastic is realized without losing its ambiguity. The panicked doctor drives the carriage off a cliff. In the wreckage Fettes finds the body of an old woman and that of MacFarlane. Fettes is left to practice medicine, which we trust him to do without robbing any graves. His horror phase is over.

Mr. Sardonicus (William Castle, 1961, US) tells of a man (played by Guy Rolfe) who digs up his father to retrieve a lottery ticket from his pocket, a ticket that had turned out to be a winner. His father's corpse has a wide, horrible smile. Guilt and fear cause the son's mouth to freeze, virtually forever,[22] in a sardonic smile that resembles the father's. The confrontation with the corpse in the open grave at night is the highpoint of horror in the film—appropriately, since this is a ghoul picture. His fears of the corpse and the grave, of which he is never free for the rest of his life, are as fixed as his smile, which is modeled on a rigid smile of death.

Psycho, the picture most responsible for making the murderous psychopath a recurring figure in the horror films of the late twentieth and early twenty-first centuries, was based on Robert Bloch's novel *Psycho*, which in turn was inspired by the discovery of the crimes committed and the life led by Ed Gein.[23] (The novel and the film were also probably influenced by Faulkner's story "A Rose for Emily," with its woman in the window and its corpse in the bed.) Because Gein's story had been covered in the magazine *Life*, many of the adults who went to see *Psycho* were familiar with it. Gein, eventually called "the mad butcher of Plainfield," idealized and was very attached to his controlling, sex-hating, deeply disturbed mother. He was a meek, soft-spoken man who never struck his neighbors as threatening, though sometimes he did seem to be laughing at some private joke. He lived alone on the deteriorating family farm after his mother's death, doing odd jobs. He closed off his mother's rooms as she had left them and lived in astounding clutter in part of the rest of the rundown farmhouse, creating a filthy mess (much of it of special value to him) that could be considered a model of his mind. In time he became a ghoul. He dug up the recently buried bodies of middle-aged and older women[24]—but never his mother. He sewed their skins into a woman suit, featuring leggings cut from legs and a vest with breasts, and some nights he would wear it. He made collections of women's dried and preserved sexual organs and turned sawed skulls into soup bowls. He murdered a woman who ran a tavern, and her face was later found in a paper bag. He was accused of cannibalism but did not practice it; still, that became part of the legend. He made a belt out of nipples and wove chair seats from strips of skin. He cured heads in brine. He cut off faces, some of which resembled his mother's, and dried them to make masks. A ghoulish artist, he decorated a shade-pull with lips. (In this and in the making of masks, he resembles Leatherface and the hitchhiker in *Texas Chain Saw*, who also were based on him. Hooper's intention was to make a film about "a whole family of Ed Geins."[25]) He imitated the Nazis he had read about in pulp magazines and made lampshades, a drum and other items out of skin. He was caught in 1957 when he shot a woman (it is not known whether he ever killed more than two) and hung up her corpse by the heels in a shed[26] to clean it like a deer. Her decapitated and eviscerated body was found with the heart in a plastic bag and the vulva in a box (with others), with hooked spikes driven into the ears so the head could be hung for display. He never showed remorse and was committed to a hospital for the criminally insane.[27] He felt both love and an unconscious hatred for his mother, and he dug up or killed women who reminded him of her. He once hoped to bring his mother back from the dead, and it is possible that when he dressed in his woman skins, he fantasized that he had done so, although it is more likely that he fantasized simply that he was a woman.

In addition to *Psycho* and *The Texas Chain Saw Massacre*, his story inspired *Deranged* (Jeff Gillen and Alan Ormsby, 1974, Canada/US) as well as *The Silence of the Lambs* and the novel by Thomas Harris on which it was based. When *Psycho*'s Norman Bates (Anthony Perkins) practiced taxidermy—which Gein was reported to do but actually did not—exhibited a nervous meekness, suffered from an Oedipus complex, felt under the influence of his dead mother, kept his mother's corpse at home (though Gein kept only parts of corpses in his house and never violated his mother's grave), kept a space dedicated to his mother and filled with her furniture in his death-charged house, dressed like her to keep her memory alive, gave expression to her hatred of sexually tempting women and appeared to be heading for an asylum at the end, he reflected the influence of Gein, who was both the ultimate ghoul and a man obsessed with the female body. When he killed his victims with a butcher knife, he prepared the way for the slashers.

Deranged may be technically weak and badly scored, but it does deliver its ghoul: Ezra Cobb (Roberts Blossom), an interpretation of Gein. *Deranged*—which includes fairly realistic scenes of the ghoul's shoveling graves open at night—shows both the sadness and the madness that accompany the ghoul's solitary position, his loneliness and his attempt to find among the dead both company and the experience of control.

Mad Killers: *Psycho* and *Henry: Portrait of a Serial Killer*

The victims of psychopathic and psychotic killers touch their madness in a way they cannot resist. Mad killers, usually the concern of the crime film, become the province of the horror film when their deeds and their reasons for committing them are not merely criminal but especially frightening, revolting, graphic, disturbing and shocking. Their madness and its expression must lend themselves to images of horror, and there may be an emphasis on the outrages to which the body may be subjected. The violent rape scene in *Irreversible* (Gaspar Noé, 2002, France), for example, shows the crime but also goes beyond any previous cinematic depiction of sexual violence into extreme horror.[28] The madness of these characters, which always results in violence, exceeds ordinary psychological disturbance. In the figure of the psychotic killer, personal identity and a hold on reality are at stake, while the psychopath challenges all our conventional notions of morality and mercy and responsibility, of caring about the victim. It is in the category of mad killers, defined most clearly by *Psycho*, that some serial killers belong, along with those who are led by their compulsive acts of murder ever deeper into outright insanity. The emphasis here is on killers whose monstrous, gruesome, violent acts are horrors primarily because of their psychological aspects.

The most disturbing child-killer in early films is the nameless knife-murderer in *M* (1931), played by Peter Lorre. He whistles a tune from Grieg when he is in the grip of his compulsion to stab a little girl. Like Jack the Ripper, he is a serial killer before the term was coined. Ordinary criminals see the child-murderer as quite different from them, a disturbed person operating on a truly immoral level. Once the killer is caught by the city's criminals and beggars, who then try him, the question becomes whether a madman can be punished for his crimes since the impulses that drive him are clearly beyond his control. Building on the figure of the knife-wielding killer but making him insane, *M* is the major link between *Caligari* and *Psycho*.

Many horror films were made about disturbed killers between *M* and *Psycho*, of which the poles are the gross *Maniac* (Dwain Esper, 1934, US) and the slick *The Bad Seed* (Mervyn LeRoy, 1956, US).[29] *Maniac*, an exploitation film loosely based on Poe's "The Black Cat," tells of a mad scientist who is killed and then impersonated by his even crazier assistant, Maxwell (Bill Woods). Madness is explained by scrolling intertitles and illustrated with clips from *Häxan*. At one point, on camera, Maxwell gouges out the eye of a cat. This may be the worst examination of insanity on film.

Hereditary madness has power in *The Bad Seed* because it is feared by the mother (Nancy Kelly as Christine) and because it appears to be manifested in her homicidal child, Rhoda (Patty McCormack), who is eight years old. It is possible, however, that Rhoda is simply evil and psychopathic on her own. She is like a child monster, but human. Rhoda's problem is that she doesn't understand or care that it's wrong to kill people to get what she wants. Although she feels anger and fear under certain circumstances, killing doesn't make her feel anything. The sweeter she is, the more dangerous we realize she is and the more we see of the moral vacuum inside her—her absence of any feelings of remorse or pity, any sense of right and wrong. She was "born blind" to such things. She knows how it looks to be nice and show love, and she imitates it. In later years she would have been called a sociopath.

A voyeuristic madman who kills women with a blade, *Peeping Tom*'s Mark Lewis set the immediate stage for Norman Bates, though the films were made too close together for Powell's film to have influenced Hitchcock's. (Hitchcock did, however, see the film before *Psycho* was released and admired it.) It is a coincidence, then, that both films feature slasher prototypes and call much attention to the camera when presenting the voyeuristic aspects of their murderers and implicating the voyeurism of the audience.

Reflexivity in *Psycho* is primarily a matter of calling attention to the presence and the probing curiosity of the camera, which sometimes is identified with the gaze of Norman Bates—who at one point uses a peephole to watch his tenant undress—but most often satisfies and implicates the voyeuristic desires of the viewer. At the very start, the camera is looking through a hotel bedroom window at a pair of lovers (Janet Leigh as Marion Crane and John Gavin as Sam Loomis). Whenever there is a killing, the camera is in a good place to see it—in fact the best place—no matter how difficult to reach, like the sudden view from above the stairs where the attack on Arbogast (Martin Balsam) takes place, or the intimate view of the murder of Marion in the shower (at whose end her dead eye is superimposed on the drain, linking the gaze, death and waste) when horror comes to her through the barrier-turned-gateway of the shower curtain, the opened frame. The voyeuristic camera is a relentless eye that will always find Marion—through a hotel bedroom window, in an apparently safe shower or through a peephole.

Norman Bates imitated Ed Gein in some respects, as has been noted. So did Leatherface when he made masks out of faces and the hitchhiker when he created furniture and art from bodies. The twist on Gein's story that novelist Robert Bloch and screenwriter Joseph Stefano added to *Psycho* (with Stefano modifying the psychology worked out by Bloch) was that Norman became his mother in his own mind as a way to keep her alive. They made him a split personality (today he would be said to be suffering from dissociative identity disorder), part of him dressing as his mother and killing, primarily, young women to whom Norman is attracted, and the other part of him being the quiet young man who cleans up after her and tries to keep her under control. It may be hard to remember that for most of the movie, the audience thinks Mrs Bates is the murderer. When Norman is caught and exposed by Marion's sister, Lila (Vera Miles), and Sam, the mother in him takes over completely, and the Norman personality is obliterated. Each personality thought, with some justification, that the other committed the crimes. For most of the picture, the mother is the chief horror figure, both as an imaginary woman (Norman dressed as his mother and speaking as her) and as the corpse discovered in the cellar. When we understand, just as we see the corpse, that the mother is dead, the focus shifts and the horror figure becomes Norman, the crazy, timid man who can erupt into violence.

When the gray wig falls off Norman's contorted face, a physical threat is augmented by a mental horror. At the same time, the camera shows us the embodied horror of the corpse of the real Mrs Bates. The climax presents both versions of the mother at once and shows that mother and son, when joined, are death in life. The image of death runs throughout the picture, but the closing shots are particularly strong in this regard, for as Norman, now mentally entirely his mother, smiles at the camera, a skull is briefly superimposed on his face as the image dissolves to show the trunk of Marion's car, which contains her body, as it is pulled out of the mud toward the camera. After this evocation of death, the mud and the contents of the trunk (the "rear" of the car) are reminiscent of feces, an evocation of and comment on the way Marion's body was disposed of: dumped into a swamp after she died in a bathroom and her blood ran down the drain, the corpse left as a waste product of homicidal rage.

Henry: Portrait of a Serial Killer (John McNaughton, 1986, released 1990, US) follows Henry (Michael Rooker) as he kills a number of people and forms a relationship, the most intimate he can manage, with Otis (Tom Towles) and his sister, Becky (Tracy Arnold). Needless to say, intimacy is not Henry's strong point, and when Becky insists on going away with him, Henry agrees while knowing he will feel compelled to kill her. At the end both Otis (whom Henry has initiated into the pleasures of random murder) and Becky have been killed, leaving Henry alone again.

One of the picture's most effective devices is to delay a detailed presentation of many of the murders until sometime after they have occurred. At such moments the film will show corpses while playing the sounds of the killings, a violent and evocative combination. When a horrific scene darts into Henry's consciousness—or when it is the right time for the film to present a flashback, regardless of what Henry is thinking—it conveys the reality of his life, an intensely graphic reality that is framed and complemented by the understated realism of the rest of the picture. Henry's absence of compassion, his bland daily life with its tense capacity for violence and the killings combine into the promised portrait of a psychopathic serial killer, loosely based on the life of Henry Lee Lucas (many of whose confessions, it now appears, were false). His lack of affect is frightening, as it should be. *Henry* encourages compassion for Becky and the random victims while it provides a convincing and at times understanding characterization of their killer.

The two young psychopathic killers in Michael Haneke's *Funny Games* (1997)[30] are, in contrast, unredeemably hateful. The more we watch and listen to them, the less we like them, but we can never be said to understand them. They are blank walls of amoral malice, and they have a twisted sense of politeness that is more than irritating. One of them (Arno Frisch as Paul) is more intelligent than the other (Frank Giering as Peter), but both of them enjoy violence and think what they are doing is amusing. The games they play with the captive family are not funny except to the sadistic home invaders. We identify with the victims and side particularly with the wife, Anna (Susanne Lothar). We want them to escape, but as Paul, looking at the camera, reminds us, we also want to be entertained by mayhem and violence. We want the action to go on so the film will reach its feature length, and we want "a real ending with plausible plot development." Thus we are implicated in what happens to the victims and in our seeing it. Reflexivity in the horror film is often a matter of making the audience ask why it wants to watch such things, as noted before, but rarely is the audience faced with such a bleak and sadistic horror to justify its interests.

Wolf Creek (Greg McLean, 2005, Australia) does not go into the psychology of the killer, Mick (John Jarratt), but his actions and his enthusiasm are insane. Ben (Nathan Phillips), Kristy (Kestie Morassi) and Liz (Cassandra Magrath) are tourists driving through the Outback. They stop for a hike, but when they return, their car won't start. Mick shows up in the middle of the night and offers to help. He tows them to his place, where he has the part they need. He has done this before, and the repetition clearly gives him pleasure. In short order Mick nails Ben to a wall, ties up Liz and tortures Kristy. When Liz escapes, Mick catches her and severs her lower spine with his hunting knife, leaving her "a head on a stick." The violence in *Wolf Creek* is ruthlessly executed, and the fear of being caught in the lair of a psychopathic killer, new victims in a long series, far from any help and surrounded by the debris of previous murders, is vividly evoked.

Mad killers bring their victims horrific violence that may be as stylized as the shower montage in *Psycho* or as unstylized as the knifework that turns Liz into a head on a stick. Whether or not their madness is analyzed and explained, they display it, are motivated by it and manifest its extremes, and the horror film is ready to make their insane vision the image of the world and how it functions: to show the world, figuratively, through Mark's homicidal viewfinder or through the lens-like orifices of Norman's peepholes.

Families: *The Last House on the Left* and *The Texas Chain Saw Massacre*

The horror family lives by its own rules. The family or near-family[31] group in a horror film is outside and apart from the conventions of civilization, unchallenged in its interpretation of the world. All or most of the members of the family have traits that make them frightening, repulsive and loathsome, and these traits and the characters themselves reinforce each other, making the whole, as a family, more horrific than the sum of its parts: a system.

The family is something most of us count on, a site of nurturance and growth. Horror turns it on its head and makes the family a site of degeneracy and destruction, though it is still characterized by tight bonds among the family members. Ideas and violent, perverse impulses bounce off the inner walls of the horror family as if hitting the walls of a house, and they can never break through to the sane outside. The father is often a more important force and determiner of values than the mother. His obsession, his craft or his temperament may be passed on to his children, so that cannibalism, for instance, could be the family legacy. Sometimes a child will turn against the will of the father and be destroyed, as in *The Last House on the Left* (Wes Craven, 1972, US), though he or she may also survive and help to save the good guys, as in *The Hills Have Eyes* (Wes Craven, 1977, US). As outsiders, these families prey on the civilized, even on other families. The horror family is often compared and set into conflict with a more conventional family, notably in *The Last House on the Left* and *The Hills Have Eyes*, which of course are by the same director.

The horror family is more than a collection of individuals, for some or all of its members are linked by blood, and it functions as a system that may appear crazy or out of control but has its own coherence. It is as a group that horror families and bands of outsiders do the most damage and pose the greatest obstacle to the survival of the conventional people. They are particularly repulsive when they are inbred, but there are many other taboos they violate.

Even if some of them are cannibals (in *Texas Chain Saw* and *The Hills Have Eyes*), that is not their primary and defining characteristic but one of their traits, one of the horror elements in the picture. It is not the fact that they are cannibals and ghouls that makes the family in *Texas Chain Saw* so formidable, so crazy together, so mutually reinforcing and so inseparable. It's that they are kin and have made their house a realm in which they are comfortable, that answers to their needs and obsessions from its slaughterhouse kitchen to its rooms full of ghoulish art. Part of the model for the horror family is the real-world dysfunctional family, part is the band of outlaws and part is the group of trolls, bad fairies or Little People[32] living in the woods or underground, or ready to leap at us from under a bridge, a destructive band of creatures who look alike—who bear, so to speak, a family resemblance. Although the members of a band of outsiders are usually not related to each other by blood or marriage, they are often as linked and purposeful as any horror family and may function as an equally integrated and murderous group; one ready example from the real world is the Manson "family."

A horror family can readily be composed of the deranged and unbalanced, and they will need a place to live. In *The Old Dark House* (1932) two groups of travelers, five people in all, take shelter from a storm in the titular building, which became the model for the large, underlit structure that harbors and hides a horror, from the farmhouse in *Texas Chain Saw* to the spaceship in *Alien*. The big house has no electricity and is the home of the Femm family. The first Femms we meet are the bickering, weird, slightly mad brother and sister, Horace (Ernest Thesiger) and Rebecca (Eva Moore), together with their creepy, mute butler, Morgan (Boris Karloff). Their 102-year-old father is kept in an upstairs room (the house features a large staircase) as the patriarch is in *Texas Chain Saw*. Even Horace is afraid of the Femm who is kept locked up in the top room, Saul (Brember Wills), who when he is released turns out to be a pyromaniac and a would-be killer. The old dark house gives an oppressive and frightening cast to the events, regardless of whether it hides a mad family or another kind of monster. The Myers family home becomes an old dark house in the course of *Halloween*.

The Virgin Spring (Ingmar Bergman, 1960, Sweden) is the story of a conventional family that is gravely hurt by three brothers who bring violence into their lives. The film is based on a fourteenth-century legend and is set in that period. The father, Töre (Max von Sydow), and the mother, Mareta (Birgitta Valberg), are stern and pious but good natured. Their only daughter is the vain and playful Karin (Birgitta Pettersson). A pregnant servant, Ingeri (Gunnel Lindblom), hates Karin and puts a frog in her bread on the day she is to carry the candles of the Virgin Mary to the local church. Ingeri also calls on the god Odin to curse Karin. Ingeri is sent to accompany Karin but feels poorly and stops for a while. Later, while hiding, she watches what happens. The three brothers, one of whom is a boy (Ove Porath), are herdsmen with stolen animals. They stop Karin on her way, and they have a picnic together until the frog jumps out of the loaf. Then the brothers turn on Karin and capture her, after which the two adults rape her. There is a particularly disgusting shot after the second adult (Tor Isedal), a mute, has raped her and lies on her, mouth open. In *The Last House on the Left*, which is based on *The Virgin Spring*, the rapist in the same position drools on his victim. Then the mute kills Karin by striking her head with a branch. They take her rich clothes and leave her body.

By chance, the brothers—the horror family—seek shelter at the home of the protagonists. After dinner one of the brothers (Axel Düberg), the first rapist, makes the mistake of offering the mother the clothes of the daughter, and at that point she realizes Karin has been murdered; he says they belonged to their late sister. She takes the clothes to her husband, and he kills the brothers. The father feels remorse for killing the boy and for the whole of his revenge. When the parents go to find Karin's body, the father rages at the God he does not understand. God witnessed and, more importantly, allowed the killing of the innocent child and the revenge. The ironic answer, or the key to God's attitude, is that God blesses this sacrifice of innocence with a miracle. When Karin is lifted off the ground, a spring appears where her head, the site of her wound, was lying. This asserts the power of God and his embrace of all aspects of life, the pure and the horrific, along with his weakness for ritual, for martyrdom and blood sacrifice. The world of *The Virgin Spring* and this God are made in each other's image. The only response it can see to horror is more horror, followed by sanctification.

The Last House on the Left preserves most of this story while updating it to the 1970s and setting it in New York State. God is left out of the picture, but there is a lake, corresponding roughly to the virgin spring, where violence occurs and blood is washed away. Because Sean S. Cunningham produced *Last House* and *Friday the 13th*, this lake may be (with the bay in *A Bay of Blood*) an ancestor of Crystal Lake, and there may be at the base of Crystal Lake not only blood, ablution, paradox and death, but also the power of a God with primitive, bloodthirsty tastes. In any case, the main reason God is left out is that *Last House* accepts the parents' revenge and does not see it as posing any moral problem. A terrible thing happens to their child, and they get even, and it does them good to accomplish their revenge without the help of the blundering police. The moral system of *Last House* is neither ambiguous nor ambivalent but simple. The vicious, ruthless cruelty and gore of the first half are complemented by the resourceful, endorsed violence of the second.

The horror "family" in *The Last House on the Left* is organized around Krug Stillo (David A. Hess), who runs things. He is also an unimaginably bad father. Junior (Marc Sheffler) is Krug's junkie son, whom Krug made an addict so that he could control him. Sadie (Jeramie Rain) is Krug's girlfriend, though it is strongly suggested that she also services Fred "Weasel" Podowski (Fred Lincoln), who has just escaped from prison with Krug and is not related to him. Though their bonds are not sanctified by marriage, they form a kind of family, with sexual ties among Krug, Sadie and Weasel, and a blood tie between Krug and Junior. They are brought into confrontation with the family of Dr John Collingwood (Gaylord St James), his wife, Estelle (Cynthia Carr), and their daughter, Mari (Sandra Cassell). The other major character, who is based on Ingeri, is Mari's lower-class friend, Phyllis Stone (Lucy Grantham). Mari is a virgin, while Phyllis appears to be more experienced. They decide to go to a rock concert for Mari's 17th birthday (the group is called Bloodlust, which the girls evidently consider a cool concept but not part of their everyday world). John and Estelle stay in their house—the one in the title, which is far from their neighbors—to prepare Mari's birthday party. As a present, they have given her a gold peace sign on a chain. Using this symbol, the movie implies that the peace movement is irrelevant as a solution to violence and that it is out of touch with the real world. Nonviolent solutions can work in the horror film (to take only one example, *The Uninvited*), but it is more common for violence to prevail in the story as well as in the worldview of the picture. Some horror movies, like many films in other genres, preach violence or encourage the audience to seek no alternative to it, constructing a trap for the characters from which violence offers the only escape.[33] While violence is often the only way to destroy a monster, it is not the only way to deal with a human, even one who represents an active threat (as at the climax of *The Curse of the Cat People*). *Last House* couldn't care less about these matters but stands as an example of the movie that deplores violence used against good characters and celebrates violence used against bad ones. That's an attitude found in many genres in many countries.

On their way to the concert, Mari and Phyllis try to buy some marijuana from Junior, whom they have never seen before, and are kidnapped by the gang. Phyllis is raped, and the next morning, Krug and the others put the girls in the trunk of their car and head upstate. By chance, their car breaks down across the street from Mari's house. They go into the woods where, before matters turn deadly, they have the equivalent of a picnic whose theme is the sexual humiliation of Phyllis and Mari. The childishness of the villains is emphasized in a scene when they force Phyllis to wet her pants and then laugh at her. The area includes a cemetery, where Phyllis is killed (by Weasel) and dismembered and disemboweled (by Weasel, Krug and especially Sadie), and a lake, where Mari is raped and then shot to death (both by Krug). In a frightful scene not found in all prints, Krug carves his name into Mari's chest. When Mari walks into the lake, she is attempting to cleanse herself for death and to find a private space.

After the three adults wash the blood off in the lake and change clothes (as in *The Virgin Spring*, Junior participates in the capture but not in the rapes and murders), the four of them ask to spend the night with the Collingwoods, not realizing at first that Mari is their daughter. After dinner, Weasel has a dream that for its brevity, simplicity and effectiveness ranks with the best nightmares in Craven's work. Weasel is lying down with his mouth open, and a chisel rests on an upper front tooth near the gum. John and Estelle stand above him, and she tells him not to move. The doctor raises a hammer and hits the chisel. We hear the impact, and Weasel wakes up. As this scene begins, we have no reason to expect it to be a dream. It could be the start of the revenge of the doctor and his wife. It is also after dinner that Estelle discovers, partly through their guests' suitcase of bloody clothes, that Mari has been killed, and by them.

Krug gets Junior, who had pulled a gun on him, to blow his own brains out. Estelle slits Sadie's throat in the swimming pool and, during lakeside fellatio, bites off Weasel's penis so that he bleeds to death. John uses a chainsaw (perhaps its first appearance as a weapon in a horror film) to carve up Krug. During most of the carnage, Mari's body, retrieved from the side of the lake, lies on the couch. Mari's corpse indicates this family will never be whole again, but the couple, shown together in the final shot, have survived the horror and strengthened their bond. The bourgeois John and Estelle have, by descending to the primitive level of the Other, triumphed over Krug and his band, the lower-class "family" who intruded into their family.

Last House includes several songs. One of them is unusual in that it takes the perspective of the outlaws, "Weasel and Sadie, junkie and Dad," with such brisk and hearty, rhythmically engaging lines as: "Let's have some fun with those / two lovely children and / off them as soon as we're do-o-one!"[34] This ballad finds the fun in repulsive violence and evil, making the whole picture seem more perverse—or just a good time at the drive-in. As in *The Virgin Spring*, the world of *Last House* is charged with violent horrors that cannot be escaped through pious or civilized behavior but must continually be guarded against, as one slip, one step into their world, one admittance of the outsiders into one's life or one act that accepts their terms, such as trying to make a drug deal or offering to share a picnic, can bring destruction. Like the virgin spring, the lake in *Last House* may seem a symbol of both the absolution and the acceptance of violence because it has seen and washed away so much blood.

The family in *The Texas Chain Saw Massacre* consists of a grandfather (whose wife is mummified), played by John Dugan, two grandsons (Leatherface [Gunnar Hansen] and the hitchhiker [Edwin Neal]) and a man who may be the father, an uncle or an older brother who is referred to as the cook or the Old Man (Jim Siedow). Leatherface wears a leather mask. He is not mute, but his squealing talk is hard to make out. The hitchhiker opens the film by constructing "a grisly work of art" out of corpses and we hear him working in the dark. The horror family encounters a partly related group that includes a sister and brother, Sally (Marilyn Burns) and Franklin (Paul A. Partain) Hardesty, along with their friends, Jerry (Allen Danziger), Kirk (William Vail) and Pam (Teri McMinn). Jerry is Sally's boyfriend, and Kirk is Pam's. Franklin is in a wheelchair and spends most of his time complaining. Franklin has a discouraging horoscope, as does Sally—really, Saturn is against all of them from the start—and it also suggests trouble when the hitchhiker marks their van with his blood as if making a sign in a private language. One by one, in search of gas and then of each other, three of the young adults enter the house of the deranged family as if they were pounding on the door of Bluebeard's forbidden chamber, which the door to Leatherface's kitchen, a silver door revealing a red wall hung with cattle skulls, figuratively evokes.[35] Kirk ignores such signs as a human tooth on the front porch (the picture's best understated horror image) and the rules against going into a stranger's house. With their hammers, their kitchen full of hooks, Leatherface's chainsaw and the hitchhiker's razor, this group's violence is inseparable from their being a family in their own private house, and is part of how they do business.

The horror they reveal to the young adults and the audience is that of an insane, degenerate and blood-related group, a family (as Hooper said, a whole family of Ed Geins) in which corpses are to be used for art, furniture and masks, while the living are to be used for meat for home consumption and sale. This is the family as a monstrous entity made up of humans—a compound human monster. The horror is also the old dark house as a gallery of artistically intense, relentlessly designed horrors, each room and its events more unendurable than the last. The house suits the family. And the noise level, which becomes extremely high between the chainsaw and all the screaming, suits the chaos and violence of the situation. Turning to the old man for help, as Sally does when she runs to the gas station, does no good, for he turns out to be a member of the family, which is what puts the stamp of horror on him. If Sally escapes, providing the picture's tense and jagged resolution, it is not as an emphatic victor but as a raw survivor driven to the point of madness, laughing hysterically as she leaves Leatherface behind her, swinging his chainsaw in the movie's final image of uncontrolled, violent, frustrated rage. The movie ends on a note of maximum, screaming tension.

In the only sequel Hooper directed, *The Texas Chainsaw Massacre 2*, the old man (Jim Siedow again) is given a name, Drayton Sawyer,[36] and is identified as the older brother of Leatherface (Bill Johnson), the hitchhiker (who was killed at the end of the original) and a new brother called Chop-Top (Bill Moseley). Chop-Top's origins are never mentioned, nor is his name, which is provided only by the credits. Chop-Top has a disgusting habit of using a coat hanger and a lighter to burn parts of his scalp and then eating the scabby bits. The family now lives in a bizarre, largely underground compound. Their business has expanded, and they win prizes for their chili. An eye for good meat, says the old man, "runs in the family." The grandfather (Ken Evert) still lives with them.

At one point the old man grasps Leatherface's chainsaw and says, "The saw is *family*." The saw is the emblem of this family's unity, the central symbol of their togetherness and destructiveness; being a family is their strength. For the old man, the saw and family are things that are reliable and known, compared with sex, which he considers an unknown. There is a good deal about sex in *Chainsaw 2*. Like the original, the sequel is largely built around the perils of one woman (Caroline Williams as Stretch),[37] and one of the tightest situations in which she finds herself is having her crotch prodded by Leatherface's chainsaw while he masturbates. The chainsaw in that scene is as phallic as possible (making Leatherface a grotesque symbol of puberty), but the old man later insists to Leatherface that he must choose the saw and family over sexuality. In the course of the picture, Leatherface goes back to using the chainsaw as a pure weapon.

Stretch is a disc jockey at a Texas radio station, and L. G. (Lou Perry) is her engineer. The most emotionally powerful and successfully horrific parts of the picture have to do with them. When both have ended up in the family's lair, L. G. is skinned alive by Leatherface with an electric carving knife. The knife is small and domestic, a highly effective, understated saw. Leatherface carefully carves off L. G.'s face (an echo of *Eyes Without a Face* as well as a nod to Ed Gein), which he forces Stretch to wear. When Leatherface is called away, L. G. gets up, then collapses. With his ribs showing and his face missing, he is a horrifying figure whose pain is evident. When he dies, Stretch puts his face back on his head, a moving moment that could only happen, let alone succeed and *be* moving, in a horror film.

In *The Hills Have Eyes* a degenerate, inbred, cannibalistic family of outsiders confronts a bourgeois family who have taken an ill-advised route across the desert. Their car breaks down in an accident, and they find they are being watched. The conventional family consists of a father (Russ Grieve as Big Bob Carter) and mother (Virginia Vincent as Ethel Carter), their two daughters (Dee Wallace as Lynne Wood and Susan Lanier as Brenda Carter), their son (Robert Houston as Bobby Carter) and their son-in-law (Martin Speer as Doug Wood), who has a new baby with Lynne, the elder daughter. They also have two big dogs, Beauty and Beast. Big Bob has just retired from the police force. He is rather bull-headed and makes the mistake of taking them off the main road when it is always a good idea in a horror movie to stay on the main road; just ask Marion Crane. The accident happens on the day before Bob and Ethel's silver anniversary.

The outsider family is run by the father, Jupiter (James Whitworth). The whore who mothered his children is called Mama (Cordy Clark), and the children include Mars (Lance Gordon), Pluto (Michael Berryman) and Ruby (Janus Blythe). Jupiter's father

(John Steadman as Fred) runs a gas station in the desert and once tried to split his son's head open with a tire iron after Jupiter burned down the house and killed his sister.

As in *Last House*, the bourgeois family turns violent, not only for vengeance, but also to survive. And not all of them do. The symbolically named Beauty is the first to be killed. Big Bob is burned alive, tied to a cactus. In a raid on the camp, Brenda is raped, Ethel and Lynne are shot and the baby is taken. Eventually, for the sake of the baby (whom all the members of the family except Ruby want to eat), Ruby takes a rattlesnake to Mars and makes it possible for Doug to kill her brother with a knife, an outburst of extreme and personally defining violence that ends the picture on a note where the victim is brought to the violator's level. Although by his actions Doug is defending himself, avenging his wife and saving his baby, which are good things, he also repels us as a murderer, partly because Ruby cries out her brother's name while Doug is repeatedly stabbing him. To emphasize the violence of Doug's action, the immersion in it and the loss of control, the screen turns red.

Jupiter was based on the apparently legendary figure of Sawney Bean, who took a woman to live with him in a cave in sixteenth century Scotland, where they had children, who through incest produced more children, until there was a tribe of 48 who lived by robbing travelers and eating them. They are said to have been caught and executed after 25 years. If the Manson "family" was part of the inspiration for *Last House* and many other films—including *The Strangers* (Bryan Bertino, 2008, US), in which the three masked invaders leave an early sign of their intrusion on a bedroom window[38]—it was the dark potential of the actual family that underlay *Texas Chain Saw* and *The Hills Have Eyes*. The hope, at least in Craven's early films, was that the ordinary family would be able to defend itself against the onslaught of the horror family, even if the fight would change them. But a film like *The Strangers* shows that ordinary people may have no chance.

Psychics and Telekinetics: *Carrie* and *Scanners*

Psychics, telepaths and telekinetics have mental powers that exceed or transgress the norm, but they rarely are mad. They can do things with their minds that others can only imagine. In a horror film these powers can turn destructive as the person who exercises them becomes a character to fear and a mystery to investigate. A telepath can read one's mind but can also send destructive visions and thoughts. A telekinetic, able to move or cause changes in objects by mental force alone, can make the physical world a dangerous place. The psychic is often presented as someone who needs a way to bring the world, especially other people, under control, sometimes so he or she can find self-expression— realize his or her full being—and sometimes so he or she can function at all. Often the act of control, the decisive exercise of power in a moment of self-definition, is an act of revenge.

Carrie (1976), based on the novel by Stephen King and the best film yet adapted from any of his works, is the story of a telekinetic, Carrie White (Sissy Spacek), who comes into power when she first menstruates. Her power is associated with blood from then on. Carrie is a retiring misfit who has always been picked on at school, and controlled by her crazy, religiously obsessed mother (Piper Laurie as Margaret) at home. She feels frightened when she has her first period in the gym-class shower—her mother never told her anything about puberty—and the other girls torment her because of it. One of them (Amy Irving as Sue) later feels bad about her behavior and convinces her boyfriend, Tommy (William Katt), to ask Carrie to the prom. When Carrie uses her telekinetic powers at home (sometimes accompanied by violins reminiscent of *Psycho*'s stabbing music[39]), Margaret decides Carrie is a godless witch.

At the prom, Tommy and Carrie are elected king and queen, and with the help of her boyfriend, a girl who hates Carrie drops a bucket of pig's blood onto them. As in the bloody shower scene, the teenagers are laughing at her again.[40] Telekinetically locking the doors and manipulating the instruments of water and fire, Carrie kills them all, now a psychic monster in total command of her powers who gives full expression to her anger.

Still covered with blood, Carrie leaves the burning school and goes home, where Margaret stabs her. Carrie makes knives and kitchen tools fly into her mother until in death she resembles her statue of St Sebastian. Then the house catches on fire and collapses. In the hugely influential coda—the shock ending after the climax and the cooling down—Sue walks in slow motion by the place where Carrie's house used to be. She then kneels down to lay some flowers on the burned ground, and is grabbed by Carrie's bloody hand as it reaches up from Hell. This turns out to be the highpoint of a nightmare. The site of horror is reduced to one we have often seen before, that of a bedroom.

This ending is comparable to the final shot of *The Great Train Robbery* (Edwin S. Porter, 1903, US), a close shot that shows a cowboy firing a pistol at the audience and that is unrelated to the plot. It was tacked on for an extra thrill at the end of the picture. Both endings bring back the central excitement and give it a full, independent expression. As has been noted before, *Carrie*, *Halloween* and *Friday the 13th* marked a significant change in the way a horror film was expected to end. The status quo was now permanently challenged, the horror still a danger as some element of it had endured or returned. The horror film became a genre in which the norms of behavior and identity were opened to intrusion but not, at the end, sealed up again. A conservative ideological pattern had given way to a potentially radical one, and a reassuring formula had been replaced by an unsettling one.

The Fury (Brian De Palma, 1978, US) is the story of a teenager, Gillian (Amy Irving), whose psychic activities generate an electromagnetic field that can make people bleed, especially when she touches them. She is frightened and alarmed by the bleeding. She feels in telepathic contact with a more powerful psychic her age, Robin (Andrew Stevens), whom she hasn't met and who is being held by a group of government agents and researchers who want to study, manipulate and use him. Their leader is the unscrupulous Childress (John Cassavetes), who took charge of Robin after convincing him that his father, Peter (Kirk Douglas), was dead. Gillian wants to find Robin and sees in him the possibility of a companion who could help her. However, by now Robin has become a barely controllable psychic and telekinetic monster, and he uses his powers to kill several people. Peter takes Gillian away with him to find Robin, a meeting that leads to the deaths of both father and son. Robin looks at Gillian just before he dies and passes his extra-special power to her, and at the end she uses her expanded force to explode

Childress, coming into her full power in a moment of revenge and justice that begins with her kissing his eye, which instantly blinds him.

From the blood that runs out of Childress's eyes to the nosebleed suffered by an obnoxious girl at school, the expression of Gillian's power is linked with blood.[41] So is Carrie's power, and so is scanning, discussed below. One reason for this connection may be that to show bleeding can be a visual way to imply a flow of something unseen, the wave of psychic power. Blood also encodes the psychic manifestations as dangerous. At the end, Gillian becomes both a psychic monster and an avenging hero, using the powers of which she had once been afraid. Her power is also linked with vision. At one point Gillian grips a researcher's hand as she sees a traumatic scene through Robin's eyes, and she holds on so long that it gives the woman a cerebral hemorrhage. These telepathic scenes, this movie says, cost blood to view.

Scanners (David Cronenberg, 1981, Canada) concerns mutants who have great telepathic and other psychic abilities. Their mothers were given a drug while they were pregnant, which made their babies "scanners." When they scan—or telepathically invade and probe and even control—someone, that person may bleed, especially from the nose. As the film's chief scientist, Dr Paul Ruth (Patrick McGoohan), defines it, telepathy is "the direct linking of two nervous systems separated by space." Dr Ruth, who invented the drug that makes scanners, has two sons, Darryl Revok (Michael Ironside) and Cameron Vale (Stephen Lack). Cameron is at first unable to function because of the cacophony of others' thoughts that he always hears in his head, but he gradually gains control over his powers. Revok, the psychic monster here, can make people kill themselves or each other, can make them see anything in their minds and can make a man's head blow up. At the end there is a battle to the death between the brothers, and they merge into a being that has Revok's body and Cameron's self—that is, Cameron's mind, eyes and voice. This being, who will use his powers for good, is the culmination of the theme of Cameron's development but also constitutes an evolutionary leap. As in *The Fury*, the climax in *Scanners* is an exercise of psychic power in the interest of justice by a figure who has gone beyond the limits of ordinary being. Some monsters are allowed to win, even if they make us bleed.

The Infected: *Rabid* and *28 Days Later*

This is plague territory. A disease makes its way through a population, breaking down civilized behavior and even civilization. The infectious bites in *Night of the Living Dead* and its sequels are similar in their range, but they are different in that they kill the victims before having their full effect and making them hungry zombies. Those grouped into the category of the infected are alive, not undead. If the disease finally proves fatal, that puts an end to them. *Rabid* (David Cronenberg, 1977, Canada) makes a tragedy out of the story of the carrier of a plague, while *28 Days Later*[42] (Danny Boyle, 2002, UK) takes a more action-oriented look at the general destruction wrought by a "rage virus."

In *Rabid* Marilyn Chambers, a star of hardcore pornography in real life, plays Rose, a young woman who is taken to a clinic after a motorcycle accident and subjected to experimental plastic surgery by Dr Keloid (Howard Ryshpan), whose name refers to scar tissue formed by excessive repairing and who is for all practical purposes a mad scientist. After the operation Rose develops a hunger for blood, nothing but blood, and it has to be human. She has also grown a little organ under her armpit with which to extract it. The needle-tipped, bloodsucking, distinctly phallic protuberance retracts into what looks like a tiny anus. Those from whom she takes blood—and she usually takes it during an embrace—develop a fatal sickness comparable to rabies and become flesh-hungry and uncontrollably violent, with their bites spreading the disease. If mutable tissue[43] is the ultimate cause of Rose's affliction, sex becomes a recurring part of how she creates her victims. At the root of the horror in this film and other disease films is the body, the site of infection, the thing to protect or to flee.

Rose both enjoys and fears the blood episodes that have made her, in her words, "a monster," and at first she does not relate them to the plague. But she is a monster and an infector. Like a werewolf on a nightly prowl, she searches for people to feed on. An ironic episode takes place in a porn theatre where Rose is in the audience and drains the blood from a male patron, reversing the situation in which Chambers would be on the screen and the men in the audience would be stimulated by or taking energy from her image.[44]

The infected become human monsters. Eventually—once her boyfriend (Frank Moore as Hart) has made her consider the possibility—she confirms that her bloodsucking makes her the carrier of the plague. She confirms it in a way that must, if she is right (and she hopes that she is proving she is wrong), lead to her death. She plans to see whether her feeding would infect a randomly chosen man, who would of course then try to kill her. At the end, Rose's body is put into a garbage truck that has been gathering other casualties of the violence. Ultimately, she sets herself up to become a victim of the epidemic she started, for this is the only way she could atone, and the only way to escape her condition. She could not stop the plague, but she could stop herself, and her suicide is satisfyingly tragic, even if it does not fix the situation.

Cabin Fever (Eli Roth, 2002, released 2003, US) shows how even friends will turn on each other to remain safe from contagion, and to motivate this behavior, the film presents disease—a flesh-eating virus—in the most physically unpleasant terms it can devise. Eventually all of the characters die or are as good as dead, whether they helped each other and showed compassion or not. After all, disease (which kills most of us in the real world, and gives rise to many valid fears) acts without regard to our moral condition.

28 Days Later opens with some animal-rights protesters' releasing lab chimpanzees that have been used in testing a "rage virus" and then getting bitten by them. The infection, carried in blood and saliva, is communicated by bites and by other contact with infected bodily fluids.[45] The similarity to AIDS is no doubt intentional on the part of the filmmakers, and is another example of the horror film's often creating images and figures for matters that frighten us in the real world.

It is 28 days after this release of the virus that the story picks up, showing a devastated England and an almost uninhabited London. Infected people attack and bite others, and their victims are immediately possessed by a killer rage and go on to attack still others. Their condition is incurable, and the math is on their side—a geometrical progression of what the picture calls "the infected."

We follow a small group of the uninfected as they negotiate a world without law, government, media, electricity and other benefits of civilization, which has broken down as the virus has spread. Jim (Cillian Murphy) wakes from a coma and soon meets Mark (Noah Huntley) and Selena (Naomie Harris), who give him shelter. When Mark is bitten, Selena kills him. When it looks as if the two of them will survive together for a while—like the couple in a horror film, though she doesn't come right out and say it—Selena asks Jim whether he would like them to "find a cure and save the world or just fall in love and fuck." Dismissing both possibilities, she says that "staying alive's as good as it gets," though she later revises that opinion and finds love, especially family love, to be of value. Frank (Brendan Gleeson) and his daughter, Hannah (Megan Burns), join up with them, and they go to the countryside in search of some soldiers who have set up a rescue operation. One soldier points out that if the virus wipes out humanity, that would be a return to normality for the planet, since man has been around for such a short time. Implicitly, the issue becomes what people have done, and will do in the future, to justify the life of the species—to find what about us is worth saving. The soldiers, who intend to use Selena and Hannah for breeding and who shoot some of the uninfected to consolidate their power, do not represent a viable solution, so the picture sees to it that all of them are killed. At the end, when the infected have begun to die of starvation and after Jim and Selena have finally made a romantic connection, they and Hannah are shown to be on the verge of rescue by other soldiers who will, we hope, behave better. Along with our humanity (a virtue of the best of the uninfected), it is love and goodness and courage that prove to be worth saving, a point that the horror film, in its investigation of human nature and culture, has repeatedly made.

Cannibals: *Eaten Alive!* and *Cannibal Holocaust*

It shows no respect for our person when a horror figure treats us as meat. The mouth of the cannibal is like our own—not canine, like that of a wolf, or imagined, like that of a werewolf. The Other, when a cannibal, is as like us as any monster could be—homo sapiens—while unlike the civilized person in his or her eagerness to outrage the boundaries of the body. Cannibalism challenges the boundary between the self and the Other by violating and confusing it, putting a human at each side of the encounter while also treating the consumed one as an object instead of a subject.[46]

It is possible to fear that in some ultimate breakdown of civilized values (values such as organized respect for persons and property and morals) one could become the victim of cannibalism, and treated as an object for the pleasure, sustenance and empowerment of others, rather than as an autonomous subject. That fear may be linked, in the cannibal picture, to the assault on life: from the real killing of animals on camera to the fictitious rapes and castrations that often precede the eating of the victims. The films insist that any form of life can be killed and eaten, and its death can be watched. Real death is mixed with enacted death in these pictures, to make all the deaths feel part of the same ruthless realism, with every animal and human liable to have its private boundaries violated and its life taken. The mix is an attempt, uncivilized in itself, to make the fiction seem more authentic. (The realism in *Freaks* was not at anyone's expense.) The atrocities committed against animals in almost all of these pictures, most of which were Italian and many of which were shot partly in the Amazon in the 1970s and early 1980s, make it clear that the filmmakers consider anything fair game for their sadistic voyeurism, anything that will increase the sense that one is drenched in real violence and death. It offers little consolation to learn that many Italian movies, going back to the documentary *Mondo Cane* (produced by Gualtiero Jacopetti, assisted by Franco Prosperi, 1962, Italy), have a tradition of abusing animals or filming their deaths.

As films about eating, cannibal films encourage vomiting. Cannibalism is the incest of eating and may evoke a taboo as strong as that against incest. To make a cannibal film is, at least to some degree, to challenge the basis and nature of society, to confront the civilized norm with its opposite and sometimes to criticize the behavior of the civilized. For a time, then, some Italian filmmakers felt it important to keep alive a region of primitive fantasy where cannibals were a real threat and the limits of behavior were tested.

There are cannibals in *The Texas Chain Saw Massacre* and in *Motel Hell* (Kevin Connor, 1980, US), where the victims are consumed as sausages and smoked meats by customers unaware of what they are eating, which makes them only accidental cannibals. The family members in *Texas Chain Saw* are, of course, fully aware of what's on the table. There is a fine line between pictures that are primarily about cannibals, such as *Cannibal Holocaust*, and those that include cannibalism among the villains' several characteristics, such as *Texas Chain Saw*. Flesh-eating zombies also belong to a different class of monster than mortal cannibals, for they are undead. It should be noted, however, that the Italian zombie pictures, beginning with Fulci's *Zombie* (*Zombi 2*), enjoyed their heyday at about the same time as the cannibal pictures, presenting spectacles that were comparable (for example, both often showed guts being pulled out of a freshly-opened body) and that appealed to many of the same fears.[47] As much eating of human flesh as there is in *Sweeney Todd: The Demon Barber of Fleet Street* (Tim Burton, 2007, US/UK)—or preparation for it, as in *Blood Feast*—the focus on cannibalism is at its sharpest in the tale of the tribe of cannibals who live in the jungle and generally make short work of outsiders. They are cannibals before they are anything else. That is their specific ticket to horror.

The first of these films was *Deep River Savages* (Umberto Lenzi, 1972, Italy), also known as *Man from Deep River*, and it contained enough real footage of animal fights, skinnings and on-camera killings[48] to make animal atrocities—as well as the graphic sex it also featured—recurring elements of the Italian cannibal movie. According to actor Giovanni Lombardo Radice, "the torture of animals was rooted in Italian cinema since the Sixties as a form to express a longing for fascism and, of course, to titillate the worst elements of a simple public."[49]

In *Last Cannibal World* (Ruggero Deodato, 1977, Italy), also known as *Jungle Holocaust*, the primary victim is a cannibal woman, Pulan (Me Me Lai), who is eaten by her own people, apparently as punishment for running away with the white outsider (Massimo Foschi as Robert Harper) who had been captured by her Stone Age tribe. Robert had forced Pulan to help him escape, and then raped her, which—in this macho fantasy—brought them closer. His attack on her body may be said to foreshadow or ritually set up the attack by the cannibals, who kill, gut, roast and eat her in onscreen detail.

As noted above, some sexual assault on a victim often comes before his or her death and consumption in a cannibal picture. These movies primarily offer a spectacle of assault on the body, and the sexual assault is physical enough to violate and tear down the first boundaries of the body.

Two women are eaten while they are alive (just after one of them has been raped, but not by a cannibal) in *Eaten Alive!* (Umberto Lenzi, 1980, Italy), also known as *Eaten Alive by Cannibals*. Diana (Paola Senatore) lies naked and outstretched on the ground while cannibals eat her breast (psychologically, an almost unmatchable act of oral aggression) and half of her leg, both of which have been cut off. We could expect her to be writhing from her wounds, but she hardly moves, perhaps dazed and in shock but in fact posed as a reclining nude might be in a painting. She is horrifically repulsive but also coded as desirable. She is a unified spectacle of sexuality and gore as well as a center of pain, an object and a subject. Earlier in the film a snake had eaten a monkey, its face shown in close-up, and a character had pronounced this "the survival of the fittest." A man and woman who have come in search of Diana do survive, but Diana is a former city-dweller, presumably less "fit," and becomes a victim of the jungle. Yet the same happens to her extremely fit native guide (Me Me Lai as Mowara), who screams when she is carved up but also ends up supine and almost passive—like some kind of sacrifice to the male gaze—while she is eaten alive before she is killed and cooked (in shots reused from *Last Cannibal World*). The women endure the horror and manifest it in their naked, wounded bodies, stripped before the violence not only so they may be presented as objects of desire, but also so that the camera can more readily show an assault on the body.

The law of the jungle is used in many of these films to justify, as realism, the portrayal and acceptance of extreme violence. So are fantasies about life in the jungle. Here is Lenzi's defense of *Cannibal Ferox*, also known as *Make Them Die Slowly* (Umberto Lenzi, 1981, Italy), a film we will take up shortly:

> Look, when you must shoot a scene with the one animal fighting with another animal, you need the one weak... I want to explain why I film many violent scenes between animals and the people. In these primitive tribes, the struggle for life is very hard, and is important to show how much is difficult to live without a civilization, authority and other things. But I don't love the violence, and showing the violence things in the movie for me is one way to condemn it... The fantasy, violence, maybe sometime is one way to put somebody in peace with himself. Maybe, I don't know... This movie is a story about the violent events of life...about the daily struggle for life in the primitive tribes of the Center America.[50]

Deodato's *Cannibal Holocaust* (1980) concerns a quartet of documentary filmmakers who are not above staging "events" for the camera but who find the real thing and pay for their interference when they set out in search of Amazonian cannibals. The director is Alan (Gabriel Yorke), the assistant director is Alan's girlfriend, Faye (Francesca Ciardi), and the cameramen, who shoot in 16mm and often show each other filming, are Jack (Perry Pirkanen) and Mark (Luca Barbareschi). When they don't come back after several months, an anthropologist (Robert Kerman as Professor Monroe), with the backing of his university and the TV company Alan had worked for, goes to the jungle to find them.

In the Amazon, one of Monroe's guide's assistants finds a muskrat and says they will eat meat that day. The muskrat is held in an open, vulnerable position and screams when a long knife is stabbed and worried into its throat twice until it dies. Then a captive tribesman eats its stomach. This real-world killing was arranged for the camera. It is a real horror, unforgettable because the small animal expresses its fear and suffering, both when screaming and in an extremity of silent agony, with such totality that we cannot help sharing the sense of mortal pain and deeply pitying the muskrat. This act is by no means an ordinary efficient killing, but something the man takes pleasure in prolonging. It is, of course, inexcusable to make a real horror happen in order to shoot a movie, and this scene is a prime example of the offense. The scene offers a resonant, harrowing look at documented horror, which will be taken up in the last chapter of this book. Unlike the muskrat, the skinned crocodile in *Last Cannibal World* makes no sound, nor does the turtle that is butchered before it is entirely dead in *Cannibal Holocaust*. Cries of pain and fear may make us feel more for the victim, but the silent spectacles remain painful and revolting and turn us just as strongly against the filmmakers.

About halfway through the movie, Monroe finds a cannibal tribe that has held onto the skeletons of the filmmakers and their cans of film, which both, they think, are full of evil spirits. Monroe takes the cans back to New York, where the footage is developed, and he is engaged by the TV company to introduce it.

The more Monroe sees of the footage, the more he resists having anything to do with the project. The filmmakers had violated every tenet of good journalism, let alone anthropology, actively provoking and attacking their subjects instead of neutrally observing them. Eventually the TV executives agree with Monroe, and they order the footage to be destroyed—but it is stolen and sold by the projectionist, as an end title informs us. One thing the executives point out to Monroe is that Alan often faked footage, which they say is not a forbidden practice, as a good deal of documentary and news footage is staged for the camera.[51] A film that shows executions by firing squad and that looks authentic is offered as one of Alan's exemplary fabrications. Even so, one suspects the actions are real, another example of horror documentary.

The second half of the film shows what was found in the cans. The filmmakers' cameras reveal them to have a taste for violence to which only Faye objects—and at one point she is more angry at their wasting film on their gang-rape of a young cannibal woman than at the rape itself. When they have found a Stone Age tribe, they set fire to a building and keep the people inside. They consider it wonderful footage and plan to pass it off as the massacre of one group of cannibals by another. Beginning with his shooting of a pig in the village he eventually burns, Alan calls what he does, and what he tells his crew to do, an example of the "survival of the fittest…the daily violence of the strong overcoming the weak." They witness weird and violent practices of the cannibals—as Monroe had observed a ritual in which a man kills his wife for adultery by pounding her genitals with a mud ball full of nails and then braining her.

Most of the violence in this movie is carried out against women (as when the raped cannibal woman is punished by her tribe by being impaled up her vagina and out her mouth), even if the three male filmmakers also are killed. The violence against women and animals in the Italian cannibal movie appears to express a desire to dominate both women and the natural world, with eating or raping the victim an ultimate act of control.

At the climax, the cannibals capture the filmmakers one by one, and the others keep the camera rolling, recording each other's deaths. Jack is castrated before he is chopped up, and Faye is raped several times before she is beheaded. Almost to the very end, Alan seems to think he can get away and win an award for this footage. Alan and Mark keep shooting as a matter of professionalism (or perhaps to put the barrier of media between themselves and death, as if they were safe observers) until the last one is killed. The dropped camera briefly shows the cameraman's—Alan's—head on the ground. The implication is that the inhumane, bloodthirsty, ambitious, meddling filmmakers have brought this on themselves and that the whites are, to quote Monroe, "the real cannibals." But this movie has no moral foundation from which to judge others, even its characters. However historically important it is, it manages to be repulsive, sexist and stupid as well as hypocritical, for it pretends to deplore the violence it is only too ready to show.

As previously mentioned, *Cannibal Holocaust*'s device of having the victims film their own encounters with the horror has inspired pictures from *The Blair Witch Project* to *[REC]*, *Diary of the Dead* and *Cloverfield*.

The villain and primary victim in *Cannibal Ferox* is Mike (Giovanni Lombardo Radice), who provokes the cannibals and deserves what he gets. The main character, Gloria (Lorraine De Selle), is a graduate student doing field work in the Amazon during a vacation, accompanied by her brother, Rudy (Danilo Mattei), and their friend, Pat (Zora Keslerová). Gloria's thesis is that cannibalism doesn't exist. The three come upon Mike and Joe (Walter Lucchini), drug dealers on the run, who join them. Eventually it is revealed that the reason the cannibals (in whose village they unwisely stay) are so hostile is that the sadistic, coked-up Mike recently terrorized them and even castrated a tribesman after gouging out one of his eyes, leaving him to bleed to death while tied to a stake in the center of the village. (In this movie equal violence is done to men and women.) During his current visit, Mike shoots a young woman. When it is their turn for revenge on the Americans, the cannibals eat Joe, kill Rudy and probably eat him too[52] and string Pat up by hooks through her breasts until she dies. They castrate Mike, eating his penis—but cauterizing the wound, leaving *him* tied up in the center of the village. Later they kill Mike by slicing off the top of his skull to eat his brain. Gloria gets away and, perhaps to keep anyone else from interfering with the tribal people driven to such extremes, she continues to maintain in her thesis that cannibalism is a colonialist fantasy. The English-language edition opens with a title card acknowledging that the film's subject matter is "disgusting and repulsive" and that the film includes "at least two dozen scenes of barbaric torture and sadistic cruelty graphically shown." This is as effective an introduction to the picture's sadistic voyeurism as the title card that opens[53] *Cannibal Holocaust* by announcing, "For the sake of authenticity some sequences have been retained in their entirety."

Slashers: *Scream*

Unlike Michael, Jason and Freddy, conventional slashers can be killed. Otherwise things are much the same. There is often an initiating traumatic event that sets out the terms of the killer's obsession or relates his or her origin; there is a madman or madwoman picking off teenagers and others; there is a last opponent, usually female, who kills the slasher; there is often a mask for the slasher's face and a knife or other sharp implement for his or her hand and there are many other codified expectations, most self-consciously laid out in *Scream* (Wes Craven, 1996, US). But there were differences too.

Prom Night (Paul Lynch, 1980, Canada), released just after *Friday the 13th*, did much to establish the terms of the mortal slasher film, as did a slightly later picture, *Terror Train* (Roger Spottiswoode, 1980, Canada/US). They both starred Jamie Lee Curtis, the star of *Halloween*, which was an influence on both pictures. Both of them open with prologues in which someone is treated cruelly, motivating the slasher's revenge years later. In both, the slasher wears a mask (in *Terror Train*, a series of costumes), and his identity is revealed only at the end. And in both films Curtis plays the final girl, defining the figure in *Halloween* and in these two pictures as an intelligent, resourceful young woman who is forced to become violent to protect herself, who is not a sexpot like some of her friends and who is selected by luck as much as by the values for which she stands (the morals, strengths, and ways of living the picture endorses[54]) to confront the slasher and survive. These characteristics of the final girl were also defined, of course, by Alice in *Friday the 13th* the same year, though Alice overcomes Mrs Voorhees by herself while the final girls in *Halloween* and *Terror Train* are saved by men. Alice had the greater influence on later films.

Naturally there were variations on the formula, especially at first. *He Knows You're Alone* (1980), as previously mentioned, opens with a reflexive sequence[55] in which the slasher (Ray, played by Tom Rolfing) knifes a young woman through the back of her seat at a horror movie. Here the movie screen is comparable to a window in the apparently safe world of the auditorium, with the restful theatre seat the equivalent of a bed, a site for experiencing what in this case is a true and sexually charged nightmare. There is a false horror on the screen and a real one in the seat behind the victim, and they are coordinated. We learn only later about the origin of the slasher's obsession—with killing women who are about to become brides, after his own fiancée rejected him (she was wearing her bridal gown when he stabbed her just before she was to marry someone else).[56] The film closes by beginning the cycle again with a new killer (the film's primary variation from earlier formulas), prone to the same controlling and judgmental obsessions, whose fiancée—the heroine—rejects him for another man and dies for it on her wedding day: an open ending that is also a repetition of the primary threat, which is typical of the slasher film. *The Burning* (Tony Maylam, 1981, US/Canada) has a formulaic prologue in which the person who will become the slasher—as a killer, he uses a pair of sharp gardening shears—is tormented and accidentally burned, but the slasher is finally killed by two young men. In *Friday the 13th* the slasher is a woman.

The sub-subgenre continued to develop with *My Bloody Valentine* (George Mihalka, 1981, Canada), in which the killer is a miner who logically wears a mask and has access to sharp tools, notably a pickax. The psychological trauma that shaped him is revealed at the end along with his identity. But there is no doubt who the killer is in *The Slumber Party Massacre* (Amy Holden Jones, 1982, US), *Silent Night Deadly Night* (Charles E. Sellier Jr, 1984), *The Mutilator* (Buddy Cooper, 1985, US), *Inside* (Alexandre Bustillo and Julien Maury, 2007, France), the remake of *Prom Night* (Nelson McCormick, 2008, US/Canada) and many other slasher films that, following the lead of *He Knows You're Alone*, abandoned the POV shots and masks[57] to concentrate on less stylized killers who were identified from the start. As much as the mortal slasher goes back to *Psycho* and the Mrs Bates outfit, there is no need for a slasher to wear a mask or costume; Mrs Bates's big knife is the more definitive influence. In *Inside*, it is the pair of scissors with which she kills, one after the other, those who would interfere with her plan and with which she cuts the baby out of the victim that mark the killer as a slasher.

The slasher film that turned overtly and even comically reflexive is best represented by Wes Craven's *Scream, Scream 2* (1997), *Scream 3* (2000) and *Scream 4* (2011), most of which were written by Kevin Williamson. The killers and most of the victims in *Scream* are high-school students who have seen many slasher films and know the rules down to every detail of the formula, and in *Scream 2* the killers know the rules of sequels. The threatened students try to defend themselves by mastering those rules.

In *Scream* the killers, whose identities are revealed only at the end of the picture (along with the fact that there are two of them, which we didn't know), wear hooded black cloaks with ghostlike black-and-white masks and primarily use knives. In the opening sequence they torment a victim (Drew Barrymore as Casey) over her portable phone, quizzing her about the details of "scary movies," which she has innocently admitted to enjoying. (As they do this first time, they typically dress in their costumes, threaten by phone and then attack. They use windows and doors and the phone itself—in this case another interface between horror and the familiar world—to gain entrance to the house or draw the victim outside.) When we meet the heroine (Neve Campbell as Sidney), she is talking with her boyfriend, Billy (Skeet Ulrich), about their relationship as if it were a movie with an MPAA rating. When the same voice that phoned Casey phones Sidney, it tries to convince her she is in the equivalent of a horror movie before she is attacked. Adults involved in the story include Dewey (David Arquette), an inexperienced policeman, and Gale (Courteney Cox), a TV journalist who is writing a book about the murder of Sidney's mother from the year before. One of the students (Jamie Kennedy as Randy) works in a video store and talks the most about the rules of the slasher film. Sidney and her friend Tatum (Rose McGowan) wonder who would play Sidney if her life were made into a movie. Just before Tatum is killed, she asks the costumed slasher whether she can be "the helpless victim" in the movie game he apparently wants to play, "psycho killer." "Please don't kill me, Mr Ghost-Face," she says before she realizes he isn't kidding, "I want to be in the sequel." Billy tells Sidney that life is "all one great big movie" and "you can pick your genre"—as if they could will themselves into a romantic comedy rather than a horror film.[58] While a group of students is watching *Halloween* on video and one of them discusses the slasher film's "obligatory tit shot," Sidney undresses in another room and Billy's body hides her breasts—a reflexive refusal to go along with the cheapest aspects of the formula, declaring in the clearest possible terms that Sidney is in a movie.

When both killers go after her just after she and Billy have had sex for the first time and Billy has apparently been knifed, Sidney plays the final girl—because *Scream* has to work as a slasher movie, not just as a film about slasher movies. After she has discovered the identity of the villains, one of whom turns out to be Billy and the other of whom (Matthew Lillard as Stu) Billy knifes as part of their alibi—but too deeply and too often— Billy is shot by Gale, then shot again by Sidney when he formulaically revives. In the big revelation scene (part of the formula ever since the climax of *Friday the 13th*), Billy admits they framed the man now on Death Row for their murder of Sidney's mother. Arming herself with the weapons of the enemy and undoing them with their own symbols of power, overcoming—by partially becoming—what has oppressed and frightened her, as the best horror victims do when they turn on their attackers, Sidney uses the phone to rattle both Billy and Stu, the costume in her attack on Billy and the TV set that is showing *Halloween* when she topples it onto Stu.

The characters are aware of movie conventions and are living a life that resembles a movie, but they are not aware that they really are in one. The only way a slasher movie could really happen, *Scream* implies, is if it happened to people who had seen a lot of slasher movies. It also implies that if one should happen to be in a situation that resembles a slasher movie, the way to survive is to go deeper into one's role, to inhabit deliberately the world that resembles art and find there the formula that leads to a solution. In the narrative context this picture constructs, to be reflexive is to be realistic. In contrast, to be reflexively minded in *Scream 4* is to be too "meta"—the characters are impatient with the attitude, the new cliché—even if being "meta" does again help one discover the primary killer.

In *Scream 2*, which is self-consciously a sequel, the characters have moved on to college, a movie (*Stab*) has been based on the events of *Scream*, and again there are two killers: Mickey (Timothy Olyphant), who is the extreme movie fan, and Mrs Loomis (Laurie Metcalf), who is Billy's mother, out to avenge her son as if she were Mrs Voorhees— a character we don't expect to be a reflexive model or symbolic reference here because she was from the original *Friday the 13th*, not from a sequel. *Scream 2* opens, taking a cue from *He Knows You're Alone*, with the stabbing of two members of the audience at a sneak preview of *Stab*.[59] *Stab*, which presents the actions of *Scream* but with different actors, is advertised as having been based on a true story, and thus the world of *Scream* remains the underlying reality. Mickey defends sequels in a film class, and it is clear that he is trying to create the equivalent of a sequel to the events of *Scream*: in the terms used in this fictional world, a real-world *Stab 2*. "Some freaked-out psycho trying to follow in Billy Loomis's footsteps" is what Dewey warns Sidney about, and that would—and does—constitute a sequel. At one point, Sidney hits Gale much as she had in the original[60]—but scenes that are repeated here are repeated reflexively, with a deliberateness we recognize, as instances of what happens in sequels.

Scream 3 had the formal requirement of turning the three films into a trilogy as if that had been the plan all along. The rules for the concluding chapter of a trilogy, as defined by Randy in a posthumous videotape, dictate that there be an unexpected back story, that revelations and actions take the characters back to the beginning, that the killer may have become nearly invulnerable and that anyone, including the main character, can die. These rules apply to the real world in which the characters find themselves, which is behaving like the last episode of a trilogy, another of whose characteristics is that "all bets are off." This last rule creates the sense that one is watching something not governed by formula, though there is of course a formula.

As *Scream 3* begins, *Stab 3* is in production, and the people making it are being stabbed by a new ghost-faced slasher. Sidney is trying to avoid publicity and more stress, but the new killer, who is the image of the previous ones, tracks her down and phones her, which pulls her back into the action. Dewey and Gail have had a relationship that failed; now they are back to sparring, and by the end they are engaged. Sidney and Dewey kill the slasher after much back story. The movie and the trilogy (but not the whole series, as it turned out; the point of this ending is that when made, it was clearly intended to be final) end with an image of Sidney's finally feeling safe and free as she decides not to set the house alarm, which she has been setting compulsively throughout the picture, and allows the wind to blow the unlocked door open.

Sidney is freed not only from her own compulsions, but also from being subject to the compulsions that motivated the killer. She is not part of a couple, but that is not an element we miss[61] when the heroine is shown as a single, healthy person who has friends again, who has survived the slashers that pursued her in film after film, and who has conquered fear enough to let the door stay open. It is a well-earned and solid resolution. She and her friends are about to watch a movie, and it could be any kind of movie ("You have to come and see," a young man says). There are other kinds of movies than slasher films (that is, to infer the film's last reflexive statement, there are other ways to live), and being open to the possibilities of film is one of the most life-affirming as well as reflexive things about this closed ending, a release from the realms of horror and the horror film at once.

Part III

RELATED GENRES

7

HORROR COMEDY

The monster is the key to the basic horror structure, but sometimes the horror figure will emerge as the film itself, as in *Dead of Night*, or the best analogy for the horrific situations and events in a movie will turn out to be a movie, as in *Peeping Tom* and the *Scream* series. Horror films, and not only the reflexive ones, set traps for their audiences and their characters, frightening and appalling them while presenting horror as the inescapable journey. They also offer avenues of release and safety, which may be a matter of undergoing a period as a monster or merging one's characteristics with those of a monster. One learns from horror and grows from confronting it, as the lawman with the fear of water does in *Jaws*. Monsters can be killed, and their dying or their corpses are often the last or next-to-last thing shown in a monster movie, to declare that the monster is dead and to focus sympathy if it is appropriate. Supernatural powers can be opposed by other forces, from religion to love, and supernaturally animated beings can be destroyed through ritual and courage. Human monsters can be killed by other humans. But not all horror movies are movies about killing monsters and vanquishing threats. In many the monsters survive, and in some cases the normal world and the world of horror are integrated. This happens in horror comedies as well as in horror documentaries. When horror is crossed with other genres, such as science fiction, a new subgenre that is set between them is formed: in this case science fiction horror. The assumptions of those subgenres reveal much about the assumptions of the master genres they integrate.

Monster Comedies: *Young Frankenstein*

The most uncompromising horror comedy may be *Bambi Meets Godzilla* (Marv Newland, 1969, Canada), an animated film that is two minutes long. Bambi munches grass, then gets stomped flat. It is funny in an awful way.

Comedies often confront chaos or some other radical upset, and sometimes absorb it into their worlds by the conclusion. In the same way, they can integrate the monsters and disturbances of horror into a world that is and remains fundamentally comic.

The chief job of the horror comedy is to make us laugh at material that is frightening and repulsive, like the crushing of Bambi. The brain transplant in *Bud Abbott and Lou Costello Meet Frankenstein* is serious business, but because it is Lou's brain and he does such a comical version of being scared, we feel simultaneously concerned about Lou and amused at his plight. Comic relief is often used in the horror film, releasing tension to intensify the moments of horror when they come, but what we are concerned with here are movies that attempt to be comedies from start to finish, working with horror material.

To succeed, such pictures must be funny and scary at once—that is, they must work as horror films and as comedies—but it may be difficult to be frightened by something at which we are laughing, so in some cases horror and humor will be evoked by turns in the course of the film. Our mixed feelings for Lou are an example of fear and humor evoked together, and so is the repulsed amusement with which we watch Seymour's plant demand to be fed in *The Little Shop of Horrors*.

Some of the films that have most successfully integrated horror and comedy have been animations. In *Hair-Raising Hare* (Chuck Jones, 1946, US) Bugs Bunny confronts a mad scientist and a monster. Every conventional horror element that appears is parodied, but is also presented as dangerous. Comedy and justice triumph in *Corpse Bride* (Mike Johnson and Tim Burton, 2005, UK/US), a romantic ghost story set in an atmospheric horror landscape. In *Monsters, Inc.* (Pete Docter, 2001, US) monsters are afraid of kids yet also need them, as the screams of children frightened in their bedrooms at night provide the power that runs the monsters' city. There is an economy here, based on the vital energy of horror. Throughout the course of *Monsters, Inc.*, which teaches children not to be controlled by their fears, laughter is presented as a more powerful force than screaming, and the value of having a monster around—especially when getting scared is fun—is strongly asserted. The fun of getting scared is part of what the horror film provides, and that fun can readily be channeled into comedy.

Young Frankenstein (Mel Brooks, 1974, US) gets many of its laughs by making reflexive jokes, trading on the audience's familiarity with every bit of the Universal Frankenstein series. Many aspects of the story are put in a parodistic context or a raunchy one. It is often the clash of tones that provokes the laughter, the inappropriate or surrealistic meeting of over-the-top comedy and horror. But the film is not just a parody; it is also an homage. Brooks used some of the original *Frankenstein* lab equipment, one example of his respect for his sources. It would be easy simply to make fun of Frankenstein and the Monster, but that would not produce great comedy. Even the Abbott and Costello movie demonstrates that the monsters must to some degree be played straight, just as in *Bedazzled* damnation must remain a real possibility. Frederick Frankenstein (Gene Wilder) must take himself seriously so that we have the option of laughing at him. The mise-en-scène is richly detailed, atmospheric and shadowy; this black-and-white picture offers an honest imitation of a classic horror style. At that point it is free to be hilarious without being superior or silly. That is one reason it works while so many horror parodies do not.

Fritz and Ygor are combined into the hunchbacked assistant, Igor (Marty Feldman). Feldman inhabits the role as a comedian but remains in character. Victor Frankenstein's notebook is called *How I Did It*. The blind man (Gene Hackman) pours hot soup in the Monster's lap. Making the Monster (Peter Boyle) larger than a normal human means that he will have large genitals, a joke that is played out till the end of the picture. The biggest change in the old plot comes when Frankenstein decides to teach the Monster himself (thus taking a major turn away from the tragedy that followed his abandoning his creation in the novel and in the movies, a change altogether in keeping with comedy), and at that moment he comes into his own and embraces his destiny, pronouncing his name "Frankenshtine" rather than "Frahnkensteen" for the first time.

It is also a big change that Elizabeth (Madeline Kahn) ends up as the Monster's bride (Frankenstein's own bride is happily his lab assistant, Inga, played by Teri Garr)— a mating that has been prepared ironically by the 1931 and 1935 movies' scenes of having the Monster come into Elizabeth's bedroom. In this movie, too, the Monster comes into Elizabeth's bedroom through the window and carries her off. When she wakes, she has the bride's white stripes in her hair, and she and the Monster make love. The bedroom-window scene still has the power, even in a comedy, to make horror present, to charge it with sexuality and to bear a person into its world.

A mental transference experiment leaves the Monster speaking, more intellectual and relatively less interested in sex (a comic punishment for the formerly standoffish but secretly lusty Elizabeth) while Frankenstein becomes more sensitive to music and better endowed. Monster and creator have been brought closer together physically and mentally, an implicit possibility ever since Henry revived on the table in *Bride of Frankenstein* and Minnie cried, "He's alive!"—but not an ending found in any other Frankenstein movie. Usually the monster is destroyed and the doctor survives. Here they both live and both marry. Comedy's continuing and self-renewing life energy and its traditional happy ending can be applied to horror, made to embrace it. Igor plays the love theme as the picture ends on a romantic high note—the triumph of sex and comedy in marriage.

Supernatural Comedies: *The Return of the Living Dead*

Many horror comedies depend on the final neutralizing, civilizing or expulsion of horror. After she is married, the witch (Veronica Lake as Jennifer) in *I Married a Witch* (René Clair, 1942, US) does not use her powers. At the end of *Bedazzled*, Stanley begins to make a new life for himself without the Devil's help. In *Ghostbusters* (Ivan Reitman, 1984, US) eruptions of the supernatural are finally dispelled or contained. But there are also comedies whose horrific elements are neither eliminated nor integrated into the normal world, such as *The Return of the Living Dead* (Dan O'Bannon, 1985, US). The combination of horror and humor is marked in that film and in *Shaun of the Dead* (Edgar Wright, 2004, UK), which opens by playing hilariously on our expectations about zombielike movements. *Return* and *Shaun* live up to the potential of their horror elements, treating horror with integrity. It is such an attitude that allows the supernatural plight of the Corpse Bride, for example, to be moving. Without caricaturing or diminishing it, great horror comedies like *Bedazzled* make the horror material funny.

Turning a picture based on *Night of the Living Dead* into a comic horror, as *The Return of the Living Dead* manages to do, is as difficult as it would be to convert *Hellraiser* into a situation comedy—though that could be done. Once the trail had been cleared, there were many zombie comedies, notably *Shaun of the Dead*, *Fido* (Andrew Currie, 2006, Canada) and *Zombieland* (Ruben Fleischer, 2009, US). For such a film to work, the comic aspects and the gore must be realized with equal zest. In *Return*, the dead are brought back from their graves by a gas released when Frank (James Karen) is showing his new assistant, Freddy (Thom Mathews), around the medical supply house where they work. Its holdings include cadavers and, in the basement, some old containers on which the army has stenciled a number to phone in case they are discovered, a number no one has ever called. Frank explains to Freddy, as if he were telling a campfire tale, that *Night of the Living Dead* was based on a real case and that the drumlike tanks in their very basement contain zombie corpses from those chemical-weapons experiments. Frank hits one of those containers to demonstrate how strong and safe it is, and it ruptures, releasing the gas sealed in with the corpse. Those not directly zombified by the gas become zombies after they are bitten and die, and all these walking corpses, which are limber, are hungry for brains. Frank and Freddy find that a cadaver and a split dog, which is gruesomely funny, have come to life. The pinned butterflies are waving their wings—a wonderful moment of horror beauty. With the help of the boss, Burt (Clu Gulager), they try to stop the cadaver by putting a pickax through its brain because something like that worked in *Night of the Living Dead*, but it doesn't work here. "You mean the movie lied?" asks Freddy. They decide the way to stop the cadaver is to cremate it in the nearby mortuary with the help of the mortician, Ernie (Don Calfa), but the ashes, even when reduced to smoke, have much the same effect as the gas, and when rain bears the smoke and ash to earth, the contaminated fluid soaks down to the corpses in the graveyard near the medical supply house.

Freddy's friends, young adults who care mostly about partying, wait in the cemetery ("Oh let's do *that*," one of them says sarcastically) for Freddy to get off work. They include his girlfriend, Tina (Beverly Randolph), and a nymphomaniac, Trash (Linnea Quigley). Trash takes off her clothes and tells them about a sexual fantasy she had about the most horrible way to die: being stripped naked and eaten alive by disgusting old men. When much of this fantasy later comes true, she doesn't enjoy it, and the scene isn't played for laughs.

Meanwhile, Frank and Freddy have been feeling the effects of the gas. Paramedics find they have no blood pressure or pulse and are at room temperature—in fact that they are dead—though they are still talking, and suffer terribly as they begin to go into rigor mortis. These scenes are, quite literally, painfully funny. In a more serious scene, a captured zombie explains to Ernie that eating brains assuages "the pain of being dead." Frank, whose body has become a site of unified comedy and horror, cremates himself while Freddy develops a hunger for Tina's brains. At last Burt calls the number on the containers, and the army nukes the city, thinking it is wiping out the problem but actually generating its own zombie-making fallout. It is misrule at its height—a theme in many comedies—and the monsters and the chaos will spread.

Human Comedies: *Arsenic and Old Lace*

Scary Movie (Keenen Ivory Wayans, 2000, US) fails when it simply makes fun of the slasher film, but it has some good moments—for example, when the camera moves in on a screaming young woman and hits her on the head. To parody a horror film is the easiest route to horror comedy, but it is also easy to find a host of parodies—some of which have a knowing and obnoxious reflexivity—that are not funny or scary, such as *Saturday the 14th* (Howard R. Cohen, 1981, US). Original situations that are both comical and frightening in themselves outshine most parodies, the best of which are made with a rich appreciation for the parodied. Crazy killers and the people who respond to them can be made to be very funny and can be readily shown in original situations, as in the exemplary horror comedy *Arsenic and Old Lace* (Frank Capra, 1942, released 1944, US), based on the play by Joseph Kesselring.

It is Halloween. Mortimer Brewster (Cary Grant), a dramatic critic who is famous for his negative attitude toward marriage, has just married Elaine Harper (Priscilla Lane), the girl next door, and on the way to take the train to Niagara Falls, they stop their cab at the Brewster house in Brooklyn. While Elaine packs, Mortimer goes to give the news of the marriage to his maiden aunts, Abby (Josephine Hull) and Martha (Jean Adair). Once he finds a corpse in the window seat and Abby and Martha tell him that the man is not the first of their victims—they have long been poisoning lonely old men and burying their bodies in the cellar—Mortimer panics, becomes distracted, forgets his honeymoon plans along with Elaine and the waiting cab, and tries to fix everything. The delay this introduces, while we are hoping he will just get out of a situation that turns progressively more crazy and dangerous and get on with the interrupted honeymoon, heightens the comedy and the tension. Mortimer thinks he can pin the murders on his uncle, "Teddy" (John Alexander), who thinks that he is Teddy Roosevelt and that he has been burying yellow fever victims in the Panama Canal, which is in the cellar. His digging new locks for the canal is both amusing and grisly, for it is a serious matter to have a dozen or more bodies buried in the basement of one's house. We have only to think of the crawl space in which serial killer John Wayne Gacy buried many of his victims. Abby, Martha, Teddy and the menacing Jonathan (Raymond Massey), Mortimer's brother, are a horror family. Jonathan, a sadistic murderer, accompanied by his plastic surgeon, Dr Einstein (Peter Lorre), shows up with a corpse of his own to dispose of, at first just looking for a place to hide long enough for Dr Einstein to change his face, but later intending to come home for good. His face currently looks like that of Boris Karloff, for Dr Einstein, who drinks too much, had last changed Jonathan's face after seeing *Frankenstein*. When Mortimer, who has briefly left the house, returns with the papers to have Teddy committed, Jonathan ties up Mortimer and prepares to kill him. The police intervene, and Jonathan is arrested. The bodies in the cellar aren't found, and Dr Einstein gets away. Abby and Martha have themselves committed so they will not be separated from Teddy, and in the process they reveal to Mortimer that he was adopted. Mortimer is relieved that he does not carry insanity in his genes (making him a better potential father) and at last leaves with Elaine, so that the film ends, as so many comedies do, with an affirmation or reaffirmation of marriage.

It is possible to imagine the same characters treated without humor, though the picture would be completely changed by this: a couple that hopes to make a quick stop at the old dark family house but is ensnared in the plots of the mad old ladies, their deluded brother and their murderous nephew with the monstrous face. There is a horror story there, lodged in the figures of the Brewster family and their house, but nearly every aspect of it is given the comic treatment. What makes the cellar burials funny is Teddy's assumptions about them. The body in the window seat is a dead man in the room, but it is also an object to be comically concealed and revealed. While Mortimer's reactions to the corpses and to his aunts' assumptions are flagrantly comical and at times overdone,

Abby's understatement—her matter-of-fact, sweet attitude about the way she and Martha have been bringing peace to lonely old gentlemen with their poisoned elderberry wine—is richly amusing. Even the dark threats of Jonathan are treated both gravely and comically. Although there is nothing inherently funny about them, they contribute to the general insanity and produce tension—and tension in this seamless movie is inseparably comic and scary. *Arsenic and Old Lace* is comparable to the majority of horror films in that it offers (but as comedy) a battle between the forces of death and those of life: life whose comic or serious demand for experience, for sexual fulfillment and sometimes for chaos cannot be suppressed.

It is simple, then, to imagine horrors taking place within a comic structure. They do not lose their horror core; if they did, the pictures would become farces. In many horror comedies, the scary forces have to stand up to a great deal of kidding, while rituals can sound and look silly. That means the horror forces must be strong and vivid. Unlike a ghost comedy of the 1940s, where there usually are no real ghosts, a comedy like *Beetle Juice* takes its basic premise, that ghosts are real, seriously. It becomes funny without making fun of itself, and a resolution that is both supernatural and comic is worked out.

Both comedy and horror generate disruptions to the status quo and try to resolve them, but both also have an infinite streak. What is essential about them is not necessarily time-bound but can continue without end, all along displaying its fundamental nature, like a perfect Marx Brothers joke or an undead being. Horror does not depend, then, on resolution or its failure. A resolved plot and a destroyed monster just make it easier for the surviving characters. But the movie is about the monster, the horror, the implied and displayed essence of destructiveness, repulsiveness and evil, not merely what happens to it. Like the ever-renewed energy of comedy, horror can exist in a state without boundaries. When they are mixed in a standard horror movie, comedy becomes comic relief, but in a horror comedy (a great subgenre for laughter in the dark and for the attempt to relieve anxiety and discomfort with humor) comedy proves dominant, perhaps because a comedy can be about any subject, can accept any stream into its all-embracing river.

8

HORROR DOCUMENTARY

Beyond comedy, there is another situation in which horror seems to have no boundaries and threatens to become infinite: when the horror is real. Our feelings about real horror can be boundless while we are in its grip. There is no consigning the evil to fiction. There is no beauty, no transfiguring or metaphoric imagery, no fantasy. Horror documentaries do not set out to entertain, but they are relevant to the genre in that they attempt to present horror on film. They often accomplish this without imposing a resolution on the material, especially where events have not provided one, leaving the horror open. To consider the documentary is vital to a complete view of the relations between horror and the horror film.

Death on Camera

The World War II documentary *Nuremberg: Its Lesson for Today* (Pare Lorentz, 1946, US) includes authentic footage taken inside a working gas chamber, and we see people die on camera, especially one man. *Nuremberg*, which contains some of the footage that was used in evidence at the Nuremberg trials, was supposed to have been shown widely after the war to educate people about the kind of evil the Allies had been fighting, but it was finally deemed too horrific for that and was released only in Germany. In the United States it was banned for 40 years. Some of the captured German footage it used, notably of Jews being thrown into a mass grave, appeared in later documentaries including *Night and Fog*.

What does it mean to see a man die on film? It is an event we witness without being able to affect it, for it is not only an image, but also an image from the past.[1] Our compassion and outrage are aroused but cannot find resolution. There is no narrative to put his suffering and death in context, no history in which he or anyone in his situation was saved. We are overwhelmed by the horror we see and feel because we know the event shown is real. We may feel strongly that the camera should not be there, although we may also feel glad that the evidence is being recorded. Dying is terrible to watch. The film that shows this death is not a narrative horror film, but it is certainly a film that generates and is permeated with horror.

Why was the film made—to check the gas chambers' efficiency? To document for the Reich that people were being exterminated? To provide a sadistic pleasure to those who might watch it? To express power? To have a record of death?

The final insult to this man was to photograph him as if he were an object fit for voyeurism, conquest and study—to take, in every sense, his last moment.

The best horror documentaries take a clear look at horror and allow us to integrate an understanding of it, or the attempt to confront it, into our vision of life. Some of them, like *Nuremberg*, take a stand against the monstrous actions they document. Some, like *Blood of the Beasts* (Georges Franju, 1949, France), a short that shows what happens to animals in slaughterhouses, present terrible events and situations that are left to speak for themselves. Others, like *Häxan*, examine horror topics (such as real Satanic cult activity or the folklore of werewolves) in an objective tone.

There are also horror docudramas, such as *Black Sun 731*, that recount true horror stories[2] but nevertheless set out to be entertaining, even if making entertainment out of atrocities can leave a bad taste. Their repulsiveness and their attraction are inseparably based on their underlying reality. An example of a more restrained horror docudrama is *The Deliberate Stranger* (Marvin J. Chomsky, 1986, US), the story of serial killer Ted Bundy, made for TV. *Black Sun 731* uses convincing special-effects makeup for most of its re-creations, while corpses are used for a few. We react to the effects as we often do in horror films, with a grateful awareness of their artificiality, but behind these are the real Unit 731 events of which we are also aware. Even if they are created and arranged images, not actualities (the exceptions are a scene in which a real cat is killed by rats and a scene in which the rats are burned), we relate them back to their origins, their referents. These re-creations show that a horror image can refer to real horror without exploding a narrative structure or disrupting the flow of the movie. But the *inclusion* of real horror, like the killing of the muskrat in *Cannibal Holocaust* or the cat in *Black Sun 731*, can derail the picture and our suspension of disbelief, yanking us out of the illusion and making us want to reject the image or denounce the filmmakers.[3]

Part of this is a matter of rejecting the narrative frame. It is hard to place, or accept, a frame around that tortured, dying muskrat. We reject it as part of the plot, as part of any story, and the frame of Monroe's narration is no more able to contain it than is the overall narrative frame of *Cannibal Holocaust*. We insist that this is real and no fiction. Not every horror can be put in a frame that keeps it in a structured relation with the rest of an artwork. Some horrors exceed all limits, even reflexive ones that can embrace an entire work.

Freaks, a fiction that includes the authentic, achieves much of its power from our realization that the human anomalies on the screen are real, though the characters they play are not. It is an exceptional example of integrating reality into a narrative film, and although it was widely banned, it does not use reality immorally, as *Cannibal Holocaust* does.

Real horror may stimulate rejection or compassion, but in some films it encourages the simple desire to accept (as the viewer of *The Act of Seeing With One's Own Eyes*, to be discussed shortly, is given the opportunity to accept) the more frightening and repulsive aspects of reality, or, as in *Night and Fog*, to try to comprehend them—in either case, to come close to them with a camera. Reality need not extinguish the horror response but may amplify it.

Real horror and real fear are often appealed to by the horror film in generating its moods and monsters. Real horror and fantastic horror are both part of the foundation of the genre. When we look at the horror artwork, real horror is not necessarily banished from our minds because, as said before, we may refer what we see to what we know and feel about horror in the real world—what we know and feel about crazy killers, for example, or snakes. But it is also possible for real horrors—like some imagined ones and some good imitations of real ones—to exceed our ability to appreciate them fully, to take in the enormity of what they show and imply, let alone to find an analogy for them in our experience. They can function as a limit to representation or as a goad to it: try to show *this*. For the horror film deals readily with the unknowable, which is comparable to the unfilmable in *Peeping Tom*, as well as with the unknown that may become known and with spectacle. Ineffable, infinite horror (sometimes an experience of the sublime) often centers on the overwhelming, but as we have seen, it can also tread on the unspeakable, on pure nameless horror and on insights that resist our understanding and our attempts to express them. The spectacle of a monster or a horrific event—or a suggestive prop, like the human tooth on the porch in *Texas Chain Saw*—makes the horror expressible if not necessarily comprehensible.

Some realities are impossible to show completely or in their full, transcendent horror. There must be room for transcendent suggestion, for the shot whose implications go beyond what it can put on the screen, like that of the pile of hair in *Night and Fog*. As both *Night and Fog* and *Nuremberg* demonstrate, a realistic horror treatment can ennoble and deepen its subject, filling the viewer not only with the fear of what people can do, but also with awe at the human capacity to endure horror, to manifest it and sometimes to survive it.

Autopsy: *The Act of Seeing With One's Own Eyes*

One image that may manifest horror and evoke it is that of the corpse—not a genocidally murdered one or a supernaturally reanimated one but a simple dead one. Horrific reality can be looked at as long as the filmmaker does not take a cruel or twisted or as-if-innocent approach to presenting it; that is made clear by Brakhage's *The Act of Seeing With One's Own Eyes* (1971), a silent documentary. The title is based on one meaning of "autopsy," to see for oneself, and the half-hour film covers several autopsies in a morgue—or watches them, for Brakhage, the literal viewer and the holder of the camera (not to mention Brakhage the editor), is always a presence implicit in the image, and his presence makes ours possible and lets us see with our own eyes. The bodies are violated, but without cruelty. We may be moved by the fact of death and fascinated by the evidence of it but do not feel any moral reaction. There is no story of how anyone died, no one to blame or fear. (What one fears is being autopsied.) A face is folded over and down to reveal the top of the skull, a skull is sawed open to expose the brain, naked bodies are examined and turned stiffly over, ribs are snipped, a liver is sliced with a butcher knife and torsos lie cut open and stripped of organs. Stomach-turning actions imitated in the goriest horror films are shown as matters of fact, close up and in color, performed on bodies that could not be more vulnerable except for the fact that death has placed them beyond being affected by what happens to them. We may be frightened and repulsed as well as moved by the image of the completely physical body and compare it with our own, for it is almost impossible to watch *The Act of Seeing* without thinking about one's own death and the possible fate of one's corpse. We also think of the gory contents of the body, which the autopsy takes from the inside and displays. Gore and bones are always present in us, and we may feel like vomiting when they are exposed. They show the nature of physical being, which we can accept and celebrate as well as hide from. As objective as Brakhage's film is, it responds to what the subjective filmmaker focuses and cuts to see, the facts of death. In its film-long silence it bears witness to the holiness and horror of the meat that can house spirit.

Looking at Horror

Brakhage's film is nonfiction, the record of an exploration and a confrontation, and it allows the autopsies to be presented in a tone of compassion, framing the horror in the most literal and cinematic sense of all, the act of looking at it through a camera. There is no other frame in this movie. In no way are we distanced from the spectacle of the dead and what is done to them. Although it is a hard film to watch (and even Brakhage lets the image go out of focus sometimes), it is kind. Its look at real horror is honest and completely effective.

Real horror appears in a variety of narrative films, as we have seen: by reference, by implication or by inclusion. Except where the integration of narrative and documentary is strong, as in *Freaks*, included horror can undermine the frame of fiction. Reference and implication are not problematic.

Within the frame of fiction, the horror film's images and events touch on the genuine fear and revulsion that may be inspired by our imagination, by our apprehension, by the expectations we hold of the genre and its recurring visual and narrative traditions and by our knowledge of what can happen in reality. The films are also inspired, of course, by what the filmmakers fear themselves or expect to be scary and by the horror moments they imagine. The genre is anchored in all of these. From the imaginary to the real, it finds its ground in horror.

The screen can be a window—as the bedroom window can be a metaphor for the screen, the literal way the horror film finds its way into our consciousness—through which we look out at the world transfigured by art or presented without a mask. It is a window in which horrors may show themselves, charging our dreams with the force of a nightmare, and our understanding with a frightening balance between what we know and what we fear to know.

As we have seen in films from *Vampyr* and *Hour of the Wolf* to *A Nightmare on Elm Street*, the horror film does often problematize vision, and not only when it is being reflexive. Part of the charge on the viewer is to see well. The genre offers a consistent system dedicated to revealing and confronting horror, a mental theatre in which a gaze or a camera that is often self-conscious faces a scene at which it is dangerous, upsetting, frightening or thrilling to look. No other film genre is so devoted both to what it shows and to the problem of watching it.

There is a battle between evil and good, articulated and extended in the horror film, that goes back through the history of art, literature, religious texts and folktales, and that is part of the way people have long speculated about and organized their visions of the metaphysics, the ethics and the values of the world. For horror films are made the world over, appealing to what may be a shared, essential, human core of fears as each one develops the mythology, the ideology and the ways to stimulate fear and disgust that are appropriate to its culture and period. What is often at stake is the balance of the universe. In horror movies, life and the good—or what the filmmakers define as good—often defeat death and evil, for we want some of our myths to be reassuring and our values to be defined and upheld (a primary function of a body of myth) even as we revel in and tremble at myths that are frightening and new and that spell the end of our old understanding, making necessary a new relationship with the universe and the dark.

If we fear being bitten or tortured, we may imagine it as we have seen it in a movie. Of course the average moviegoer, even the horror enthusiast, does not go through life gripped by fears of the dark, of violence, of nightmares, of losing blood, of death and undeath, of monsters, of being eaten alive and of slashers, and certainly not all at once. These are things that *can* scare us, latent fears that the horror film brings out, frightening us by stimulating our ability to be scared and linking it with a story, a monster, an image, a mood. Even if the central goal of the horror film is to frighten us, it also attempts to help us defeat our fears and to resolve or dispel what it has activated—in most cases through the climax and catharsis that are part of even those films whose endings let the threat reappear.

The horror film offers many images of the intrusion of horror into the world—not only in the bedroom-window scene, but also by way of the viewfinder that frames how the killer sees the victim in *Peeping Tom* and the screen that shows a horror film while a woman in the audience is stabbed in *He Knows You're Alone*. From the camera to the screen, the horror film has found ways to call attention to its look at the frightening and repulsive, ghastly and dreadfully beautiful, supernatural and monstrous, transcendent and terrible, cruel and painful aspects of the known and unknown world. It is a look at the frightening, put in a frame—both narratively and by the camera—that encourages us to enjoy being frightened and to feel power at the overcoming of the monsters and their horrors, and relief as they are dispelled.

NOTES

1. Horror

1 This is true for many people even if there is a vast critical literature on the genre.

2 The English word *uncanny* is used in this book in its dictionary sense, to denote the "peculiarly unsettling, as if of supernatural origin or nature; eerie" (*American Heritage College Dictionary*), but Freud's interpretation of the German word *unheimlich*—that the material is both familiar and unfamiliar, homelike and not, at once, and that it is familiar but unrecognized and unsettling because it has been repressed—is relevant throughout. See Sigmund Freud, *The Uncanny*, translated by David McLintock (New York: Penguin, 2003), 121–62.

3 For a historically based introduction, see Walter Kendrick, *The Thrill of Fear: 250 Years of Scary Entertainment* (New York: Grove Weidenfeld, 1991). On the horrific aspects of folklore and popular culture, see Harold Schechter's *The Bosom Serpent: Folklore and Popular Art*, 2nd ed. (New York: Peter Lang Publishing, 2001) and *Savage Pastimes: A Cultural History of Violent Entertainment* (New York: St. Martin's Press, 2005).

4 Stephen King argues in *Danse Macabre* (New York: Everest House, 1981), 34–7, that there is a descending scale from terror (which can be disembodied) to horror (which involves a physical component) to revulsion. His first aim is to terrify, and if he cannot do that, to horrify; then "if I find I cannot horrify, I'll go for the gross-out."

5 This association goes back at least to *Kwaidan* (Masaki Kobayashi, 1964, released 1965, Japan) and is not found only in later J-horror.

6 *Oxford English Dictionary*, "horror," *n.*, 3.a.

7 *Oxford English Dictionary*, "horror," *n.*, 4.

8 Edmund Burke, *A Philosophical Enquiry into the Origin of our Ideas of the Sublime and Beautiful* (Oxford and New York: Oxford University Press, 1990), 36–7, 53–9. For more on the nameless and the unnamable, see Bruce F. Kawin, *The Mind of the Novel: Reflexive Fiction and the Ineffable* (McLean, IL and London: Dalkey Archive Press, 2006).

9 Rick Worland, *The Horror Film: An Introduction* (Malden, MA and Oxford: Blackwell Publishing, 2007), 9: "particular monsters can be thought of as embodying particular threats or fears."

10 Hershel Toomim and Robert Joneson, "Anxiety, Anger, Depression, TBI and HEG," presented at the International Society for Neuronal Regulation, 2003. Also see University of Washington, "Finding Fear: Neuroscientists Locate Where It Is Stored In The Brain," *ScienceDaily* 7 July 2009. http://www.sciencedaily.com/releases/2009/07/090707093753.htm (accessed 28 March 2011).

11 The film was made in P. R. China with government approval, was apparently released there in 1987, and then opened in Hong Kong in 1988. Those who interviewed Tun Fei Mou at Montreal's Fantasia Film Festival in 1998 are the source for the 1987 release date; the interview is included on the DVD of Mou's *Black Sun: The Nanking Massacre* (Unearthed Films).

12 Quoted in Georges Sadoul, *Dictionary of Films*, edited by Peter Morris (Berkeley and Los Angeles: University of California Press, 1972), 398, and later in this book (see page 32).

13 Dearden directed the primary narrative frame (the Walter Craig story) and the story of the hearse driver. Hamer directed the story of the haunted mirror, Crichton the golf story and Cavalcanti the stories of the tower room and the ventriloquist's dummy.

14 Noël Carroll, *The Philosophy of Horror or Paradoxes of the Heart* (New York and London: Routledge, 1990), 12–13. Also see Brigid Cherry, *Horror* (New York and London: Routledge, 2009), 156–63.

15 Carroll, *The Philosophy of Horror*, 37–42, summarizes the nature and necessity of monsters and discusses why *Psycho* is not a horror film.

16 In *Focus on the Horror Film* (Englewood Cliffs, NJ: Prentice-Hall, 1972), editors Roy Huss and T. J. Ross divided the genre into "gothic horror," "monster terror" and "psychological thriller." My three categories grew from those and are similar to Rick Worland's more recently formulated "frightful tales of monsters, madmen, and supernatural evil"; Worland, *The Horror Film*, 2. However, not all human horror figures are insane.

17 *Black Sun 731* differs from conventional horror films in that it is a docudrama. For the full story of Ishii's experiments, see Hal Gold, *Unit 731 Testimony* (Tokyo: Yenbooks, 1996).

18 Robin Wood, "An Introduction to the American Horror Film," in Barry K. Grant and Christopher Sharrett, eds, *Planks of Reason*, rev. ed. (Lanham, MD and London: Scarecrow Press, 2004), 107–41. "Normality is threatened by the Monster" is on 117.

19 Canto 3, stanza IX, lines 1–2.

20 The shocking and depressing ending of *Night of the Living Dead* was of its period; consider the following year's *Easy Rider* (Dennis Hopper, 1969, US) and *Medium Cool* (Haskell Wexler, 1969, US). However, the shock ending typified by *Friday the 13th* was intended as a chilling thrill, not a staggering defeat.

21 Anticipating the *Book of the Vampire* by two years, a book and a manuscript provide crucial evidence in *The Cabinet of Dr. Caligari*.

22 The tape is accompanied by an untranslated book, the source of the incantations that are read on the tape.

23 *Beowulf: The Oldest English Epic*, edited and translated by Charles W. Kennedy (New York: Oxford University Press, 1978), 44.

24 Kennedy, *Beowulf*, 28.

25 Lines 451–6. Text from Wordsworth and Coleridge, *Lyrical Ballads 1798*, ed. W. J. B. Owen, 2nd edition (London: Oxford University Press, 1969), 7–32.

26 Lines 119–22.

27 On the failure of death and for an excellent introduction to the genre, see R. H. W. Dillard, "Even a Man Who Is Pure at Heart: Poetry and Danger in the Horror Film," in W. R. Robinson, ed., *Man and the Movies* (Baltimore: Penguin, 1969), 60–96.

28 See Dillard, "Even a Man Who Is Pure at Heart" and James B. Twitchell, *Dreadful Pleasures: An Anatomy of Modern Horror* (New York and Oxford: Oxford University Press, 1985).

29 In a radio interview sometime in the early 1980s.

30 Leo Tolstoy, *War and Peace*, translated by Richard Pevear and Larissa Volokhonsky (New York: Vintage, 2008), 143.

2. The Monster at the Bedroom Window

1 Sex and horror are, of course, linked throughout the genre, including when sex is treated as potentially fertile romantic love.

2 Earlier significant horror films include *The Haunted Castle* (Méliès, 1897), less than a minute long and apparently the fifth extant horror film (the earlier four, discussed in Chapter 4, were made by Méliès in 1896: *A Terrible Night*, *The Vanishing Lady*, *The Devil's Manor*, and *A Nightmare*); many versions of *A Christmas Carol*, beginning in 1908; two short adaptations of *Dr. Jekyll and Mr. Hyde* (1909 and 1912); two adaptations of *Frankenstein* in the US, *Frankenstein* (1910, a one-reel short released by Edison) and *Life Without Soul* (Joseph W. Smiley, 1915, US) and, in Germany, the first versions of *The Student of Prague* (1913) and *The Golem* (1914).

3 Siegfried Kracauer, *From Caligari to Hitler: A Psychological History of the German Film* (Princeton: Princeton University Press, 1947), 61–76.

4 A mindscreen is the visual and aural field of the mind's eye, whether the character (or a narrator, the filmmaker, or a reflexive narrative system) is having a fantasy, dreaming, remembering or telling a story. Bruce F. Kawin, *Mindscreen: Bergman, Godard, and First-Person Film* (McLean, IL and London: Dalkey Archive Press, 2006).

5 The first window reveals an optically printed view of the animated Kong, while the second admits a full-sized mechanical hand. The same thing happens in the next scene discussed.

6 This entire scene was censored out of the domestic release version.

7 Angela Carter, *The Bloody Chamber and Other Adult Tales* (New York: Harper and Row, 1981), 142–53. The script was co-written by Carter and Jordan.

3. Fear in a Frame

1 This happens after Allan has given blood. In a darkened hallway, a dark door opens into a lit room and then closes; then a doorway of light opens inside the dark door, as if the door had opened again, albeit in an impossible manner.

2 Sadoul, *Dictionary of Films*, 398.

3 For a brilliant reading of the camerawork and many other aspects of this film (and of *Day of Wrath*, which is discussed later in this book), see David Bordwell, *The Films of Carl-Theodor Dreyer* (Berkeley and Los Angeles: University of California Press, 1981).

4 The restoration is available on DVD from The Criterion Collection, and the set includes the script. It is clear from the mixes in the French and English versions (reviewed on film) that the German version was edited and mixed first, for the music and effects cease when dialogue in French or English is cut in; that gives the German version greater textual authority.

5 Carl Theodor Dreyer, *Four Screenplays*, translated by Oliver Stallybrass (Bloomington and London: Indiana University Press, 1970). Also contains the script for *Day of Wrath*.

6 She is blind in the script and in most of the film.

7 The difference is that her hand and the skeleton hand move in opposite directions.

8 Dreyer, *Four Screenplays*, 123: "The shot is taken in such a way that the spectator is uncertain whether the hand is real or not."

9 This may have been inspired by *A Corner in Wheat* (D. W. Griffith, 1909, US), whose villain is suffocated by a cascade of grain.

10 The only difference is that now they are covered with the closing credits.

11 Leo Marks, *Peeping Tom* (London: Faber and Faber, 1998).

12 In the script his eyes remain open. Mark's 16mm projector runs out at the end, but there is no reddish light; instead Mark's screen "fades slowly into greyness." Marks, *Peeping Tom*, 182–3.

13 For more extensive definitions and treatments of reflexivity and self-consciousness, see Robert Alter, *Partial Magic: The Novel as a Self-Conscious Genre* (Berkeley: University of California Press, 1975), the key work on the subject. Also see Kawin, *The Mind of the Novel* and *Mindscreen*.

4. Monsters

1 *The Haunted Castle* was Méliès's fifth (surviving) horror film. In the world's first known horror film, Méliès's *A Terrible Night* (1896), a big bug disturbs a man in bed, and the overall effect is comical but unnerving; *A Terrible Night* has been called a dream film but may not be. In Méliès's second horror film, *The Vanishing Lady* or *Escamotage d'une dame chez Robert-Houdin* (1896), a magician changes a woman into a skeleton, then back into her flesh-and-blood self. In the third, *The Devil's Manor* (1896; sometimes confusingly called *The Haunted Castle*), a bat flies around in a spooky room, then changes into a devil, who conjures up things and people and makes them vanish; two men examine the place but are frightened as a demon, a skeleton and so on appear and disappear; one man runs away, but the other vanquishes the devil with

a cross. In the fourth, *A Nightmare* (1896), a man has a vivid bad dream in part of which the moon chews his hand. The first five horror films, then, presented a frightening event in bed, a horror spectacle, a haunted house, a nightmare and a series of supernatural transformations. For the films, see the Flicker Alley DVD, *Georges Méliès: First Wizard of Cinema (1896–1913)*.

2 Robert Louis Stevenson, *The Complete Shorter Fiction*, edited by Peter Stoneley (New York: Carroll & Graf, 1991), 448.

3 Stevenson, *The Complete Shorter Fiction*, 479.

4 Stevenson, *The Complete Shorter Fiction*, 482.

5 It should come as no surprise that movies add love stories where they are "missing." It appears to be one of the only ways they can organize a horror story and what is at stake in it, as well as a familiar way to make us like and judge the characters and to exploit the unconscious eroticism of the screen.

6 Another was directed by Murnau: *Der Januskopf* (F. W. Murnau, 1920, Germany). It appears to be lost.

7 *Frankenstein* was released in November 1931, and *Dr. Jekyll and Mr. Hyde* on 31 December 1931 (opening widely two days later), so influence is unlikely.

8 The selfish and hedonistic young June is, in this context, very like Mr Hyde. For more on this picture, see Vivian Sobchack, "The Leech Woman's Revenge: On the Dread of Aging in a Low-Budget Horror Film," reprinted in *Uncontrollable Bodies: Testimonies of Identity and Culture*, edited by Rodney Sappington and Tyler Stallings (Seattle: Bay Press, 1994). The article has also been updated online: http://old.cinema.ucla.edu/women/sobchack/default.html (accessed 26 June 2011).

9 Mary Shelley, *Frankenstein: A Norton Critical Edition*, edited by J. Paul Hunter (New York: W. W. Norton, 1996), 30–32. The text is that of the 1818 edition.

10 William Everson notes in *Classics of the Horror Film* (Secaucus, NJ: Citadel Press, 1977), 53, that the producers changed their minds about whether the Monster should be blind: "For some reason, Universal had a great many second thoughts about the production…and changes were made during and after production. One of the basic decisions was to follow through directly from *The Ghost of Frankenstein* and to leave the Monster blind. Lugosi played the role that way, and effectively. Later, the idea was scrapped—but not to the extent of re-shooting all of the existing footage, so that Lugosi's movements and actions sometimes become inexplicable for one who was not now supposed to be blind." If the Monster is not blind, there is no reason to leave him with Ygor's brain, so he is back to his old criminal brain without any explanation, just as after *Bride* he lost the ability to speak without explanation.

11 Shelley, *Frankenstein*, 136.

12 For the Edison press release containing the shot-by-shot synopsis, see "Frankenstein Meets the Edison Company" in Huss and Ross, eds, *Focus on the Horror Film*, 66–9. It reads in part: "The story of the film brings out the fact that the creation of the monster was only possible because Frankenstein had allowed his normal mind to be overcome by evil and unnatural thoughts… With the strength of Frankenstein's love for his bride and the effect of this upon his own mind, the monster cannot exist… Standing directly before the mirror we see the remarkable sight of the monster's image reflected instead of Frankenstein's own. Gradually, however, under the effect of love and his better nature, the monster's image fades and Frankenstein sees himself in his young manhood in the mirror. His bride joins him, and the film ends with their embrace, Frankenstein's mind now being clear of the awful horror and weight it has been laboring under for so long." The film itself can be found on YouTube.

13 In the original legend the amulet contains a sacred religious text.

14 In the novel Victor acknowledges that he is the Monster's creator and eventually that he has responsibilities to him as his creator, but he does not compare himself to God or say that he stands in God's place. The Monster, who has read *Paradise Lost*, compares himself to Adam and may imply a comparison between Victor and God that is not to Victor's advantage.

15 Johann Wolfgang von Goethe, *Faust: A Tragedy*, edited by Cyrus Hamlin, translated by Walter Arndt (New York: W. W. Norton, 1976), 172 (part II, act II, "Laboratory," line 6,835).

16 It was with the title of *Frankenstein Meets the Wolf Man* in 1943 that Universal let "Frankenstein" refer to the Monster and not to Henry or other members of the Frankenstein family.

17 There were, of course, many other significant movies about the Frankenstein Monster, including Hammer's color *The Curse of Frankenstein* (Terence Fisher, 1957, UK), which brought red blood into Frankenstein's lab and started a series, but one of the most beautiful and chilling was *The Spirit of the Beehive* (Victor Erice, 1973, Spain), in which a little girl (Ana Torrent) imagines seeing the Monster after she has seen the 1931 movie.

18 *Oxford English Dictionary*, "monster," *n.* and *a.*, 3.a.

19 The sequel before *The Creature Walks Among Us* was *Revenge of the Creature* (Jack Arnold, 1955, US). Actually the Creature shows no romantic interest in the woman in the third film, but he does pay attention to her. On the Creature's romantic nature see Frank D. McConnell, "Song of Innocence: *The Creature from the Black Lagoon*," *Journal of Popular Film* II, 1 (Winter 1973), 15–28.

20 It is revealed at the very end, when something is seen falling from the sky into the ocean, that it came from outer space.

21 One of the artists who worked on the film, Eric Leven, said this about the monster's not being destroyed: "In most giant monster movies…the story ends up in the Army command center, with scientists trying to figure how to nuke the creature, and we feel sympathy for the creature. This movie was different because we stay with, and we sympathize with, these young human characters as they lose their friends and family. The monster was a big rampaging beast, and we never get a chance to think of it as a sympathetic character." Quoted in Joe Fordham, "Ground Zero," *Cinefex* 113 (April 2008), 66.

22 Carroll discusses the opposition this character or those like him may have to face, particularly from authority figures: *The Philosophy of Horror*, 100–102.

23 A child was threatened at the start of the picture. Thus in the course of the film, the world is made safe again for children, who were certainly part of the audience as well as symbols of the vulnerability within the adult, the child in us that first felt the fear of monsters and to which these films often encourage us to relate.

24 *The Lost World: Jurassic Park* was not a remake of *The Lost World*. It was an adaptation of Michael Crichton's novel *The Lost World*, which was itself influenced by the 1925 movie.

25 The last shots go on to show birds, the descendants of the dinosaurs, flying serenely, and an exterior of the helicopter that is flying home.

26 With all its talk of "pure blood," the movie may also be implying that the races belong sexually apart.

27 *Spielberg on Spielberg*, Turner Classic Movies, 2007. He said he had to "suggest the shark without showing the shark."

28 Shane M. Dallmann, "Cujo: 25th Anniversary Edition," *Video Watchdog* 143 (September 2008), 9.

29 There is a similar situation, with a similar denial of the power of the disembodied monster, in *The Hand* (Oliver Stone, 1981, US), where a graphic artist who has lost his drawing hand in a traffic accident imagines that the hand is crawling about on its own and killing those he considers his enemies. It is made clear at the climax that the artist, not his hand, is the killer and that he has been forgetting the crimes.

30 This comparison and some of the text leading up to it have been excerpted, with revisions, from my article "The Mummy's Pool," *Dreamworks* I, 4 (Summer 1981), 291–301, reprinted in Grant and Sharrett, *Planks of Reason*, 3–19.

31 On the ways the human community defines itself and its values while uniting to oppose monsters, see Gregory A. Waller, *The Living and the Undead: From Stoker's* Dracula *to Romero's* Dawn of the Dead (Urbana and Chicago: University of Illinois Press, 1986).

32 Of course there is often an ambivalent or even a negative attitude toward science in science fiction. In Kurt Vonnegut's novel *Cat's Cradle*, for example, a scientific breakthrough is responsible for the end of the world.

33 The ship's name is a reference to Joseph Conrad's *Nostromo*. The ship carries ore, the satiric equivalent of the novel's silver treasure. Scott's first feature, *The Duellists* (Ridley Scott, 1977, UK), was based on a Conrad story.

34 Ripley calls Mother a bitch when the self-destruct cancellation fails to work. After the ship has exploded, she says she got the son of a bitch, the Alien, as if the monster were Mother's child.

35 It is significant that Godzilla is killed by a change made to the water (its oxygen is destroyed), which is its home and the site of its first attacks. Godzilla is a monster from underwater as well as a giant.

36 The principal helps the teenagers break into the high school to get fire extinguishers.

37 Actually the original marketer and his new partner, an ice-cream executive, who have plans to release a modified version of the stuff.

38 The father discusses *Frankenstein* and emphasizes the nominal confusion between the Monster and its creator, which may imply that he feels like a monster, not just its co-creator.

39 On the "monstrous-feminine" (Barbara Creed's term) in *The Brood* and *Alien*, see Cherry, *Horror*, 111–16.

40 The term comes from Carol J. Clover, *Men, Women, and Chain Saws: Gender in the Modern Horror Film* (Princeton: Princeton University Press, 1992), 35–41. The character is a resourceful woman who is the last one alive to fight and destroy the monster, usually in a slasher film. This discussion of *The Funhouse* is based on my review in *Film Quarterly* XXXV, 1 (Fall 1981), 25–31.

41 A mad scientist had a similar idea in *I Was a Teenage Werewolf* (Gene Fowler, Jr, 1957).

42 The very end of the picture, which speaks of a citywide wave of sexual violence, may imply that she also had sexual partners living elsewhere.

43 For more on this topic see James Frazer, *The Golden Bough: A Study in Magic and Religion* (New York: Macmillan, 1963).

44 That describes the end of the unrated version. In the rated version, which was followed by a sequel, she gets away from the cave, though she runs into a final shock.

5. Supernatural Monsters

1 A caterpillar and a butterfly belong to a single species, even though they may have been read as an analogue in nature for interspecies transformation.

2 H. P. Lovecraft, *Supernatural Horror in Literature* (New York: Dover, 1973), 12.

3 Pazuzu is named in the novel and shown but not named in the release version of the movie.

4 The remake is longer, has better production values and more advanced special effects and stars Conrad Veidt as the student, but it is not a better picture than the original and lacks much of its power.

5 In the novel, this line is Renfield's. Bram Stoker, *Dracula: A Norton Critical Edition*, edited by Nina Auerbach and David J. Skal (New York: W. W. Norton, 1997), 130.

6 See Montague Summers, *The Vampire in Europe* (New York: E. P. Dutton, 1929) for a rich and detailed history written by someone who clearly believes vampires exist.

7 What often does change is the nature of the earth in the coffins. In a few films, such as both versions of *Nosferatu*, it comes from cemeteries used for victims of the Black Death; in Stoker's *Dracula* it must come from sanctified ground (though Van Helsing can render it even more holy and make it impossible for Dracula to inhabit). Because some vampires in folklore were buried at crossroads, the ground in which they were buried would not have been consecrated. Most films simply specify that the coffins contain the earth in which the vampire was buried, consecrated or not.

8 See Stoker, *Dracula*, 209–13, for Van Helsing's list of the vampire's powers and limitations.

9 This appears to be Stoker's invention.

10 The first film adaptation of Stoker's novel, also unauthorized, is now lost. It was *Drakula*, directed in Hungary in 1921 by Károly Lajthay.

11 Waller, *The Living and the Undead*, 120.

12 "Nosferatu" in this picture means "the vampire" (or the most formidable of vampires), though it can also refer to the undead in general. It is not his name, which is Count Orlok, but his species.

13 All intertitles and descriptions of the editing in *Nosferatu* are taken from the newly translated restoration (Friedrich Wilhelm Murnau Foundation, 2006) based on a 1922 print. On US video, the restoration is available from Kino in a 2-disc set, *Nosferatu: The Ultimate DVD Edition.*

14 In the restored version, the book is entitled *Of Vampyres, Terrible Phantomes, Magic, and The Seven Deadly Sins.*

15 "...ein gar sundlos Weyb" (an entirely sinless woman) is how the title reads; the English version of the restoration unfortunately translates this as "an innocent maiden."

16 Stoker, *Dracula*, 42. The novel's most intense early moment of horror comes on 43–4 when Dracula gives his former lovers a bag with a child in it.

17 For R. H. W. Dillard, the Van Helsing type is "the hero of the horror film" though he is not the central character; "he copes with events beyond human control. He is the older and wiser guide who reveals the mystery to the votary." Dillard, "Even a Man Who is Pure at Heart," 68–9.

18 The first journal read by another character is Lucy's; Van Helsing reads it along with her letters and other papers.

19 He does, however, read a great deal—especially about England before he goes there—and he does write a few business letters to which we don't have access.

20 The closest thing to this antitextuality in the movies is the fact that the vampire can't be reflected in a silver mirror or captured on silver-based film. Logically, it shouldn't appear in a movie at all, but it is still implicitly opposed to film and photography.

21 Seward, Van Helsing, Arthur and Quincey. Jonathan and Mina become part of the group soon after Lucy is delivered from undeath, though at first the group tries to exclude Mina for her protection.

22 The stake was not connected in Stoker's mind with the history of Vlad the Impaler. Stoker knew something about Vlad Tepes but did not mention his nickname or his practice of impaling great numbers of victims. The association of staking and impalement, where the stake is revenge against the impaler in his own coin, may have developed through folklore or may have been a happy coincidence; in any case, vampires were being staked long before Stoker's novel appeared. Van Helsing's stake may also be considered a metaphor for the stake at which witches and werewolves were burned.

23 Dillard, "Even a Man Who is Pure at Heart," 65–6.

24 Waller, *The Living and the Undead*, 108–9.

25 They have the "power of combination," which is denied to the vampire. Stoker, *Dracula*, 210.

26 Act I and act III, scene 1 are set in the library in Seward's sanitarium, act II in Lucy's (Mina's; the names have been switched) bedroom and act III, scene 2 in a vault in Carfax Abbey. For a plot summary, see Waller, *The Living and the Undead*, 361–62.

27 For more on the American and British versions of the play and how they departed from the novel, see David J. Skal, "'His Hour Upon the Stage': Theatrical Adaptations of *Dracula*," in Stoker, *Dracula: A Norton Critical Edition*, 371–80. For a vision of Dracula in one of his more repellent moments, see the novel, 53, and for Mina's first impressions of him, see 155.

28 For a comparison of the 1931 film and the 1927 play, see Waller, *The Living and the Undead*, 85–93.

29 In the novel on which the film is based (by John Ajvide Lindqvist, who also wrote the script), Eli was born male and castrated before being turned into a vampire.

30 In a 1941 introduction to the re-release of *Häxan*, director Benjamin Christensen tells about the experiences of a friend who had duplicated the recipe for "the witch's ointment." The short is included on The Criterion Collection's DVD of *Häxan*.

31 Donald C. Willis, *Horror and Science Fiction Films: A Checklist* (Metuchen, NJ: Scarecrow Press, 1972), 529. All the Méliès films discussed in this book are available on the Flicker Alley DVD, *Georges Méliès: First Wizard of Cinema (1896–1913)*.

32 Some critics have read the "confession" as a lie; some see it as a moment of madness and sad conviction. Others consider the confession to be straightforward and say that Dreyer did believe in witchcraft. Georges Sadoul, *Dictionary of Films*, edited by Peter Morris (Berkeley and Los Angeles: University of California Press, 1972), 409.

33 The film is loosely based on an early nineteenth-century ghost story by Gogol, "The Vij."

34 For a definitive study of Bava's films, see Tim Lucas, *Mario Bava: All the Colors of the Dark* (Cincinnati: Video Watchdog, 2007).

35 In 2007 Argento released *Mother of Tears: The Third Mother* (in Italian, simply *La terza madre*), which also has a large house, this one in Rome, investigated by a young woman (Asia Argento as Sarah)—the daughter of a powerful spiritualist whose ghost sometimes appears to her—who sets out to destroy the witch. This time the witch takes on the guise of a young woman who wants to bring about a new age of witchcraft and, as Rome is consumed by random acts of violence, attracts witches from all over the world to join her.

36 *Suspiria 25th Anniversary*, on the 3-disc DVD of *Suspiria* (Anchor Bay).

37 Daniel Myrick and Eduardo Sánchez called their company Haxan Films. The actors also contributed much of the dialogue and some of the action.

38 Shirley Jackson, *The Haunting of Hill House* (New York: Fawcett, 1977), 5.

39 *Poltergeist* was produced by Spielberg, who made it the horror picture to accompany *E.T. The Extra-Terrestrial* (Steven Spielberg, 1982, US) in a diptych, since the science fiction picture sometimes looks as if it was shot in the same neighborhood.

40 The remake, *The Ring* (Gore Verbinski, 2002, US/Japan), fails to recreate the horror of this sequence; the eye is especially inadequate. The remake also softens the ending.

41 Seen through the elevator door, the floor at which she gets off is in black and white. When she gets out of the elevator, the floor is in color.

42 They were conceived by Romero in collaboration with his co-author on *Night of the Living Dead*, John Russo.

43 Wade Davis, *The Serpent and the Rainbow* (New York: Simon and Schuster, 1985), 12. On pages 11 and 12, Davis explains his preference for the term "vodoun" rather than "voodoo" for the traditional religion of the Haitian people.

44 The movie *The Serpent and the Rainbow* (Wes Craven, 1988, US) did not tell Davis's story but did at least present zombies as people who had been drugged and hadn't really died.

45 The script was by Curt Siodmak, who had just written *The Wolf Man*, and Ardel Wray.

46 Similarly, Charles asks Legendre to zombify Madeline to keep her from marrying Neil. In both these films zombification is employed to control the victim's sexuality.

47 Fulci's zombies may be examples of both kinds of zombie, for they are flesh eaters who appear to be animated by voodoo.

48 The part as written did not call for an actor of any particular race, and no changes were made when Jones was cast.

49 Waller takes up this theme in *The Living and the Undead*, with special emphasis on *Dawn of the Dead*.

50 The only problem is that the TV shows daytime footage when it should be showing interviews made at night, but this is a continuity error rather than an attempt to say anything about the media.

51 Once Ben had established the pattern, there is a black character at or near the moral center of each of the *Dead* films.

52 Anthony C. Ferrante, "Return of the Living Dead Director," *Fangoria* 171 (April 1998), 20–21.

53 In *Virus*, the ones who realize the damage the virus will cause are political and ecological terrorists, and they are killed right away.

54 The film was released in Italy as *Zombi 2* so that it wouldn't be confused with *Zombi*.

55 James Frazer, *The Golden Bough*. 426. For both versions of the myth of Osiris, which are condensed here from Frazer, see 420–27.

56 The sculpted missing genitals may have been expressed in the movies as the Mummy's romantic compulsiveness and fixation.

57 The first victim, a standard figure in the horror film, is the one who pays for being the first to encounter the monster, the one whose knowledge of what is going on is fatal.

58 There are some faithful vampires, including Edward in the *Twilight* series, and Dracula is finally reunited with his original bride in Coppola's *Bram Stoker's Dracula* (1992, US).

59 Kharis did of course die when he was buried alive. Saying he "never really died" is another way of saying he became undead.

60 *The Mummy's Hand* is usually considered the first sequel to *The Mummy*, even though none of the modern story of *The Mummy* is acknowledged in *The Mummy's Hand*. After Imhotep or Kharis is buried, the stories diverge. But the attempt to resurrect the spirit of the princess shows up in *The Mummy's Ghost*, and all the films include a threat to a modern woman. Also, as we shall see, Kharis and the priest(s) can be seen as aspects split off from Imhotep. So there appears to be enough of *The Mummy* in the Kharis pictures to call all of them the Mummy sequels.

61 She died of natural causes (as we assume her father did) so that a scene wouldn't have to be written in which Kharis killed her.

62 The local paper is *The Bayou Times*, and some of the characters are Cajun.

63 Willis, *Horror and Science Fiction Films*, 334. The earliest mummy films appear to have been *Cleopatra* (Georges Méliès, 1899, France), in which Cleopatra is resurrected; *The Haunted Curiosity Shop* (Walter R. Booth, 1901, UK), in which a mummy comes briefly to life before dissolving into a skeleton; *The Mummy of the King* (1909, France), in which a professor revives the mummy of Ramses; *The Mummy* (1911, US); *The Vengeance of Egypt* (1912, UK), in which a cursed ring stolen from a mummy brings death to all who possess it and *The Dust of Egypt* (George D. Baker, 1915, US), in which the mummy of a princess is revived. Roy Kinnard, *Horror in Silent Films: A Filmography, 1896–1929* (Jefferson, NC: McFarland, 1995), 12, 13, 32, 44, 52, 71.

64 See Mircea Eliade, *The Myth of the Eternal Return*, translated by Willard Trask (New York: Pantheon, 1954), also called *Cosmos and History*. Also see Bruce F. Kawin, *Telling It Again and Again: Repetition in Literature and Film* (Niwot: University Press of Colorado, 1989), 65–70, 90–94.

65 Brad Steiger, *The Werewolf Book: The Encyclopedia of Shape-Shifting Beings* (Detroit and London: Visible Ink Press, 1999), xxvii.

66 Steiger, *The Werewolf Book*, x. Between 1520 and 1630, 30,000 people were charged.

67 *Metamorphoses*, book I.

68 The best of these is Sabine Baring-Gould, *The Book of Werewolves: Being an Account of a Terrible Superstition* (New York: Dover, 2006), first published in 1865.

69 For the biography of Albert Fish, see Harold Schechter, *Deranged: The Shocking True Story of America's Most Fiendish Killer* (New York: Pocket Books, 1990).

70 Baring-Gould, *The Book of Werewolves*, 101–32.

71 Baring-Gould, *The Book of Werewolves*, 126.

72 The film is lost, but it is described in Kinnard's *Horror in Silent Films*, 59. According to Steiger (*The Werewolf Book*, xxx), a real wolf was used in the transformation scene. The transformation was achieved with a dissolve. No director is on record, but the company was Bison, and the producer was Henry MacRae.

73 Applied to the skin, the fluid from a blossom can stop a werewolf from transforming for one night.

74 In some folklore, one of the ways to cure a werewolf is to call it by its real name.

75 Larry's elder brother was killed in a hunting accident, leaving Larry the oldest son and only inheritor; he has come back from America to learn how to carry on the line.

76 Even if psychology is a false god in *The Wolf Man*—its repeatedly offered explanations are finally refuted or at least shown not to apply in the case of a real werewolf—there is a father-and-son emphasis in the final confrontation that encourages a Freudian interpretation.

77 The story, "The Forbidden," is in *Clive Barker's Books of Blood*.

78 See Alan Dundes, "Bloody Mary in the Mirror: A Ritual Reflection of Pre-Pubescent Anxiety," *Western Folklore* 57 (1998), 119–35, and Mikel J. Koven, "Candyman Can: Film and Ostension," *Contemporary Legend* new series 2 (1999), 155–73. Bloody Mary can also be called Mary Worth; see "I Believe in Mary Worth" in Jan Harold Brunvand, ed., *Encyclopedia of Urban Legends* (Santa Barbara: ABC CLIO, 2001), 205–6. Thanks to Cathy Preston for running this down.

79 Eliade, *The Myth of the Eternal Return*.

80 The tail credits say that Michael is shown when he is 6 and when he is 23, while the dialogue and intertitles say there are 15 years between the events. In *Halloween II* Loomis says that Michael is 21.

81 Clover, *Men, Women, and Chain Saws*, 35–41.

82 The "Kih" and "Mah" sounds of this sentence were synthesized to create the eight-beat "Ki/Ma" voice-over.

83 There are a few shots from the POV of the spider in *Tarantula*, but the emphasis is always on the victim's fear.

84 What begins as Horatio's "In the most high and palmy state of Rome" (I, i), which speaks of bad omens and the rising of the dead, ends as Hamlet's "I could be bounded in a nutshell and count myself a king of infinite space, were it not that I have bad dreams" (II, ii).

6. Humans

1 Aside from all the confusion of art and reality in this picture, there are also such reflexive moments as the policeman's telling the driver, in an urgent chase scene, to slow down because there's no hurry; Dr Gogol's quoting Dr Caligari when talking to Stephen (he says he now understands his case and thinks he can help him); and the housekeeper's quoting the opening sequence of director Freund's previous horror film by saying that Yvonne's statue "went out for a little walk."

2 The sign outside his shop reads "Orlac and son, Jewelers," with "and son" crossed out; it appears he didn't want to pay for a new sign.

3 It was not until 2005 that the first successful face transplant was made—ironically, in France. Denise Gellene, "From Her Lips to Doc's Cheers," *The Denver Post*, 13 December 2007, 22A.

4 Leslie Fiedler, *Freaks: Myths and Images of the Secret Self* (New York: Simon and Schuster, 1978), 16.

5 Fiedler, *Freaks*, 328, 347.

6 *The American Film Institute Catalog: Feature Films, 1931–1940* (Berkeley and Los Angeles: University of California Press, 1993), vol. I, 700.

7 Ibid.

8 Mikita Brottman, *Offensive Films* (Nashville: Vanderbilt University Press, 2005), 18.

9 This time the sculptor is Henry Jarrod (Vincent Price), the whole story is set in New York, the treacherous partner is killed early in the picture and becomes an exhibit, a newspaper subplot is dropped in favor of making police the primary investigators and the woman who almost becomes the core of a sculpture is named Sue (Phyllis Kirk). In a typical minor change, the artist falls into the hot wax without being shot first, and the policeman is the one who then saves the woman while her boyfriend is recovering.

10 Artist and work are also destroyed together when the artist falls into the vat of wax, since he has made the wax the vehicle of his artistic expression.

11 A second woman (Pamela, played by Baybi Day) also lives with them.

12 The inner movie stars John Trent rather than Sam Neill; that's the only difference on the marquee and the poster. On the screen, the inner movie is presented via a montage of scenes from the real movie.

13 Brottman, *Offensive Films*, 75, 199n.

14 The flat color of the walls also resembles that of dried blood.

15 For both the soldiers and the captives, conventional heterosexual intercourse has been forbidden.

16 What we see is purportedly a reconstruction of the original snuff film sent to a "bizarre cartoonist" by a fan of his work.

17 The one made by the cameraman who is one of the killers, which takes up most of *Flower's* running time.

18 Adam could also saw off his foot and use the gun to save himself—though only Lawrence has a bullet; however, he breaks his saw when trying to cut through his chain.

19 Lawrence says he is going for help, but until the final sequel we never find out what happened to him, even if we know that his family has been saved. No help is sent back for Adam, but in *Saw III* (Darren Lynn Bousman, 2006, US/Canada) Amanda is revealed to have mercifully suffocated him.

20 Narrative coherence is at stake in *Saw II*, where what appears through the use of cross-cutting to be contemporary with the present actually turns out to have taken place in the past. As part of the game, the events are shown on monitors later than they happened, thanks to a recording on tape. What is deceptive is that the filmed and videoed events are spliced together in the cutting as if they were happening together. At the climax of the film we reinterpret the cross-cutting we have been watching all along. We literally can't understand what we have seen until we can understand this game.

21 Baring-Gould, *The Book of Werewolves*, 143–5.

22 At the end, a doctor causes him to relax his smile by injecting him with a placebo and leaving him in a dark room with his father's corpse. Thus the affliction is proved to have been psychological in origin. It turns out, however, that his mouth remains rigid in its new, closed position, and he remains the victim of his guilt and fear.

23 For the biography of Ed Gein, several aspects of whose life inspired the novel and film of *Psycho* as well as other works, see Harold Schechter, *Deviant: The Shocking True Story of the Original "Psycho"* (New York: Pocket Books, 1989).

24 He may also have dug up a few younger women, though the evidence for this is not solid. Schechter, *Deviant*, 100–101.

25 Bill Cooke, "*The Texas Chain Saw Massacre*," *Video Watchdog* 151 (September 2009), 47.

26 The summer kitchen, attached to the rear of the house with its own door, but described by Gein as a "wood shed." Schechter, *Deviant*, 81, 96.

27 In 1978 he was transferred to a mental health institute, where he died at the age of 78 in 1984. Schechter, *Deviant*, 236.

28 Beyond that the film explores one aspect of what might be called the horror condition—the state of being trapped in or dedicated to a horror—by showing how rape and murder can be fated and irreversible, for the action unfolds in reverse chronological order, building to a closing moment of stability and hope that is actually at the beginning of a chain of terrible events. By going back to the beginning of the story, the film tries to reverse its events and somehow avoid them, but what happened in it remains inexorably what happened, and there is no way to begin on a different course or make different decisions.

29 *The Bad Seed* was based on the novel by William March and more directly on the play by Maxwell Anderson.

30 Haneke's American remake was released in 2008; the films are similar.

31 In a "near-family," only some, or even none, of the members of the group are related by blood or marriage.

32 A reference to the Welsh legends so important in the work of Arthur Machen (*The Three Impostors*), not to the little people in *The Devil-Doll*.

33 Bruce Kawin, "Me Tarzan, You Junk," *Take One* VI, 4 (March 1978), 29–33.

34 Songs by David A. Hess. Songs have become rare in horror films, except under tail credits. One of the last songs to be an integral part of a nonmusical horror film was "I've Written a Letter to Daddy" in *What Ever Happened to Baby Jane?* (Robert Aldrich, 1962, US), a dark tale set not between families but within the family, in which two sisters destroy each other's lives.

35 Schechter, *The Bosom Serpent*, 35–7.

36 In the tail credits he is called "Cook," so Drayton Sawyer may be an assumed name, with "Sawyer" a joke.

37 Sally is the focus of the second half of *Texas Chain Saw*.

38 They write "hello" on it; their leaving the curtain open to reveal the window declares that they have already been inside.

39 The music is similar to *Psycho*—and Margaret uses a butcher knife on Carrie, and the high school is named Bates High—to link a controlling, insane, sex-hating mother with her troubled child as if they were two sides of a single madness (this time gendered entirely female, not a compound of mother and son) and to imply that Carrie's problem is psychological—not that her powers are neurotically motivated but that she is a mental horror figure in the tradition of Norman Bates, with telekinetic powers rather than a psychosis. None of these references is in the novel; in crossing to the cinema, *Carrie* became part of a series of film horrors and took *Psycho* for its new foundation, in company with De Palma's other homages to Hitchcock and a growing number of films about crazy killers.

40 The laughing is presented from Carrie's POV (accompanied by her memory of her mother's prediction that she would be laughed at if she went to the prom) and may be augmented to the point of illusion by her humiliation and anger, for she sees the gym teacher laughing too, which would be out of character.

41 Gillian is a Fury both in her association with blood and in the just vengeance she takes on Childress.

42 *28 Days Later…* is the US release title.

43 This is another instance of the "flesh" theme in Cronenberg's early films.

44 As a porn actress given phallic power, Chambers is already a figure of reversal in this movie.

45 In the sequel, *28 Weeks Later* (Juan Carlos Fresnadillo, 2007, UK/Spain), one character is infected by a kiss.

46 For further observations on the subject and object in horror, see Julia Kristeva, *Powers of Horror: An Essay on Abjection*, translated by Leon S. Roudiez (New York: Columbia University Press, 1982).

47 They are discussed together in Jay Slater's very useful *Eaten Alive!: Italian Cannibal and Zombie Movies* (London: Plexus, 2002).

48 Slater, *Eaten Alive!*, 46.

49 Slater, *Eaten Alive!*, 163.

50 From the commentary track on the laserdisc and DVD of *Cannibal Ferox* (Grindhouse).

51 This was the film's central revelation, daring at the time. Slater, *Eaten Alive!*, 105–6. The practice dates back at least to *Nanook of the North* (Robert Flaherty, 1922, US), if not to the Lumières' *Leaving the Factory* (Louis and Auguste Lumière, 1895, France).

52 When some meat is offered to Gloria and Pat, Gloria famously says, "Don't! It could be Rudy."

53 The title card comes just after the credits and is part of the original movie, unlike the title card in *Make Them Die Slowly*.

54 As Sean Cunningham put it in an interview, the final girl "has embodied the moral code that society thinks allows you to go forward in life." *Going to Pieces: The Rise and Fall of the Slasher Film* (Starz, 2006).

55 In a later reflexive moment, a psychology student (Tom Hanks) expresses his doubtless valid opinion that horror movies give one the vicarious thrill of conquering death—"you can face death without any real fear of dying; it's safe"—and says that is why it is a pleasure to be frightened in the controlled worlds of art and roller coasters.

56 He also kills several men, including an old man who makes bridal gowns, whom he stabs with scissors. Then he stabs (with a knife) a sexually active young woman who is not engaged to anyone, along with the married professor with whom she is having an affair—so promiscuity is as much his target as are brides and a man who dresses brides.

57 One exception is the Santa costume in *Silent Night Deadly Night*, which functions as a kind of mask for the character whose violence is triggered by his psychological associations with the suit.

58 By implication, this scene is picked up in the very different ending of *Scream 3*, where one *can* choose another genre.

59 In *He Knows You're Alone* the victim goes to the theatre's bathroom before she is killed in the auditorium. In *Scream 2* a man is killed in the theatre bathroom before his girlfriend is killed in the auditorium.

60 She slaps her instead of slugging her because most events repeated in sequels take place with variations.
61 The final girl is usually alone at the end. The couple theme is picked up by Dewey and Gail.

8. Horror Documentary

1 On this aspect of spectatorship see Stanley Cavell, *The World Viewed: Reflections on the Ontology of Film*, enlarged ed. (Cambridge, MA and London: Harvard University Press, 1979).
2 The film was scrupulously researched, but more evidence and first-hand testimony appeared after it was released.
3 For another example of inclusion, consider the real decapitations that Mou cut into many of the re-enacted executions in *Black Sun: The Nanking Massacre* (T. F. Mou, 1995, Hong Kong).

FILMS CITED

28 Days Later or *28 Days Later...* (Danny Boyle, 2002, UK)

The Act of Seeing With One's Own Eyes or *Autopsy* (Stan Brakhage, 1971, US)

Alien (Ridley Scott, 1979, US/UK)

Alien: Resurrection (Jean-Pierre Jeunet, 1997, US)

Alien³ (David Fincher, 1992, US)

Aliens (James Cameron, 1986, US/UK)

The Amazing Colossal Man (Bert I. Gordon, 1957, US)

An American Werewolf in London (John Landis, 1981, UK/US)

Angel Heart (Alan Parker, 1987, US/Canada/UK)

Arsenic and Old Lace (Frank Capra, 1942, released 1944, US)

Attack of the 50 Foot Woman (Nathan Juran as Nathan Hertz, 1958, US)

Au secours! or *Help!* (Abel Gance, 1923, France)

Audition (Takashi Miike, 1999, Japan)

The Bad Seed (Mervyn LeRoy, 1956, US)

Bambi Meets Godzilla (Marv Newland, 1969, Canada)

Basket Case (Frank Henenlotter, 1982, US)

A Bay of Blood or *Twitch of the Death Nerve*, literally titled *Ecology of Murder* (Mario Bava, 1971, Italy)

The Beast with Five Fingers (Robert Florey, 1946, US)

Beauty and the Beast (Jean Cocteau, 1946, France)

Bedazzled (Stanley Donen, 1967, UK)

Beetle Juice or *Beetlejuice* (Tim Burton, 1988, US)

The Beyond (Lucio Fulci, 1981, Italy)

The Birds (Alfred Hitchcock, 1963, US)

The Black Cat (Edgar G. Ulmer, 1934, US)

Black Christmas (Bob Clark, 1974, Canada)

Black Sun 731 or *Men Behind the Sun* (T. F. Mou, 1987, China)

Black Sun: The Nanking Massacre (T. F. Mou, 1995, Hong Kong)

Black Sunday. See *The Mask of the Demon*

The Blair Witch Project (Daniel Myrick and Eduardo Sánchez, 1999)

The Blob (Irvin S. Yeaworth, Jr, 1958, US)

Blood Feast (Herschell Gordon Lewis, 1963, US)

Blood of the Beasts or *Le Sang des bêtes* (Georges Franju, 1949, France)

Blow Out (Brian De Palma, 1981, US)

The Body Snatcher (Robert Wise, 1945, US; produced by Val Lewton)

The Boogens (James L. Conway, 1981, US)

The Boys from Brazil (Franklin J. Schaffner, 1978, UK/US)

Brainstorm (Douglas Trumbull, 1983, US)

Bram Stoker's Dracula or *Dracula* (Francis Ford Coppola, 1992, US)

Breakfast at the Manchester Morgue. See *Let Sleeping Corpses Lie*

Breaking Dawn—Part 1 or *The Twilight Saga: Breaking Dawn—Part 1* (Bill Condon, 2011, US)

Bride of Frankenstein (James Whale, 1935, US)

Bride of the Gorilla (Curt Siodmak, 1951, US)

The Brood (David Cronenberg, 1979, Canada)

Bud Abbott and Lou Costello Meet Frankenstein (Charles T. Barton, 1948, US)

The Burning (Tony Maylam, 1981, US/Canada)

Cabin Fever (Eli Roth, 2002, released 2003, US)

The Cabinet of Dr. Caligari (Robert Wiene, 1919, released 1920, Germany)

Candyman (Bernard Rose, 1992, US)

Cannibal Ferox or *Make Them Die Slowly* (Umberto Lenzi, 1981, Italy)

Cannibal Holocaust (Ruggero Deodato, 1980, Italy)

The Canterville Ghost (Jules Dassin, 1944, US)

The Car (Elliot Silverstein, 1977, US)

Carrie (Brian De Palma, 1976, US)

The Cat and the Canary (Paul Leni, 1927, US)

Cat People (Jacques Tourneur, 1942, US; produced by Val Lewton)

Children of the Damned (Anton Leader, 1963, UK)

Child's Play (Tom Holland, 1988, US)

Christine (John Carpenter, 1983, US)

Cleopatra (Georges Méliès, 1899, France)

Close Encounters of the Third Kind (Steven Spielberg, 1977, US)

Cloverfield (Matt Reeves, 2008, US)

Color Me Blood Red (Herschell Gordon Lewis, 1965, released 1966, US)

The Company of Wolves (Neil Jordan, 1984, UK)

A Corner in Wheat (D. W. Griffith, 1909, US)

Corpse Bride or *Tim Burton's Corpse Bride* (Mike Johnson and Tim Burton, 2005, UK/US)

Creature from the Black Lagoon (Jack Arnold, 1954, US)

The Creature Walks Among Us (John Sherwood, 1956, US)

Cujo (Lewis Teague, 1983, US)

The Curse of Frankenstein (Terence Fisher, 1957, UK)

The Curse of the Cat People (Robert Wise and Gunther Von Fritsch, 1944, US; produced by Val Lewton)

Curse of the Demon. See *Night of the Demon*

The Curse of the Werewolf (Terence Fisher, 1961, UK)

Dawn of the Dead (George A. Romero, 1978, released 1979, Italy/US)

Day of the Dead (George A. Romero, 1985, US)

The Day of the Triffids (Stephen Sekely, 1962, UK)

Day of Wrath (Carl Dreyer, 1943, Denmark)

The Day the Earth Stood Still (Robert Wise, 1951, US)

Dead of Night (Alberto Cavalcanti, Charles Crichton, Basil Dearden and Robert Hamer, 1945, UK)

Dead Ringers (David Cronenberg, 1988, Canada/US)

Deep River Savages or *Man from Deep River* (Umberto Lenzi, 1972, Italy)

The Deliberate Stranger (Marvin J. Chomsky, 1986, US)

Demon Seed (Donald Cammell, 1977, US)

Demons (Lamberto Bava, 1985, Italy)

Deranged (Jeff Gillen and Alan Ormsby, 1974, Canada/US)

The Descent (Neil Marshall, 2005, UK)

The Descent: Part 2 (Jon Harris, 2009, UK)

The Devil-Doll (Tod Browning, 1936, US)

The Devil's Manor (Georges Méliès, 1896, France)

Diary of the Dead or *George A. Romero's Diary of the Dead* (George A. Romero, 2007, US)

Doctor X (Michael Curtiz, 1932, US)

Donovan's Brain (Felix Feist, 1953, US)

Don't Look Now (Nicolas Roeg, 1973, UK/Italy)

Dr. Cyclops (Ernest B. Schoedsack, 1940, US)

Dr. Jekyll and Mr. Hyde (August Blom, 1909, Denmark)

Dr. Jekyll and Mr. Hyde (Lucius Henderson, 1911, released 1912, US)

Dr. Jekyll and Mr. Hyde (John S. Robertson, 1920, US)

Dr. Jekyll and Mr. Hyde (Rouben Mamoulian, 1931, wide release 1932, US)

Dr. Jekyll and Mr. Hyde (Victor Fleming, 1941, US)

Dracula (Tod Browning, 1931, US)

Dracula (John Badham, 1979, US/UK)

Drakula (Károly Lajthay, 1921, Hungary)

The Driller Killer (Abel Ferrara, 1979, US)

The Duellists (Ridley Scott, 1977, UK)

The Dust of Egypt (George D. Baker, 1915, US)

Easy Rider (Dennis Hopper, 1969, US)

Eaten Alive! or *Eaten Alive by Cannibals* (Umberto Lenzi, 1980, Italy)

Eclipse or *The Twilight Saga: Eclipse* (David Slade, 2010, US)

E.T. The Extra-Terrestrial (Steven Spielberg, 1982, US)

The Evil Dead (Sam Raimi, 1983, US)

The Exorcist (William Friedkin, 1973, US)

The Exterminating Angel (Luis Buñuel, 1962, Mexico)

Eyes Without a Face (Georges Franju, 1959, France)

Fantasia (Walt Disney, 1940, US)

Faust (F. W. Murnau, 1926, Germany)

Fido (Andrew Currie, 2006, Canada)

Fiend Without a Face (Arthur Crabtree, 1958, UK)

Final Destination (James Wong, 2000, US)

The Fly (Kurt Neumann, 1958, US)

The Fly (David Cronenberg, 1986, Canada/US)

Forbidden Planet (Fred M. Wilcox, 1956, US)

Frailty (Bill Paxton, 2002, US/Germany/Italy)

Frankenstein (J. Searle Dawley, 1910, US)

Frankenstein (James Whale, 1931, US)

Frankenstein Meets the Wolf Man (Roy William Neill, 1943, US)

Freaks (Tod Browning, 1932, US)

Freddy vs. Jason (Ronny Yu, 2003, Canada/US/Italy)

Freddy's Dead: The Final Nightmare (Rachel Talalay, 1991, US)

Friday the 13th (Sean S. Cunningham, 1980, US)

Friday the 13th (Marcus Nispel, 2009, US)

Friday the 13th Part 2 (Steve Miner, 1981, US)

Friday the 13th Part III (Steve Miner, 1982, US)

Friday the 13th: The Final Chapter (Joseph Zito, 1984, US)

Frogs (George McCowan, 1971, US)

The Funhouse (Tobe Hooper, 1981, US)

Funny Games (Michael Haneke, 1997, Austria)

The Fury (Brian De Palma, 1978, US)

The Ghost of Frankenstein (Erle C. Kenton, 1942, US)

Ghostbusters or *Ghost Busters* (Ivan Reitman, 1984, US)

The Ghoul (T. Hayes Hunter, 1933, UK)

The Giant Claw (Fred F. Sears, 1957, US)

Ginger Snaps (John Fawcett, 2000, Canada)

The Godsend (Gabrielle Beaumont, 1980, UK)

Gojira or *Godzilla* (Ishiro Honda, 1954, Japan); US version with new material by Terry Morse, *Godzilla King of the Monsters!*, 1956

The Golem (Paul Wegener and Henrik Galeen, 1914)

The Golem: How He Came Into the World (Carl Boese and Paul Wegener, 1920, Germany)

It Lives Again (Larry Cohen, 1978, US)

It! The Terror from Beyond Space (Edward L. Cahn, 1958, US)

It's Alive (Larry Cohen, 1974, US)

It's Alive III: Island of the Alive (Larry Cohen, 1987, US)

Der Januskopf (F. W. Murnau, 1920, Germany)

Jason Lives: Friday the 13th Part VI (Tom McLoughlin, 1986, US)

Jason X (Jim Isaac, 2002, US)

Jaws (Steven Spielberg, 1975, US)

Jungle Holocaust. See *Last Cannibal World*

Ju-on: The Grudge (Takashi Shimizu, 2003, Japan)

Jurassic Park (Steven Spielberg, 1997, US)

Kalevet or *Rabies* (Aharon Keshales and Navot Papushado, 2010, Israel)

King Kong (Merian C. Cooper and Ernest B. Schoedsack, 1933, US)

Kingdom of the Spiders (John "Bud" Cardos, 1977, US)

Kwaidan (Masaki Kobayashi, 1964, released 1965, Japan)

Land of the Dead or *George A. Romero's Land of the Dead* (George A. Romero, 2005, Canada/France/US)

Larger than Life (Ellory Elkayem, 1998, New Zealand)

Last Cannibal World or *Jungle Holocaust* (Ruggero Deodato, 1977, Italy)

The Last House on the Left (Wes Craven, 1972, US)

The Last House on the Left (Dennis Iliadis, 2009, US)

The Last Wave (Peter Weir, 1977, Australia)

Leaving the Factory or *Workers Leaving the Lumière Factory* (Louis and Auguste Lumière, 1895, France)

The Leech Woman (Edward Dein, 1960, US)

The Leopard Man (Jacques Tourneur, 1943, US; produced by Val Lewton)

Let Me Dream Again (G. A. Smith, 1900, UK)

Let Sleeping Corpses Lie or *Breakfast at the Manchester Morgue* or *The Living Dead at Manchester Morgue* or *Don't Open the Window,* literally titled *Do Not Speak Ill of the Dead* (Jorge Grau, 1974, Spain/Italy)

Let the Right One In (Tomas Alfredson, 2008, Sweden)

Life Without Soul (Joseph W. Smiley, 1915, US)

Lifeforce (Tobe Hooper, 1985, UK)

The Little Shop of Horrors (Roger Corman, 1960, US)

Little Shop of Horrors (Frank Oz, 1986, US)

The Living Dead at Manchester Morgue. See *Let Sleeping Corpses Lie*

Lost Continent (Sam Newfield, 1951, US)

Lost Horizon (Frank Capra, 1937, US)

The Lost World (Harry Hoyt, 1925, US)

The Lost World: Jurassic Park (Steven Spielberg, 1997, US)

M (Fritz Lang, 1931, Germany)

The Mad Ghoul (James P. Hogan, 1943, US)

Mad Love (Karl Freund, 1935, US)

Madman (Joe Giannone, 1982, US)

The Magnetic Monster (Curt Siodmak, 1953, US)

Make Them Die Slowly. See *Cannibal Ferox*

Man from Deep River. See *Deep River Savages*

The Man with the X-Ray Eyes. See *X*

Maniac (Dwain Esper, 1934, US)

Maniac (William Lustig, 1980, US)

Mark of the Vampire (Tod Browning, 1935, US)

Martin (George A. Romero, 1978, US)

Mary Jane's Mishap (G. A. Smith, 1903, UK)

The Mask of the Demon or *The Mask of Satan* or *Black Sunday* or *Revenge of the Vampire* (Mario Bava, 1960, Italy)

May (Lucky McKee, 2002, US)
Medium Cool (Haskell Wexler, 1969, US)
Men Behind the Sun. See *Black Sun 731*
The Mole People (Virgil Vogel, 1956, US)
Mondo Cane (Gualtiero Jacopetti and Franco Prosperi, 1962, Italy)
The Monolith Monsters (John Sherwood, 1957, US)
Monsters, Inc. (Pete Docter, 2001, US)
Motel Hell (Kevin Connor, 1980, US)
Mr. Sardonicus (William Castle, 1961, US)
The Mummy (uncredited, 1911, US)
The Mummy (Karl Freund, 1932, US)
The Mummy of the King (uncredited, 1909, France)
The Mummy's Curse (Leslie Goodwins, 1944, released 1945, US)
The Mummy's Ghost (Reginald LeBorg, 1943, released 1944, US)
The Mummy's Hand (Christy Cabanne, 1940, US)
The Mummy's Tomb (Harold Young, 1942, US)
Murders in the Rue Morgue (Robert Florey, 1932, US)
The Mutilator (Buddy Cooper, 1985, US)
My Bloody Valentine (George Mihalka, 1981, Canada)
Mystery of the Wax Museum (Michael Curtiz, 1933, US)
Nanook of the North (Robert Flaherty, 1922, US)
Near Dark (Kathryn Bigelow, 1987, US)
New Moon or *The Twilight Saga: New Moon* (Chris Weitz, 2009, US)
Night and Fog (Alain Resnais, 1955, France)
Night of the Demon or *Curse of the Demon* (Jacques Tourneur, 1957, UK)
Night of the Living Dead (George A. Romero, 1968, US)
Night of the Zombies. See *Virus*
A Nightmare or *The Nightmare* (Georges Méliès, 1896, France)
A Nightmare on Elm Street (Wes Craven, 1984, US)
A Nightmare on Elm Street 3: Dream Warriors (Chuck Russell, 1987, US)
Nosferatu: A Symphony of Horror (F. W. Murnau, 1922, Germany)
Nosferatu: Phantom of the Night (Werner Herzog, 1979, Germany)
Nuremberg: Its Lesson for Today (Pare Lorentz, 1946, US)
The Old Dark House (James Whale, 1932, US)
The Omen (Richard Donner, 1976, UK/US)
The Other (Robert Mulligan, 1972, US)
The Others (Alejandro Amenábar, 2001, Spain/US)
Paranormal Activity (Oren Peli, 2007, revised and released 2009, US)
Peeping Tom (Michael Powell, 1960, UK)
Persona (Ingmar Bergman, 1966, Sweden)
Pet Sematary (Mary Lambert, 1989, US)
The Phantom of the Opera (Rupert Julian, 1925, revised 1929, US)
Pharaoh's Curse (Lee Sholem, 1957, US)
Piranha (Joe Dante, 1978, US)
Poltergeist (Tobe Hooper, 1982, US)
The Possession of Joel Delaney (Waris Hussein, 1972, US)
Prom Night (Paul Lynch, 1980, Canada)
Prom Night (Nelson McCormick, 2008, US/Canada)
Psycho (Alfred Hitchcock, 1960, US)
Rabid (David Cronenberg, 1977, Canada)
The Raven (Louis Friedlander, also known as Lew Landers, 1935, US)
Rebel Without a Cause (Nicholas Ray, 1955, US)

[REC] (Jaume Balageró and Paco Plaza, 2007, Spain)
The Return of the Living Dead (Dan O'Bannon, 1985, US)
Revenge of the Creature (Jack Arnold, 1955, US)
Revenge of the Vampire. See *The Mask of the Demon*
The Ring (Gore Verbinski, 2002, US/Japan)
Ringu or *Ring* (Hideo Nakata, 1998, Japan)
Rosemary's Baby (Roman Polanski, 1968, US)
The Ruins (Carter Smith, 2008, US/Germany/Australia)
Salò or The 120 Days of Sodom (Pier Paolo Pasolini, 1975, Italy/France)
Saturday the 14th (Howard R. Cohen, 1981, US)
Saw (James Wan, 2004, US/Australia)
Saw II (Darren Lynn Bousman, 2005, US/Canada)
Saw III (Darren Lynn Bousman, 2006, US/Canada)
Saw V (David Hackl, 2008, US/Canada)
Saw 3D or *Saw: The Final Chapter* (Kevin Greutert, 2010, US/Canada)
Scanners (David Cronenberg, 1981, Canada)
Scary Movie (Keenen Ivory Wayans, 2000, US)
Scream (Wes Craven, 1996, US)
Scream 2 (Wes Craven, 1997, US)
Scream 3 (Wes Craven, 2000, US)
Scream 4 or *Scre4m* (Wes Craven, 2011, US)
The Serpent and the Rainbow (Wes Craven, 1988, US)
Se7en or *SE7EN* (David Fincher, 1995, US)
The Seventh Victim (Mark Robson, 1943, US; produced by Val Lewton)
Shadows of Forgotten Ancestors (Sergei Paradjanov, 1964, USSR)
Shaun of the Dead (Edgar Wright, 2004, UK)
Sherlock Jr. or *Sherlock, Jr.* (Buster Keaton, 1924, US)
The Shining (Stanley Kubrick, 1980, US/UK)
Shivers or *They Came from Within* (David Cronenberg, 1975, Canada)
Shock Waves (Ken Wiederhorn, 1977, US)
The Silence of the Lambs (Jonathan Demme, 1991, US)
Silent Night Deadly Night or *Silent Night, Deadly Night* (Charles E. Sellier Jr, 1984, US)
The Sixth Sense (M. Night Shyamalan, 1999, US)
The Slumber Party Massacre (Amy Holden Jones, 1982, US)
Snow White and the Seven Dwarfs (Walt Disney, 1937, US)
Son of Dracula (Robert Siodmak, 1943, US)
Son of Frankenstein (Rowland V. Lee, 1939, US)
The Spirit of the Beehive (Victor Erice, 1973, Spain)
Squirm (Jeff Lieberman, 1976, US)
Sssssss (Bernard Kowalski, 1973, US)
The Stepford Wives (Bryan Forbes, 1975, US)
The Strangers (Bryan Bertino, 2008, US)
The Student of Prague (Stellan Rye and Paul Wegener, 1913, Germany)
The Student of Prague (Henrik Galeen, 1926, Germany)
The Stuff (Larry Cohen, 1985, US)
Super 8 (J.J. Abrams, 2011, US)
Suspiria (Dario Argento, 1977, Italy)
Sweeney Todd: The Demon Barber of Fleet Street (Tim Burton, 2007, US/UK)
Tarantula (Jack Arnold, 1955, US)
The Terminator (James Cameron, 1984, UK/US)
A Terrible Night (Georges Méliès, 1896, France)
Terror Train (Roger Spottiswoode, 1980, Canada/US)

The Texas Chain Saw Massacre (Tobe Hooper, 1974, US)

The Texas Chainsaw Massacre 2 (Tobe Hooper, 1986, US)

Them! (Gordon Douglas, 1954, US)

They Came from Within. See *Shivers*

The Thing (John Carpenter, 1982, US)

The Thing From Another World or *The Thing* (Christian Nyby, 1951, US; produced by Howard Hawks)

The Third Mother or *Mother of Tears: The Third Mother* (Dario Argento, 2007, Italy)

This Island Earth (Joseph M. Newman, 1955, US)

Three…Extremes (Fruit Chan, Takashi Miike and Park Chan Wook, 2004, Hong Kong/Japan/ South Korea)

The Tingler (William Castle, 1959, US)

Topper (Norman Z. McLeod, 1937, US)

Tremors (Ron Underwood, 1990, US)

Twilight (Catherine Hardwicke, 2008, US)

The Twilight Saga. See individual titles

Twitch of the Death Nerve. See *A Bay of Blood*

Two Thousand Maniacs! (Herschell Gordon Lewis, 1964, US)

Ugetsu (Kenji Mizoguchi, 1953, Japan)

The Ugly (Scott Reynolds, 1997, New Zealand)

The Uninvited (Lewis Allen, 1944, US)

The Unknown (Tod Browning, 1927, US)

Vampyr (Carl Dreyer, 1932, Germany/France)

The Vanishing Lady or *Escamotage d'une dame chez Robert-Houdin* (Georges Méliès, 1896, France)

The Vengeance of Egypt (uncredited, 1912, UK)

Village of the Damned (Wolf Rilla, 1960, UK)

The Virgin Spring (Ingmar Bergman, 1960, Sweden)

Virus or *Hell of the Living Dead* or *Night of the Zombies* or *Zombie Creeping Flesh* (Bruno Mattei, 1980, Italy)

Voodoo Island (Reginald LeBorg, 1957, US)

The Walking Dead (Michael Curtiz, 1936, US)

The Werewolf (uncredited, 1913, US)

The Werewolf (Fred F. Sears, 1956, US)

WereWolf of London (Stuart Walker, 1935, US)

Wes Craven's New Nightmare or *New Nightmare* (Wes Craven, 1994, US)

What Ever Happened to Baby Jane? (Robert Aldrich, 1962, US)

White Zombie (Victor Halperin, 1932, US)

The Wicker Man (Robin Hardy, 1973, UK)

Willard (Daniel Mann, 1971, US)

The Witch (Georges Méliès, 1906, France)

Witchcraft Through the Ages. See *Häxan*

The Wizard of Oz (Victor Fleming, 1939, US)

Wolf Creek (Greg McLean, 2005, Australia)

The Wolf Man (George Waggner, 1941, US)

X or *The Man with the X-Ray Eyes* (Roger Corman, 1963, US)

Young Frankenstein (Mel Brooks, 1974, US)

Zombi (a cut of *Dawn of the Dead* supervised by Dario Argento, 1979, US/Italy)

Zombie or *Zombi 2* or *Zombie Flesh Eaters* or *Island of the Living Dead* (Lucio Fulci, 1979, Italy)

Zombie Creeping Flesh. See *Virus*

Zombie Flesh Eaters. See *Zombie*

Zombieland (Ruben Fleischer, 2009, US)

Zombies of Mora Tau (Edward L. Cahn, 1957, US)

SELECTED BIBLIOGRAPHY

Alter, Robert. *Partial Magic: The Novel as a Self-Conscious Genre*. Berkeley: University of California Press, 1975.

Baring-Gould, Sabine. *The Book of Werewolves: Being an Account of a Terrible Superstition*. Mineola, NY: Dover, 2006.

Barker, Clive. *Clive Barker's Books of Blood*. 6 vols. London: Sphere Books, 1987.

Bataille, Georges. *The Trial of Gilles de Rais*. Translated by Richard Robinson. Los Angeles: Amok, 1991.

Bordwell, David. *The Films of Carl-Theodor Dreyer*. Berkeley and Los Angeles: University of California Press, 1981.

Brottman, Mikita. *Offensive Films*. Nashville: Vanderbilt University Press, 2005.

Budge, E. A. Wallis. *The Mummy: A History of the Extraordinary Practices of Ancient Egypt*. New York: Bell, 1989.

Burke, Edmund. *A Philosophical Enquiry into the Origin of our Ideas of the Sublime and Beautiful*. New York and Oxford: Oxford University Press, 1990.

Butler, Ivan. *Horror in the Cinema*. New York: Barnes, 1970.

Carroll, Noël. *The Philosophy of Horror or Paradoxes of the Heart*. New York and London: Routledge, 1990.

Carter, Angela. *The Bloody Chamber and Other Adult Tales*. New York: Harper and Row, 1981.

Cherry, Brigid. *Horror*. New York and London: Routledge, 2009.

Clarens, Carlos. *An Illustrated History of the Horror Film*. New York: Capricorn, 1967.

Clover, Carol J. *Men, Women, and Chain Saws: Gender in the Modern Horror Film*. Princeton: Princeton University Press, 1992.

Davis, Wade. *The Serpent and the Rainbow*. New York: Simon and Schuster, 1985.

de Givry, Grillot. *Witchcraft, Magic & Alchemy*. Translated by J. Courtenay Locke. New York: Dover, 1971.

Dillard, R. H. W. "Even a Man Who Is Pure at Heart: Poetry and Danger in the Horror Film." In W. R. Robinson, ed., *Man and the Movies*. Baltimore: Penguin, 1969.

Dreyer, Carl Theodor. *Four Screenplays*. Translated by Oliver Stallybrass. Bloomington and London: Indiana University Press, 1970.

Eisner, Lotte H. *The Haunted Screen: Expressionism in the German Cinema and the Influence of Max Reinhardt*. Translated by Roger Greaves. Berkeley and Los Angeles: University of California Press, 1969.

————. *Murnau*. Berkeley and Los Angeles: University of California Press, 1973.

Eliade, Mircea. *The Myth of the Eternal Return*. Translated by Willard Trask. New York: Pantheon, 1954.

Everson, William K. *Classics of the Horror Film*. Secaucus, NJ: Citadel Press, 1977.

Fiedler, Leslie. *Freaks: Myths and Images of the Secret Self*. New York: Simon and Schuster, 1978.

Frazer, James. *The Golden Bough: A Study in Magic and Religion*. 1 vol. abridged ed. New York: Macmillan, 1963.

Freud, Sigmund. *The Uncanny*. Translated by David McLintock. New York: Penguin, 2003.

Gold, Hal. *Unit 731 Testimony*. Tokyo: Yenbooks, 1996.

Gordon, Mel. *The Grand Guignol: Theatre of Fear and Terror*. Rev. ed. New York: Da Capo, 1997.

Grant, Barry K., ed. *Film Genre Reader III*. Austin: University of Texas Press, 2003.

Grant, Barry K. and Christopher Sharrett, eds. *Planks of Reason: Essays on the Horror Film*. Rev. ed. Lanham, MD and London: Scarecrow Press, 2004.

Guazzo, Francesco Maria. *Compendium Maleficarum: The Montague Summers Edition*. Translated by E. A. Ashwin. New York: Dover, 1988.

Haggard, Howard W. *Devils, Drugs, and Doctors: The Story of the Science of Healing from Medicine-Man to Doctor*. New York: Halcyon House, 1929.

Huss, Roy and T. J. Ross, eds. *Focus on the Horror Film*. Englewood Cliffs, NJ: Prentice-Hall, 1972.

The Internet Movie Database. www.imdb.com. Accessed 2007–2011.

Jackson, Shirley. *The Haunting of Hill House*. New York: Fawcett, 1977.

James, Henry. *The Turn of the Screw and Other Short Novels*. New York: Signet Classics, 2007.

Kawin, Bruce F. *The Mind of the Novel: Reflexive Fiction and the Ineffable*. McLean, IL and London: Dalkey Archive Press, 2006.

_____. *Mindscreen: Bergman, Godard, and First-Person Film*. McLean, IL and London: Dalkey Archive Press, 2006.

_____. "The Mummy's Pool." *Dreamworks* I, 4 (Summer 1981). In Grant and Sharrett, *Planks of Reason*, above.

_____. *Telling It Again and Again: Repetition in Literature and Film*. Niwot, CO: University Press of Colorado, 1989.

Kendrick, Walter. *The Thrill of Fear: 250 Years of Scary Entertainment*. New York: Grove Weidenfeld, 1991.

Kennedy, Charles W., ed. and trans. *Beowulf: The Oldest English Epic*. New York and Oxford: Oxford University Press, 1978.

King, Stephen. *Carrie*. New York: New American Library, 1974.

_____. *Danse Macabre*. New York: Everest House, 1981.

_____. *The Shining*. New York: New American Library, 1977.

Kinnard, Roy. *Horror in Silent Films: A Filmography, 1896–1929*. Jefferson, NC and London: McFarland & Co., 1995.

Kracauer, Siegfried. *From Caligari to Hitler: A Psychological History of the German Film*. Princeton: Princeton University Press, 1947.

Kramer, Heinrich and James Sprenger. *The Malleus Maleficarum*. Translated by Montague Summers. New York: Dover, 1971.

Kristeva, Julia. *Powers of Horror: An Essay on Abjection*. Translated by Leon S. Roudiez. New York: Columbia University Press, 1982.

Le Fanu, Sheridan. *In a Glass Darkly*. New York and Oxford: Oxford University Press, 1993.

Lentz III, Harris M. *Science Fiction, Horror & Fantasy Film and Television Credits*. 2 vols. Jefferson, NC and London: McFarland & Co., 1983.

Lovecraft, H. P. *The Dunwich Horror and Others*. Edited by August Derleth and S. T. Joshi. Sauk City, WI: Arkham House, 1984.

_____. *Supernatural Horror in Literature*. New York: Dover, 1973.

Lucas, Tim. *Mario Bava: All the Colors of the Dark*. Cincinnati: Video Watchdog, 2007.

Machen, Arthur. *The Three Impostors and Other Stories*. Edited by S. T. Joshi. Oakland, CA: Chaosium, 2000.

Marks, Leo. *Peeping Tom*. London: Faber and Faber, 1998.

McConnell, Frank D. "Song of Innocence: The Creature from the Black Lagoon." *Journal of Popular Film* II, 1 (Winter 1973).

McDonagh, Maitland. *Broken Mirrors/Broken Minds: The Dark Dreams of Dario Argento*. New York: Carol/Citadel, 1994.

Messadié, Gerald. *A History of the Devil*. Translated by Mare Romano. Tokyo, New York, and London: Kodansha, 1996.

Pagels, Elaine. *The Origin of Satan*. New York: Random House, 1995.

Pirie, David. *A Heritage of Horror: The English Gothic Cinema 1946–1972*. New York: Avon/Equinox, 1974.

Poe, Edgar Allan. *Edgar Allan Poe: Poetry and Tales*. New York: The Library of America, 1984.

Prince, Stephen, ed. *The Horror Film*. New Brunswick, NJ and London: Rutgers University Press, 2004.

Remy, Nicolas. *Demonolatry*. Translated by E. A. Ashwin. London: John Rodker, 1930.

Rose, Carol. *Giants, Monsters & Dragons: An Encyclopedia of Folklore, Legend, and Myth*. New York and London: W. W. Norton, 2001.

Schechter, Harold. *The Bosom Serpent: Folklore and Popular Art*. 2nd ed. New York: Peter Lang, 2001.

_____. *Deviant: The Shocking True Story of the Original "Psycho".* New York: Pocket Books, 1989.

_____. *Savage Pastimes: A Cultural History of Violent Entertainment.* New York: St. Martin's Press, 2005.

_____. *The Whole Death Catalog: A Lively Guide to the Bitter End.* New York: Ballantine Books, 2009.

Schechter, Harold and David Everitt. *The A to Z Encyclopedia of Serial Killers.* New York: Pocket Books, 1996.

Scot, Reginald. *The Discoverie of Witchcraft.* New York: Dover, 1972.

Shelley, Mary. *Frankenstein: A Norton Critical Edition.* Edited by J. Paul Hunter. New York and London: W. W. Norton, 1996.

Siegel, Joel E. *Val Lewton: The Reality of Terror.* New York: Viking, 1973.

Sinistrari, Lodovico Maria. *Demoniality.* Translated by Montague Summers. New York: Dover, 1989.

Skal, David J. *The Monster Show: A Cultural History of Horror.* New York: Penguin, 1993.

Slater, Jay. *Eaten Alive!: Italian Cannibal and Zombie Movies.* London: Plexus, 2002.

Sobchack, Vivian. "The Leech Woman's Revenge: On the Dread of Aging in a Low-Budget Horror Film." In Rodney Sappington and Tyler Stallings, eds, *Uncontrollable Bodies: Testimonies of Identity and Culture.* Seattle: Bay Press, 1994.

Steiger, Brad. *The Werewolf Book: The Encyclopedia of Shape-Shifting Beings.* Detroit and London: Visible Ink Press, 1999.

Stevenson, Robert Louis. *The Complete Shorter Fiction.* Edited by Peter Stoneley. New York: Carroll & Graf, 1991.

Stoker, Bram. *Dracula: A Norton Critical Edition.* Edited by Nina Auerbach and David J. Skal. New York and London: W. W. Norton, 1997.

Summers, Montague. *The History of Witchcraft and Demonology.* Secaucus, NJ: Citadel Press, 1971.

_____. *The Vampire in Europe.* New York: E. P. Dutton, 1929.

Telotte, J. P. *Dreams of Darkness: Fantasy and the Films of Val Lewton.* Urbana and Chicago: University of Illinois Press, 1985.

Turner, Alice K. *The History of Hell.* New York: Harcourt Brace & Co., 1993.

Twitchell, James B. *Dreadful Pleasures: An Anatomy of Modern Horror.* New York and Oxford: Oxford University Press, 1985.

Waller, Gregory A. *The Living and the Undead: From Stoker's* Dracula *to Romero's* Dawn of the Dead. Urbana and Chicago: University of Illinois Press, 1986.

Warren, Bill. *Keep Watching the Skies!* 2 vols. Jefferson, NC: McFarland, 1982, 1986.

Weaver, Tom, Michael Brunas and John Brunas, eds. *Universal Horrors: The Studio's Classic Films, 1931–1946.* 2nd ed. Jefferson, NC and London: McFarland & Co., 2007.

Weldon, Michael J. *The Psychotronic Encyclopedia of Film.* New York: Ballantine, 1983.

_____. *The Psychotronic Video Guide.* New York: St. Martin's/Griffin, 1996.

Wells, H. G. *The Island of Dr. Moreau.* Mineola, NY: Dover, 1996.

Willis, Donald C. *Horror and Science Fiction Films.* 4 vols. Metuchen, NJ and London: Scarecrow Press, 1972, 1982, 1984, 1997.

Wilson, Colin. *The Mammoth Book of True Crime.* New ed. New York: Carroll & Graf, 1998.

Wilson, Colin and Damon Wilson. *A Plague of Murder: The Rise and Rise of Serial Killing in the Modern Age.* London: Robinson, 1995.

Wood, Robin. "An Introduction to the American Horror Film." In Grant and Sharrett, *Planks of Reason,* above.

Worland, Rick. *The Horror Film: An Introduction.* Malden, MA and Oxford: Blackwell Publishing, 2007.

Wright, Dudley. *The Book of Vampires.* Mineola, NY: Dover, 2006.

INDEX

CPSIA information can be obtained at www.ICGtesting.com
Printed in the USA
BVOW060905250612

293375BV00009B/2/P